# STOPPING HITLER

AN OFFICIAL ACCOUNT OF HOW BRITAIN PLANNED
TO DEFEND ITSELF IN THE SECOND WORLD WAR

# STOPPING
# HITLER

## AN OFFICIAL ACCOUNT OF HOW BRITAIN PLANNED
## TO DEFEND ITSELF IN THE SECOND WORLD WAR

Captain G.C. Wynne

Frontline Books

# STOPPING HITLER
## An Official Account of How Britain Planned to Defend Itself in the Second World War

This edition published in 2017 by Frontline Books,
an imprint of Pen & Sword Books Ltd,
47 Church Street, Barnsley, S. Yorkshire, S70 2AS,

Based on file reference WO 277/37 (entitled *Defence Plans for the United Kingdom 1939-45* and compiled by Captain G.C. Wynne) at The National Archives, Kew, and licensed under the Open Government Licence v3.0.

Text alterations and additions © Frontline Books

ISBN: 978-1-47389-552-2

CIP data records for this title are available from the British Library

For more information on our books, please visit
**www.frontline-books.com**
email info@frontline-books.com
or write to us at the above address.

Printed and bound by Gutenberg Press Ltd
Typeset in 10.5/12.5 point Palatino

# Contents

**Part IV**

**1942-45: The Threat of Raids and of Rocket Bombs**

Appendices

# Foreword

The purpose of this monograph is to give a general account of the plans made for Home Defence during the war period 1939-1945. It is arranged in four parts corresponding to the four different threats which developed with the changing situations of the war.

For the United Kingdom the defensive phase lasted from 1939 to 1942. It is dealt with in Parts I to III. The intention of the text is to provide the strategical setting for, and to summarize, the plans of the Defence Services. The Chiefs of Staff review of the situation as each threat developed, and the plans and appreciations to meet it, are given in full as Appendices. Part IV deals with the threats which arose after the United Kingdom had become the base for the Allied counter-offensive into Europe.

*Captain G.C. Wynne*
*Historical Section, Cabinet*
*19 May 1948*

# Publisher's Note

As far as possible, this 'official history' is reproduced in the form that it was originally written. Aside from correcting obvious spelling mistakes, most frequently in places names, or typographical errors, we have strived to keep our edits and alterations to the absolute minimum. A direct consequence of this policy is that there are occasional inconsistencies in the text.

# Glossary

| | |
|---|---|
| A.C.I. | Army Council Instruction |
| Admiralty C.B. | Admiralty Monograph (In Admiralty Historical Section) |
| Admiralty M | File in Admiralty Record Office |
| A.H.B. | Air Historical Branch (in Air Historical Section) |
| A.L. | Archivist and Librarian's File (Cabinet Historical Section) |
| A.M.B. | Air Ministry Bulletin (in air Ministry Record Office) |
| A.R.D. | Air Raid Damage and Shelter Policy |
| A.R.P. | Air Raid Precautions |
| B/Defence/Invasion | Ministry of Defence File |
| Cabinet | Cabinet Conclusions |
| Cab. Reg | Cabinet Registry File |
| C.B.C. | Crossbow Committee |
| C.C. | Combined Commanders: Papers |
| C.D.C. | Civil Defence Committee |
| C.I.D. | Committee of Imperial Defence |
| C.O.S. | Chiefs of Staff |
| C.P. | Cabinet Papers |
| D.C.M. | Ministerial Committee on Disarmament |
| D.C.O.S. (A.A.) | Deputy Chiefs of Staff (Anti-aircraft) Committee |
| D.O. | Defence Committee (Operations) |
| D.P.(P) | Ministerial Committee on Defence Plans (Policy) |
| D.P.R. | Ministerial Committee on Defence Policy and Requirements |
| D.R.C. | Defence Requirements Committee |
| H.D. | Home Defence Committee |
| H.D.S. | Home Defence Scheme |

| | | |
|---|---|---|
| H.F. | | Home Forces |
| | G.H.Q. | General Headquarters |
| | E.C. | Eastern Command |
| | S.E.C. | South-Eastern Command |
| | S.C. | Southern Command |
| J.I.C. | | Joint Intelligence Committee |
| J.P.C. | | Joint Planning Committee |
| K.P.I.D. | | Key Point Information Directorate |
| L.F. | | Land Forces |
| Misc | | War Cabinet (Miscellaneous) |
| P.D.(E) | | Passive Defence (Evacuation) |
| P.D.C. | | Port Defence Committee |
| V.P.A. | | Vulnerable Points Adviser |
| *War at Sea, The* | | Preliminary Narrative (A7) in 2 volumes, compiled by the Admiralty Historical Section. |
| W.M. | | War Cabinet Meeting |
| W.P.(G) | | War Cabinet Papers (General) |

# Part I

HOME DEFENCE PLANS 1933-39
The Threat of a Knock-out Blow
from the Air

Chapter 1

# The Attempt to Prevent German Aggression 1933-36

**Effect of the Ten Year Rule**

After the conclusion of the 1914/18 War British policy was diverted to the promotion of peace and to the reduction and limitation of armaments. The signing of the Covenant of the League of Nations by the chief countries of the world in 1919 led to the hope that international disputes might be settled by arbitration, and aggressors outlawed by a system of collective security.

The prospect of another European conflict seemed, in fact, so remote that the Cabinet accepted the assumption that no major war would take place for ten years. That assumption, for the purposes of the Estimates for the Defence Services, was re-affirmed in 1928. The little urgency attached to the armed strength of this country is illustrated by the fact that in 1931 the total effective expenditure on the Navy, Army, and Air Force together (£88,900,000) was less than the State dole to relieve unemployment (£89,222,000). Our absolute naval strength had been so diminished as to render the Fleet incapable of affording efficient protection to our trade in the event of war. The Army had been pared to the bone, and was so small that it was not capable of fulfilling our international commitments. The Air Force, which in 1918 had been among the strongest in the world, both in quality and quantity, ranked fifth in terms of first-line strength.

In 1932 the principle of collective security under the League of Nations met its first test. The attack on Shanghai on the 2nd February by Japan was a deliberate act of aggression against China, a fellow member of the League, and demanded intervention. But no concerted arrangements for the application of armed force, nor even for the enforcement of sanctions under Article XVI of the Covenant, were found practicable. As a consequence the League came to be regarded not as a "super-State with an international police force" but rather as "an organization to prevent conflict by building

1

up the machinery for conciliation". The Japanese incident gave the warning that international law had as yet only moral force behind it.

In 1932, too, the situation in Germany became menacing. A National-Sozialistiche (Nazi) party, with a dictator, Herr Hitler, as its leader and the crooked cross of the Swastika as its emblem, became the strongest political party in the country. The party programme, proclaimed openly in Herr Hitler's political testament, "Mein Kampf", was based on the belief that "Germany deserves to be master of the World"; and the aim was "peace established by the victorious sword of a people of overlords which can bend the world to the service of a higher culture". France and Russia were to be destroyed; France as an act of revenge and liberation, and Russia in order to gain "soil and territory" for an increase in the German population from 50 millions to 250 millions within the next hundred years. In October 1933 Germany withdrew from the League of Nations with the declared intention to re-arm. Re-armament and the re- establishment of munition and aircraft factories had, in fact, already taken place on a considerable scale.

The reaction of the British Government to these threats was to cancel the Ten Year rule; and to appoint a Defence Requirements Committee, including the Chiefs of Staff of the three Defence Services, to prepare a programme to make good the Service deficiencies. But in order to calculate the defence requirements a defence plan was necessary; and it was on the nature of the plan that the Cabinet and the Chiefs of Staff were to differ for the next five years, almost till the outbreak of war.

Ministers and Chiefs of Staff were agreed that Germany was the potential enemy against whom our long-range defence policy should be directed. They agreed, too, that German aggression would probably take the form of a "sudden air attack of great and possibly unknown strength" in an attempt to gain a rapid decision. They also agreed that the best defence would be to create a strong striking force of bomber aircraft in order to reduce the scale of attack and to be able to retaliate "with unprecedented Powers of destruction". The Chancellor of the Exchequer, Mr. Neville Chamberlain, expressed the general opinion when he wrote that "it stands to sense that our policy should be to construct the most terrifying deterrent to war we can think of, and recent advances in design of aircraft and engines give us the weapon best calculated to effect that purpose". The difference of opinion did not lie in the weapon, but in the way to employ it.

### The Chiefs of Staff Plan 1934-35
The Chiefs of Staff maintained that an Air Striking Force based on this country would not be a deterrent to German aggression. They estimated that a 3 to 1 ratio of bomber aircraft would be needed, and at best we could

not hope to attain more than parity with the German air force in the next five years. Even with a 3 to 1 ratio they doubted if this country could risk the inevitable retaliatory measures on vital targets such as London. With a quarter of the population concentrated in the south-eastern corner of England, about London, we were incomparably more vulnerable to air attack than was Germany.

For that reason the Defence Requirements Committee planned for defence in the event of war rather than to create a deterrent to German aggression. And they placed in the forefront of their programme, as being "vital for Britain's security", the occupation of a forward zone on the Continent at the very outset of hostilities. We would require a forward zone as an advanced base for our Air Striking Force of bomber aircraft near to vital German targets; and, equally important, in order to keep the German air-bases as far away as possible. The occupation of such a zone would also be necessary to give depth to our anti-aircraft defence. Our fighter aircraft in England would need warning of approaching bombers at least 100 miles from the coast if they were to have time to climb and be ready to intercept. It was important, too, that Dutch and Belgian ports should not fall into German hands as bases for their light naval forces and submarines.

To carry out the occupation operation the Chiefs of Staff recommended as among the most urgent of the defence requirements that the Regular Army at Home be restored to the status of an Expeditionary Force ready to co-operate at the earliest possible moment, "within a fortnight of the outbreak of war," in the defence of the Low Countries or of France. "It must be a thoroughly mobile force organised, trained and equipped on the most modern lines".

This "distant defence" of the United Kingdom was to be backed by "close defence" provided by fighter aircraft and anti-aircraft guns. Taking 1942 as the possible date by which Germany might be ready to go to war, the German air force was by then expected to have a first line strength of 1,440 aircraft, including 1,230 bombers of which 960 would be suitable for employment against this country from air bases in Germany. The actual scale of attack on target areas was put at an average of 75 tons of bombLiss daily during the first weeks of a war.

A scheme for the Air Defence of Great Britain was worked out by the Home Defence Committee.[1] Of the 35 fighter squadrons (420 first line aircraft) to be allotted to Home Defence 10 were to be sent to advanced

---

[1] The Committee had been formed out of the Home Ports Defence Committee in December 1922 to "deal, in conjunction with the Army and the Air Force, with all questions relating to the defence particularly the anti-aircraft defence, of the United Kingdom".

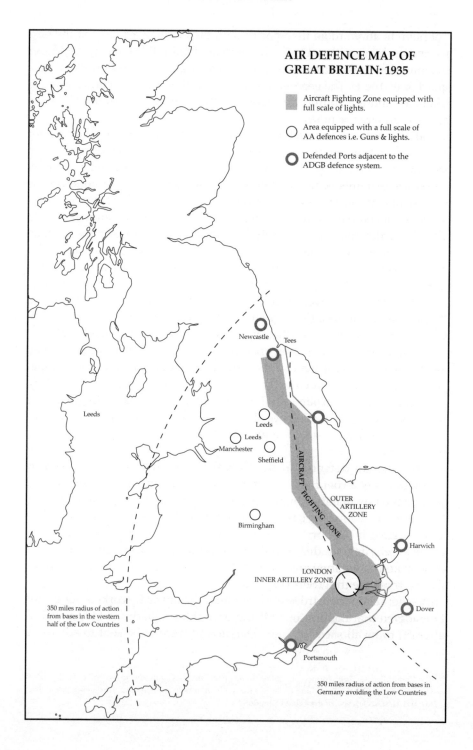

**AIR DEFENCE MAP OF
GREAT BRITAIN: 1935**

Aircraft Fighting Zone equipped with
full scale of lights.

Area equipped with a full scale of
AA defences i.e. Guns & lights.

Defended Ports adjacent to the
ADGB defence system.

Newcastle
Tees

Leeds

Leeds

Leeds
Manchester
Sheffield

AIRCRAFT FIGHTING ZONE

OUTER
ARTILLERY
ZONE

Birmingham

Harwich

LONDON
INNER ARTILLERY ZONE

350 miles radius of action
from bases in the western
half of the Low Countries

Dover

Portsmouth

350 miles radius of action from bases in
Germany avoiding the Low Countries

bases in the forward zone on the Continent, 16 were to be stationed in the Portsmouth-Huntingdon area covering south-east England, and 9 in the Huntingdon-Tees area covering the industrial Midlands and the North-East coast (see Map 1). The general idea was a continuous defence zone, 26 miles deep, around the South-East and East coasts, from Portsmouth to East of London and thence northwards to the Tees. This zone was sub-divided into an outer Artillery Zone 6 miles deep, to contain 34 anti-aircraft (eight-gun) batteries, and 19 searchlight companies (each of 24 lights); and behind it an Aircraft Fighting Zone, 20 miles deep, in which the fighters would meet the German bombers after they had been broken up during their passage through the outer artillery zone. The fighter zone was also to contain 58 searchlight companies to assist the fighters in interception at night.

Behind the coastal zone was to be the inner artillery zone of local defences, or gun defended areas: that of Greater London was to be 20 miles in diameter with 12 anti-aircraft batteries and 6 searchlight companies while other important centres to be protected included the main industrial centres of the Midlands. The total equipment for the ground anti-aircraft defences in this scheme amounted to 57 anti-aircraft batteries and 90 searchlight companies.

To man the defences would, according to a War Office calculation, require 43,500 all ranks; and the intention was to convert for the purpose as a start two of the 14 Territorial Divisions. It was suggested, too, that the Observer Corps be expanded to cover eastern England and the Midlands, south of a line from the Tees to Preston. To prevent the demoralisation of the civil population by sustained air attack, Air Raid Precautions, including the provision of respiratory gas-masks, were to be accelerated.

The Chiefs of Staff also pointed out that our home population depended to the extent of 60 per cent. on overseas trade for the food by which it lived, apart from raw materials for industry; and the Navy would have to be put on a sufficiently sound basis to carry out its vital tasks of protecting our coasts and our sea-borne trade against attack, and also of controlling an enemy's maritime trade.

For these several purposes the Chiefs of Staff advised the re-armament of the three fighting Services as a balanced force "with their roles not differing very much from those they filled in the 1914/18 War". They considered that the best means to prevent war was to re-arm on a lavish scale in order to show to Germany and Continental neighbours that we intended to meet force by force. They regarded re-armament in that sense as urgent; and they asked that public opinion should be enlightened as to the reasons for the heavy financial outlay involved. Backed by a strong Britain the League of Nations was expected to become far more effective as an instrument for keeping the peace, and as a deterrent to war.

## The Government Plan 1934-35

The Cabinet rejected the Chiefs of Staff plan on the grounds that political and financial considerations were overriding. Ministers believed, too, that a mechanized German army could overrun the Low Countries before the proposed Expeditionary Force could be transported there. The despatch of the Force from this country would require previous military conversations amounting to an alliance. Such a course would not only be contrary to the spirit of the Locarno Treaty, which was one of mutual good relations, but the British public was unlikely to accept any preparatory measures that might lead to a commitment to land operations on the Continent. Financially, too, it was "necessary to cut our coat according to our cloth", and, in the words of the Chancellor of the Exchequer, "to put it bluntly, we are presented with proposals impossible to carry out". The future of the country, he said, depended on the recovery and maintenance of sound finance and a healthy trading position; "without these we cannot provide resources for Imperial or national defence".

The creation of a powerful deterrent to war, in the shape of a strong air force, and an efficient air defence system for Great Britain was to have priority at the expense of the Army and the Navy. The full air requirement of 75 squadrons recommended as a five year programme by the Committee, in order to achieve parity with the German air force by 1939, was approved. The Army requirement was cut by half, and of that amount priority was to be given to the Army's share in the ground anti-aircraft defences. No mention was made of a possible Continental commitment. Naval expenditure was to be reduced by postponing the recommendation to send capital ships to protect our interests in the Far East, and by the intention to attempt to make a naval limitation agreement with Germany.

At the same time the Cabinet approved a statement to be made in the House of Commons on the decision to achieve parity in the air with any neighbour. It was hoped that the statement would in itself act as a deterrent to any contemplated aggression by Germany, and also inspire confidence at home. The pledge of air parity was followed by a reference to the need for a forward zone. "Since the day of the air the old frontiers are gone. When you think of the defence of England you no longer think of the cliffs of Dover; you think of the Rhine. That is where our frontier lies". The Cabinet might appear to have accepted the plan for a forward zone; but by their conclusions on the re-armament programme England's land frontier in the event of war was to remain along the cliffs of Dover. The creation of a powerful Air Striking Force as a deterrent to German aggression had become a political rather than a military consideration.

Chapter 2

# Britain on the Defensive

**German Military Occupation of the Rhineland**

The potential expansion of the German air force had been under-estimated. In December 1936 the Air Staff put the possible weight of a German air attack on this country at eight times their estimate of 1934; and the date by which Germany might be ready for war was advanced three years, from 1942 to 1939. By that time (April 1939) the German first line air strength was expected to amount to 2,520 aircraft, including 1,710 bombers of which 1,485 might be suitable for employment against this country from bases in Germany. The improved carrying capacity of these long-range bombers might enable an average of 644 tons of bombs to be dropped daily on the target area during the first three weeks of a war, as compared with the 1934 estimate of 75 tons.

The possible British reply by 1939 was put by the Chiefs of Staff at less than one sixth of the German bomb-lift, or 100 tons daily and for a shorter period; and the vital German targets were more distant and less vulnerable.

The conception of a powerful Air Striking Force based on this country as a deterrent to German aggression consequently ceased to have either a military or a political meaning. The lack of respect for our air strength was, in fact, shown by the military occupation of the Rhineland by Germany in March 1936. That action, carried out in defiance of the Locarno Treaty and of the League of Nations, was equivalent to a declaration of war; but the German army crossed the Rhine bridges unopposed, and began at once to construct defence works along the Belgian, Luxemburg and French frontiers. The one sure foundation upon which a forward zone for either the United Kingdom or France might have been built against German aggression westwards had gone; and there remained only the doubtful security of the Belgian and French frontier fortifications.

Italy and Japan, seeing the swing of the balance of power in Europe, made common cause with Germany. Belgium, too, broke off plans for joint military co-operation with France; and in October 1936 declared her neutrality.

The vision of collective security under the League of Nations had vanished; and in view of the all-round greater speed of German re-armament, the problem which confronted the United Kingdom before the close of 1936 was no longer to create a deterrent to German aggression so much as that of a struggle for survival.

The Committee of Imperial Defence asked that the Air Defence system be re-cast "on the assumption that Germany might attempt a knock-out blow on this country from the air, and that the blow would be delivered with the maximum intensity at the outbreak of war". The Civil Air Raid Precautions services would have to be prepared to deal with an alarming casualty rate of the order of 200,000 persons a week, including 66,000 killed and 25% gassed.[2] A single German bomber, too, could carry 2,000 incendiary bombs which would suffice to cause widespread destruction in built-up areas unless the fire-fighting services were efficient.

**The Chiefs of Staff Plan 1937**
The changed outlook was expressed in a memorandum of the 15th February 1937 by the Chiefs of Staff on "Planning for a war with Germany". They assumed that war might break out in the latter part of 1939 with Germany as the aggressor; and that Germany would try to exploit her preparedness by a rapid victory within a few months. The initial object would probably be to knock-out quickly either Great Britain or France and Belgium. An attempt to deliver a knock-out blow from the air on Great Britain was considered the more likely, owing to the strength of the French frontier fortifications. The risk of a seaborne or airborne invasion was regarded as negligible so long as our naval and air forces were in being. The danger was that the country might be defeated by air attack alone, without the need for invasion.

The method of the knock-out blow from the air had been popularised and elaborated by several writers, and notably by the Italian General Douhet in his book "The Command of the Air" (1928). His advice to an aggressor was to "mass your strength in the air". An independent Air Force might suffice by itself to win a war quickly and decisively by "putting the enemy population in an intolerable condition of life through aerial offensives". The procedure was to be an intensive bombing of densely populated areas,

[2] According to the statistics of the 1914/18 War one ton of bombs on crowded areas had caused an average of 50 casualties (17 killed and 33 wounded).

8

transportation arteries and main industrial centres with high explosive and incendiary bombs, and with poison gas – the high-explosive bombs to demolish the target, the incendiaries to set fire to it, and the poison gas to prevent the fire-fighters from extinguishing the fires. The enemy's will to resist would be broken and his capacity to make war destroyed.

If a knock-out blow was attempted the Chiefs of Staff expected that the German air striking force would be used ruthlessly. An attack on the scale estimated, continuous and concentrated, might paralyse transport and supply services in a few weeks, and so undermine the morale of civil population as to force the Government to discontinue the war. To counter such an attack would require all our resources.

A successful attack on France and Belgium would in the opinion of the Chiefs of Staff be "equally disastrous" for Great Britain; and for that reason they recommended that our land and air forces should be ready to give immediate support on the Continent in order to ensure co-operation between the French and the Belgians to stem a German advance westwards. They did not believe that the movement of an Expeditionary Force to the Continent could be prevented by enemy action, given the number of ports on both sides of the Channel and the many defensive and protective measures available.

For this distant defence the Chiefs of Staff repeated their opinion that the Regular Army at Home should be ready, trained and equipped on the most modern lines for employment as a Field Force on the Continent at the outbreak of war. They pointed out that in its existing state, with the range of its field guns and howitzers only about half that of foreign field artillery, "it would be murder to send our Field Force overseas to fight against a first class power". They also recommended an increase of the Air Striking Force as the best means of reducing the scale of German air attack by counter-bombing at the source. Out of a total Home air-requirement of 2,331 first line aircraft by the end of 1939, the Air Staff asked for 1,442 bomber aircraft to keep abreast of the German air striking force, estimated at 1,458 aircraft by that date.

For close defence, to meet the new estimate of the weight of attack by 1939, the minimum requirement of fighter squadrons was increased to 38, and later to 51; the number of searchlights was doubled, to 4,684; and the anti-aircraft gun requirement was trebled to 1,296. Owing to the longer range of the German bombers the Air Fighting Zone was to be extended to include the Tyne, Forth and Clyde defences, and widened from 20 to 50 miles to give the fighter defence a larger field of action. To man the additional guns and searchlights would require another 50,000 men, and it was proposed to convert two more Territorial divisions for the purpose. A system of cable-carrying balloons to trap low-flying bombers, or to force them to keep to high altitudes over vital targets had been approved; a total of 450 were to be sited in the London area, and manned by 5,000 auxiliary and Territorial troops. The balloon barrage was to be extended to other vital areas as production allowed.

A more hopeful outlook for close defence had been opened up by the development by the Air Defence Research Committee since April 1935 of an invention for radio direction finding (R.D.F.) by reflected electrical echoes. Applied to the purpose of locating approaching aircraft the instrument gave promise that warning might be obtained at 80 to 200 miles from the coast. The intention was to erect a chain of 22 R.D.F. coastal stations, from the Isle of Wight to the Tees, by the end of 1939. Given the warning signal at that distance fighter aircraft might have time to climb and be ready to meet the German bombers at or near the coast. The outer, or coastal, artillery zone was therefore abandoned, and the guns were moved back to reinforce the gun-defended areas.

Another improvement in close defence was the 8-gun fighter types of aircraft, the Hurricane and the Spitfire; by placing the machine guns in the wings the fighter fire-power had been quadrupled. It was confidently hoped that the greatly improved speed, armour and fire-power of these new models would give them a decisive advantage over the German bombers.

The Chiefs of Staff did not consider their 'Ideal' minimum requirement to be by any means an over-insurance; and yet only a fraction of it was available. The Air Force was a year behind its programme. Of the approved 38 fighter squadrons only 27 were mobilisable in March 1938; and 20 were still equipped with obsolescent aircraft which were slower than the majority of the German bombers. Reserves of aircraft were estimated at only 1½ operational weeks. The anti-aircraft ground defences were far below requirement. The 252 3-inch guns in hand were of old pattern and their range inadequate; the production plant for the new 3.7 inch and 4.5 inch heavy guns was ready, but only seven of the 640 guns approved had been delivered. Of the approved 3,027 searchlights 969 were available; and the cable-carrying balloon barrage had not yet reached the stage of practical value. The vital and secret R.D.F. system was still in its infancy, with four stations covering the approaches to London.

The civil, or passive, defence side of the Air Defence system was also embryonic, with no centralised control or co-ordination. Air-raid shelters for the civil population were practically non-existent; and fire-fighting arrangements to meet the effect of heavy bombing raids had not yet been organised. The provision of gas-masks was the satisfactory feature; and, although much other preparatory work had been done the air raid precautions had not yet reached a stage when air-attacks could be faced with any confidence.

The Chiefs of Staff forecast that owing to the comparative weakness of our armed strength a war with Germany would have to be a long war if it was to be won. After the initial German onslaught had been defeated, the war would enter its second phase during which we would have to rely upon our industrial and economic power, backed by the resources of the Empire, to build up our armed strength in preparation for the third phase, the counter-offensive against Germany. The intervention of Russia, and possible material assistance from America, "would go far towards making the Allied counter-offensive possible".

**The Government Plan 1937-38**
Ministers agreed that the cornerstone of our Imperial Defence policy was to maintain the security of the United Kingdom. "Our main strength lies in the resources of man-power, production capacity, and the powers of endurance possessed by country. Unless these can be maintained substantially unimpaired not only in peace but particularly in the early stages of a war our ultimate defeat in a major war be certain, irrespective of what might happen in other secondary spheres".

They also approved the Chiefs of Staff forecast of the probable course of a war with Germany; but in the detail of the defence measures they still maintained that political and financial considerations must be overriding. Priority was still to be given to financial stability in order to pay for re-armament in peace-time, and to be able to purchase from world resources during a war so as to win it. "Britain must confront her potential enemies with the risks of a long war which they cannot face; and if we are to emerge victorious from such a struggle it is essential that we should enter it with sufficient financial strength to enable us to make the fullest use of resources overseas and to withstand the strain." The Treasury held that the maintenance of financial stability in this sense was an essential fourth area in defence, alongside the three Defence Services, without which purely military effort would be of no avail.

The first military aim was to protect the country from a knock-out blow from the air, and to that end the Air Force was to be given priority. Ministers did not share the Air Staff's view that counter-attack by the Air Striking Force on the enemy's aerodromes and industrial plant was the best means of defence. They contended that since our main object was the defence of this country we should concentrate upon defensive fighter aircraft for direct action against the German bombers, combined with anti-aircraft ground defence. The concentration on a policy of close defence and direct action was encouraged by the invention of radio-location and by the improved types of fighter aircraft. Ministers accordingly decided for the maximum production of fighter aircraft at the expense of the Air Striking Force; and

11

anti-aircraft guns and searchlights were to have priority in Army expenditure. A request by the Secretary for War that the production of anti-aircraft guns be postponed till the worst gun deficiencies of the Field Force were made good was refused. Ministers reasoned that "first things must come first", and that "the problem before us is to win the war over London".

Second place in Home Defence expenditure was given to measures "to preserve the trade routes on which we depend for essential imports of food and raw materials". The Admiralty was to continue to replace out-of-date ships, and to maintain in Home Waters a naval force able to meet the requirements of a war with Germany. The Admiralty request for a new standard of naval strength to allow for a Fleet to protect our interests in the Far East was still under discussion.

The Chiefs of Staff repeated demand for a Field Force of 5 divisions, backed by 12 Territorial divisions, equipped for a war on the Continent was again ruled out. Ministers considered that we could not afford to maintain such a force in complete readiness in peace-time while at the same time supporting a very powerful Navy and Air Force. Instead they gave us their third objective the maintenance of the Regular Army at Home as an Expeditionary Force for "Imperial Police duties" overseas; and "as the operations involved are unlikely to be waged with the sustained intensity or scale as operations on the Continent it should be possible to effect a very substantial reduction in the scale of reserves and also in the provision of tanks, especially of the heavy calibres".

Both Regular and Territorial troops would also be needed to assist the civil authorities at Home in the event of sustained air attacks to keep order and to maintain transport and other essential services. Coast defence came last in the Army's Home Defence tasks in view of the expert assurance that the danger of sea-borne or air-borne invasion on any considerable scale was negligible.

The fourth objective, "which can only be provided after the other objectives have been met, is co-operation in the defence of the territories of any allies we may have in war". In other words the despatch of an expeditionary force to Europe was to come last in priority. The Air Force was to some extent to supplant the Army, and not merely supplement it; but "should France be overrun an army would have to be improvised".

### Decision to Send the Field Force to France
Events in Europe during the next twelve months led to a change in that list of priorities. To compensate for the loss of the Czech Army of 30 divisions by the Munich Agreement in September 1938, the French Government asked for assistance on land, as well as the naval and air support to which

British co-operation was limited in the event of a war against Germany. Unless a Field Force was sent, France might not face the prospect of bearing the brunt of the fighting on land. The situation which would arise with German possession of the French Channel ports was so grave that, in the opinion of the Chiefs of Staff, the despatch of the Field Force to the Continent should be placed first instead of last on the list of the Government's priorities.

On the 22nd February 1939 the Cabinet agreed to that recommendation; and in April, after the annexation by Germany of the Czech State and the open threat to Poland, Ministers decided to bring 13 Territorial divisions up to war establishment and, when so brought up, the number was to be doubled. To provide the man-power for this expansion, conscription was introduced on the 17th April; and to provide the additional arms and equipment a Ministry of Supply was set up on the 14th April. Apart from the decision to prepare the Field Force for war on a Continental scale, the plan for Home Defence remained unaltered.

On the 2nd September, the day following the German invasion of Poland, Britain and France declared war against Germany. The Government assumed that the United Kingdom would remain a secure base; and that within it an armed force would gradually be built up for the counter-offensive into Germany. A long defensive phase was seen to be inevitable; and production programmes were based on a three-year war. The authorised target figure by the Spring of 1942 was the provision and maintenance of an army of 55 divisions, and an output of aircraft at the rate of 2,550 a month.

Chapter 3

# Defence Against Air Attack

**Scale of Attack**

At the time of the outbreak of war in September 1939 an attempt at a knock-out blow on this country by the German air striking force was still regarded as the "worst case" our defence might be called upon to meet.

The Home Defence air strength was less than half the estimated air strength of Germany – roughly 500 first line fighter aircraft against 1,000, and 950 British and French bombers against Germany's 2,000. An Air Staff appreciation in April 1939 (given as Appendix I) estimated the possible scale of attack at 700 tons of bombs every 24 hours for the first two weeks; after which period casualties and breakdowns might reduce the weight of attack by about 50 per cent.

Of Germany's long range bombers over a third, an average of 650, might be employed daily on attacks which would probably be ruthless and sustained. The most likely objectives would be food supply and distribution centres, particularly the Port of London, and densely populated areas. As Germany had recognised Dutch and Belgian neutrality it was assumed that the attacks would be delivered from air bases in Germany.

Despite Germany's air superiority our Air Defence had at least two reasons for confidence. The chain of secret R.D.F. stations along the East coast was nearly complete, so that our fighters were expected to be able to meet the German bombers over the coast, and secondly the German bomber was unarmoured and practically unarmed.

The German bomber had been designed on experience gained in the Spanish Civil War (1936/38) where the opposing fighters had lower speeds; armour and armament had been sacrificed to gain greater speed so as to rely upon its power of evasion for safety. As England was out of range of the German fighters from air-bases in Germany the bombers would be unescorted. Our new fighters, the Spitfire and the Hurricane, were faster

14

than the German bombers (305 to 365 miles an hour against 250 – 312); and it was believed that, given sufficient warning by the R.D.F. stations, they might be able to meet and destroy the German raiders with comparatively slight loss to themselves.

### The Air Defence of Great Britain (A.D.G.B.)

The most important element in the Air Defence system was therefore the Fighter Force and the R.D.F. warning stations. Of the approved number of squadrons, 51, only 37 squadrons (590 first line aircraft) were mobilisable, with 30 per cent. instead of the required 100 per cent. maintenance reserves. Their re-equipment with the new Hurricane and Spitfire types was, however, nearly complete.

Of the 22 approved R.D.F. stations 19 had been established along the East and South coasts covering an area from Ventnor (Isle of Wight) to the River Tay (Gallows Hill), and a station at Kirkwall (Orkneys) covering the base of the Home Fleet at Scapa Flow. The stations had an effective radius of 80 – 200 miles; and although the instrument had a blind area below 1,000 feet altitude the bombers were expected to approach at a high level, up to 20,000 feet or more, in order to be able to drop their bombs and return to base before our fighters could intercept.

The Aircraft Fighting Zone, between the coast and the gun-defended areas, had been extended as a perimeter defence around the industrial heart of England and Scotland; and it was divided into 21 fighter sectors of which 16 were on the eastern side of the country, and of those sixteen 7 were within reach of the London area. To assist the fighter defence at night, a continuous search-light belt, with lights 6,000 yards apart, was formed in the eastern half of the zone, from the Solent, and east of London to the Humber and the Tyne–Tees area, with an addition between the Forth and the Clyde. For tracking the bombers inland 28 Observer Corps districts had been formed, out of 32 proposed, with a network of communication to Fighter Command and local military authorities.

The other close defence weapon, the anti-aircraft gun, was expected to be a deterrent rather than a means of destruction, as its accuracy of fire was unsatisfactory. The application of radio-location (R.D.F.) to the ranging of A.A. guns, as also of searchlights, was being investigated, and the production of suitable sets had been approved; but the problem of finding the height as well as the direction of an approaching aircraft had not yet been solved. Barrages had to be fired on orders from the Gun Operations Room based on rough calculations by the intersection of bearings from sound-locators two miles apart; or, as an alternative, the gunners could use their height-finders and predictors which were ineffective above 25,000 feet and had too slow a traverse to follow low-flying aircraft.

15

The guns were sited in the gun-defended areas so as to produce the maximum volume of fire during the run-up of about two miles to the target area, at which period the bomber would have to keep on a constant course. An average 36-gun density (nine four-gun stations) covering the approaches to the target area was considered an adequately powerful deterrent for the most important objective. London, for example, was allotted 480 heavy guns on that calculation (a maximum fringe density of 48 and a minimum of 16, giving an average of 36).

**The Record of Home Defence Measures**
A Home Defence Scheme, begun in 1937 to "knit together the whole of our Home Defence arrangements", described the state of readiness of the active and passive defence measures, and of the control organization. The second edition of the scheme, renamed the "Record of Home Defence Measures" was amended up to the 22nd August, eleven days before the outbreak of war.

Although the requirement of heavy A.A. guns had been raised to 2,232, only 695 had been delivered by the outbreak of war (127 4.5-inch, 298 3.7-inch and 270 3-inch). For example, London and the Thames approaches had 253 guns in position instead of the authorised 480. The Birmingham–Coventry area, main production centre for fighter aircraft aero-engines, had 35 (Birmingham 23, Coventry 12) instead of 120. The twenty main fighter aerodromes near the East Coast averaged one 3-inch gun instead of four. Scapa Flow, base of the Home Fleet, had 8 instead of the approved 24.

The increase in fighter and heavy A.A. gun defence was expected to tend to force the Germans to resort to low-flying attack. For the low altitude air defence of London the approved 450 cable-carrying balloons were complete; and the expansion of Balloon Command, R.A.F., on an Auxiliary Air Force basis, to an establishment of 1,455 first line balloons, organised in 47 squadrons, to cover vital areas in the provinces was in progress. The possibility of low-flying attack also called for additional light A.A. guns, and for the development of the 2-inch multiple barrelled (U.P.) rocket projectors, still under trial, capable of discharging large quantities of projectiles simultaneously. The delivery of the light A.A. weapons was however even more backward than that of the heavy equipments. The total requirement of 1,112 light A.A. guns approved in 1938 had been increased to 1,924 (2,000 barrels) in February 1939 in order to give protection to 1,622 vulnerable and key points against low-flying attack. Of that total only 97 (54 Bofors and 43 2-pdr.) had been delivered at the outbreak of war.

The approved totals of heavy and light A.A. equipments included, when they became available, a mobile reserve of 168 mobile heavy and 252 light guns to be at the disposal of A.A. Command in order to strengthen the defence of any area, such as docks, aircraft factories, oil supply depots, which might be indicated by Intelligence reports as possible immediate objectives for air attack.

Operationally the Air Defence System was under the C.-in-C., Fighter Command, R.A.F.; he was to act in consultation with the C.-in-C. Anti-Aircraft Command who controlled the guns and searchlights. The manning of the anti-aircraft guns and searchlights had been the responsibility of the Territorial Army since 1935; and from the 1st April 1939 the A.A. establishment had been increased from five to seven A.A. divisions; and their strength on mobilisation totalled 106,690.

The counter-offensive element was provided by the Air Striking Force under Bomber Command. Of an approved total of 85 squadrons of bomber aircraft 57 had been formed, of which 40 were mobilisable at 25 bomber station headquarters in North-East, East and South-East England. Their purpose would be to reduce the scale of air attack by bombing the German operational aerodromes, the German air force maintenance organisation and the main supply industrial centres, such as the Ruhr region.

**Internal Security and Coast Defence**

Next in priority to Air Defence were the arrangements for internal security, which included aid to the Civil Power and the garrisoning of aerodromes, and of other vulnerable and key points against sabotage and attack. The Army was to be ready to assist to keep order among the population and to maintain essential services in the event of major and sustained air attacks. In the London Area, for example, the minimum requirement was considered to be the presence of seven of the best disciplined battalions available: one Guards battalion was allotted to each of the four Metropolitan districts and three were retained as a central reserve. The large number of troops in depots and training centres near provincial towns and industrial areas were considered to be adequate for the purpose.

The guarding of aerodromes was an Army responsibility, and at the outbreak of war local guards 50 to 100 strong were provided to "protect them against saboteurs or small mobs of disaffected persons". The protection of the numerous Service establishments and other Vulnerable Points was the responsibility of the Service concerned; and Navy, Army, Air Force and War Department Police Guards were reinforced by National Defence companies of the Territorial Army, formed for that purpose and called-up during the precautionary stage before the declaration of war.

A number of key points essential for the country's industrial effort, such as oil fuel installations, railway vital points, broadcasting stations, store depots, factories of outstanding importance and public utility undertakings, had also to be protected by military guards. The list of key points was kept up-to-date by a special department (Key Points Intelligence Directorate) of the Ministry of Home Security.

### Civil Defence Measures

The Record shows that for Air Raid Precautions, and civil defence generally, the country was not fully prepared either as regards trained personnel or protective measures. Volunteers for the Civil Defence Services, including Air Raid Precautions personnel, additional police and firemen, were far below the estimated requirement of 1,150,000; and comparatively few had been trained. Protective measures were inadequate; the provision of shelters, for example, was limited as a rule to protection against blast, splinters and gas. A long-term policy for the construction of deep bomb-proof shelters was not regarded as a practical proposition; and the decision was left with local authorities according to circumstances.

Compulsory evacuation from crowded danger areas was not contemplated; but it was estimated that about one third of the population of such areas would wish to leave. In the case of London, the London Transport Board aimed at moving two million persons within 24 hours to a distance of 30 to 50 miles by rail, road and the underground railways.

The Record also gives the states of readiness of other civil defence arrangements such as lighting restrictions, control of transport and supply by rail and road, man-power distribution, the maintenance of essential services such as oil-supply, coal, gas, electricity, food and water.

### Control Organisation

Executive action on Home Defence matters was to be taken through the normal ministerial and departmental channels. The war-time Home Security organisation had been founded by the appointment in November 1938 of a Minister for Civil Defence: and the eleven regional commissioners who were to co-ordinate the civil defence schemes with local military requirements had had ten months in which to settle to their task. Co-ordination between military and civil planning was to be effected by direct meetings between the Chiefs of Staff and a member of the Ministry of Home Security.

The Record assumed that Government control would continue to function in London. War Rooms in Whitehall had been prepared in strutted basements; A Central War Room under the same roof as the War Cabinet, and War Rooms for each of the Service Departments and for the Home Security organisation headquarters. Specially protected basement reserve War Rooms were also being made ready in the outkirts of London for the War Cabinet, Admiralty and Air Ministry. In the event of evacuation becoming necessary a scheme for the move of Government departments to

18

the West Country was on the point of completion: the War Cabinet to Worcester, the Admiralty to Bath and Malvern, the War Office to Cheltenham and Droitwich, the Air Ministry to Bath, Gloucester, Worcester, etc.). Alternative accommodation was being arranged in the northern counties, at Harrogate, Blackpool, St. Anne's-on-Sea, etc., in the event of special emergency.

Chapter 4

# The Julius Caesar Plan:
# 27 October 1939

**Air Power Considered to Have Made the Risk of Invasion Negligible**
The advent of air-power had changed the prospects for an invasion of this country. It was believed that the preparation of an expeditionary force would be unable to escape the watch of our air-reconnaissance patrols, and that the expedition could be bombed and shelled to destruction before reaching these shores.

Coastal Command R.A.F. was responsible for reconnaissance over possible invasion ports on the Continent (17 of the 19 squadrons approved for Coastal Command were ready to operate at the outbreak of war); and Bomber Command had an adequate striking force to attack any concentration of shipping. Our naval supremacy in Home waters was guaranteed by the Naval Pact with Germany in 1935.[3]

In the circumstances the Committee of Imperial Defence had approved that "so long as our Navy and Air Force are in being, a sea-borne invasion could be defeated without the help of land forces ... and the danger of airborne attack on a large scale is negligible". The land forces to be retained in the United Kingdom needed to be adequate only "to man the anti-aircraft ground defences and to maintain order and essential services in the event of major and sustained air attacks".

The Chiefs of Staff appreciations of 1937 and 1939 regarding invasion are given as Appendix 2. In accordance with their assurances all the Regular divisions in the country were sent to France as soon as mobilised, to be followed by Territorial divisions as they became fit for service.

Not only was the Home Army reduced to a token force of semi-trained troops, but priority was given to the Field Force in France for trained

---

[3]  For relative strengths of the British and German Fleets at the outbreak of war see *The War at Sea* Vol. 1, Sec. 1.

officers and the full output of equipment, artillery and transport from production. For the same reason – the belief that preparations against invasion were unnecessary – coast defence had come last in priority in defence measures, and the 28 "defended ports" were far below the approved requirement in armament as shown in Appendix 3.[4]

## Civil Invasion Preparations Cancelled

As the War Office did not propose to make specific preparations to deal with large scale seaborne or airborne raids, or invasion, civil defence schemes to meet such a contingency were "unnecessary and, indeed, impracticable".

Entries in the Government War Book for civil anti-invasion measures, such as the evacuation of the population from coastal areas, removal of supplies, etc. inserted purposely after the 1914/18 War to ensure that they were not overlooked, had been cancelled in 1937.

## Risk of a Large Scale Raid Considered

During the first weeks of the war the activities of German submarines off the North and West coasts resulted in a reduction of our light naval force in the North Sea to provide escorts for trade protection. When the nights began to lengthen in October, the War Cabinet agreed that a convoy of German transports might slip through our naval and air patrols, and land an armed force on the coast. The Chiefs of Staff were accordingly asked to reconsider the risk of a large scale raid, and to take the necessary steps to meet it. Our naval and air forces could be rapidly strengthened sufficiently to intercept any reinforcements of troops and supplies; but even a local success, such as the destruction of a port or of some vital objective near the coast, might have a political and moral effect sufficient to tie up many more troops at home. The requirement therefore was to destroy the landing force as soon as possible before any serious damage could be done.

The Commander-in-Chief, Home Forces, was asked to "prepare immediate plans to meet an invasion on a large scale, based on a course of enemy action which had previously been ruled out an unlikely". The

[4] All three Services had their share of responsibility for the defence of ports. The Navy provided the necessary local naval forces (auxiliary mine-sweeping and anti-submarine vessels, and other light craft) and the off-shore, or seaward, defences such as minefields, booms, baffles, nets, and the permanently mounted torpedo-tubes. The Army provided and manned the fixed coastal artillery; and Territorial units were available locally as mobile reserves to oppose small-scale seaborne or airborne raids. The Air Ministry was responsible for providing the aircraft required for general reconnaissance in co-operation with the fixed defences. For defence against air attack ports and dockyards were incorporated in the A.D.G.B. system. Except at naval dockyards executive responsibility lay normally with the commander of the Army garrison in co-ordination with the other Service commanders through a combined Area Headquarters

outcome of that request was the "Julius Caesar" plan produced by G.H.Q. Home Forces on the 27th October (see Appendix 4).

The maximum German force which might evade our sea control was estimated at a division, or 15,000 fully equipped troops, in twenty 4,000–5,000 ton transports supported by 10,000 airborne troops in 1,000 civil aircraft.

Until the airborne troops had captured a port from the landward side, cleared opposition from the vicinity of the docks and anchorages, and from ground commanding the entrance to the port, it was considered to be "supremely dangerous for a seaborne landing to be attempted"; so that "if the initial air landing operation is a failure the operation as a whole cannot proceed and has definitely failed". Consequently the defeat of the airborne force was the principal aim of the plan. With equipment limited to rifles and light machine guns, and a restricted ammunition supply, the airborne troops were expected to have little staying power unless quickly supported from the sea.

The most likely objective was an aerodrome, or landing grounds, near a port of considerable size, such as Harwich or the Humber, where a number of quays, wharves and cranes were available for rapid disembarkation; but defence precautions were taken at all ports between Peterhead and Newhaven where ships could come alongside, in particular Aberdeen, Dundee, Yarmouth, Lowestoft and Ramsgate.

The main defence was by fighter aircraft and anti-aircraft guns which would destroy the troop-carrying aircraft in the air; but parties of aircraft might evade the air defence, or might land before daybreak or in bad visibility. The ground defence was based chiefly on the location of mobile reserves within call; and the success of the plan would depend upon the ability of the local coastal forces to "pin down" the German airborne formations, and upon the time taken by the mobile reserves to reach the area of operations.

To give the earliest possible warning additional air reconnaissance and naval patrols were to be ordered to cover the German coastal and North Sea areas by day and on moon-light nights; and certain bomber squadrons were to be maintained in immediate readiness to bomb ship concentrations. With those precautions it was estimated that a minimum of eight hours' notice could be given of any attempted large scale raid. The code-word "Julius", denoting that an invasion was impending, brought the Home Defence forces to a state of readiness at eight hours' notice; the code-word "Caesar" signified that an invasion was imminent.

It was expected that the landing force, seaborne and airborne, would be eliminated within seven days. That calculation provided the basis for the short-term period for the immobilisation of ports and the denial of facilities to the enemy. The civil population not in immediate danger were to be encouraged to remain in their homes; but the exodus of those persons in the danger zone was to be controlled and directed so that military two-way roads into the area of operations was kept clear of all civil traffic.

The C.-in-C. Home Forces put the minimum Army requirement for the plan at seven divisions: two for the Eastern and one each for the Northern and the Scottish Commands, and three in G.H.Q. Reserve. In Yorkshire, Lincolnshire and East Anglia armoured detachments were to be ready to move at once to break up the landing force before a port could be seized. The dispositions of Home Forces early in May 1940, when nine divisions were available for the plan.

The Julius Caesar plan may be regarded as an annex to the Record of Home Defence Measures; and together they formed the foundation of the plans for Home Defence during the first Winter of the War.

# Part II

1940: The Threat of Air Attack
Preparatory to Invasion

Chapter 5

# The German Offensive Against
# the Western Powers

**The Occupation of Norway, Denmark and Holland**
The expected onslaught from the air at the outset of the War did not
materialize. The German air striking force had been created not as a
weapon for forcing a decision by independent air action, but rather as
a means for preparing the way for the rapid advance of an army
through enemy territory. Several authorities in this country had
believed that an air attack would not be launched until the German
army, with which half the German air force had been trained, was ready
to exploit a success.

The postponement of air attack throughout the Winter gave the
needed time to improve the air defence preparations. The task was
interrupted in the Spring (1940) by the opening of the German offensive
against the Western Powers. The occupation of Norway and Denmark
in April, and the invasion of Holland on the 10th May brought about the
critical situation which had long been foreseen, but so inadequately
faced, by the Cabinet and the Chiefs of Staff.

The assumptions upon which the Air Defence of Great Britain had
been based were transformed. German bombers based on Dutch
aerodromes would be able to have fighter escorts over the most
vulnerable parts of the country. The Chiefs of Staff admitted, too, that
their former assurances on the negligible risks of invasion were no
longer valid.

**Precautions Against Seaborne and Airborne Landings**
Additional precautions were ordered by the Chiefs of Staff within the
framework of the Julius Caesar plan. Light naval forces adequate to
intercept a seaborne expedition from Dutch harbours were placed in
readiness. The East Coast mine-barrage, laid from off Scotland to the

Humber to cover possible landing places from German harbours only, was extended southwards to include the Thames estuary; and all East and South-East coast ports from the Wash to Newhaven were prepared for short-term (7 days) immobilisation. Naval brigades were formed as an additional garrison for naval ports and dockyards; and the Coastguard, a civil organisation under the Ministry of Shipping, was taken over by the Admiralty.

Likely airborne landing grounds, such as straight stretches of arterial road and other open spaces within 5 miles of ports, possible landing beaches and air-fields up to 20 miles of the East Coast, from Sunderland to Hastings, were ordered to be obstructed by road-blocks, overhead wires, poles or trenches; all roads leading to ports and coastal aerodromes had blocks placed in position, and bridges in the area were prepared for demolition.

Church bells throughout the country were only to be rung as a warning signal of enemy parachutists or airborne landings; the order to that effect was issued by the Ministry of Home Security on the 13th June after discussion with the Ecclesiastical authorities.

### The Local Defence Volunteers (Home Guard)

According to the Julius Caesar plan airborne troops and parachutists who succeeded in landing were to be dealt with by the A.A. gun and searchlight detachments in the network of the Air Defence system. The Observer Corps, watching the greater part of the country was in direct communication with the military authorities in each area. In addition the Police Force, with a peace strength of 60,000, was to be armed, and rifles distributed to the County Police for "Flying Squads" to deal with parachutists.

Those precautions were, however, considered inadequate to meet the increased threat. To ensure that parachutists should be dealt with at once the War Cabinet authorised, on the 13th May, the creation of a Local Defence Volunteer Force. This citizen force, voluntary and unpaid, with part-time duties except in an emergency, was required to deal without delay with an enemy arriving by whatever means in the vicinity of their villages and parishes.

Volunteers soon reached the half a million mark. Enrolment was only restricted by the shortage of rifles; 100,000 old rifles out of the repair shops were available up to the end of May, and to make good the deficiency until the arrival of consignments of rifles ordered from Canada and the United States, civilians were asked to hand over any shot-guns in their possession.

## The Home Defence Executive

Anti-invasion schemes by civil departments and local authorities, considered unnecessary before the war, had to be extemporised. Voluntary evacuation from East and South coast towns was encouraged; but if invasion occurred the population throughout the country were to stay where they were, and keep of the roads, particularly in coastal areas. The coastward roads would be required for military movements, and would be subject to deliberate air attack by German bombers. In view of possible Fifth Column activities and sabotage with 73,000 aliens at large in the country, all enemy aliens and members of subversive organizations were rounded up and interned.

To avoid assistance to airborne or seaborne troops railways were prepared for immediate immobilization; and the Ministry of Transport undertook the removal of signposts and milestones throughout the country. Place-names were removed from railway stations, shops, vans, advertisement hoardings, etc., and local maps from stationers' shops. Arrangements were made to immobilise gas, electricity and water undertakings, to place all petrol pumps out of commission and to deny to a landing force coastal and inland bulk storage supplies of essential foods and commodities. Stocks at East and South coast ports were to be moved inland in an emergency or, if necessary, destroyed.

For the supervision of these tasks, and for the co-ordination of military and civil plans, the Chiefs of Staff set up a Home Defence Executive, under the chairmanship of the C.-in-C. Home Forces, with representatives of the Admiralty, Air Commands, Air Ministry and the Ministry of Home Security. The Executive held its first meeting on the 11th May.

## The 1st Armoured Division Goes to France

As the threat of invasion was not regarded as immediate the War Cabinet, on the 11th May, at the request of the C.-in-C. British Expeditionary Force, authorised the despatch to France of the 1st Armoured Division which included all the medium and cruiser tanks in the country. These tanks were equipped with the 2-pdr. anti-tank gun; and their departure left only 168 light reconnaissance tanks, armed with machine-guns, as the armoured force for Home Defence.

## The Loss of the French and Belgian Ports

The main German offensive against Belgium and France opened on the 14th May, the day after Dutch resistance ceased. Within a week, by the 20th May, a German armoured column had reached Abbeville on the Channel coast. On the 22nd, with a southern flank established along the

Somme-Aisne river line, German armoured forces swung northwards on a wide front towards Boulogne and Calais while other German forces pressed westwards through Belgium and French Flanders.

On the 24th the Prime Minister[5] asked for an effort to be made to close the Straits of Dover to enemy shipping by the use of long-range guns – the largest Dover guns at the time, two 9.2-inch, had a range of 17,000 yards and the Straits at their narrowest were 38,000 yards across. On the same day an area ten miles deep around the East and South coasts, from Kinnaird's Head (Aberdeenshire) to Christchurch (Hampshire), was declared a prohibited area in which control of the movement of persons was to be in the hands of the military authorities.

On the 26th the French Premier, M. Reynaud, intimated that French resistance might soon be at an end. By the 27th the German forces had occupied Boulogne and Calais; and the British, French and Belgian divisions in the northern sector of the battlefront, north of the Somme, were being pressed from east and south into a narrowing bridgehead around Dunkirk. That night evacuation to the English coast was in full swing.

On the 28th the C.-in-C. Fighter Command told the War Cabinet that owing to the additional commitment to protect the Allied forces on the Continent the Fighter Force for Home Defence had been "reduced almost to cracking point". The Prime Minister thought that the enemy might take advantage of the situation to send in a heavy attack against the United Kingdom. The Chiefs of Staff agreed; and on the following day, the 29th, they warned the War Cabinet "as a matter of urgency and as military advisers to the Government" that it was highly probable the German Command was now setting the stage for a full-scale attack on this country and that the attack might be imminent.

On the 12th June Mr. Churchill, after a meeting with the French Premier, told the War Cabinet that effective resistance by France as a great land power was coming to an end. "We must now concentrate everything", he said, "on the defence of this island." He viewed the new phase of the war with confidence. A declaration that we were firmly resolved to continue the war in all circumstances would prove the best invitation to the United States of America to lend us their support. "We shall continue the blockade" he added, "and win through, though at the cost of ruin and starvation throughout Europe." On the 17th June the French Government accepted the German terms for an armistice.

---

[5] Mr. Winston Churchill became Prime Minister in the place of Mr. Neville Chamberlain on the 10th May: the day of the invasion of Holland.

Chapter 6

# Defence Against a Large Scale Raid

**Scale of Attack**

The imminent threat to which the Chiefs of Staff had referred with such urgency on the 29th May was not that of a full-scale invasion, which was expected to take the Germans some weeks to prepare, but that of a large scale raid, airborne and seaborne, following on the heels of the Dunkirk withdrawal, which might lead to invasion if a footing was established.

The raid might be carried out by a method which hitherto had not been seriously considered. The Chiefs of Staff estimated that a fleet of up to 200 fast motor-boats, carrying 100 men apiece, could assemble in Dutch and Belgian estuaries and harbours unseen by our air reconnaissance, and might make the crossing in the dark hours or in thick weather. The boats, self-propelled and of shallow draught, might be run up on the open beaches simultaneously with a landing of up to 20,000 airborne troops and parachutists inland. The seaborne force would probably be accompanied by armoured fighting vehicles in specially buoyant landing craft which could also be landed on the open beaches.

The Chiefs of Staff admitted that naval and air action might be unable to prevent such a landing; they admitted, too, that if the German force became firmly established ashore the Home Army "had not got the offensive power to drive it out". The result would depend upon the ability of the Navy and the Air Force to prevent the reinforcement of the bridgehead.

The Admiralty, in an appreciation of the 29th May, forecast that the Germans would employ their maximum effort and accept almost catastrophic losses, making the best possible use of air, Fifth Column and armoured vehicles in the first wave. "The success or failure of the

31

first wave would decide whether the enterprise ever reached the scale of an invasion."

## The Airborne Threat
In each country invaded the Germans had at the outset occupied or destroyed the aerodromes. Their technique of airborne attack had been demonstrated on the first day of the invasion of Holland when parties of fifty or more parachutists, armed with submachine guns, had established themselves in groups on Dutch aerodromes. The Dutch experience had been that such groups could not be dealt with rapidly by ground forces without some more effective weapon than rifles. Airborne troops, too, who were landed persistently by every form of air carrier, were usually armed with weapons of high fire-power, and could only be dealt with satisfactorily by similar weapons.

The Air Staff pointed out on the 24th May that German parachutists could be brought over and dropped on, or near, our main fighter aerodromes in South-East England before preventative action could be taken. Of the 5,000 trained German parachutists, 500 might be landed simultaneously at each of the seven vital south-eastern fighter sector head-quarters (Tangmere, Kenley, Biggin Hill, Hornchurch, North Weald, Debden and Duxford). Such a force would suffice, in the Air Staff's opinion, to destroy hangars and aircraft, and wreck the Operations Room arrangements controlling Air Defence to such an extent that troop-carriers with reinforcements might land in numbers without effective opposition.

A critical situation in the air defence of the country would immediately arise. Sustained bomber attacks on the aerodromes the following day might well succeed in achieving air superiority over London and South-east England for a sufficient period to cover the landing of the first wave of a seaborne expedition.

## Ground Defence of Aerodromes
The A.A. gun defence of vital aerodromes was at once strengthened, and the Air Staff urged that the local guards should be reinforced by the best troops available, armed with light automatic weapons on a much higher scale than normal. The existing guards averaged about 100 semi-trained soldiers many of whom had not fired a musketry course; and the Air Staff point of view was that at vital aerodromes no airborne force should be allowed to obtain any footing at all. On the other hand, the C.-in-C. Home Forces, who was responsible for the defence of aerodromes, held that the available trained troops were better employed as counter-attack formations placed within call, at 2 to 3 hours' notice.

Although the difference of opinion on this matter persisted, the Home Forces policy was not changed, the emphasis in the defence of all important Vulnerable and Key Points being placed upon a mobile reserve of Field Army troops within call for counter-attack. Aerodrome local guards were doubled by the employment of R.A.F. station personnel armed with rifles; and open lorries were fitted with Bren machine-guns, mounted in vertical large-diameter concrete pipes, to move out quickly into the centre of the aerodrome against a landing party.[6]

**The Seaborne Threat**

The C.-in-C. Home Forces (General Sir E. Ironside, from being Chief of the Imperial General Staff, had succeeded General Sir W. Kirke as C.-in-C. Home Forces on the 27th May) confirmed the Chiefs of Staff opinion as to the weakness of our land defence. "We are at the present time" he wrote on the 31st May, "very ill-prepared to meet a German offensive which may have an initial strength of 20,000 airborne and 20,000 seaborne troops who will be relatively well trained. A large part of the Army at Home is as yet insufficiently trained and equipped with artillery and armoured fighting vehicles to take the offensive, and must act on the defensive in prepared positions".

The detail of the state of the Home divisions on the 31st May is shown in Appendix 5. Owing to the priority given to the Expeditionary Force they were far below strength in every respect. They averaged little over a half of their establishment of 15,500 men; about a sixth (mostly out-of-date 18-pdr.) of the 72 field guns, and a sixth of the 48 2-pdr. anti-tank guns to which they were entitled; and the deficiency of machine guns was even greater.[7] For mobile reserves they depended upon civilian owned 32-seater motor coaches which would take 8 to 24 hours to collect; and no organization existed for controlling this transport and

---

[6] In order to reduce the number of local guards a Vulnerable Point Adviser (major-general's rank) was appointed in August to decide more carefully the probable scale of attack for each locality, and the protection required, whether against sabotage or airborne attack or both. By August the Army were being asked to give protection to 375 aerodromes, R.D.F. stations, and fuel storage depots requiring 25,000 troops including 10,000 from Field Army units; and local guards for 2,800 key points, in addition to other vulnerable points of importance. The Defence Services, required 17,000 men from Field Army units and 41,000 of Home Defence units. The National Defence companies formed to provide these local guards at the outbreak of war had been replaced and absorbed by Home Defence battalions.

[7] The G.O.C. 1st London Division, responsible for the vital coast sector of Kent, from the Isle of Sheppey (east of Chatham) to Rye, complained to Eastern Command on the 31st May that "I am very weak in field artillery; I have no anti-tank guns, and an inadequate supply of anti-tank rifles and ammunition; I have no armoured cars, no armoured fighting vehicles, and no medium machine guns. (1st Lond. Div. Diary: 31 May 1940).

the civilian drivers in the difficult conditions of active operations against a landing force.

The successful evacuation of the British Expeditionary Force from Dunkirk and Northern France "revolutionised the Home Defence position". Of the 400,000 of our best trained troops sent across the Channel after the outbreak of war 350,000 had returned; and the incorporation of the 12 Field Force divisions into Home Forces brought the Field Army strength up to 27 divisions, excluding semi-trained troops. Another 400,000 men were due to be taken into the Army within the next two months under the conscription call-up. Contingents of Dominion troops had already joined the Field Army in this country; the 1st Canadian Division, which arrived in January, was to be followed shortly by the 2nd, and 9,000 Australian troops and 6,000 from New Zealand had arrived in mid-May.

The shortage was not of man-power. It was that of modern weapons – of up-to-date artillery, anti-tank guns and armoured fighting vehicles, of machine guns and light automatics for the infantry, and of ammunition of all kinds and suitable transport vehicles. Most of this essential Army equipment had had to be left behind in France, and the losses could be made good only by degrees out of current production.

## Revision of the Julius Caesar Plan

The Julius Caesar plan had assumed that a seaborne expedition would have to land in the vicinity of a port; as a consequence extensive stretches of vulnerable open beach on the East and South coasts, and a number of good anchorages, remained largely unprotected and deserted. The problem for the C.-in-C. Home Forces was how to dispose his ill-equipped Army to meet a landing on these unprotected open beaches, and "to defeat a rapid thrust inland by an armoured force supported by dive-bombing aircraft".

The Battle of France had shown "the catastrophic results which could be achieved by armoured fighting vehicles operating through country unprepared for defence". The landing force would have to be "destroyed before it could do any serious damage to London and the industrial Midlands"; and the Army would also "have to be ready to intercept any reinforcements which might escape the vigilance of the Navy and the Air Force". The task was complicated by the extent of the possible landing places. Of the 485 miles of beach on the East and South coasts suitable for the landing of armoured fighting vehicles and other arms 178 miles were along the coasts of East Anglia, Kent and Sussex in the probable invasion area.

The Operation Instructions to meet the new threat, issued by the C.-in-C. Home Forces on the 5th and 15th June are given as Appendix 6. Their purpose was "to prevent the enemy from running riot and tearing the guts out of the country as had happened in France and Belgium". The defence, he explained, had to be in great depth in order to provide against airborne attack inland as well as against seaborne attack on the coast. The three main elements in the revised plan were: (1) a crust acting as an outpost zone on the coast "to give warning of, delay and break up, the initial attack"; (2) a G.H.Q. line of anti-tank obstacles down the east centre of England; and (3) mobile reserves in rear of that anti-tank line.

The G.H.Q. line lay from Richmond (Yorkshire) through Newark and Cambridge to the Thames (Canvey Island) following waterways, steep inclines and other tank obstacles wherever possible; south of the Thames it continued by Maidstone and Basingstoke to Bristol. So sited, as will be seen in Map 2, it covered London and the main industrial centres in the Midlands. Between the G.H.Q. line and the coast were planned intermediate (Command, corps and divisional) anti-tank stop lines. Five of these lines lay across East Anglia to check an advance from the vulnerable beaches about Lowestoft either along the open upland of the north-eastern extremity of the Chilterns on London, or towards the Midlands; and three crossed Kent, Sussex and Surrey as the forward defences of London to the south-east and south. The stop-lines were to contain about 2,500 brick or concrete block-houses to cover road junctions, bridges and tank obstacles …

The coastal divisions, by using the stop-lines, were to confine, break-up and delay an advance inland by a mechanized force. In addition, various methods of checking it were being organized. The majority of the field guns available (786 in all by mid-June) were sited near the coast to cover the more likely landing beaches, and anti-tank mines and obstacles placed on the beaches; roads leading inland were blocked, and stocks of incendiary grenades and sticky bombs were available at every guard-post; auxiliary units, regular and irregular, were being trained to "harry or pursue the German tanks or cut off their crews from supplies of food, water and petrol"; and of the 2-pdr. anti-tank guns, which had proved so effective in France, most of the 167 available by mid-June were kept back in the G.H.Q. line.

These static defence and harrying tactics were intended to give time for the mobile reserves to arrive. The C.-in-C. Home Forces told the Defence Committee that four armoured divisions in reserve would solve the country's defence problem; instead he had less than half the strength of one armoured division. All the heavier tanks had had to be left behind in France; and by the end of June new production, working

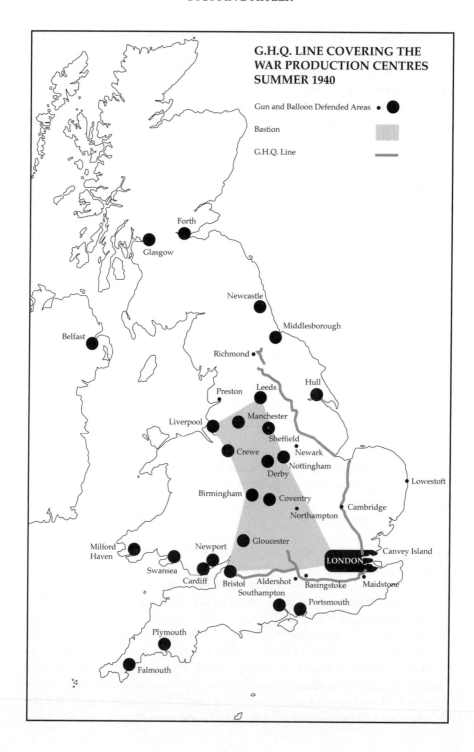

**G.H.Q. LINE COVERING THE
WAR PRODUCTION CENTRES
SUMMER 1940**

Gun and Balloon Defended Areas   ● ⬤

Bastion

G.H.Q. Line

day and night shifts, enabled 81 medium (infantry) tanks to be issued to the 1st Armoured Division. They were disposed partly at Aldershot and partly near Northampton. Also in G.H.Q. reserve were three of the better equipped infantry divisions disposed in the area Aldershot – North London – Northampton so as to be able to move rapidly by brigade groups for independent action to any threatened area along the 400 miles of coast between the Wash and Southampton.

The G.H.Q. reserves were to be ready to strike with the least delay at an enemy wherever he might penetrate. In addition, the 2nd Armoured Division with 178 light reconnaissance tanks was disposed in the Northampton–Newmarket area so as to be able to operate against the flank and rear of an enemy advancing inland from the East Anglian coast or north of the Wash. An allotment of R.A.F. reconnaissance aircraft had been arranged to assist.

The general plan of the defence was therefore a combination of mobile columns and static defence over a wide area. General Ironside admitted that the coastal divisions had few troops in local reserve for counter-attacks; but counter-attacks, if they were to be effective, could not be carried out without the requisite weapons, and the divisions still had very little artillery or transport, and were only partially trained. In the circumstances he thought that there could be little advantage in keeping larger local reserves for counter-attacks.

**Criticism of the Revised Plan**
Both the detail and the dispositions of the plan were strongly criticised. Much of the construction work in the stop-lines had been given out to civilian contractors, and by the 19th June civilian labour 150,000 strong was being employed on the work. Owing to the urgency it was inevitable that mistakes were made.

Many of the road-blocks were valueless, as armoured vehicles could go round them; and many of the pill-boxes were sited facing the wrong way, or where they could serve no purpose, or could not be occupied. "We are becoming pill-box mad", wrote one divisional commander on finding that the garrisoning of the block-houses consumed most of his man-power. The lure of so much concrete was inclined to lead away from first principles, and the stop-lines came to be regarded as a succession of unsupported linear defence positions. Divisional commanders were also worried about the smallness of their local reserves in the knowledge that even under favourable conditions substantial reinforcements could not arrive in under 12 hours.

The Vice-Chiefs of Staff maintained that the idea of holding the coast with outposts and contemplating a main line of resistance after half the country had been overrun seemed to be nothing short of suicidal. The only policy, in their view, was to resist the enemy with the utmost resolution from the moment he set foot on shore. The Chiefs of Staff agreed that the balance of the defence leant too far on the side of a thinly held crust on the coast, with insufficient mobile reserves in the immediate vicinity of the points at which penetration might occur.

The Prime Minister, in his observations on the discussion, suggested that the German "Storm-troop" idea of the 1914-18 War should be copied. "There should be at least 20,000 Storm-troops or 'Leopards', drawn from existing units, ready to spring at the throat of any small landings or descents … the safety of the country depends upon having a large number of 'Leopard' brigade groups which can be directed swiftly, i.e. within four hours, to the points of lodgement. All depends on rapid, resolute engagement of any landed forces which may slip through the sea control. This should not be beyond our powers provided the field troops are not consumed in beach defences, and are kept in high condition of mobility, crouched and ready to spring".

The defence of any part of the coast, he added, was to be measured not by the forces on the coast, but by the number of hours within which strong counter-attacks by mobile troops could be brought to bear upon the landing places. "It ought to be possible to concentrate 10,000 men fully equipped within six hours, and 20,000 men within twelve hours, upon any point where a serious lodgement has been effected. The withholding of the reserves until the full gravity of the attack is known is a nice problem for the Home Command".

He agreed with the principle of the Julius Caesar plan that no serious invasion was practicable without the capture of a harbour and its quays. "In the unhappy event of the enemy capturing a port, larger formations with artillery would be necessary"; and he suggested that "four or five good divisions should be held in general reserve ready to deal with such an improbable misfortune".

## Alteration in the Character of the Defence
The continued respite from German interference until the end of July gave time for a great improvement in the re-equipment of Home Forces, particularly with artillery and armoured fighting vehicles; and the system of static defence and stop-lines was able to be largely abandoned.

It was left to General Sir Alan Brooke, who succeeded General Sir E. Ironside as C.-in-C. Home Forces on the 20th July, to give to the defence a more offensive character. At a meeting of the G.O.C.'s Army Commands at the War Office on the 6th August he explained his intentions, and their gist was contained in his opening sentences. "The idea of linear defence must be stamped out; mobile offensive action must be the basis of our defence. What is required to meet the dual threat of seaborne and airborne attack is all-round defence in depth with the maximum number of troops trained and disposed for a rapid counter-offensive".

The whole defence lay-out was to be closed up nearer to the coast. Local mobile reserves were to be within closer striking distance of probable landing areas; and, during July and August, the G.H.Q. reserves were moved forward to Cambridge, Hertfordshire and Surrey, their distance from the coast being reduced by about half.

The stop-lines, constructed with such urgency, were to be regarded as of secondary importance. Work upon them was to be limited to forming nodal points for all-round defence at the principal road junctions and communication centres, the more important of which were to be fortified as "anti- tank islands". The stop-line garrisons were to be withdrawn to strengthen the local mobile reserves; and in an emergency the strong-points were to be occupied by any troops in the neighbourhood.

The artillery policy, too was transformed. With the reduction in importance of the rearward lines, the anti-tank guns were to be moved up to cover the beach obstacles and exits, and the field artillery returned to a mobile role. Heavy artillery were to be sited within range of likely airborne and seaborne landing places.

---

[8]  H.F. Artillery Inst. No. 3: 31 July 1940. The German Command had made no preparations for a large scale raid on this country. It was not until the 2nd July that planning for the invasion of England was ordered.

Chapter 7

# Defence Against Air Attack

**The New Scale of Air Attack**
With the German air bases spread out from Norway to Brittany the main advantages possessed by our Air Defence in September 1939 no longer existed. German long-range bombers could be escorted by long-range fighters over the entire country, including the West coast ports and the shipping approaches; short-range dive-bombers and fighters could cover southern England south of a line from the Humber to the Bristol Channel.

The Chiefs of Staff appreciation of the 25th May as to the possible course of German action after the fall of France is given as Appendix 7. In spite of the greatly increased air threat they doubted whether the heavy and sustained air attacks required for a knock-out blow would be practicable owing to the all-round improvement in our air defence since September 1939. Instead they believed that the German Command would attempt to obtain a high degree of air superiority over the country as a preliminary to invasion, assisted by Fifth Column activities.

**Directive to Commanders-in-Chief**
After discussion between the Chiefs of Staff and the Commanders-in-Chief of the three Services on the 26th July an Air Staff memorandum was issued as a directive to govern the action of the three Services in the event of invasion.

The directive is given in full as Appendix 8. It maintained that until Germany had defeated our fighter force an invasion by sea was not a practical operation of war. The first phase of an invasion was therefore likely to be a large scale air offensive against our fighter defence, that is, fighter aircraft in the air, fighter aerodromes and organisation and the aircraft industry.

The German Command might not risk a seaborne invasion until our naval forces also had been seriously weakened. Another preliminary phase, simultaneous with the attack on the fighter force, might therefore be a heavy air attack on our naval forces and naval bases, particularly those on the South-East and East coasts, extending north to the Home Fleet base at Scapa Flow. During the preliminary air offensive, too, heavy attacks were to be expected on centres of war production and of distribution of food and supplies in order to cause the maximum disorganisation in the country preparatory to invasion.

If bridgeheads were formed on the coast the German Command would have to establish a line of sea-communication from the Continent in order to sustain a major invasion. To secure such a line of supply would require clear air superiority over our fighter force to enable the German bombers to operate freely against our naval forces in the narrow waters between the opposing coasts.

The preliminary air offensive was expected to last for some weeks before the high degree of air superiority required to land and maintain an invading force, adequate to overrun the country, could be obtained.

The Chiefs of Staff considered that the ability of the country to avoid defeat depended on whether the morale of the population could withstand the strain of unrestricted bombardment, on whether our fighter defence would be able to reduce the scale of air attack to within reasonable bounds, and on our capacity to resist invasion until the autumn. The respite from a serious invasion threat during the winter months would enable Fighter Command to attain a degree of expansion difficult for the German air force to master, and by the spring of 1941 the Army would be trained and equipped adequately to make invasion an even more formidable undertaking.

**Priority for Fighter Command**
The crux of the problem lay in air defence, in which the maintenance of the fighter force had a completely dominating position. The Chiefs of Staff asked that the country's energies should be concentrated primarily on the production of fighter aircraft and the training of crews; and that the protection of fighter aircraft production centres should have priority in ground defence.

By mid-July the heavy losses in fighter aircraft during the withdrawal of the Expeditionary Force from France had been made good; and Fighter Command had 59 squadrons in operations and 9 forming (fighter production was averaging 250 to 300 a month, including about 90 Spitfires and 120 Hurricanes). To meet the new scale of attack, and to keep abreast of Germany's estimated fighter strength (1,550 including over 500 long range fighters) the fighter force was to be raised to 76 squadrons (1,126 first line aircraft) as soon as possible.[9]

A vital factor to maintain Fighter Command in operation was the widest possible dispersion of aerodromes and satellite landing grounds. The 70 operational fighter and bomber aerodromes already in use by the summer of 1940 were to be increased to the full limit of suitable flat land available in this country.

The chain of R.D.F. stations along the East and South coasts was to be extended to the West coast. The danger gap below the 1,000 foot altitude, which had been the weakness of the system at the outbreak of war, was being overcome by the establishment of smaller (C.H.L.) stations which were able to detect lower flying aircraft approaching the coast. By mid-June seventeen of these low-location stations had been installed out of the 21 projected; their range was 30 miles, compared with at least 80 miles of the larger R.D.F. stations.

Ten new fighter sectors were formed in the Aircraft Fighting Zone, mostly to cover the north, north-west and south-west areas. By July 3,900 searchlights were available to illuminate the Aircraft Fighting Zone and the Gun-Defended Areas out of the approved total of 4,128. The balloon barrage, which had proved its value as a deterrent to low-flying attack was to be provided for more vulnerable points, and the authorised establishment raised from 2,000 to 2,600 first-line balloons with 100 per cent. reserves.

While the main effort in aircraft production was placed on fighter aircraft during the emergency of 1940, a strong counter-offensive force of bomber aircraft had to be maintained to reduce the scale of air attack at its source and to bomb vital objectives in Germany, as also to attack shipping concentrations in the invasion ports. By August Bomber Command had 613 first line aircraft spread over 25 operational stations, compared with Germany's estimated 2,000 bombers (1,600 long-range and 400 short-range dive bombers).[10] It was expected that during 1941 the emphasis of aircraft production would be able to be transferred to bomber aircraft.

### Revision of the A.A. Ground Defences

The new scale of attack required considerable changes in the lay-out of A.A. Command. The re-distribution of guns was approved in August by

[9]  According to German records (Fuehrer Conferences on Naval Affairs 1940 (A.L.721 p. 88) the German air force in the west had 1,308 first line fighters (including 375 long-range) at the beginning of August.

[10]  German records give the strength of the German air striking force in the West at the beginning of August as 1,451 bombers (1,105 long range and 346 short-range).

the Chiefs of Staff in their review of the Air Defence arrangements which is given as Appendix 8.

Fighter aerodromes received at once their full allotment of 4 heavy guns and, in addition, 2 light A.A. guns and 8 to 12 A.A. machine guns for use against low-flying or airborne attack. The A.A. protection at naval bases on the East and South-east coasts was raised by 30 to 50 per cent.; and at Scapa Flow, the base of the Home Fleet the 8 guns in position at the outbreak of war had been increased to 88 by July, and by October 100 guns were in position. With all main shipping approaches diverted to the north-about route around Ireland the A.A. gun defences of the West coast ports – Bristol-Avonmouth, Liverpool-Mersey, and the Clyde – were able to be strengthened at the expense of the South coast ports. Additional defence was also given to supply distribution centres and vital war production areas.

Immediate requirements had to be met by transferring mobile guns from places which could best spare them, and from war production centres not of primary importance.

The need was so urgent that London's A.A. guns had been reduced by July from 114 to 92: but with the air attacks in September these guns and more were back, so that by October the number of heavy A.A. guns in the London area had risen to 199.

The heavy A.A. guns deployed had nearly doubled since the outbreak of war (1,209 by July, 1940 compared with 689 in September, 1939); nevertheless that total was little more than half the requirement authorised in February, 1939, i.e. 2,232. As a result of their review the Chiefs of Staff approved a further increase of 1,512, making an authorised total of 3,744, of which 50 per cent. were to be mobile; but the average monthly output during 1940 was only 85 (20 4.5-inch and 65 3.7-inch) to meet all demands, Home and overseas.

The unsatisfactory method of directing the fire of the heavy A.A. guns had not improved. The sound-locator system broke down against the high-flying and massed German air attacks, and the barrages used in August and September were largely uncontrolled. It was not until October that the radar (radio direction and ranging) principle of the R.D.F. Stations was applied to anti-aircraft gunfire control. The difficulty had been the inability of radar to give the height; and in October an elevation finding attachment solved the problem but was inaccurate when the angle of sight increased to more than 45°. There was a very large blind zone right over the guns and for some distance around them; but the improved results showed that the future of anti-aircraft shooting would have to be associated with the radar principle.

The deficiency of light A.A. guns was even greater than that of the heavy guns; less than a quarter (431) of the authorised 1,860 light A.A. guns had been delivered. To that approved total the Chiefs of Staff in August added 2,250 which brought it to 4,410. The new requirement was for an average of six light A.A. guns each for another 425 vulnerable and key points, (150 Service, chiefly ports and aerodromes, 200 new industrial key points and at 75 places to cover balloon barrages and to oppose mine-1aying aircraft). The strength of A.A. Command had increased to over 157,000 …

Experience had shown that German dive-bombing attacks had been one of the most powerful means of breaking down the defence. G.H.Q. Home Forces had accordingly arranged with A.A. Command for the provision of 120 heavy and 84 Light A.A. guns for the protection of anti-invasion troops. Army base areas which might be subject to bombing were to be arranged in areas already covered by A.D.G.B. artillery zones.

**Civil Defence Services**
The vital importance of all measures designed to enable the population to resist the demoralizing effect of sustained bombing attacks was being brought home to every individual by the daily progress of events. It was estimated in June that as a whole these measures, such as air-raid shelters, auxiliary fire brigades and the entire Air Raid Precautions organisation with its many ramifications, were about 75 per cent. up to the 1939 programme. Even so the Chiefs of Staff pointed out that against the new scale of attack the 1939 programme was inadequate; and in their opinion the existing quasi-peacetime organisation gave no guarantee that the country could hold out.

The detailed progress of Civil Defence (Air Raid Precautions) measures during 1940 is described in the Official History of Civil Defence. An example was the rapid development of underground air-raid shelters. A large proportion of the houses in the London Civil Defence Region had basements convertible into shelters, or back-gardens in which shelters had been dug; and, in addition, by the end of September, public underground shelters were available to accommodate 1,300,000 persons, not including the deep Underground Railway Stations in which over 100,000 persons were sheltering during raids at that time. The organisation for sounding the air raid sirens is described in Appendix 18.

Chapter 8

# Defence Against Invasion

**Scale of Attack**
The probable strength of the initial landing force to establish bridgeheads in this country was put at about 5 divisions, or 75,000 troops, supported by an airborne force of up to 15,000 on the first day. The most likely ports of departure, to give the shortest sea-passage, were between the Dutch estuaries and Cherbourg; and the most probable landing places, to allow for maximum fighter cover, were between the Wash and Newhaven.

The German Command was estimated to have up to 100 divisions available for further conquests. That figure allowed for 76 divisions to keep order in the occupied countries of Europe, and 20 for internal security in Germany and a general reserve. Of their ten armoured divisions five were known to be stationed in France and the Low Countries, as well as four of their six motorised divisions. Sufficient sea-transport was probably available to carry 30 divisions to these shores.

The seaborne expedition was likely to be covered by the maximum available strength of the German air force. The naval escorts would probably include all the light naval forces the German navy could muster, estimated at 10 destroyers, 24 torpedo-boats, 40 to 50 motor torpedo-boats and 40 to 50 submarines. Heavier surface forces were estimated to have been reduced by August to one battle-ship and 3 6-inch cruisers; but the Admiralty doubted if the German Naval Command would risk its battle cruisers in the southern part of the North Sea.

**Principles of the Defence**
The traditional principles governing the defence of these islands against

45

invasion were re-affirmed by the Prime Minister and Minister for Defence, in a paper of the 6th August which is given as Appendix 10.

The three stages of a seaborne expedition would be: 1. the concentration of shipping and troops at the points of departure; 2. the sea-passage; and 3. the establishment of a bridgehead in this country.

An airborne attack would probably be launched previous to, or simultaneous with the arrival of the seaborne expedition. The predominant and first task of our armed forces was to concentrate upon the seaborne expedition, as it was the most dangerous. Next in importance was the necessity to ensure the protection of the fighter squadrons, their maintenance organisation and the aircraft industry. Third in importance was to dispose of the airborne invasion.

The Air Force and the Royal Navy were the decisive elements in the defence, both in defeating the initial landing force and in the prevention of a supply line to the bridgeheads. Should the Air Force be worn down by prolonged air fighting and by the destruction of its aircraft supply the power of the Navy remained decisive against invasion.

**Air Defence**
The tasks of the Operational Command of the Royal Air Force were laid down in the Air Staff memorandum of the 30th July (see Appendix 8).

Coastal Command had the primary task of air reconnaissance over the enemy coastal areas to give early warning of shipping and troop concentration, and the departure of convoys.

Bomber Command would use its maximum force to attack and destroy with bombs and machine-gun fire any shipping in the probable embarkation ports, convoys on passage and at the landing beaches. Its task was also to reduce the scale of air and airborne attack by attacking enemy aerodromes and troop carrying aircraft on the ground; but attacks on shipping, if reported, were to have priority.

Fighter Command was to provide protection, to the limit of its range, to Bomber Command in attacks on troops and shipping; and also to naval forces both in harbour and when engaged in destroying the enemy's transports and escort vessels. In its action against seaborne attack priority was to be given to strike at dive-bombers operating against our naval forces. Fighter Command would also have to protect its own aerodromes and maintenance organisations against both air and airborne attack by striking at the enemy's bombers and troop-carrying aircraft.

To assist the Army to destroy any enemy that might succeed in landing on our shores 168 Army Co-operation aircraft were at the disposal of Home Forces.

**Naval Defence**

An Admiralty appreciation on invasion at the end of May is given as Appendix 11 and the instructions for the disposition of the Home Fleet as Appendix 12.

Four flotillas of destroyers, a total of 36, under the C.-in-C. Nore were to be based in or near the likely invasion area, one each at the Humber, Harwich, Sheerness and Dover, or, as an alternative, Portsmouth (see Map 3). Supporting forces for these destroyers included two cruisers at Sheerness and another at the Humber; the destroyer force in the Channel would be supported by such battleships as could be made available based on Plymouth, with escorts as could be spared. The heavier 6-inch cruisers would remain with the main Home Fleet at Scapa Flow. The heavy ships of the Home Fleet – 2 battleships, one battle cruiser and 8 cruisers – were to be organised into two forces, either of which would be overwhelmingly strong, the one to contain a Northern outbreak and the other to counter a dash to the south from Norwegian or German harbours.

The greater part of the destroyers were at sea every night, and at rest during the day. In this way they would encounter enemy vessels in transit during the night, and by day they could reach any landing point in their area in two or three hours. They could immediately break up the landing craft, interrupt the landing and fire upon the landed troops who, however lightly equipped, would have to have some proportion of their ammunition and equipment carried on to the beaches from the boats. For their most powerful intervention on the beaches, from dawn onwards, the destroyers would require strong air support from fighter aircraft, and co-operation was to be arranged with Fighter Command according to circumstances.

In all, of the 700 armed patrolling vessels at the Admiralty's disposal for reconnaissance work, 200 to 300 were always at sea in the threatened area between the Wash and Newhaven, and the maximum number of small craft that could be spared from escort duties (about 17 corvettes, 17 sloops and 15 motor torpedo-boats). In Home Waters, too, were 35 submarines.

A mine-sweeping force of 25 fast mine-sweepers and 140 mine-sweeping trawlers was disposed between Sunderland and Portsmouth to maintain a searched channel between those two ports. Also an Auxiliary Patrol of about 400 trawlers and small vessels was disposed round the coast between Invergordon and Portland to give warning of an invading force.

By early July the Admiralty considered that the dispositions of its light naval forces and supporting cruisers in the narrow waters of the

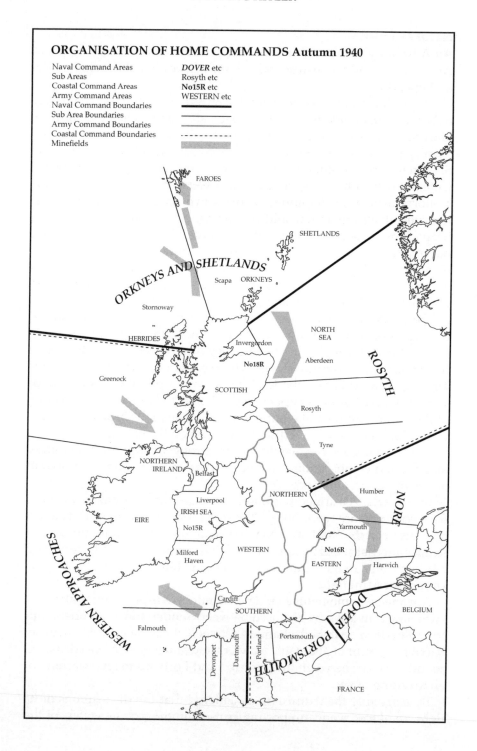

ORGANISATION OF HOME COMMANDS Autumn 1940

Naval Command Areas          *DOVER* etc
Sub Areas                    Rosyth etc
Coastal Command Areas        **No15R** etc
Army Command Areas           WESTERN etc
Naval Command Boundaries
Sub Area Boundaries
Army Command Boundaries
Coastal Command Boundaries
Minefields

FAROES

SHETLANDS

ORKNEYS AND SHETLANDS

Scapa    ORKNEYS

Stornoway

NORTH
SEA

HEBRIDES

Invergordon

ROSYTH

No18R        Aberdeen

Greenock

SCOTTISH

Rosyth

Tyne

NORTHERN
IRELAND    Belfast

NORTHERN        Humber

NORE

Liverpool

EIRE        IRISH SEA

No15R

Yarmouth

Milford
Haven           WESTERN        No16R

EASTERN        Harwich

WESTERN APPROACHES

Cardiff

SOUTHERN        BELGIUM

Falmouth

Devonport    Dartmouth    Portland    Portsmouth

PORTSMOUTH

DOVER

FRANCE

probable invasion area made a surprise crossing by the Germans in small craft, though possible, a most hazardous undertaking. A typical anti-invasion operation order for light naval forces, Operation Plan J.F. for Portsmouth Command, is given as Appendix 13. In the broader parts of both the North Sea and the Channel a seaborne expedition would be faced by even greater peril as part of the voyage would have to be made in daylight.

During August, decisions were made by the Admiralty regarding the despatch of heavy ships to the narrow waters of the North Sea. They were not to be sent unless enemy heavy ships came out in support of a seaborne expedition accepting the risks involved. If their presence was reported it was essential that our heavy ships should move south against them, also accepting risks, and engage them at the earliest opportunity. The route inside the East Coast mine-barrage was recommended (see Map 3).

On the 13th September, when a large scale invasion appeared imminent, heavy ships of the Home Fleet were ordered from Scapa to Rosyth where they remained until November. The Battleship *Revenge*, too was ordered to Plymouth, and later (11th October) to Spithead.

## Naval and Air Co-Operation

The organisation for reconnaissance by naval and air patrols over the sea-barrier had been supplemented by mid-June by arrangements for watching the whole coast by coastguards and special coast-watchers.

Inland the watch was taken up by the Observer Corps which passed its information through R.A.F. channels to Fighter Command, and also direct to the local military commanders. By mid-July the naval and air arrangements to counter invasion were such that, in the opinion of the First Sea Lord, the "maintenance of a line of supply by the Germans to this country unless they had overcome both our air force and our navy seems practically impossible".

## Defensive Minefield

The defensive mine-fields in Home waters in 1940 are shown in Map 3. With the occupation by the Germans of the Dutch and Belgian coast in May 1940 the East coast mine-field, laid at the outbreak of war from the North of Scotland to the Humber to protect East coast shipping against attack from German harbours, was extended southwards to the Thames estuary. The Dover Straits mine-field, laid in September 1939 to cover the transport of the Expeditionary Force to France, was strengthened; and mine-fields were also laid off the South coast ports.

49

The laying of the Cornwall–Ireland (Eire) mine-barrage to block the southern entrance to the Irish Sea began on the 26th July; and on the 11th September the same mine-laying squadron, the 1st, began to' lay the North-Western Approaches mine-fields off Northern Ireland.

The Northern mine-barrage from the Orkneys (later from Cape Wrath) was begun on the 10th July, and continued to the Faroes in September. The extension to Iceland was taken in hand in November.

## The Danger of Fog, Smoke and Gas

An invader was expected to use every available means for concealing his departure and places of arrival. The gravest danger, in the opinion of the Prime Minister, was fog, as it would favour the infiltration tactics by which the Germans would most probably attempt to secure their lodgements. For that reason he asked, during the peak of the invasion menace in September that the strongest possible air barrage be put down upon the invasion ports during the night and early morning should conditions of fog prevail. The Chiefs of Staff agreed that fog would not be a deterrent to the landing of an invasion force, and might be used to the enemy's advantage. The probable effects of fog on the action of sea, air and land forces was examined in detail in a memorandum of the 22nd September by the Vice Chiefs of Staff.

The use of smoke screens on a large scale to cover an invasion, though considered technically practicable, was a two-edged weapon which might prove more a hindrance than an aid to an invading force and its supporting aircraft. The subject was dealt with at length in a memorandum by the Joint Intelligence Committee on the 20th July. An invader was more likely to rely on darkness, the period of which could be predicted, or in low visibility, rather than on smoke which required particular wind and atmospheric conditions.

The Air Staff took the view that though gas might be used against troops it was unlikely to be employed against the civil population or industrial areas. The possible scale of attack was put at 880 tons of gas bombs or gas spray per day over a period of a month; and, in view of reports that the German aircraft were being prepared for carrying gas containers, the Prime Minister directed the Chiefs of Staff to study the possibility of instant retaliation upon the German population on the largest possible scale in the event of a gas attack on this country.

## Defence of Ports, and Coast Defence

In May 1940 a high priority for immediate defence was given to all the undefended minor ports and landing beaches on the East and South coasts at which armoured fighting vehicles and transport might land. To meet the sudden demand the Army's resources were quite inadequate; and the Admiralty, on the 19th May agreed to lend to the War Office for coast defence purposes 150 6-inch guns from its own stocks – earmarked for mounting on merchant ships.

This initial Admiralty loan proved quite inadequate; and by the end of the year it had increased to 420 guns (140 6-inch, 20 5.5-inch, 30 4.7-inch and 230 4-inch). A large proportion of these guns were sited so as to cover anti-tank obstacles and possible landing approaches along the East Kent and East Anglian beaches; even so, many vulnerable places along the coast remained without gun defences. The manning, as the provision, of the coast defence armament was an Army responsibility; but the Army had not the trained men for the purpose, and of the 46 new batteries half were manned by the Navy and Royal Marines until Army detachments could be provided.

The "defended" ports were reclassified in November 1940 into 33 major and 50 minor defended ports, and the armament in position at each on the 30th November is shown in Appendix 3. The calibre of the armament was limited mainly to the requirements for close defence against destroyers, armed merchant vessels, mine-layers, boom-smashers, submarines and motor torpedo-boats. The counter-bombardment (9.2-inch) guns were outranged by the guns of modem 8-inch cruisers; but that disadvantage was counter-balanced by the assumption that squadrons of Bomber Command would be available at short notice to engage enemy capital ships approaching the coast.

The number of A.A. guns at each port is shown in the K.P.I.D. tables; and further details of naval measures for the defence of ports and dock-yards in the summer of 1940 are given in the Admiralty monograph.

**Land Defence**
The purpose of the Home Army was primarily to make an enemy come in such large numbers as to afford a proper target for our naval and air forces, and to make enemy preparations and movement noticeable to air reconnaissance.

The disposition of the Home Army assumed that the Navy had a good prospect of intercepting a seaborne expedition on passage and that, outside the narrow waters at least, any landing force could not be maintained by sea; also that our Air Force would be able to render untenable any landing outside the limit of enemy fighter cover, and precarious within that limit.

The Army's anti-invasion task was therefore to be in a position to destroy that part of the first wave of a seaborne and airborne expedition which might reach this country, and to be ready to intercept any reinforcements which might escape our naval and air control.

A revised estimate of the strength of a seaborne landing was made by the First Sea Lord in July and summarised by the Prime Minister in his paper on Invasion on the 6th August (see Appendix 10). Given favourable conditions he put at 12,000 the strength of a force which might land between the Wash and Dover in high speed motor-boats from the innumerable harbours and stretches of canal between Terschelling and Cap Gris Nez. That figure excluded 20 per cent. of the expedition which our coastal naval patrols might be expected to stop. In addition armoured fighting vehicles and artillery might be brought across in special landing craft.

The stretch of coast from Dover to Land's End was less menaced because the Navy and Air Force would take care that no mass of enemy shipping and still less protecting warships, passed through the Straits of Dover to the French Channel ports. Our air reconnaissance over the French harbours was good, and their nature and lay-out was such that the Germans could not hope to make preparations for an invasion on an extensive scale unseen; but by using small craft and given suitable weather the First Sea Lord considered that 5,000 troops might be brought across and landed. The Prime Minister doubled that figure for greater security.

The West coast from Cornwall to the Mull of Kintyre was the least vulnerable. An expedition would be open to attack by our cruisers and flotillas; and the strong mine-field from Cornwall to Ireland covered the Bristol Channel and the Irish Sea from southward attack. With the Home Fleet at Scapa and Rosyth an expedition from Norway was unlikely. But in favourable weather 10,000 troops might be landed on our Northern coast and islands.

In thick weather too, an expedition from North German ports of about fifty moderate sized fast ships, carrying up to 75,000 troops, might not be detected till close to the coast, and could be run ashore on selected beaches between Rosyth and Southwold (Suffolk). Allowing for considerable losses during unloading, the First Sea Lord estimated that 50,000 might get ashore with a proportion of armoured fighting vehicles.

**Disposition of Home Forces**
The coastal area was to be held as an outpost zone. The greater part of the mobile reserves were behind the Wash – Newhaven sector where landing forces would have the maximum fighter cover and would be nearest to the probable initial objective, London. Landings on other coastal sectors and islands were to be contained by the local garrisons,

relying on the Navy and Air Force to isolate the landing force from reinforcements and supplies. No immediate land assistance to the local garrisons was to be expected.

The infantry divisions were still "backward" as regards training. Half of them had had little collective training; and those which were fit to operate as brigade groups were untrained in motorised movement for a mobile role. Four divisions were fully equipped and eight were fairly equipped; but the remainder were deficient in many important items, particularly in transport despite the requisitioning of all vehicles of a suitable type.

The deficiency of light anti-aircraft guns to protect the troops against dive-bombing attack also caused grave concern; only four batteries (48 guns) were at that time (August) available for co-operation with the Field Army in the event of invasion. The beach and forward defences in the more vulnerable areas had been strengthened with men and materials, particularly with guns (6-pdr. and 4-inch), anti-tank mines and obstacles.

The mobile reserves were placed mainly so as to give protection to the more vulnerable and important ports on the assumption, as in the Julius Caesar plan, that the German Command would have to capture a port in order to carry through an invasion to success. By early September the available armoured units were equipped with 240 medium (infantry) tanks, for close support of the infantry near the probable landing areas, and 108 cruiser tanks; both these tank models were equipped with the 2-pdr. gun. The number of light reconnaissance tanks had nearly trebled, to 514, since mid-June. The number of 2-pdr. anti-tanks guns had also been trebled, to 498, by production during the previous three months June, July and August; and production of field guns during the same period (194 25-pdrs. and 231 converted 25-pdrs.) had increased the quantity available by 50 per cent.

The G.H.Q. reserve consisted of two corps, north and south of London: the IV Corps (2nd Armoured Division, 42nd Division, 43rd Division, and 31st Infantry Brigade Group) in the Hertfordshire area (Chesham–Royston) and the VII Corps (1st Armoured Division, 1st Canadian Division, and 1st Army Tank Brigade) in Surrey (Leatherhead–Reigate). The time that armoured and mechanized reinforcements were expected to take to reach an area of operations is given in the instructions for the VII Corps (see Appendix 14). The difficulty of communication due to the scarcity of army cable, telephone and wireless sets was temporarily overcome by the use of the G.P.O. telephone system. Also, civilian wireless sets were issued to units, and an army broadcasting station was set up to give the latest information.

The Local Defence Volunteers, renamed the Home Guard on the 31st July, had become a most valuable adjunct to Home Forces. Already nearly 500,000 strong, its localised function provided a network of defended villages, parishes and towns to break up and delay airborne attack and, in the coastal sector, seaborne attack by reinforcing the static defences. As their training advanced, mobile detachments were formed among the younger men, using motor-cars, motor cycles and bicycles, in order to deal more quickly with an emergency.

The C.-in-C. Home Forces was confident that any part of a seaborne force which escaped our sea-control would probably be prevented from obtaining a footing on land; and "even should a landing force have an initial success it would probably be destroyed before it had penetrated to any depth inland".

## Further Criticisms

The sister Services were not satisfied. The difference of opinion on the defence of the coast, like that over the ground defence of aerodromes, arose from the fact that the Army had made no allowance for exceptional circumstances.

The First Sea Lord referred in particular to the Kent coast, from the North Foreland to Dungeness, the one part of the sea barrier where our full naval strength could not be developed. The Germans with their long-range guns about Cap Gris Nez could already deny to our naval forces quite half the Dover Straits.

Assuming that by a surprise attack in fog or in some other way they could get possession of Dover and capture its gun defences, they would then be in a position to deny the whole Dover defile to our naval forces. If they could do this they might be able to send a stream of craft across from Calais to Dover with tanks, guns and everything they needed for a full-scale battle. "With the vast quantities of war material which Germany possesses today, compared to which our own material is almost as nothing, there really might be the prospect of an invasion succeeding if once they get a solid footing in this country and even a moderately secure supply line. All we could do to stop that supply line would be by air attack which we know from experience is not enough, at least by night."

For that reason, the First Sea Lord added, "while it might be accepted on other parts of the coast that our coast defences are a "crust" and the main body of resistance would be found farther back, that rule must not apply to the Dover area where the coast-line must be held at all costs. Under no conditions could we accept that the Germans get any footing there at all". He did not think the matter had been looked at in that way by the C.-in-C. Home Forces, and suggested that the Chiefs of Staff should raise it immediately.

The Chief of the Air Staff, Sir Cyril Newall, had also pointed out that from the air point of view the most favourable moment for defeating a seaborne attack was during the approach and disembarkation when a large scale of air attack could be delivered without endangering our land forces or the civil population.

## The Defence of the Kent and Sussex Beaches Doubled in Strength

The objections were met in part during the following weeks. On the 30th September the C.-in-C. Home Forces told the Chiefs of Staff that another corps of 2 divisions would be needed in South-East England to make the position there reasonably secure; and in his defence plan for the spring of 1941, 3 additional divisions were placed in Kent and Sussex, and an extra Field Army division behind the more vulnerable East Anglian beaches.

The coast defence garrisons were doubled in strength in those two vital areas, and the beaches there were to be held as the main line of resistance.

## The Dover Guns

The unsuccessful efforts made during 1940 to close the Dover Straits to enemy shipping by gunfire are described in the History of the Long-range Dover guns. By September the only methods of attacking enemy shipping in the further half of the Straits was by aircraft and mine-laying.

Our super-charged 14-inch gun with a theoretical range of 49,000 yards had been mounted in the Dover area, but was unable to reach the French coast (38,000 yards). A 13.5-inch gun loaned by the Navy, and expected to be able to lob shells into Calais and Boulogne, was not installed till the end of the year. On the other hand the Germans were estimated to have twelve long-range guns in position about Cap Gris Nez, and emplacements ready for twenty; they had already shelled Hawkinge aerodrome at a range of over 40,000 yards.

Close-defence guns in the Dover area by the end of September included eight 12-inch howitzers, some well back from the coast, five 9.2-inch guns (17,600 yards) some forward and some back to cover the coast, seven 6-inch guns (12,000 yards) and twelve 5.5-inch guns. In addition 27 guns equipments, up to 6-inch calibre, had been mounted between the North Foreland and Dungeness for coast defence. The intention was to increase the Dover batteries by eight gun equipments for counter-battery across the Straits and to control shipping, 27 guns for long ranges and 38 medium and short range guns for close defence.

**Civil Invasion Preparations**

The task of solving the numerous urgent problems which would arise for co-ordinating military and civil plans in the event of a German landing was the responsibility of the Home Defence Committee of the War Cabinet and of the Home Defence Executive at G.H.Q. Home Forces. The Chief Civil Staff Officer, Sir Findlater Stewart, was chairman of both committees.

Voluntary evacuation from coastal towns between Yarmouth and Folkestone was encouraged, and the population was warned that if invasion occurred, all civilians were to stay where they were, and to keep off the roads. By mid-July out of a population of 280,000 in the coastal towns of East Anglia, 127,000 had been evacuated voluntarily and by special arrangements for children and old people; and of the 207,000 in the coastal towns of Kent, 80,000 had moved inland.

In September the C.-in-C. Home Forces asked that the evacuation programme be extended westwards to Brighton (inclusive) and also from obvious bombing targets inland such as the road junction towns of Ipswich, Colchester and Canterbury.

In any particular operational area the military commander was to take control, being advised on civil matters by the Regional Commissioner. Should any territory be effectively occupied by the Germans the older men of the Police Force and of the Civil Defence Services, including Air Raid Precautions personnel were to "stay-put" with the civilian population, and carry on with the work for which they had been trained. Younger men, trained in the use of arms, were to withdraw and co-operate with the Home Guard and the Regulars in the neighbourhood. Ambulances would be left in any occupied territory; but all other transport was to be either removed or immobilised.

The denial of resources to a landing force was of vital importance; and arrangements for the removal or destruction of all such supplies were the responsibility of the Home Defence Executive. Special precautions had to be taken about petrol; the abundant supplies left in the roadside garages in Northern France had been a major factor in the rapid German armoured advance to the coast.

The thinning-out of garage pipes by 50 per cent (over 100,000) around the coastal area from the Moray Firth to the Bristol Channel began on the 1st June with the issue of Petroleum Order No.3 (under the Defence Regulation 19B); and local Military authorities were given detailed instructions regarding the destruction of the remainder in an emergency.

Chapter 9

# The Control Organization

**System of Command**

The Naval and Army Commands in 1940 are shown on Map 3. The system of Command in the event of invasion was set out by the Chiefs of Staff in a memorandum of the 4th July.

The C.-in-C. Home Fleet, working directly under the Admiralty, commanded the naval units based in this country. The shore organisation was in six Commands (Rosyth, Dover, The Nore, Portsmouth, Plymouth, North Western Approaches (Liverpool), Orkneys and Shetlands); a seventh was the C.-in-C. convoy operations in the North Western Approaches established on the 4th September with headquarters in Liverpool.

The Air Ministry co-ordinated the work of the four operational Air Commands (Coastal, Fighter, Bomber and Army Co-operation) each of which had its own commander-in-chief.

Operational control of all army units in the United Kingdom was vested in G.H.Q. Home Forces. The threat of invasion had found the G.H.Q. organisation unprepared for active operations, and by the end of May it had been re-cast as the headquarters of a Group of Armies in the field. Each of the six peace-time administrative Commands was regarded as analogous to an Army headquarters; and Corps headquarters were created within the Commands. In the Eastern Command, for example, the sectors north and south of the Thames became the XI and XII Corps respectively. Within corps the normal organisation of divisions and brigades was retained as far as possible. Administration of the Home Commands was so firmly rooted in the War Office through Commands that the administrative duties of G.H.Q. Home Forces were restricted to ensuring that the arrangements made suited the plans.

The Northern Ireland and Iceland Commands were under War Office control as were units due to proceed overseas, training units, commandos and the Free French contingent; other foreign units, chiefly Polish and Czech., in the country were under Home Forces. In the event of invasion, however, all units in the United Kingdom were to come under operational control of Home Forces.

**Co-ordination of Command**

Arrangements to ensure co-ordination of command, according to the established practice of the three Services, were already in force; intelligence reports obtained by the combined efforts of the Navy and Air Force were dealt with by a combined staff.

With the start of the invasion battle on these shores the conduct of inshore and land operations was to come under the operational control of the C.-in-C. Home Forces. He would direct the land forces, and as far as possible the R.A.F. Commands would carry out his wishes. He had at his battle headquarters an operational staff which, in addition to his own Chief of the General Staff, included a naval Staff Officer (Rear-Admiral) and an air Staff Officer (Air Vice-Marshal); and he was in direct cable communication with the Admiralty and the Royal Air Force Commands. Area Combined Headquarters, containing Navy, Army and Air Force Coastal Command staffs, were at Rosyth, the Nore, Plymouth and Liverpool.

This system of control ensured unity of command while allowing for decentralisation for the execution of orders.

For the co-ordination of military and civil defence measures the Home Defence Executive set up on the 10th May was considered too unwieldy, and by the end of that month it had become a branch of G.H.Q. Home Forces controlled by the Chief Civil Staff Officer with a Joint civil and military staff. It was available at all times to convey the wishes and instructions of the C.-in-C. Home Forces to the civil ministries; and during operations it was to become an executive branch of the Staff for all civil matters.

A combined Home Defence operations room was established at St. Paul's School, Hammersmith; and an Advance Headquarters, Home Forces, was in readiness in the Cabinet War Room, as the Prime Minister considered it absolutely essential that the C.-in-C. Home Forces and his senior Staff Officers should be available for consultation with the Chiefs of Staff, the War Cabinet and himself.

The Chiefs of Staff were confident that this system would stand any test which might be imposed upon it.

## The Government to Remain in the London Area

The preparations made soon after the outbreak of war to move the War Cabinet and Government Departments to places in the West Country in the event of an emergency were abandoned in view of the German occupation of the French coast.

The West Country had become easily accessible to air attack, and it was decided that if the Government was driven out of Whitehall by air attack it would move to other quarters within the defended area of London until able to return to Whitehall. The accommodation in the West Country was used as an overflow for staffs not required in London.

Chapter 10

# The Battle of Britain

**The German Air Plan**

After the French surrender the German Command regarded the war in the West as won. Air attack, combined with a submarine blockade, was expected to force the British Government quickly to appreciate that further resistance was useless. At first the German Command believed that Britain would surrender without the need for invasion; but early in July, owing to the challenging speeches made by the Prime Minister, preparations were begun for an invasion though only as a last resort.

The strategic deployment of Germany's available air strength for action against the United Kingdom was completed during July, under cover of minor air attacks on shipping, harbours and airfields. The 2nd and 3rd German Air Fleets were assembled on Dutch, Belgian and French aerodromes to be directed against Southern England and the Midlands; and the 5th Air Fleet, from bases in Norway, was to pin down our northern air squadrons by attacks on the Newcastle area. Out of 1,451 bomber aircraft (including 346 short range dive-bombers) available at the beginning of August, 801 were with the 2nd and 3rd Air Fleets, and also 1,149 fighter aircraft out of a total of 1,308 (including 346 short-range fighters).

The opening day for the air offensive was to be the 13th August (Eagle Day). Air superiority over Southern England was expected to be achieved within four days by sustained air attacks on our fighter force in the air and on the ground, and on its ground units and production factories. The air offensive to break the fighter defence was then to be continued northwards, sector by sector, first to a line King's Lynn–Leicester; until all England could be covered by day air-attacks without

60

interference. By that means the country was expected to be disorganized and made ready for invasion within four weeks, by the 15th September.

The Invasion Plan
The drafting of an invasion plan (Operation Sea Lion) was ordered on the 2nd July. On the 15th the German Command issued Directive No. 16 to prepare for the invasion of England (see Appendix 15).

The plan was to make four bridgeheads – three between Folkestone and Beachy Head, and one between Brighton and Selsey Bill – with an initial landing force of 100,000 troops as a first wave. They were to be reinforced by a succession of waves of troops as fast as the landing craft could be turned round (see Appendix 16).

The first operational objective was a line Thames Estuary–North Downs–Southampton (see Map 4). Another landing in the Weymouth area was to assist in the conquest of the south-western counties; the second objective being a line from the Blackwater estuary at Maldon (Essex) to the Severn estuary, including the occupation of London. Two diversions were to be made by cruisers and empty transports – one towards the North-East coast of England and the other towards Iceland; a commerce-raiding cruise by a pocket battle-ship into the Atlantic was hoped to draw off a part of the Home Fleet.

The movement of shipping from German northern ports to the embarkation ports began on the 1st September. On the 3rd at time-table was issued for the preparatory invasion period, including the laying of mine-barrages on the flanks of the invasion corridor. The time-table is reproduced as Appendix 17. The German Naval Staff advised that moon and tide conditions would be possible only between the 19th and 26th September; and the date for the launching of the invasion was accordingly altered from the 15th to the 20th, the landing to take place early on the 21st, two hours after high tide.

**Change in the Air Plan**
Neither the first four days nor the first two weeks brought any sign of a decision in the air battle over Southern England. In spite of a further order by the German Air Command on the 20th August for "ceaseless attacks to bring the enemy fighter formations into operation" our fighter defence showed no weakening, and the German casualties were unexpectedly severe (during the first week, 12th-19th August, German records give their losses as 174 aircraft). Bomber Command, R.A.F., too, continued to make frequent daylight attacks on the barges and shipping assembling in the invasion ports; as well as carrying out nightly raids into Germany. On the 26th August Berlin was bombed for the first time.

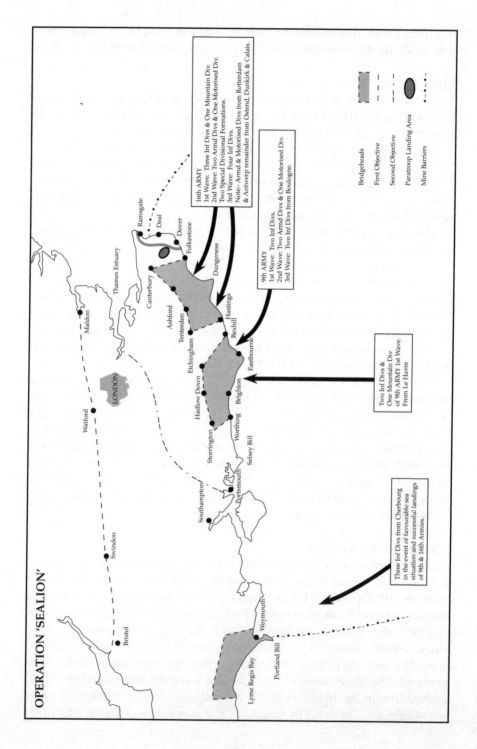

OPERATION 'SEALION'

16th ARMY
1st Wave: Three Inf Divs & One Mountain Div.
2nd Wave: Two Armd Divs & One Motorised Div.
Two Special Divisional Formations.
3rd Wave: Four Inf Divs.
Note:- Armd & Motorised Divs from Rotterdam
& Antwerp remainder from Ostend, Dunkirk & Calais.

9th ARMY
1st Wave: Two Inf Divs.
2nd Wave: Two Armd Divs & One Motorised Div.
3rd Wave: Two Inf Divs from Boulogne.

Two Inf Divs &
One Mountain Div
of 9th ARMY 1st Wave.
From Le Havre.

Three Inf Divs from Cherbourg
in the event of favourable sea
situation and successful landings
of 9th & 16th Armies.

Bridgeheads
First Objective
Second Objective
Paratroop Landing Area
Mine Barriers

Ramsgate
Deal
Dover
Folkestone
Dungeness
Hastings
Bexhill
Eastbourne
Brighton
Worthing
Storrington
Selsey Bill
Portsmouth
Southampton
Weymouth
Lyme Regis Bay
Portland Bill
Thames Estuary
Canterbury
Ashford
Tenterden
Etchingham
Hadlow Down
Maldon
LONDON
Watford
Swindon
Bristol

As no quick decision was being obtained by concentrating against the fighter defence the German Command decided to switch the main weight of the air offensive on to London. Greater success was expected from this change of target.

While the main object of wearing down our fighter defence would not be relaxed, the morale of the civil population would be severely strained and the "economic war from the air", by the destruction of supply services, was to be "embarked upon with full fury". The German Command announced on the 4th September that in retaliation for the bombing of Berlin they intended to "wipe out the cities" of England.

## German Shipping Losses in the Invasion Ports

The air onslaught on London which began on the 7th September and continued for the next two months did not interfere with the activities of Bomber Command nor with operations by our light naval forces against the invasion ports. On the night of the 8th/9th September Calais and Boulogne were bombarded by units of the 2nd Cruiser Squadron, and on the following night destroyers of the 21st Flotilla shelled both harbours. Sweeps at night by destroyers and other light craft along the French coast against enemy shipping were made whenever weather permitted. On the 13th Bomber Command R.A.F. sank 80 barges in a raid at Ostend.

These offensive operations were sufficient demonstration to the German Command that, in the words of the German Naval C.-in-C., "the most important pre-requisite for the invasion, i.e. clear air superiority in the Channel area, has not been achieved". On the 14th the German Command agreed that the degree of air supremacy necessary to justify executing Operation Sea Lion on the 20th had not been reached, and it was accordingly postponed.

By the 15th September our air reconnaissance and intelligence reports estimated that only sufficient sea-transport for three divisions was assembled in the French Channel ports between Dunkirk and Cherbourg, and for eight divisions in Dutch and Belgian harbours. The Royal Air Force continued to carry out bombing raids on the assembling invasion armada; and German records give the losses to their transports and barges at the embarkation ports between the end of August and end of September as 12 per cent.

Some of the barges which put to sea for training purposes, or to escape the raids, were sunk either by bombing or bad weather; and about 36 bodies of German soldiers were washed up on the English coast at various points between Yarmouth and Cornwall during that period giving rise to the belief in this country that an invasion fleet had actually sailed.

---

## The Royal Navy Alone Might Have Prevented Invasion

The German Naval Command gave its opinion more than once during September that even if the British Air Force was grounded the German air force would be unable to prevent the Navy from attacking a seaborne expedition. The contention was that the German air force did not possess the necessary weapons for attacking naval forces, and that the bombs in use were of far too small a calibre to prevent heavy ships from coming to grips with the landing force. "Even if the first wave of the expedition has been successfully transported, resolute naval forces of the enemy will still be able to place themselves between the first wave; already landed, and the succeeding transports".

Other factors which, in the opinion of the German Naval Command; increased the risk were that the German troops and Staff officers had no training or experience in amphibious assaults, and that assault shipping was limited mainly to barges, river-boats and tugs which were only capable of standing up to a calm sea.[7]

## The Invasion Plan Postponed Indefinitely

In spite of the warnings of the German Naval Command it is probable that if the Royal Air Force had been defeated the invasion operation would have been launched. Troops and ships were kept in readiness till the 12th October when the operation was postponed indefinitely.

## Scale of the Air Attacks on London

For the attempt at a knock-out blow on London bomber units of the 5th German Air Fleet in Norway moved south to reinforce the 2nd Air Fleet. Daylight attacks by formations of 200 to 300 bombers of all types were carried out daily on the London area, including the docks. The majority of the high-explosive bombs used were up to 550 lbs. calibre (250 kgs.); heavier bombs up to 2½ tons (2,500 kgs.) and air mines were dropped on special targets.

The attacks met a very different defence than if they had been delivered a year earlier as expected. Both our fighter force and the anti-aircraft ground defences were double the strength, and the air raid shelter policy and the civil defence arrangements generally had been greatly improved. The German losses in aircraft during their day-light attacks in September were so severe that in October the German Air Command changed from daylight to night raids, and employed smaller formations. A "fire-raiser" group of bombers had the special task of dropping incendiary bombs at the start of attacks in order to mark the target area.

The air battle over London lasted for two months. On every day or night, except seven, from the 7th September to the 7th November, the

London area was attacked by an average of 166 aircraft. During the last fortnight of the onslaught 1,800 bombers dropped 1,900 tons of high-explosive and 17,500 incendiary bombs on the target area. The civilian casualties in London alone during the two-month period amounted to 13,555 killed and 18,259 seriously injured; whereas the casualty rate for such an onslaught forecast by the Air Ministry in 1937 was 200,000 a week, including 66,000 killed.

## Failure of the German Air Plan

The story of the epic defeat of the German air effort to gain supremacy over England is told in the official Air History. Fighter Command not only defeated the German attempt to destroy its squadrons and maintenance organization, but at the same time was able to reduce the scale of attack on London to tolerable proportions.

The victory was due to the fighter pilots whose skill and courage was backed by confidence in the superiority of their aircraft. It was due, too, to the stubborn endurance of the people of London assisted by the Civil Defence arrangements. Many other factors contributed. The invention of radio-location which enabled our fighter defence to break-up the German bomber formations before they could deliver the full weight of their bomb-load; the wide dispersal of fighter aerodromes, and the park-like English landscape which made their location difficult from the air; and the inadequacy of the German bomber in armour, armament and bomb-load for the task given to it.

The German records affirm that the Battle of Britain was not fought out to a decision owing to the conviction of the German Command that a clash with Russia was inevitable and imminent. For that reason the German air force could not be unduly weakened. On the other hand, their records admit during the three winter months after mid-November the majority of their airfields in the West were waterlogged and unfit for operational work; only a few had runways and concrete taxying lanes. The German air effort of 1940 ended during the latter half of November by attacks on Liverpool and on the war production centre of Coventry.[11]

On the 16th January 1941, before the aerodromes in Western Europe were serviceable, Operation Sea Lion was again postponed. The German Command had made its decision to take the offensive against

---

[11] German Records: A.M.B. 25187: 15 Sept. 1947. The attack on Coventry on the night of the 14th/15th November caused heavy casualties and damage. According to German records 600 tons of high explosive and incendiary bombs were dropped by 454 aircraft on the target area. The civilian casualties were 506 killed and 883 seriously injured; and widespread fires caused great destruction.

Russia. Their technique of completing one task at a time was abandoned. The conquest of the United Kingdom was to wait until the close of the Russian campaign.

Between the 22nd May and early June the mass of the German air striking force moved to the Eastern front leaving only 8 bomber groups in the West instead of 44. Before their departure heavy raids were carried out on London and other industrial centres. The most severe was that on London on the night of the 16th/17th April when 711 aircraft in a double attack dropped 1,026 tons of high-explosive and 150 tons of incendiary bombs on the target area, resulting in 1,179 civilians killed and 2,232 seriously injured; also 2,200 fires occurred in the City causing widespread damage.

For the subjugation of Russia the German Command believed that ground combat forces would be more essential than the maintenance of air supremacy. The production of tanks, artillery and transport was given priority at the expense of the German air force. Production of aircraft only sufficed to replace wastage, and no new types of aircraft were developed. The intention of the German Command was to build the largest possible air force after the conclusion of the Russian campaign. Millions of soldiers would be transferred from the Army to the air force and the aircraft industry which would then be given absolute priority.

The decision in the battle for the conquest of the United Kingdom, and the decision of the War itself, would depend upon the duration of Russian resistance. The German Command accepted that gigantic gamble owing to their belief in a rapid victory in the East.

### Air Raid Warnings and States of Readiness; the "Invasion Imminent" Signal of the 7th September 1940

The organization for sounding the Air Raid sirens is described in Appendix 18, and the States of Readiness for the three Defence Services, in the event of an attempt at invasion, in Appendix 19.

The information and events which led to the "Invasion imminent" signal (Cromwell) being given by the C.-in-C. Home Forces on the evening of the 7th September 1940 are outlined in Appendix 20.

# Part III

Home Defence Plans 1941-42:
The Threat of Air Attack
Combined with Invasion

Chapter 11

# Effect of the Battle of the Atlantic on Home Defence

## The Danger Area Shifts to the Western Approaches

It was expected that the German Naval Command would take advantage of the great strategical possibilities offered by the occupation of Trondheim and Lorient to attempt to strangle the import trade of the British Isles by submarine attack and by naval raiding forces. On the 17th August the German Command proclaimed a "total blockade of the British Isles"; and, during September, simultaneous with the attempt by the German air force to gain air supremacy, the submarine campaign was intensified particularly in the waters off the west of Scotland and in the North-Western Approaches.[12]

Our ability to carry on the war depended upon the maintenance of supplies through the West coast ports by the north-about route around Ireland. In September imports dropped to about 800,000 tons or 23 per cent. less than for May 1940 (over 1,000,000 tons). The minimum requirement had been put at 60 per cent. of the May figure, so that although the falling off was considerable the decline was as yet far from being a total blockade. In addition to that threat, the march of events in South-East Europe compelled us to accept the risk of sending reinforcements to the Middle East to the limit of our shipping capacity.

[12] Fuehrer Naval Conferences 1940 (A.L.721): P. 65, 91, 92. On the 11th July the German Naval C.-in-C. told the German Command he was convinced that Britain could be forced to ask for peace simply by cutting off her import trade by means of submarine warfare combined with air attacks on convoys and heavy air attacks on main centres, such as Liverpool. He did not advocate an invasion, and referred to the many difficulties involved. Herr Hitler agreed that invasion should be regarded only as a last resort.

## Diversion of Naval Forces from Anti-Invasion Duties to Trade Protection

At the end of October the First Lord of the Admiralty, Mr. A.V. Alexander, pointed out to the Defence Committee that our shipping losses in the North-Western Approaches were most serious, the tonnage lost being in excess of replacement by purchase and new construction. He added that if the existing rate of losses were to persist our reinforcement programme overseas would have to be curtailed, and it might prove impossible to maintain large forces in the Middle East.

The C.-in-C. Home Fleet, Admiral Sir C. Forbes, agreed that unless our anti-submarine craft on the North-Western Approaches were substantially increased there would be a grave danger of losing the war by the interruption of our life-line with the United States and the Empire.

That threat to our overseas trade routes caused the diversion to trade protection of more than half of the naval light forces allotted to anti-invasion duties; and the Prime Minister asked the President of the United States to sanction the purchase of fifty American destroyers as a reinforcement.

By the Spring (March 1941) the Battle of the Atlantic had spread to the whole of that ocean. In addition to their ocean-going submarines the Germans had a number of efficient surface warships and raiders in Northern Waters, and it had become necessary to convoy right across the Atlantic. Shipping was being attacked too, off the West coast of Africa. In the circumstances, heavier ships of the Home Fleet had to be dispersed to distant ports, ready to join as escort if necessary.

## Reduced Anti-Invasion Naval Forces Based on Plymouth and Rosyth

The vital need to guard adequately our Atlantic trade routes was not the only cause of the reduction in immediate naval assistance to counter an attempted invasion. Owing to the threat of dive-bombing attack and to the continuous sowing of mines by German aircraft the naval authorities proposed to base the naval anti-invasion forces on ports down the Channel, such as Plymouth, rather than on the restricted East coast; and the East coast cruiser squadron on Rosyth (see Map 3).

The Defence Committee accordingly noted on the 31st October that the Army would have to be prepared to hold the beaches in South-East England, with such assistance as the Air Force could afford, until the arrival of naval forces strong enough to intercept the enemy's sea passage. That "period before relief" of the troops guarding the beaches was estimated at 12 hours, i.e. the time of passage at 20 knots from Plymouth to Dover.

### Erection of Beach Scaffolding as a Delaying Measure

As some compensation the Admiralty was asked to consider the erection along the most vital beaches, particularly in the North Foreland–Dungeness area, of fixed tubular steel scaffolding to check the first waves of an invasion attack. Experiments had shown such an obstacle to be unclimbable and proof against tanks. Compared with the proposed under-water nets, too, the scaffolding would last for three years instead of three months, and it could be made of lower grade steel. The scaffolding was to be erected above high-water mark as an anti-tank obstacle; if placed in shallow water it was proof against light craft but could be penetrated by heavy barges.

### The Admiralty to have Operational Control of RAF Coastal Command

In order to be able to deploy the maximum possible force in the air for action in the North-Western Approaches, and to enable a single authority to be responsible for bringing in the convoys, the Admiralty asked that the Air Ministry should hand over "the whole of Coastal Command, R.A.F. complete". In the opinion of the First Lord, Mr. A.V. Alexander, they could not assume full responsibility for the protection of convoys unless they had control of the operations equipment and training of the air squadrons of Coastal Command. He believed that the transfer could be effected without difficulty.

The Prime Minister thought that if they had been starting afresh in peace-time the great change proposed might be desirable; but "it would be disastrous at the present moment to tear a large fragment from the Royal Air Force". The Committee agreed that Coastal Command should remain an integral part of the Royal Air Force for administration and training, but that for all operational purposes it should come under the control of the Admiralty. In the event of a difference of view between the Admiralty and the Air Ministry the number and type of aircraft to be allotted to Coastal Command should be fixed by the Defence Committee (Operations).

The Admiralty took over operational control of Coastal Command R.A.F. on the 15th April 1941.

### The Problem of Eire

An attack upon Eire from French ports might be made either as a diversion in the event of an invasion of Great Britain or as a deliberate move to establish air and submarine bases from which to attack our vital shipping routes.

Whoever landed first in Eire would probably be attacked by the Irish; and to seize harbours and air-bases there against the will of the Government and people would involve a very gave military commitment, though it might have to be done if the threat on our Western Approaches became mortal.

The Defence Committee considered that the maintenance of a successful German landing in Eire was most improbable so long as our naval and air forces were undefeated. Should a large scale raid be attempted, and allowing for losses due to our naval and air action, up to 2 or 3 divisions might be landed from merchant ships with a proportion of tanks, and supported by a maximum of 8,000 airborne troops.

To resist such a landing the armed forces of Eire itself amounted to four brigade groups, arranged in mobile columns of about one company each, with armoured cars; and the Local Security Force, corresponding to our Home Guard, was about 90,000 strong.

Our resources in Northern Ireland were 3 Infantry divisions, one independent brigade group and 2 infantry brigades.[13] The Ulster Volunteers or Home Guard amounted to about 38,000 by the end of May 1941; and in addition 3 Garrison, 4 Home Defence and 2 Young Soldiers battalions were available for guarding aerodromes and other Vulnerable Points.

[13] Two composite brigades the 71st and 72nd with artillery had arrived in Northern Ireland (Co. Antrim) at the end of 1940 (D.O. (40) 3rd Mtg. 10 Jan.). The 5th Division was sent across in April 1941 (C.O.S. (41) 161: 27 Mar.).

Chapter 12

# Defence Preparations for 1941

### The Possible Invasion Area During the Winter 1940/41
The risk of a large scale invasion during the winter months was considered remote except through South-East England. The principal danger, in the opinion of the Defence Committee, was the possibility of a landing on the beaches between North Foreland and Dungeness by troops and tanks brought across in self-propelled barges. Such an operation might be combined with a landing from merchant ships using small harbours and suitable beaches between Orfordness (Suffolk) and Poole, including diversions on other parts of the coast.

The C.-in-C. Home Forces proposed to keep two Field Army divisions forward in the Dover area and one forward in Norfolk, the remainder of the Field divisions to be withdrawn into mobile reserve for training. Elsewhere the beaches would be held by lower category troops.

The security of the United Kingdom still had priority; and the Defence Committee agreed that "a minimum of 12 Field Army divisions at any time must lie in reserve as a Home Army apart from troops on the beaches". With that proviso the programme for overseas reinforcement aimed at sending from this country one division a month, with ancillary troops, during the six months period January–June 1941.

### Preparations to Meet Invasion in the Spring of 1941
The Defence Committee had agreed that the Air Ministry should continue to give priority to the production of fighter squadrons with the object of building up the Metropolitan Fighter Force to meet a sustained enemy air offensive in the spring. The supply of skilled fighter pilots was being affected by the requirements for the Middle East; and the C.-in-C. Fighter Command, Air Marshal Sir H. Dowding, warned the Defence Committee that it would be dangerous to assume that we

could repeat our success in the air battle over Britain, which we had won only with a narrow margin, unless the fighter force and the training organisation behind it were both expanded. The withdrawal of bombers and trained crews for despatch to the Middle East was also delaying the expansion of the bomber force. The intention was to form new Metropolitan bomber squadrons with a view to full employment during the autumn of 1941.

The scale of a possible invasion in the spring was estimated at a first wave of 25 divisions, including 5 armoured divisions, supported by about 4 airborne divisions. To meet that threat there were in the country 22 full scale field divisions, one armoured division (plus 3 being formed), 7 County divisions of a 50% lower establishment and 6 independent infantry brigades.[14]

Of the 22 field divisions 6 were under orders or earmarked for overseas and another four (two Corps) were to be held ready for operations in overseas theatres. It had been hoped to replace these divisions on withdrawal by newly raised formations, but the programme was being held up by shortage of man-power for the Army.

## The Training of Counter-Attack Troops

For Home Forces the period after Dunkirk had been a scramble to meet a threat of invasion regarded as imminent. It was not until the end of October, when the threat subsided, that opportunity had been given to pull out the Field Army formations from static defences to be trained as counter-attack troops, demanding maximum mobility and striking power. The training programme was designed to ensure that these formations would be able in an emergency to cover 150 to 200 miles in mechanized transport or march 20 to 40 miles on foot, and be ready to fight on arrival in the area of operations.

The success of the defence would depend on the rapidity and freshness with which the mobile reserves could reach the landing beaches and airborne landing areas. Routes were carefully reconnoitred for every contingency and rehearsals carried out, including practice in clearing away pockets of airborne troops landed to block communications. A high standard of traffic control and march discipline was to be maintained, anti-aircraft protection arranged, and civilian refugees kept off the roads.

---

[14] The Field Army divisions had an establishment strength of 15,500 all ranks and the full scale of supporting arms. The lower establishment (County) divisions had an establishment of 10,000 all ranks with little artillery or transport. The intention was to build up the County divisions into full-scale divisions as material became available. (C.O.S. (41) 260 (0): 25 Nov. 1941).

## Creation of a South-Eastern Command

The Eastern Command which included practically the whole of the probable invasion area, from the Wash to Bognor Regis, had been found too large and vulnerable for one command.

In February 1941 it was split into an Eastern and a South-Eastern Command divided by the Thames estuary and the London district. The western coastal boundary of the new South-Eastern Command was extended from Bognor Regis to Portsmouth (exclusive).

## The Likelihood of Invasion in 1941

Economic evidence supported the military view that Germany would make the most strenuous endeavours to win the war in 1941. A successful invasion of the United Kingdom would end it; but the operation was regarded by the Chiefs of Staff to be so much a gambler's throw in face of the progressive increase of Britain's army and air strength that the German Command was expected to try all other means before making the attempt.

The growing intensity of the Battle of the Atlantic, aiming rather at the strangulation of this country, lent colour to that opinion; and the Chiefs of Staff believed that pressure might be exerted through Spain, and from Italy or in the Balkans, in order to stretch our naval and shipping resources to the maximum before the German Command played its last card of invasion, possibly in the autumn of 1941.

That date might be advanced if America entered the war; for Germany's only hope of success would then be to invade this country before American military aid became effective. By the end of 1941, with the full effects of American assistance, we should be so strong that in the opinion of the Chiefs of Staff, Germany would be faced with the prospect of defeat or, at best, stalemate.

The review by the Chiefs of Staff in March 1941 of the preparations to meet invasion during 1941 is given as Appendix 21.

Chapter 13

# The War Situation Transformed by the Battle of Russia

**The German Thrust Eastwards Gives Further Respite for Strengthening the Home Defence Organisation**

With the opening of the Balkan campaign by the German Command on the 9th April, culminating in a large expenditure of trained airborne troops for the capture of Crete, an invasion of England in the near future became less likely. The occupation of the Balkan peninsula was followed by the start of the offensive against Russia on the 22nd June.

By the end of July it was evident that the Germans were committed to a major campaign in Russia on a front of 1,500 miles with substantially the whole of their first line forces engaged, and all their supply and transport diverted to that front. After six weeks of fighting there was no sign of an immediate decision in favour of Germany; the Russians were still fighting hard, and German progress was in general being reduced.

From a military point of view, it was inconceivable that the Germans could break off the offensive until they had achieved a major objective either as a result of the capitulation of the Russian army in the field or by making such territorial gains as would preclude the possibility of further counter-action by the Russian forces.

The profound effect of continued Russian resistance on the war situation was outlined by the Chiefs of Staff on the 31st July. An invasion of the United Kingdom would be postponed; and the possibility of German adventures in Spain and North Africa would be reduced. While the security of the United Kingdom would necessarily remain the overriding consideration in our strategy, time would be given to send reinforcements, and particularly armoured fighting vehicles, overseas to strengthen our position in the Middle East the loss of which would be a military disaster of the first magnitude. In the North Atlantic much had been done to overcome the German attack and given more ships and aircraft for convoy protection and continued American assistance the Chiefs of Staff were confident that the threat to our trade and convoy routes could be mastered.

The Chiefs of Staff agreed with the opinion of the Joint Intelligence Committee that the Germans would be unable to disengage from the Russian front the large land and air forces required for an invasion of this country before the 1st September at the earliest. Calculating that 6 to 8 weeks would be needed to transport, re-equip, concentrate and embark them in the west, and to assemble the shipping and supply organisation, an invasion could not start before the middle or end of October, by which time winter would be setting in. The probability was that Russian resistance would extend the respite for the United Kingdom until the following spring (1942).

### Appreciation by the C.-in-C. Home Forces
In view of the improbability of a decision on the Russian front in time for the German Command to mount an invasion against Great Britain before the winter the C.-in-C. Home Forces on the 1st August, wrote an Appreciation to determine the minimum requirement for Home Forces by the spring of 1942.

The appreciation is given as Appendix 22; and the following notes summarize the Home Defence plan for the spring of 1942 within its framework.

Chapter 14

# Assumptions for the Home Forces Plan for the Spring of 1942

**Change in the Probable Form of Attack**
While the Germans were developing their war-production mainly for ground forces for the Russian Campaign at the expense of their air force, the Royal Air Force was expanding rapidly. In the circumstances a prolonged battle for air supremacy prior to invasion had even less chance of success than in 1940, and the attempt was unlikely to be repeated.

Instead, the C.-in-C. Home Forces believed that the German Command would merge the efforts of its land, air and sea forces into a concentrated attack based upon surprise, speed, ruthlessness, and the rapid exploitation of success, making the fullest use of armoured forces. Of the several possible methods of attack he considered the concentrated effort to be the most probable, and the greatest threat.

**One Month's Warning of Invasion Probable**
The Chiefs of Staff accepted the view that the Germans would be unable to disengage from the Russian front and concentrate in the West for an invasion of this country without disclosing their intentions. They accordingly told the Defence Services on the 2nd August that they might expect "from now on to receive one month's warning from us of impending invasion".[15]

**Five to Seven Days Possible Delay Before the Full Deployment of the Home Fleet**
The Admiralty worked out a programme, given as Appendix 23, on the assumption of three weeks' notice by which time nearly two thirds (97)

---

[15] C.O.S. (41) 272 Mtg: 2 Aug. A "Preliminary Warning" signal was to be issued, on the same lines as the "Stand-to" and "Action Stations" signals (see Section 60).

of the total of destroyers in Home Commands and 75 per cent. of the total of coastal vessels in the United Kingdom could be transferred to anti-invasion duties, apart from heavier ships of the Home Fleet and vessels which might be recalled from foreign stations.

Such a force would be able to cope without difficulty with the German light escorts, amounting in all to about 17 destroyers, 30 torpedo boats and 60 E-boats, provided their fighter protection could be neutralised.

The Admiralty had, however, to take into account the vital need for escorting our import ships, the reinforcement convoys to the Middle East, and the convoys of war material of all kinds by the Northern route to Russia. In view of the scale of attack on these trade and convoy routes the task was of such urgency that the Admiralty felt that confirmation of actual invasion would have to be awaited before diverting light naval forces and cruisers to counter it.

The fact that an invasion was mounted did not necessarily signify when it would be launched or even that it would be launched at all. Faced with that predicament the Admiralty admitted that five to seven days might elapse after the invasion had started before the Navy in Home Waters could be fully deployed in an anti-invasion role.

The C.-in-C. Home Forces pointed out that it was the first few days of an attempted invasion which were vital, and when navel assistance was most needed. With armoured forces landed in the country five to seven days was a long time, within which it would be perfectly possible to lose this country and the war unless the Home Amy was sufficiently strong to deal with such a threat (see Appendix 22).

**Limitations on Air Defence**
The Air Staff continued to maintain that until Germany had defeated our fighter force an invasion by sea or air was not a practical operation. The C.-in-C. Home Forces, however, took the view that although the struggle for air supremacy would affect the whole course of invasion the defeat of our fighter force would be unnecessary before German troops could land in this country. They might make the sea crossing under cover of darkness, fog or smoke; and in his opinion the Air Staff calculation gave insufficient attention to the possible absence of naval assistance to our defence during the first vital days, and also to the degree of risk which the German Command would be prepared to accept to gain a decision.

The German expedition would be given the maximum fighter cover, and while our fighter force would be engaged in protecting its own organisation and in taking toll of airborne invasion our bombers would have to face heavy opposition from German fighters and anti-aircraft defence in their efforts to attack the expedition in the embarkation ports, on passage, and on the landing beaches.

In view of the large number of possible assembly ports available to the Germans between Norway and Bordeaux, the C.-in-C. Home Forces considered that the task of disorganising and disintegrating a force of some 40 divisions before it sailed would be beyond the power of our bomber force; and every replacement of merchant shipping by the smaller tank landing-craft and barges would assist the Germans in avoiding the effects of bombardment from the air. The withdrawals of our own forces from Dunkirk, Greece and Crete, undertaken with a varying degree of fighter cover and in the face of heavy bombing, led him to the conclusion that the Royal Air Force could not prevent a large German force being landed in this country.

### The Home Army to be Prepared to Defeat the Seaborne Expedition Unaided

While taking into account the casualties which our naval and air action might inflict on an invading force the C.-in-C. Home Forces maintained that for the purpose of the Home Defence plan for the spring of 1942, the sea-barrier, hitherto the country's main bulwark, would have to be regarded as an undefended no-man's-land.

In the conditions which might prevail "the Army must be strong enough to deliver a decisive blow against the maximum enemy force which can be transported to this country". He believed that it would be dangerous to accept any other assumption.

### A Pincer Movement on London Expected

The bulk of the German armoured force was expected to be directed against South-Eastern and Eastern Commands, with London and its port as the objective. It was estimated that the maintenance of the German invasion forces when landed would require 8,000 to 10,000 tons of supplies daily, and that the only single port capable of dealing with such a quantity was London.

The Chiefs of Staff had stressed the vital importance of the defence of the Kent coast, bordering the Straits of Dover as being the only place where the Germans had a chance of obtaining an initial and secure line of communications. By capturing the Kent coast and mounting guns on it, or capturing our guns, they could hope to deny the Straits to our naval forces; and they could evade our air force by making the maximum use of the dark hours. It was believed that if the Germans could use the harbours and beaches for landing supplies they would be able to maintain an invading force landed in the Kent area. The Chiefs of Staff were therefore convinced that a vast effort would be made to seize that vital area; and that airborne troops, and possibly gas, might be used to isolate it from the rest of the country.

If bridgeheads were formed in East Anglia and in Kent, the advance would probably take the form of a pincer movement on, or to the west of, London by attacks through the Eastern Counties and through South-East England, combined with a subsidiary attack from landing beaches east of Weymouth. The Joint Intelligence Committee estimated however that the casualties inflicted upon the landing forces would be so heavy that not more than 50 per cent. would advance inland from the beaches.

Chapter 15

# Defence against Seaborne Attack

**Scale of Attack**

It was assumed that the Germans would have achieved sufficient success in Russia by the Spring of 1942 to enable their forces to be withdrawn apart from security requirements, and that the maximum strength available would be concentrated for an invasion of the United Kingdom. With some 20 armoured and 250 infantry divisions the German Command would have no lack of troops for invasion; the limiting factor was shipping, and the number of craft which could issue from suitable ports at one time.

The transport available for the main attack was estimated at 3,000 especially converted self-propelled barges, about 1,000 suitable merchant vessels totalling 2 million tons, up to 2,000 unconverted barges for carrying supplies and for piers, anti-aircraft gun platforms, etc., and a number of ferries. They were known, too, to have 450 to 800 special tank landing-craft capable of carrying 7 or 8 tanks at a speed of 10 to 15 knots.

Altogether the seaborne threat was estimated at 9 armoured and 23 infantry divisions for the main attack; and, with the full establishment of a German armoured division at 400 tanks, from 2,000 to 3,600 tanks might be expected.

For military diversions heavier shipping would be available for about 11 divisions; 3 from Norway and 3 from the Baltic diverted on one or more objectives such as North Scotland, the coast of North-East England, Orkneys and Shetlands, the Faroës, Iceland or possibly Northern Ireland; and up to 5 divisions with a few tanks from the French west or north-west ports directed against Eire, and Devon and Cornwall, both as a diversion and possibly as a move to establish air and submarine bases.

Germany's weakest feature was her navy, and all her naval forces were expected to be used in support of an invasion; or as a diversion, possibly including action by the Italian Fleet, to draw our naval forces away from the invasion area.

The probable landing areas for the main attack were the East Anglian beaches (3 armoured and 9 infantry divisions), the Kent and Sussex coast (4 armoured and 11 infantry divisions), and the beaches east of Weymouth (2 armoured and 5 infantry divisions). The three attacks would probably be led by two waves of landing craft at a close interval carrying in all 5 armoured and 7 infantry divisions. This force, which would have to form the bridgeheads, might make the sea-crossing in light craft with some merchant vessels converted for running ashore and landing direct on the beach.

The main body was likely to consist of 4 armoured and 16 infantry divisions carried in merchant vessels after the bridgeheads had been formed. Another 3 armoured and 2 infantry divisions would probably be held in Baltic and German ports ready to exploit any success.

**Minimum Requirement for Home Forces**
The task of the Army, according to the assumptions made by the C.-in-C. Home Forces, was to be far greater than in 1940. Instead of a threat of the equivalent of 7 divisions landing at various points on the coast, it had to be prepared to defeat "the maximum enemy force which can be transported to this country". After allowing for 50 per cent. casualties to the German landing force due to our naval and air action and on the landing beaches, the threat by the main land attack on Southern England would amount to about 5 armoured and 12 infantry divisions.

To deliver a decisive blow against such a force the C.-in-C. Home Forces put his total minimum requirement at 8 armoured and 14 full scale infantry divisions. For coast protection he asked, in addition, for 12 lower establishment (County) divisions and for 10 Army tank brigades. For special duties he asked for 5 independent infantry brigades, 3 infantry brigade groups, and an airborne brigade. The detail of the minimum requirements for each Command, for the defence of aerodromes and other vulnerable points, for coast defence artillery and outlying garrisons, and also the scale of the expected requirement for the first reinforcement, is shown in Appendix 22.

The Home Guard was expected to attain a strength of 1½ million by the spring of 1942, with the ultimate ceiling at 2½ millions. In view of the increased reinforcement required overseas during the winter the Defence Committee proposed that certain units of the Home Guard should be incorporated with mobile formations for Home Defence in an emergency. The aim was to be able to make mobile in this manner a total of six Home Guard brigades, one in each Corps area.

## Coast Defence

The first objects of a seaborne attack was expected to be the landing of armoured forces as quickly as possible. The attack would probably be led by special tank landing-craft and anti-aircraft barges, equipped with high velocity guns; their purpose would be to produce smoke-screens and to shoot up the concrete pill-boxes and obstacles near the beaches, and generally to prepare the way for fresh waves of tank landing-craft and protect them from air attack.

The beach defences had accordingly been strengthened as materials became available, priority being given to those on the Kent and Sussex coasts and in East Anglia. The obstacles consisted mainly of wire entanglements, up to 3 belts in depth, steel-tubular scaffolding, and anti-tank ditches, concrete obstacles and anti-tank mines to block the beach-exits.

To be effective these obstacles had to be covered by fire-positions; and by August 1941, 302 6-pdr. and 4-inch guns had been disposed for the defence of the beaches, sited where possible so as to cover the obstacles. Also, 573 coast defence guns, mostly 6-inch, lent by the Admiralty, had been distributed for the defence of ports and the more vulnerable sectors of the East and South coasts.

The most dangerous sector was the Kent coast; and in January 1941 a G.H.Q. Home Forces Coast Defence Committee had recommended a minimum of one 6-inch or other coast defence gun per thousand yards for the vulnerable beaches between North Foreland and Beachy Head. Of the total requirement of 81 6-inch guns for this purpose, 57, mostly navel guns, were in position by the end of March 1941. In addition to various other medium and heavy artillery in the Dover area the field artillery of two divisions, each up to an establishment of 144 guns, was disposed so as to cover these beaches. The greatest gun concentration covered the stretches between Ramsgate and Kingsdown, and between Hythe and Littlestone.

Precautions had to be taken against the possible landing of heavily armoured 60 to 70-ton tanks, equipped with high velocity guns capable of penetrating our concrete defences, and also of dealing with any of our existing tanks. To make good this weakness in the defence as many of the mobile 3-inch and 3.7-inch guns as could be spared from the anti-aircraft defences were to be deployed in depth behind the coast defences and equipped with heavy armour-piercing shot. Some of the guns in the latest tanks, too, were being given 3-inch barrels for the same purpose. In addition, the static 4.5-inch and 3.7-inch anti-aircraft guns, at aerodromes, ports and elsewhere, were all sited as far as possible for anti-tank as well as for anti-aircraft defence.

The Admiralty had stated that it could not guarantee that enemy ships would not bombard a port, in spite of possible air action against them. Coastal artillery for the defence of ports consequently had a daily "watch and ward" role; whereas the guns covering stretches of coast against invasion would not be required until invasion became imminent. By limiting the degree of readiness of the coast defence guns the requirement in personnel was reduced from over 43,000 to 35,000 (see Appendix 22).

The instructions for the gun defences of the major and minor ports in March 1942, and for the close defence guns along the coast, are given as Appendix 24.

### Troops on the Coast

The general idea was to hold the coast as an outpost line with particular attention to beaches near ports and to steep-to beaches suitable for landing tanks. The vital ports of Dover and Folkestone were each allotted an independent infantry brigade for their special protection.

As the greater weight of the attack was expected against the Kent and Sussex beaches that 162 mile sector of the coast (between Whitstable and Chichester) was to be held by four Field Army divisions with the full scale of supporting arms. In that area the beaches were protected by company or platoon defended localities, wired for all round defence; the garrison was to fight on to the last, killing Germans, delaying their advance and threatening their lines of supply. With about a dozen defended localities on a normal brigade front of 8 to 14 miles, wide gaps had to be accepted; but the more likely landing beaches and avenues of advance were covered by fire. Two or more 4.7-inch or 6-inch batteries covered the beach obstacles in each brigade sector, and two or more 25-pdr. batteries were in close support, 6,000 to 8,000 yards from the coast.

The most likely sector for large scale seaborne landings was the 83 miles between Whitstable and Rye of which 32 miles was suitable for the landing of wheeled and tracked vehicles at all states of the tide. As an example of the defence lay-out the "Plan to defeat Invasion" in Kent by the XII Corps is given as Appendix 25.

North of the Thames estuary to the Wash the East Anglian coast was held by the same method; but the beach defences were garrisoned by County (lower establishment) divisions with two Field Army divisions in close support behind the more likely landing areas. The remainder of the 1,752 miles of the East and South coasts of Great Britain, north of the Wash and west of Weymouth, was also held by County divisions. Their deficiencies were in the process of being made good up to the standard of full-scale divisions; and meanwhile they were capable of operating only within a very limited radius, and were unsuitable as reserves.

## Counter-Attack Troops
The general disposition of Home Forces was based on the principle of having a minimum of troops on the coast to deal with seaborne attack, and a minimum to deal with airborne attack. The strength of the defence was to lie in the local and G.H.Q. reserves which were to be capable of a rapid counter-offensive and to be 100 per cent. mobile.

Normally each infantry brigade on the coast had a battalion in reserve, 4 to 6 miles behind the three forward battalions; and each coastal division had a brigade in reserve, 10 to 12 miles from the coast. These local reserves had a double task: to counter-attack any penetration of the beach defences, and to defend against airborne attack, or to reinforce essential areas such as aerodromes, anti-tank fortresses on the main inland roads, bottlenecks in the communications, etc.

The probability that the Germans would attempt to land armoured forces at the outset required that the outpost divisions should have at their disposal infantry tanks for close support and immediate counter-attack. The minimum requirement was put at 10 Army tank brigades, of which 7 were to be behind the Wash–Weymouth coast-line (3 being behind the Kent and Sussex beaches).

## Troops in G.H.Q. Reserve
The local reserves were to be used to counter-attack a landing force which had overrun the beach defences, and was threatening essential areas immediately in rear. The Army and G.H.Q. reserves were to be employed against any penetration farther inland. They were organised so as to contain a sufficient armoured element to deal with the possible armoured threat to each Command, and sufficient infantry to provide support for that armoured force, and also to deal with airborne descents in rear of the beaches. The intention was to prevent the establishment of a bridgehead through which the main body of the attack could be landed, supplied and reinforced. Any ground lost was to be regained by immediate counter-attack, and the invader was to be driven back into the sea as rapidly as possible. The training of the armoured formations and field divisions had been designed to that end.

Armoured formations were regarded as the most suitable for the purpose, and a low proportion of infantry divisions was accepted. The C.-

in-C. Home Forces asked for four armoured divisions as a requirement for G.H.Q. Reserve, mainly behind the Eastern and South-Eastern Commands, in addition to the armoured division already at the disposal of each of those Commands (see Appendix 22); but owing to the reduced force available for Home Forces by the spring of 1942 only one additional armoured division in Army or G.H.Q. Reserve was immediately available, 30 to 50 miles from the coast, for each of the two Commands.

As soon as the main German landing areas were confirmed, the reserves from the other Commands would be moved to pre-arranged concentration areas in the threatened Command according to the situation. As an example, the forward concentration areas in the South-Eastern Command, and the estimated speed of movement of the armoured and infantry formations, are shown as Appendix 26.

The revised scale by the spring of 1942 allowed the Northern Command one armoured division as an immediate reserve to meet a possible diversion attack against the Midlands industrial area through the Humber or against the Tyne-Tees industrial centres: the strength of the raid contemplated was estimated at up to 3 seaborne divisions and one airborne regiment. In the Southern Command, to meet a subsidiary landing east of Weymouth, the force for immediate counter-attack was to be one field division and one armoured division. An airborne brigade was required to assist possible counter-attacks against objectives such as the Isle of Wight, the Scilly Isles or the Isle of Thanet.

## Method of Employment of the Reserves

The best answer to the German system of infiltration was considered to be a resolute defence-in-depth, and the holding of the nodal points on the lines of communication. That method of defence would slow up an enemy advance inland, and give time to stage the counter-attack with the mobile reserves.

The essence of the defence problem for the Eastern and South-Eastern Commands was the defence of London; and in a land attack upon the capital the battle would have to be fought by the troops of those two Commands backed by the G.H.Q. Reserve. The lack of depth between the coast and London made it essential that a landing force should be stopped on or near the beaches. Selected towns on the main approach roads had been prepared as tank-proof localities, or nodal points, and the reserves were in all cases to be based on these defended localities in order to be able to manoeuvre from a secure pivot.

The handling of the reserves is discussed in an appreciation written for the South-Eastern Command by the C.-in-C. Home Forces in October 1941, and given as Appendix 27.

## The Defence of London

The entrances to London were to be held by the Home Guard which totalled nearly a quarter of a million men in the London district. There were also 20,000 police in the London area and a number of military depots and training battalions capable of providing small columns. The strong anti-aircraft and balloon barrage detachments would also be of considerable value. The Field Force requirement was to be sufficient to deal with a surprise incursion and to restore a situation by delivering a counter-attack. The minimum for the London District for that purpose was put at one infantry brigade group and two independent infantry brigades, or the equivalent of one full scale infantry division.

An attempt might be made to paralyse the machinery of Government at the moment of invasion by large-scale parachutist and airborne landings. The number of parachutists who might be able to land in the London area was estimated at 3,600, in addition to glider-borne troops landed in the outskirts. The C.-in-C. Home Forces believed, however, that so long as our fighter aircraft continued to operate over South-East England troop-carrying aircraft would suffer such heavy losses that the landing of sufficient troops within a short period to isolate London was unlikely. Small parties landed at night might be used to disorganise communications.

Another possible form of attack was a direct assault by shallow-draft craft up the Thames, or by sea-plane landings in the river. To counter such a threat the Thames estuary was covered by fixed defences on either shore and by forts in mid-stream; also by the light naval forces stationed at Harwich and Chatham. The narrower waters of the river inside the estuary were guarded by a cross-fire machine-gun defence from both banks, and by armed river-craft.

An exercise to test the London defences, proposed in July 1940, was abandoned as being likely to interfere too much with the normal life of the Metropolis; but the preparation for the exercise revealed the inadequacy of the defence arrangements to meet these threats, and the chaos that might have resulted in reality. The necessary improvements were made; and, in addition to the three brigades plus the Home Guard at the disposal of the G.O.C. London District, one of the three Field Force divisions in the vicinity was to be ready to move into London to assist.

## The Auxiliary Units

The Auxiliary units hastily improvised in the summer of 1940 to operate behind the lines of an invading force comprised at first only half-a-dozen Army officers, a few local Home Guards and a handful of civilians. On the 2nd July 1940 the establishment of Auxiliary units had been officially authorised as a part of the country's defence system, and the military and civilian units were amalgamated.

That small beginning was the foundation of what became by the Spring of 1942 a powerful and elaborate organization in which may thousands of Army, Home Guard, A.T.S. and civilian personnel worked in harmony. Starting from the threatened South-Eastern corner of England, the organization had gradually spread over half the coastal belt of Great Britain, to a depth of twenty miles inland, to John o'Groats in the north and the Hebrides, and along the south coast to Pembrokeshire in the West. It contained 600 to 700 patrols which would operate from hidden communication centres behind an invader's advance inland, and against his rearward services immediately after seaborne and airborne landings.

The organization, working under G.H.Q. Home Forces, had an operational (Home Guard) and a civilian intelligence (Special Duties Organization) personnel, which though nominally amalgamated progressed along the separate lines which their distinct roles required.

## Battle Schools

The greatest asset the German troops would possess in an invasion was considered to be their battle experience, and the fact that relatively few officers in Home Forces had experienced front line fighting. The C.-in-C. Home Forces (Lt.-General Sir B. Paget) believed that the bulk of the Home divisions were not yet fully alive to the fire-power available within their units, nor trained to make the best use of it. He thought, too, that the evil influence of linear tactics was still lurking among them.

In order to educate junior leaders in the co-ordinated use of fire-power and in the technique of the front line in a modern battle, and to give them some idea of modern battle conditions, he instituted a G.H.Q. Battle School. The school, which opened near Barnard Castle, Co. Durham, in January 1942, was intended primarily to train instructors for the divisional battle schools which were being started, and to ensure that all were thinking and working along the same lines. Large training areas were requisitioned in each Command where exercises involving armoured and infantry formations could be carried out using live ammunition, and also live bombs from aircraft.

The infantry arm remained, in his opinion, the major factor in winning battles; and modern conditions demanded of it individual and collective skill and ability. He looked to the battle schools to show that the infantry should not be regarded as "an unskilled labour exchange".

# Chapter 16

# Defence against Air Attack

## The Revised Air Defence Plan

The changed assumption as to the form of German air attack, i.e. that the air battle would be fought in direct co-operation with the seaborne and airborne landings, required a drastic re-adjustment of the Air Defence arrangements. The existing air and anti-aircraft defences would have to be concentrated in an area south of a line from the Wash to Bristol ready to fight the battle for local air-superiority over the probable invasion area east of a line from the Wash to Weymouth.

Heavy bombing attacks immediately preceding, or simultaneous with the invasion were expected against our fighter organization, on ports from which the Fleet counter-strokes might be made, on London as the centre of Government, and on rail, road and headquarters communications to hinder the movement of Army reserves to the landing areas.

The revised air defence plan for the spring of 1942, as prepared by the Commander-in-Chief Fighter Command in consultation with the Commander-in-Chief Anti-Aircraft Command, is given as Appendix 28. The Air Staff Memorandum of the 31st July 1940 defining the anti-invasion tasks of the Air Commands was still in force (see Appendix 7). More detailed instructions as to the role, organization and disposition of the Royal Air Force to meet invasion, issued by the Air Staff in February 1942, are added as Appendix 29.

## Scale of Air Attack

With the continuing wastage of German strength in the campaign in Russia the estimated German air strength in the West had been reduced to not more than 1,000 aircraft of all types, including 600 fighters and 250 bombers. If the Russian campaign was successfully concluded by

90

the Germans three months would probably be required to transfer their air strength to the West and before air operations against the British Isles could be developed to full intensity.

After allowing for a security air force for the Russian and other occupied territories the German air strength available to support an invasion was estimated at 2,100 bomber aircraft (1,540 long range and 560 dive-bombers) and 1,520 fighter aircraft of all types. Ample accommodation and alternative landing grounds were available in France and the Low Countries covering the invasion area.

**Strength of the Metropolitan Air Force**
While the estimated German air strength to support an invasion was practically the same as in the summer of 1940, the Royal Air Force had achieved an all-round expansion for Home Defence, even though our productive capacity was being stretched to the utmost to build up a force of 62 R.A.F. squadrons for the Middle East and to supply fighter aircraft to Russia at the rate of 200 a month.

The fighter force remained the only effective means for denying to the Germans local air superiority over the invasion area. For its many vital tasks the agreed minimum strength was 75 day and 23 night fighter squadrons, and 8 Army co-operation squadrons (totalling about 1,700 first line aircraft). By January 1942 66 day and 25 night fighter squadrons (totalling 1,484 aircraft) and 15 Army co-operation squadrons (totalling 120 aircraft) were available. To that total must be added 800 fighter aircraft under the Banquet plan for making use in an emergency of aircraft and crews in operational and technical training units. Fighter Command could therefore probably count upon an all-round superiority over the German fighter force.

The bomber force in the United Kingdom in January totalled 47 squadrons (10 heavy, 33 medium, 4 light) or 832 aircraft; and of another 80 aircraft (one heavy, 2 medium, 2 light squadrons), which were non-operational, the majority would be operational by the 1st March in the event of invasion. Under the Banquet plan an additional 800 bomber aircraft would be available in an emergency. Although still numerically inferior to the German bomber force Bomber Command therefore possessed a most powerful striking force to employ against an invading armada. If gas had to be used as a retaliating measure or to counter a landing, 14 bomber squadrons were trained and equipped for gas spray (see Appendix 29).

Coastal Command in January 1942 had 28 squadrons (448 aircraft) of reconnaissance and fighter aircraft employed mainly on trade protection duties, and they could be directed at short notice to anti-invasion purposes. Under the Banquet plan another 300 Coastal Command aircraft would be available.

In the event of an invasion of Ireland a special force of R.A.F. units was stationed in Northern Ireland (see Appendix 29).

## Re-Distribution of Anti-Aircraft Guns

The revised Air Defence plan required a drastic re-adjustment of the anti-aircraft defence. From being widespread over the country to meet the requirements of 1940 and early 1941 it now had to be concentrated for the maximum protection of vital targets in the probable invasion area east of a line from the Wash to Weymouth.

Priority was to be given to the protection of the 21 fighter aerodromes covering the area; and only slightly less important would be the 31 rearward airfields and air bases west of that line and south of a line from the Wash to Bristol. Special protection was to be given to the Fighter Command operational centres at Stanmore, Uxbridge and Leighton Buzzard.

Almost equally important was the defence of those R.D.F. centres upon which Fighter Command relied for early warning of impending air attacks. Out of a total of 85 coastal and inland R.D.F. stations available by August, 1941 (to be expanded to 170 during 1942) 21 were regarded as vital for anti-invasion air defence.

Next in priority came the air-defence of the aerodromes of Coastal and Bomber Commands required for locating and striking the enemy invasion forces; within that category came 8 Coastal and 14 Bomber aerodromes. Equal in importance were the naval aerodromes, ports and other vulnerable points essential for the naval anti-invasion operations.

Anti-aircraft requirements for Home Forces included the protection from air attack of the East Kent coast artillery; also centres of communication and bottle-necks such as Canterbury, Maidstone and Ashford, through which the mobile reserves might have to pass to reach the landing beaches (Attic scheme). To protect pre-arranged troop concentration areas a mobile force of 8 Anti-Aircraft Regiments (96 heavy and 114 Light A.A. Guns) was to be transferred to Home Forces as soon as invasion threatened (Bargain Scheme).

Twenty-one vital industrial and densely populated areas required additional protection from air attack, and were to be given the maximum scale. The importance of the London air and anti-aircraft defence was such that no revision of its requirement was considered advisable

The scale of defence to be allotted to each of these vital targets is shown in the revised Air Defence plan (see Appendix 28) ... The total requirement for the plan was put at 2,400 heavy and 3,300 light A.A.

guns which was considerably less than the 1940 requirement (3,744 heavy and 4,410 light). In March, 1942 the "absolute minimum dead-line" was put at 2,048 heavy (25 per cent. mobile) and 1,278 light A.A. guns, and that total was available with the exception of 236 light A.A. guns due within the next few months.[16] To meet the threat of mine-laying by night in estuaries and coastal waters – Thames estuary, Greenock, Rosyth, Humber, Harwich, Portsmouth, Belfast and Londonderry – another 48 heavy and 40 light A.A. guns were required for mounting on sea forts (Maunsell towers).

The revised scheme involved the move of 1,000 heavy and 800 light A.A. guns by a re-adjustment of existing defence units (400 heavy and 540 light for the Air Ministry for strengthening the defence of aerodromes, 160 heavy and 48 light for the Admiralty for the additional defence of ports and other naval vulnerable points, and 440 heavy and 218 light for Home Forces). The task of redistributing the guns would involve the transfer of 30,000 personnel and 23,000 tons of ammunition, and labour for 20,000 men for five weeks.

The immediate need was modified however by the assurance that one month's warning of impending invasion could be given. Work which could be completed within a month did not therefore need to be carried out until the warning was received; and it was sufficient to make preparations, such as to prepare the new sites for the heavy static guns and to earmark transport for giving the required mobility to mobile units.

## Mixed A.A. Batteries

The shortage of man-power and the large demands on A.A. Command to supply trained personnel for the Field Army led to the employment of women (A.T.S.) for all work excluding heavy manual labour such as the loading and manning of the guns. The mixed batteries were limited to the static heavy gun sites, and the proportion of women to men in these batteries became roughly two to one; the number of A.T.S. in A.A. Command rose rapidly to a maximum of over 74,000.

The G.O.C. A.A. Command in his despatch writes of the "triumphal success of the mixed units" and praises the high morale and valuable work of the women and their great courage during heavy air raids.

## Anti-Aircraft Command to be More Flexible

The aim was to be able to concentrate rapidly for the defence of any objective the enemy air force might select, docks, aerodromes, factories,

[16] C.O.S. (A.A) 418: 20 Feb. 1942. C.O.S. (42) 134, 199: 24 Feb., 3 Apr..

troop communications or concentrations, etc.; and for that purpose the Air Defence was to be kept as flexible as possible.

The increased flexibility was obtained by classing the A.A. batteries into three categories: mobile, semi-mobile and static. Mobile batteries had a full establishment of transport, and were manned by Regulars; semi-mobile batteries had a lesser scale of transport and were manned by a proportion of Home Guard; static batteries were manned by only a nucleus of Regular personnel the remainder being A.T.S. and Home Guard, or Home Guard only.

This measure enabled a proposed increase of 50,000 in A.A. Command personnel to be cancelled. Twelve A.A. divisions had been formed; and in view of the need for men to strengthen the Field Army the Prime Minister said that it seemed reasonable to fix the total of A.D.G.B. personnel "at its present figure of 280,000 men plus any additional recruitment of women it can attract". The new figure in November 1941 stood at 280,000 men and 170,000 women which was 30,000 more men than the number with which A.D.G.B. had successfully overcome the air raids of 1940.

## Improved Searchlight Lay-out

The introduction of Radar (S.L.C.) equipment during the summer of 1941 to control the searchlight beam enabled the searchlights to be re-sited singly instead of in clusters of three; and the re-arrangement resulted in the 'fighter box' method of assisting fighter interception at night. The idea will be explained later in dealing with the problem of night raiders. The other uses of searchlights were to prevent mine-laying in harbours and estuaries, to illuminate balloons for our own aircraft, and to act as a homing beacon for our aircraft at night.

The total requirement for the new searchlight lay-out was 176 batteries (each of 24 lights), with 526 personnel for each battery. The total of 92,576 all ranks represented a saving of 22,731 on the previous requirement.

The batteries were distributed as follows: 143 to cover the gun defended areas including the London A.A. Defences, 9 for defence of the principal aerodromes against low-flying attack, 5 for coastal defence against enemy mine-laying, 6 for the Orkney and Shetland defences, and 13 as additional mobile reserve batteries.

## Reduction in Balloon Command

The cable-cutting device fitted to a number of German low-flying aircraft had decreased the lethal effect of the balloon barrage defence, though counter measures were being developed. In the mean-time the moral effect, particularly for night raiders, could be maintained by a density less than that required for lethal effect.

In order to release all possible man-power for the Field Army, a reduction of 25 per cent. in the personnel of Balloon Command was to be proceeded with; the reduction in operational balloons was from 2,401 to 1,928. The London balloon barrage, for example, was to be reduced from 400 to 300 balloons by the 4th April, 1942.

Chapter 17

# Defence against Airborne Attack

### Scale of Airborne Attack

The Germans were expected to possess by the spring of 1942 3,500 troop-carrying aircraft and 4,000 gliders capable of transporting 55,000 troops and equipment over a period of three days.

The landings would probably be in the coastal belt in close co-operation with the sea-borne landings, and the airborne troops were expected to arrive in three waves: 23,000 parachutists and glider-borne troops followed by 20,000 and 12,000 troops in troop-carrying air transports.[17]

### Probable Objectives

The airborne force, composed of parachutists, glider troops, or troops in troop-carrying aircraft, was likely to be employed for four purposes. The greatest threat was a concentrated attack on the vital fighter aerodromes and their associated R.D.F. stations in an effort to cripple our air counter-offensive. In the South-Eastern Command, for example, airborne landings were expected on the Tangmere group of aerodromes and those at Redhill, Biggin Hill, Gravesend and West Malling.

Another threat was a landing in rear of the beach defences to assist a seaborne landing, and to prevent the arrival of reserves. As a preventative measure, in the South-Eastern Command for example, light tank units were stationed at points along the South Downs and near the Medway road-crossings to deal at once with parachutists and airborne forces who might attempt to block the approaches for reserves to the South coast and Kent beaches. Special precautions had also been

---

[17] C.O.S.(A.A.) 317: 27 June, 1941. For the capture of Crete in May 1940 the Germans landed 32,000 troops by air during the whole period of the attack.

taken to isolate and destroy airborne landings on open inland areas such as Salisbury Plain or the Norfolk Broads (see Appendix 22). Fourthly was the possibility of an airborne attack on London concurrently with invasion; and the preparations for its defence against such an onslaught have already been mentioned.

While fighter squadrons and A.A. guns were the main defence against airborne attack ground mobile forces were disposed inland so as to give maximum protection to essential areas. A.A. guns, static and mobile, were sited for the dual role of A.A. and anti-tank defence wherever possible; and both gun and searchlight detachments carried arms to be able to defend their own positions.

## Ground Defence of Aerodromes

Lessons drawn from the German airborne attacks on Crete in May, 1941 had radically changed the method of defence of aerodromes and other vulnerable points. To avoid the effects of preliminary bombing and machine-gun attack from the air the defence posts were to be sited in depth and not, as in 1940, close around the airfield.

The posts generally consisted of wired-in defended localities sited so as to cover the aerodrome and its approaches. The inner posts contained mortars and light machine-guns; the outer posts had heavy machine-guns and artillery. Concealed guns with a restricted field of fire were considered of more value than guns in the open with an all-round field of fire but liable to be knocked out at an early stage. Alternative sites for each defended post were to be prepared within 100 yards. The protection of aircraft storage depots presented a special problem since they relied upon dispersion for security against bombing, and they occupied areas up to 12 miles in circumference.

The Army requirement for aerodrome defence included a permanent garrison and an external force for relief and counter-attack. The number of aerodromes and landing grounds in the country had increased to 550 by August, 1941, and another 100 were due for completion during 1942 with 755 as the limit on the flat ground available. The Army's share of permanent garrison troops by April, 1942 was estimated at 118,500 men, the remaining 73,500 required being found by the Royal Air Force (see Appendix 22). Mobile troops of light tanks (Beaverettes) were to be ready to deal quickly with airborne troops landing out of range; and out of an order for 1,000 Beaverettes 600 were to be ready by April, 1942.

The estimate by the Commander-in-Chief, Home Forces, was modified by the recommendations of a Committee on Aerodrome Defence set up in November, 1941 to the effect that the permanent garrisons should be provided by an Aerodrome Defence Corps (R.A.F.

Regiment) to be formed under the control of the Air Ministry. During land operations the control would pass to the Commander-in-Chief Home Forces, and be exercised through station commanders. By May, 1942 the permanent garrisons of 32 of the main aerodromes had been taken over from the Army by the R.A.F. Regiment.

External forces for relief and counter-attack were to be provided by Field Force units in corps, Army or G.H.Q. reserve. For each vital fighter aerodrome a relief column of an infantry battalion, or its equivalent, was to be stationed within a mile and to be available within one hour. Twenty-four independent battalions were required for this purpose. In addition, a counter-attack force equivalent to a brigade was to be within call, and so placed as to be available within 2 to 3 hours (see Appendix 22).

A change of policy governing the erection of obstructions around aerodromes and on possible landing grounds against troop-carrying aircraft was agreed by the Chiefs of Staff in August, 1941. Previously the policy, laid down in August 1940, had been to obstruct all dangerous open spaces within a radius of five miles of ports, practicable landing beaches, specified aerodromes and vulnerable points.

The new policy was to obstruct open spaces within a radius of one mile around all aerodromes up to 20 miles from the coast between the Wash and the Severn, and within 20 miles of Hull, Middlesbrough, Newcastle and Edinburgh. Existing obstructions were not to be removed.

**Ground Defence of Vulnerable Points**
Up to the summer of 1941 about 50,000 troops were engaged in the protection of other vulnerable points. The introduction of Military Police (5,000 had been enrolled for this purpose by August, 1941) to protect certain establishments against sabotage, and the organisation of small mobile columns to act as a reinforcement, and to deal with an airborne threat, enabled a considerable saving in the number of permanent guards.

During 1942 the number of Military Police (V.P.) was increased to 12,000 enabling a reduction in permanent garrison troops to 25,000 (25 Home Defence battalions). The small mobile columns for relief and counter-attack near the more vital points required another 10,000 troops (see Appendix 22).

Chapter 18

# The Estimated Requirement for Home Forces Considered Excessive

**Minimum Requirement of Home Forces not Available**
By mid-October it was realised that the minimum requirement for Home Defence as calculated by the Commander-in-Chief Home Forces in his Appreciation of the 1st August, would not be available by the spring of 1942. The formation and strength of the armoured divisions, in particular, was not proceeding to programme owing to the despatch of tanks and equipment to the Middle East and Russia.

On the 23rd October the Commander-in-Chief, Home Forces, reminded the Chiefs of Staff that a reduction of full scale infantry divisions, from over 20 to 14, had been accepted on the understanding that armoured formations would be increased to 8 armoured divisions and 10 Army tank brigades. It was now evident, he wrote, that by the spring of 1942 Home Forces would be deficient of 3 armoured divisions and 5 Army tank brigades. Other formations lacking would be one full scale infantry division, 2 brigade groups and 3 county divisions; and the airborne brigade would not be complete. He added his opinion that the strength of Home Forces by the 1st April 1942 would be inadequate for the defence of the country; and he asked that "steps be taken to remedy the position before that date, when it may well be too late".

The Chiefs of Staff Committee had to take into account the urgent demands for reinforcements and drafts for the Middle East, and also the need to build up an Expeditionary force which was being trained in Scotland as the spearhead for a landing overseas. A plan for the return to the Continent to take advantage of a possible deterioration of the German morale and strength in the West was being prepared by the Commander-in-Chief, Home Forces.

These commitments required that the Home Defence Army be kept at the minimum for safety, and the Chiefs of Staff questioned whether the estimate of the scale of attack accepted by the Commander-in-Chief, Home Forces, still held good. The comparative strengths of our own and the German air forces had altered considerably in our favour; and the estimate by the Joint Intelligence Committee did not appear to take adequately into account the casualties which our superior air force would inflict on the German airborne and surface forces, nor the difficulties of mounting and launching a seaborne and airborne invasion on the scale required.

The Prime Minister, too, asked that an appreciation of the scale of attack should be made on a sound basis and in no way exaggerated. The nearer invasion ports, such as Dunkirk, Calais and Boulogne could no longer be considered as eligible invasion ports, since any concentration of shipping in them could be broken up by our daylight bombing attacks. He found it difficult to believe, too, the estimate of 3,000 especially converted barges and tank landing-craft, and that this large quantity of craft could be collected in not too distant ports and launched for an invasion. He thought that the restrictions on the use of the nearer invasion ports, and also the possibility of employing gas offensively and defensively, should be taken into account in our preparations to resist invasion in 1942.

## The Inter-Service Committee on Invasion
In order to check the estimate of the probable scale and form of German attack the Chiefs of Staff set up a "German syndicate", consisting of senior officers from the three Services, who were to consider themselves in the position of a German staff who had to prepare a plan for the invasion of the British Isles about the 1st April, 1942. They were to set out the form and scale of attack and the resources required. They could assume that the Germans would remain on the defensive on all other fronts, and that otherwise the maximum possible forces would be available.

The main difference between the Report and the Appreciation by the Commander-in-Chief, Home Forces lay in the probable form of attack. The Report took the view that circumstances would compel the Germans to concentrate their main attack through South-East England on London using the shortest possible sea-route, the Straits of Dover.

The Commander-in-Chief, Home Forces, on the other hand, had based his dispositions on the assumption that the most likely form of attack would be a pincer movement on, or to the West of London through East Anglia, and through South-East England.

In a later review of the Report and of the comments upon it by Commanders-in-Chief concerned, the Vice-Chiefs of Staff thought that the pincer movement on London suggested by the Commander-in-Chief, Home Forces, was more likely to succeed than a purely frontal attack through Kent and Sussex. They believed that the losses to shipping, due to our bombing, in an attempt to land a force in East Anglia might not be so heavy as the Report estimated; and that the enormous risks and losses which the German Command would be prepared to accept in order to achieve its purpose had been under-estimated.

The Vice-Chiefs also commented on the fact that the Report conveyed the impression that the deciding battle would take place on land; whereas, in fact, an invading force was most vulnerable when at sea or attempting to land on the beaches. Every effort would have to be made to defeat a seaborne expedition at that stage; and while full preparations would necessarily be made to allow for a subsequent land battle, our defence plans should lay emphasis throughout on the importance of attacking and defeating the enemy before he landed.

The Vice-Chiefs considered too, that the Report had placed too much stress upon meteorological factors likely to govern the actual invasion date; and not enough on the really vital factors which were a calm sea and good landing conditions on the beaches. The Report was regarded not so much as a guide on which our requirements for defence should be based, but rather as a very useful investigation which had brought to light certain questions requiring further attention.

**American Criticism**
As the vanguard of the United States armies was about to arrive in the United Kingdom the defence of the country was of direct interest to them. American estimate of the defence, according to the plan and figures imparted to them and from their own observations, was given to the Chiefs of Staff Committee in November.

They commented upon the possible inability of the Navy to concentrate light forces for anti-invasion action prior to the fifth or seventh day after invasion had started; and also upon the apparent lack of co-ordination between the Army, Navy and Air Force. Above all they criticised the dispositions of Home Forces as being unlikely to check an invasion. The defended localities along the coast were too far apart for mutual support. The gun-cover for the beach obstacles was inadequate. The local mobile reserves were not strong enough; and as they generally had a double task, against airborne as well as seaborne attacks, they might be too fully occupied with one to attend to the other. The G.H.Q.

reserves were too far from the coast; and owing to the narrow margin of time probably available for determining the enemy's main effort, they might arrive in the area of operations too late.

According to the American estimate the German air force had been discounted to too great a degree; and it was believed that the Germans, given sustained local air superiority, would be able to land from barges on the open beaches sufficient men, vehicles, tanks, artillery and supplies to overrun the vital areas of South-Eastern England in a blitz attack lasting about five days.

The American estimate pointed out the great increase in German armoured forces, and the lack of battle experiences of the British leaders compared with the German leaders. Nor did the American critics agree with the British opinion that in the initial stages of invasion the Germans would require the use of a port and a secure line of communications.

## The Prime Minister's Comments

The observations made by the Prime Minister on this American estimate applied also to the assumptions upon which the Home Forces plan had been based. He pointed out that the assumptions had been accepted in order to keep our defence up to the mark, and did not rest on any solid basis other than that of prudent apprehension. As an example, he said that the assumption "given sustained local air superiority" was very hard to accept when it was remembered how very much more powerful our fighter force was than in 1940, when it proved to be enough; and that we could attack by day any lodgements under fighter protection at any selected moment.

He thought that the great fault of the American estimate was that it ignored the time-sequence of events. An invasion on so vast a scale could not be prepared without detection. Aerial photography would reveal the process, and the Air Force would subject the armada to the heaviest bombing during what might well be a fortnight or more. From Dunkirk to Dieppe our air strength was sufficient to enable us to make daylight attacks under fighter air cover.

When the difficulties of embarkation had been surmounted it would still be necessary to marshal the ships and bring them across the sea. By that time, the Prime Minister added, it was reasonable to expect that naval assistance would be available in a very high form (see Appendix 23). The use of gas by us upon the invasion ports, either at the moment of embarkation or against lodgements, had also to be taken into account.

Commenting upon the American estimate that there might be no warning, and that our light naval forces would be engaged in the Battle of the Atlantic, the Prime Minister said that such an assumption was absurd once the scale of the invasion was raised above the level of heavy raids. The punishing naval and air action played no part in the American estimate, "and yet, in it is comprised the main and proved defence of the island from invasion".

He explained that with the wish to train an Army and to keep it keen we had naturally stressed what might happen after the enemy land, "but the Royal Navy and Royal Air Force are responsible for shattering the assembly of the armada and for cutting it down, striking into it decisively in passage". There must, he said, be no lifting of this obligation off these two forces.

The Prime Minister asked that these features of the defence should be studied as of equal importance to the resistance which would be offered by our military forces once the enemy had landed.

**Actual Strength of Home Forces in April, 1942**
The dispositions had had to be modified considerably below the minimum requirement demanded by the Commander-in-Chief, Home Forces, in August, 1941 (see Appendix 22). The strength of South-Eastern Command, considered the most vulnerable, remained unchanged at the expense of the other Commands. The Eastern, Northern and Southern Commands each lost a County division and an Army tank brigade for beach defence below the minimum requirement, and their reserves were limited to armoured formations. G.H.Q. reserve was reduced from 4 to one armoured division (plus the 42nd and Canadian neither of which would be ready before mid-Summer 1942).

Home Forces, including the six Commands or Armies and the London district, amounted to about 850,000 troops by the spring of 1942; and the total Army at Home, including Anti-Aircraft Command (under Fighter Command) and the force in Northern Ireland (under the War Office) was over 1½ million. To that figure must be added the Home Guard which had reached a strength of nearly 1,600,000 men of whom 74 per cent. were armed.

To that anti-invasion force must be added the Expeditionary Force in process of formation in Scotland under War Office control. It consisted of one armoured and 2 full-scale infantry divisions, of which in the event of imminent invasion one full-scale division would remain in Scotland at the disposal of the Commanders-in-Chief Home Forces and the remainder would return to England as formations in G.H.Q. reserve.

Chapter 19

# Civil Defence Measures

### Control Organization
The detailed civilian arrangements to meet the threat of invasion in the spring of 1942 were issued by the Home Defence Executive in September 1941, with a final revision in June, 1942.

In general the measures for control evolved during the summer and autumn of 1940 remained in force. In addition, Invasion Committees were formed out of the Civil Defence Emergency Committees in towns, villages and rural areas which enabled local authorities, local departmental officials, the police and the military authorities to meet and work out plans for action in advance for each locality. The Regional Commissioner in consultation with the Army Commander concerned had to sanction the special arrangements made; but in the event of invasion the Invasion Committees would form the focal point to which the civil population would look for guidance, and a local channel of communication for civil and military co-operation.

The crux of the control problem was the maintenance of communications. The decision, made in September 1940, was to fight the invasion battle from Whitehall so long as communications held; and the Chiefs of Staff believed that a heavy air attack on London in order to disorganise the centre of Government would form part of the German invasion plan. High priority had accordingly been given for the completion of the bomb-proof communications system known as "the Whitehall tunnel" for telephone cables, and for the construction of the heavily protected "citadels" for the War Cabinet and for other essential Government staffs in a grave emergency.

In the event of a breakdown of communications with London, or when delaying a decision would be dangerous, Regional Commissioners were invested with executive Ministerial powers.

104

## Evacuation of Coastal Towns

Other civil plans for assisting the military authorities were those for the enforcement of a stand-firm policy and the control of civilian movement, including the evacuation of coastal towns and the control of refugees. The disastrous results of mass movements of civilians on the roads during the invasion of France in 1940 had not been forgotten; and arrangements were made to keep the roads free for carrying out the military defence plan.

In the autumn of 1940, on the threat of invasion, 40 to 50 per cent. of the population of the East and South coast towns had voluntarily moved inland; but during the winter a large proportion had returned. Plans had been prepared for the compulsory evacuation of 19 towns between Great Yarmouth and Hythe, totalling over half a million persons; with the extension of the probable invasion area westwards the Brighton group of towns as far west as Littlehampton with another 300,000 persons, were brought into the scheme, making 38 towns in all. Evacuation was to begin 9 days after the receipt of the month's warning signal (see Section 75), and it was to be completed 5 days before the warning period expired. The aim was to have only 4 or 5 per cent. of civilians to maintain essential civilian services for defending the area.

If a subsequent refugee movement from coastal or inland towns developed, the police and military were to divert it to pre-arranged reception areas.

## Denial of Resources to an Invader

The Civil invasion preparations also included plans for denying to the enemy all resources which might be to his immediate advantage. The policy was based on the assumption that the invader would be ejected in a relatively short period, and that he would be too harried to use any resources not immediately available. A "scorched-earth" policy required long distances to take effect, as in Russia, and it would not pay over the short distance with good roads between the coast and London.

The schemes for the immobilisation of ports were for a period of 7-10 days by dismantling and removing essential equipment. Railway facilities were to be denied by removing all engines from coastal sheds and threatened areas on the "Stand-to" signal. Plans were also in readiness for the immobilisation of all motor vehicles and bicycles; and for the reduction of food and petrol stocks to an essential minimum before invasion started, with the alternative of most careful arrangements for their certain destruction if necessary.

105

## Maintenance of the Civilian War Effort and of Civil Life

The Civil anti-invasion preparations necessarily included measures to keep up war production by maintaining rail and road transport wherever possible. Pre-arranged restriction zones, on the assumption of an invasion area east of a line from the Wash to Weymouth, were to be imposed by the Railway Executive Committee on instructions from the Ministry of War Transport.

Arrangements for power-supplies were the responsibility of the Emergency Service organisation of the Board of Trade; and plans had been completed in collaboration with the Ministry for Home Security for the maintenance and restoration of essential services. For the supply of food during an invasion period the country was divided into 109 separate zones (London was sub-divided into 28 zones), in each of which bulk stocks of food were stored sufficient to feed the normal population for 14 days.

Food Executive Officers had been appointed in each Borough and Urban and Rural Districts assisted by numerous voluntary food organisers. Special arrangements, too, had been made for the issue of communiques on the situation through the office of the Minister of Defence during the invasion period.

## Civil Defence (Air Raid Precautions)

The full scope of the Civil Defence preparations to meet heavy air attacks during the winter and in the spring of 1942 were outlined in a memorandum by the Minister for Home Security in July 1941.

The basis of the Civil Defence organization had remained as originally planned in 1938 with its chain of command from the A.R.P. Controller through the Chief Wardens of towns and districts, divisional and group wardens down to warden posts. The immediate need, particularly in the more vulnerable towns such as London, was for deep shelters, the provision of which had been neglected on the grounds of expense and labour. Adequate shelter against blast and splinters was available, and in December 1940 the shelter policy was overhauled. Deep shelters were to be provided according to the degree of vulnerability of the town or district, for which purpose the country was divided into three (A, B and C) Zones. In London, places such as the underground tube stations, were adapted for the purpose.

The great losses caused by fires from incendiary bombs, particularly in the City of London, resulted in the re-organization of the fire brigade services on a national basis; and the National Fire Service was formed in August 1941 with compulsory powers for the direction of labour. The strength of the Fire Service at that time in England, Scotland and Wales was over 105,000 out of a total establishment of 132,950. To ensure more prompt action against fires the power to deal with incendiary bomb attacks was delegated from departmental to regional responsibility.

The evacuation of population from the more vulnerable towns was on a large scale. By July 1941 there were about 1,300,000 official evacuees in reception areas in England and 149,000 in Scotland; and that total was in addition to the planned compulsory evacuation schemes for the coastal areas on the threat of invasion. Some 300,000 beds were ready in hospitals for air-raid and Service casualties.

The total man-power in the Civil Defence Services at this period, was about 172,500 whole-time workers, including 53,000 women; to that total must be added over 2 million part-time workers, and also the still greater army of fire-guards or fire-watchers throughout the country.

The story of Air Raid Precautions will be found in the Official History of Civil Defence; but this general account would not be complete without some reference to the high degree of collaboration and interaction between all sides of the life of the nation which had been reached by the spring of 1942 to meet the threat of air attack and invasion.

# Chapter 20

# The German Plan for Invasion Fades Out

### The Plan Postponed Indefinitely

Following the postponement of the German plan for invasion (Operation Sea Lion) in January 1941 until the close of the proposed offensive against Russia, deception measures were maintained through the spring and early Summer of 1941.

In July of that year the German Command again postponed the operation until the spring of 1942, on the assumption that by that time the Russian campaign would be completed. The project as not seriously considered again.

# Part IV

1942-45: The Threat of Raids
and of Rocket Bombs

Chapter 21

# The United Kingdom as a Base for the Counter-Offensive

**General Situation in the Spring of 1942**

Before the outbreak of war the Chiefs of Staff had forecast that the United Kingdom would require a period of two years of defensive war in order to build up sufficient armed strength for a counter-offensive.

By the Spring of 1942 not only had that difficult defensive phase been surmounted, but the situation was far more favourable than the Chiefs of Staff had anticipated. Active intervention by the United States, which had appeared "doubtful" in 1939, had been provoked by the bombing of the American naval base at Pearl Harbour by Japan on the 7th December, 1941; and within a few weeks the vanguard of the American armies was arriving in this country. The intervention of Russia, too, regarded as hopeful in 1939, had succeeded beyond expectations. The supreme German effort to capture Moscow in 1941 had been checked; and it seemed inevitable that the German Command would have to resume the Eastern offensive in 1942 in order to obtain essential oil from the Caucasus, and to break the Russian army, before taking on further commitments.

The Anglo-American policy in face of this situation, discussed at Washington in February, 1942, was to send war material to Russia as a first priority, and also to take offensive action by sea, air and land as major diversions. The United Kingdom was to be administered and planned as a base for the accommodation and supply of British and American forces destined for offensive operations on the Continent (Operation Round-up). Three British Armies were being assembled: the First in Scotland, the Second in the Midlands, and a Canadian Army in South-East England; the South-Western counties and Northern Ireland were allotted for the assembly and training of American troops.

Chapter 22

# Defence Against Sea and Airborne Raids

**Protective Measures Against Raids**

The campaign against Russia was re-opened by a Russian counter-offensive which delayed the German offensive towards the Caucasus till mid-June; and it was evident that Germany would be fully occupied throughout the summer. On the 19th June the Chiefs of Staff approved a memorandum for the C.-in-C. Home Forces to the effect that an invasion of this country was impossible so long as the Russian army remained undefeated; and that, even so, three months must elapse before sufficient forces could be re-grouped in the West for an invasion. As a complete Russian collapse before August was unlikely, preparations to meet an invasion before the spring of 1943 were considered unnecessary. In the meantime precautions against sea and airborne raids were not to be relaxed.

To deal with these raids a defence screen was arranged to meet a maximum scale of attack by 100,000 troops. The raids would probably be directed against the most vulnerable objectives near the coast, such as London, the Tyne-Tees area, the Forth Bridge and Rosyth, and possibly the Orkneys, Shetlands and Caithness. Local garrisons were to be provided by L.E. (lower establishment) divisions, independent brigades and Young Soldier and Home Defence battalions or the Home Guard, some of these formations being trained as local mobile reserves for counter-attack.

Field Army formations, as major mobile reserves, were stationed in readiness in the St. Albans–Aylesbury area for London, East Anglia and the Midlands, and in the Edinburgh–Glasgow area for the North and Scotland. In addition field army divisions in training could be diverted at once to Home Defence positions at the preliminary warning of an impending raid or invasion.

## Home Forces Plans for the Spring of 1943

On the 28th September the C.-in-C. Home Forces[18] wrote an appreciation for the Home Defence plan for the spring of 1943. He believed that Germany had already lost the last chance of a successful invasion of this country; but he accepted the possibility of one desperate final gamble by the German Command if Russia should be defeated.

In that event the Germans would probably use every device to obtain surprise, and might employ, smoke, flame-throwers and gas, in one concentrated effort to over-run the country. He expected the main attack to be diverted through South-Eastern Command on London; and estimated its strength at 10 armoured divisions (about 2,000 tanks) and 21 infantry divisions.

To meet that threat the C.-in-C. Home Forces put his minimum requirements at 6 armoured and 22 infantry divisions; and he pointed out to the Chiefs of Staff that Home Forces would be deficient to the extent of one armoured and 3 infantry divisions owing to the dispatch of reinforcements to the Middle East during 1942 and to the departure of the First Army to North Africa in November (Operation Torch).

## Invasion Risk Considered Negligible

The Chiefs of Staff, on the other hand, believed the danger of invasion in the spring of 1943 to be negligible. The combined British and American air force would then be able to drop 47,000 tons of bombs in seven days on the invasion ports and troop concentrations; a quantity which was double the bomb-lift in the spring of 1942. They believed that the effect of such a weight of attack would be to make the ports inoperative during that period and to destroy about 20 per cent. of the invasion craft.

The strength of our light naval forces, too, had considerably increased during the year owing to production and to American assistance. Our naval dispositions, which could be strengthened during the preliminary warning period, were such that on the day of assault a large force of light naval units could quickly be concentrated to repel the invasion transports; and within four days the full weight of reinforcements from the Western Approaches would be thrown into the naval attack. Given adequate air protection, it was believed that these naval forces would prove the greatest counter to invasion.

The Chiefs of Staff also thought that diversions of any strength outside the main enemy fighter cover, between the Wash and

[18] Lt. General Sir B. Paget had succeeded General Sir Alan Brooke as C.-in-C. Home Forces on the 25th Dec. 1941.

Weymouth, need not be feared. The War Office had been examining the possible scale of invasion from this country onto the Continent, and they had concluded that the ferrying ashore of a landing force from transports under constant bomber attack was almost impossible. To north and west of the fighter-covered area the Army requirement might therefore be restricted to the defence of harbours; and South-Eastern Command could be kept at maximum strength. They reminded the C.-in-C. Home Forces that five United States Army divisions would be in this country by the spring.

In view of Britain's armed strength as a whole, the Chiefs of Staff were agreed that it was "inconceivable that the Germans would be able to attain the requisite degree of air superiority for an invasion to be practicable before 1944, if ever"; and that no risk would be involved in re-organising the forces in the United Kingdom to form the largest possible balanced offensive force.

### Church Bells to be Rung Again

In the Chiefs of Staff opinion, too, the risk of sea and airborne raids had greatly diminished. The only probable purpose for such raids at that stage of the war would be to gain information about our preparations to invade the Continent, and the targets for such information were so distant from the coast that the German Command was unlikely to waste sea or air transport for it.

The outward sign of this confidence was the permission given on the 14th April to ring the church bells from Easter Sunday (1943) onwards. For three years since June 1940, they had been silent except as a signal of parachutist or airborne attack.

### Re-organisation of Home Forces

The spring of 1943 therefore saw the continued reduction of Home Forces, and the integration of its divisions and services into the complex of force which was taking shape for the invasion of the Continent, (renamed Operation Overlord).

The total of British troops of all categories overseas at this time was approaching the million mark, leaving 1½ million in the United Kingdom of whom one-third were in Field Army formations. The problem for the C.-in-C. Home Forces was to find every suitable man to bring the Expeditionary Force to the required strength, and to provide the manifold services, such as transport, signals, lines of communication, etc. essential on a large scale to maintain a modern army in the field for offensive operations.

The many scattered garrisons of aerodromes and vulnerable points, and the units of A.A. Command, had to be reduced to a minimum, and trained for the new task. The remainder were to be used to maintain the structure of the Home Defence organisation until all possible threats had been removed. The Home Guard, too, which was nearing 1½ millions strong; and not included in the above totals, was to be kept at a high state of efficiency.

In the transformation of Home Forces for an offensive role a "worst possible case" was taken into account. It was pointed out that after our invasion armies had been launched onto the Continent Germany might defeat Russia and, bringing an overwhelming force against us in the West, compel us to a costly withdrawal. In such an event defences along the coast which would take 9-12 months to re-establish might be required at once. To meet such a possibility the coast defences were dismantled in two stages: the first by a reduction from 185 to 142 Regular and from 75 to 47 Home Guard batteries. The second stage was to be deferred until the situation on the Continent was favourable.

To ease the difficulty of maintaining an efficient Home Army while at the same time providing the large drafts and reinforcements for overseas, a holding organisation to produce up to 40,000 trained men per month was formed under War Office control. The scheme was to establish six Holding divisions, with a proportion of armoured units, to which men would be sent from the training units.

These divisions would give the final two months training for drafts overseas, and provide the man-power needs both for forces overseas and at Home. Home Forces was thereby relieved of the two major difficulties with which it had had to contend during 1941/42; that of units being continually under strength and the constant changes in personnel.

Chapter 23

# Defence Against Air Raids

**Improved Night Interception Measures**

The withdrawal of the mass of the German air striking force from the West at the end of May 1941 to support the offensive against Russia had transformed the scale of air attack on this country. The average operational strength of German bomber units in the West during 1942 and 1943 was 60, whereas 600 had been available for the raids in the autumn of 1940 and early 1941.

Night raids had become the practice of the German air force since the heavy losses incurred during the daylight raids in September 1940; and night interception was the most urgent problem for the Air Defence of Great Britain. At first the intention was to illuminate and hold the bomber by searchlights while the fighter pursued according to daytime interception methods. The system failed owing to the inability of the searchlights to support the fighter in continuous engagement. The searchlights, relying upon sound location for directing their beams, too often lagged behind the bomber and became a hindrance rather than a help; low flying raiders, too, were able to slip through unobserved, and frequently they were at heights at which the search-lights were ineffective.

A new method was adopted; and searchlights were left out of the picture. The positions and tracks of approaching bombers were plotted at section operations rooms from the R.D.F. Stations and the G.L. (later G.C.I.) radar sets. From these readings the night fighter was to be put behind the bomber, and in such a position that the echo of the bomber would show on his own A.I. radar set which had a maximum range of 2 to 3 miles. The fighter would then overtake the bomber until it became visible to the naked eye, and shoot it down. Practical results were, however, disappointing. The A.I. sets could only be fitted to twin-engined multi-seater fighters which were often slower than the German

116

bombers. The A.I. set itself, too, proved to be unexpectedly capricious and many German bombers escaped after a pick-up, and even after visual contact had been made.

Until the early summer of 1941 the A.A. guns had therefore had to play a major part in the defence against night raiders; and their results were greatly improved by the introduction in October 1940 of Radar (G.L.) sets which enabled the uncontrolled barrages of September 1940 to be replaced by "unseen" barrages controlled by radar from the gun operations rooms. The experience turned the A.A. gunners into skilled technical operators. and during the last six weeks of the massed German air attacks, from the 1st April to the 12th May, 72 bombers were shot down by the guns and 82 "probables" recorded.

Scientific research during the summer of 1941 gave fighter aircraft a better chance of night interception with searchlight assistance. Among the many inventions devised to assist air defence at that time was the application of the radar principle (S.L.C.) to direct the searchlight beam accurately on to the moving target. As a result a new fighter and searchlight defence layout was able to be evolved.

The country was divided up into fighter boxes, 44 miles by 14 miles in size, around the gun defended areas; the size of the box being the space within which a night fighter would have time to intercept a bomber. The fighter was to circle a stationary vertical searchlight beam until given an indication that a bomber was entering the box. Searchlights spaced singly at 6 miles interval at the ends of the box constituted an indicator zone; while at the centre the lights were placed as close as was possible without mutual interference between the radar sets, about 3½ miles, so as to give maximum illumination to the killer zone. The series of boxes, side by side, formed a continuous belt of indicator and killer zones.

The initial distrust of the night fighter crews of searchlight assistance was gradually overcome by making the R.A.F. and Searchlight Controls interchangeable. The box system remained the basis of searchlight deployment till the end of the war.

The evolution of the night interception plan is an example of the constant variations required in air defence policy to keep abreast of scientific developments and changing conditions. The full story of Fighter Command's achievements in night interception is told in the Official History of the War in the Air.

### Re-organisation of A.A. Command

The flexibility given to A.A. Command as part of the Air Defence plan for the spring of 1942 assisted it to counter the air raids in the following months.

Overland night raiding started again in April 1942 when the German air force singled out open towns and cathedral cities for attack, the so-called Baedeker raids, as a measure of retaliation for Bomber Command's massed attacks on German cities. The mobility given to A.A. Command enabled the rapid transfer of 252 mobile heavy guns from gun defended areas for the defence of 28 of these previously undefended targets as soon as the German intention was realised.

The summer of 1942 also saw the beginning of the low-level daylight raids on coastal towns in reply to our fighter sweeps across the Channel. Between April and September 57 coastal towns were attacked between Aldeburgh (Suffolk) and St. Ives (Cornwall). The raiders approached at heights below 1,000 feet, confusing radar detection and escaping the shore-watchers till the last minute. Light A.A. guns and machine guns were the best available counter weapons, but their supply had been severely limited by the urgent demands for the Middle and Far East.

By June 104 light A.A. guns had been allotted to the "fringe target towns", and experience quickly showed that places provided with guns and balloon defence suffered relatively lightly compared with those with little or no air defence, such as Exeter. By March 1943 the fringe defences had been increased to 917 40mm guns, 192 20mm guns and 674 light machine guns of various kinds.

Against the strong air attacks in May and June, when 15 raids were made by about 300 aircraft on coastal and inland towns of which the worst sufferers were Eastbourne and Hastings, the A.A. guns shot down 25 aircraft and 13 probables, while the R.A.F. accounted for 17 shot down and 4 probables.

To meet the threat of mine-laying by night in harbours and estuaries sea forts (Maunsell Towers) were constructed in the Thames and Mersey estuaries, each mounting 4 heavy A.A. guns, 2 light 40mm guns, one searchlight and a radar set. The four forts completed in the Thames estuary by October 1942 also closed a serious gap in the London defences.

During the summer of 1942, too, A.A. Command had to provide additional protection to the Southern anchorages, by the move of 102 heavy and 176 light A.A. guns, for the embarkation of the First Army for North Africa (Operation Torch), and also for the disembarkation ports of the American divisions in this country. Before the end of the year planning was already in progress for the invasion of the Continent (Operation Overlord).

During the spring of 1944 the anti-aircraft defences of the embarkation ports, supply bases and lines of communication of the Southern por.s, from Great Yarmouth to South Wales were built up to a total of 1,374 heavy and 1,120 light A.A. guns, 538 balloons and 17 smoke screens.[19] That total included large contributions of guns from the Field Force and the United States Army.

The organisation of Fighter Command stood up to these many demands and sudden changes; but A.A. Command found its corps and division organisation too rigid, and also too cumbersome for the dissemination of orders. In October 1942 it was replaced by seven A.A. groups working in co-ordination with the R.A.F. groups. Establishments were graded according to the operational commitments in each group area. The new organisation was extremely flexible as the grade of any group could be changed to meet current needs; or group boundaries could be altered to allow the insertion of another group in the area.

[19] A.L. 146 (K.P.I.D. tables) Chemical instead of oil smoke screens were developed early in 1943, and new methods of rapid multiple ignition. Smoke screens were also used to protect 19 of the main reservoirs in the country in view of possible retaliation after the successful British air attacks on German reservoir and canal dams in May 1943 (H.F. Bundle 31/1,4))

Chapter 24

# Defence Against the Flying and Rocket Bombs

**Report of Secret German Weapons Confirmed**
Information concerning a German experimental station at Peenemünde on the Baltic coast confirmed reports in April 1943 of the existence of a long range rocket-assisted projectile. Further information indicated that experiments were also being made with pilotless aircraft; and photographs from reconnaissance aircraft disclosed over 90 probable launching sites under construction in coastal areas in Northern France. The supposed launching sites were heavily bombed by the R.A.F. and by the United States Eighth Air Force during the following winter 1943/44.

**The Defence Plan**
A plan to counter the threat of these secret weapons was approved by the Chiefs of Staff in January 1944. The scale of attack was estimated at 200 missiles an hour, and the probable targets as London, the Solent and Bristol.

London was to be protected by a belt of 528 heavy and 804 light A.A. guns sited on a line south of Redhill–Maidstone–Thames estuary. In front of the gun-belt was to be the fighter zone in which the aircraft were to maintain a 24-hour watch up to the French coast. A searchlight belt of 19 batteries (456 lights), in front of the range limit of the gun-belt, was to co-operate with the fighters by illuminating the flying bombs at night. Behind the gun-belt was to be a barrage of 480 cable-carrying balloons as a final check. The reason for placing London's defence deployment well inland was to reduce enemy jamming of the radar equipment, and also to allow the fighters the maximum area for manoeuvre.

To protect the Solent area the Isle of Wight air defences were to be re-adjusted; and for Bristol a similar lay-out to that of London was planned on a smaller scale, with the gun-belt to the north of Shaftesbury.

## Description of the Flying (V.1) Bomb
The flying bomb was a jet-propelled expendable aircraft with an explosive warhead equivalent to a 1-ton high blast bomb. The overall length of the aircraft was 21½ feet, and the wing span 17½ feet. Control in flight was effected by an automatic pilot monitored by a magnetic compass housed in the nose of the aircraft; and the bomb was put into a dive by the action of tail detonation. The speed of flight varied from 230 to 400 miles an hour, and the range was about 160 miles normally at a height of 2,000 to 3,000 feet.

The total stock of flying bombs in June 1944 was put at 8,000 to 14,000, with production at 1,000 to 1,500 a month. Of the 90 launching sites 72 were employed, and it was seen that many of the sites damaged by bombing could be quickly repaired. Priority was therefore given to bombing the supply communications and storage depots as being the most likely method of reducing the scale of attack.

## Deployment of the Defence
The first flying bombs arrived over London in the early hours of the 13th June, and the sustained attack started on the 15th. On that day, the 15th, the defence plan was put into effect (Operation Crossbow). Within a week (22nd June) 8 squadrons of high performance fighter aircraft were deployed, to operate in the fighter zone.

The Expeditionary Force (Operation Overlord) had landed successfully in France on the 6th June, and the quantity of A.A. guns required to cover its supply ports and communications against air attack stretched to the limit the reserves of A.A. Command.

The necessary guns for Operation Crossbow had to be found by removing or stripping to a minimum the gun defended areas in the North-east, North and West of the country. By the same date (22nd June) 192 heavy and 192 light A.A. guns were deployed in the pre-arranged gun-belt; 11 searchlight batteries (264 lights) were in the searchlight belt; and 480 cable-carrying balloons in the balloon belt, with another 1,000 in prospect.

## First Results Unsatisfactory
The attacks were concentrated upon London; and it was expected that the anti-aircraft defence would obtain good results, the missile flying on a steady course and with no evasive action. During the first three weeks, however, about two-thirds of the flying bombs that reached the coast passed through the defence lay-out unscathed; and it became apparent that neither fighters nor guns were being given full scope. With the great speed of the bombs the fighters often had to break off

the pursuit owing to the difficulty of distinguishing the boundary of the gun-belt. The guns, too, had to be sure that the break on the radar tube was not a friendly fighter before opening fire.

The successes by the guns, amounting to less than 10 per cent., were particularly disappointing. The heavy guns were mostly the mobile 3.7-inch gun which had become the standard gun; and the conversion of the 4.5-inch by adding a special 3.7-inch barrel had begun in October, 1943. The rate of fire of the gun had been increased by the invention of an automatic fuze setter during 1942 by up to 250 per cent.; and the proximity fuze enabled the explosion of the shell to be controlled automatically by the proximity to the target.

The main difficulty however was that the traverse of the mobile gun could not deal with the low flight of the flying bomb requiring a higher rate of traverse than the mobile gun could manage, and only the static gun could cope with it. The 2,000 to 3,000 feet level was in fact too low for the mobile heavy guns and too high for the light guns to be effective. The answer was either to emplace the mobile guns or to replace them by static guns; and before the answer could be fully applied a new defence lay-out had been arranged.

**Alteration in the Defence Layout**
At a meeting at Fighter Command headquarters on the 13th July it was decided to move the gun-belt to the coast. The fighter pilots would be able to identify the position of the gun-belt by the coast-line; radar sets would be free of inland interference, and enemy jamming methods were not apparently being used; flying bombs brought down by the guns would probably fall into the sea instead of on land.

The move to the new gun-belt, between Cuckmere Haven (west of Eastbourne) and St. Margaret's Bay (east of Dover) began on the 14th July, and was completed in four days. The mobile heavy batteries were largely replaced by static mixed batteries for which platforms had to be extemporised out of steel rails, sleepers and ballast.

The move involved the transport of 23,000 men and women, and 30,000 tons of ammunition, also the laying of 3,000 miles of inter-battery cable. The accuracy of the fire of the guns was increased by the arrival from America at this time of the new radar (S.C.R.584) set designed to work successfully at high angles of sight; and it was operated with the auto-follow system by which the sets were kept on the target, once located, by an automatic electric control. Results rose from 17 per cent. in the first week to 55 per cent. in the fourth week.

The new defence lay-out on the 20th July, is shown on Map 5. The forward fighter zone extended over the Channel beyond the boundary of the gun-belt, marked by boats and buoys, 10,000 yards from the English coast. Thirteen day and seven night fighter squadrons were operating, and more night fighters were available if required. Patrols were extended to include the approach to the Thames estuary; and 25 aircraft were on patrol at any one time. The heavy and light A.A. guns were deployed to a depth of 3,000 yards along the coast; and additions, including 20 American A.A. batteries of 90mm guns, brought the total by the 10th August to 703 heavy and 2,002 light (1,312 40mm and 790 20mm) A.A. guns.

The balloon barrage, approximately in its original position, about the line of the North Downs, was rapidly expanded until by the 10th August a concentration of 2,003 balloons, the largest yet assembled, had been deployed. In the wide area between the balloon barrage and the coast was the inland fighter zone within which the fighters operated under a running commentary control.

The search-light belt, also remaining about its original position, was to co-operate with the inland fighter zone at night to illuminate the flying bombs for easier destruction (search-lights assisted fighters to destroy 142 or about 30 per cent. of the bombs entering the inland zone at night). An additional deployment of A.A. guns was made in the Thames estuary area to meet flying bombs approaching from the east.

By the 19th August the eastward advance of the British Expeditionary Force along the French coast enabled the westward end of the defence system to be closed, and the eastern end was extended to Sandwich. The re-adjusted lay-out continued to show improved results until the 5th September by which time the armies in France and Belgium had captured the remainder of the launching sites.

## Results and Casualties

From the 15th June, when the sustained attacks by flying bombs began, until the 4th September, when the last launching sites were overrun, 8,081 flying bombs were plotted by radar as having been launched. Of the bombs that arrived 3,765 were destroyed by the combined defences and 2,325 caused incidents and damage. Of the number destroyed 1,903 were shot down by fighter aircraft, 1,585 by A.A. guns and 276 were brought down by the balloon-cable barrage.

The total casualties caused in this country by flying bombs were 5,812 killed, 17,080 seriously wounded and 22,847 slightly wounded. Property damage in the greater London area during the first three months from the start of the attack included 24,000 houses destroyed beyond repair and over a million damaged, apart from public buildings; churches, factories, etc.

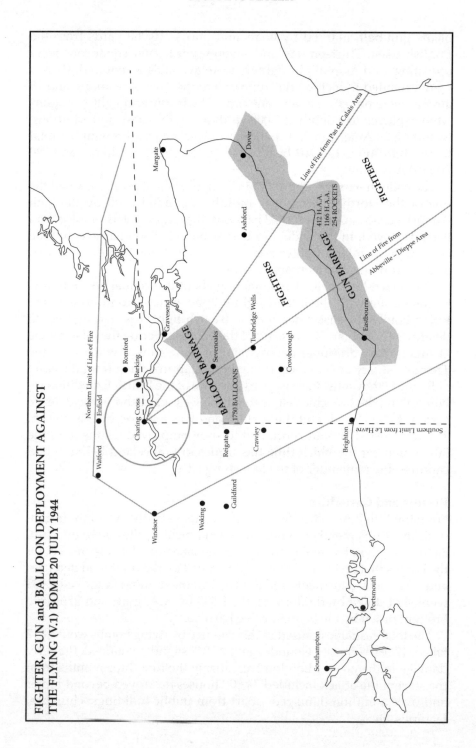

FIGHTER, GUN and BALLOON DEPLOYMENT AGAINST
THE FLYING (V.1) BOMB 20 JULY 1944

## Launchings from Piloted Aircraft

The Germans continued to send over flying bombs by launching them from piloted aircraft, and from sites near The Hague and Rotterdam. The extension of their range to 200 miles was made possible by introducing wooden wings and a lighter warhead.

Spasmodic attacks of this kind continued till the 15th January, 1945; and to meet them a new gun-belt was deployed from Whitstable to Great Yarmouth, including the Maunsell sea-forts in the Thames Estuary.

Of the total of 1,012 bombs plotted in this last phase of the flying-bomb offensive only 495 came within range of the guns, many being inaccurately aimed or passing to the flanks of the new belt, and 66 reached London.

## The Long Range Rocket (V.2) Bomb

On the 8th September, 1944, three days after the flying-bomb launching sites had been captured, another and more fantastic kind of bomb fell in the London area. This new missile had a cylindrical body, 45 feet long, with a tapering point that gave it the appearance of an enormous explosive shell. It weighed 13½ tons, including a warhead of 1,900 to 2,000 lbs.

It was propelled at first by a jet of gas resulting from the combination of liquid oxygen and ethyl alcohol; and the trajectory took the form of a parabola with the maximum height at about 50 miles, and a landing angle of 45°. Control was either by radio equipment or by an integrating accelerometer which obviated the use of radio by means of an activator gyroscope control. The range was estimated at about 200 miles, and the maximum speed at over 3,000 miles an hour, with a landing speed of 1,800 miles an hour. Those estimated figures gave the measure of this alarming threat.

The launching sites were on Walcheren and in The Hague district of Holland, and also farther north in Friesland and east of the Zuider Zee. The targets were principally London and Norwich. In all 531 of the bombs fell on land in this country; the most serious incident being at Deptford on the 23rd November when 160 people were killed and 108 injured by a single explosion. The worst incident from a single rocket bomb occurred at Antwerp in Belgium, where, in November 1944, a direct hit on a crowded cinema killed 500 persons; and at least 300 were injured.

The total killed by the V.2 rocket-bombs in this country was 2,754 (2.4 per rocket fired), 6,522 severely injured, and 15,438 slightly injured.

In spite of the immense speed of the rocket the five or six minutes of its flight enabled calculations to be made by radar equipment as to its position and where it would land. On the 23rd December, 1944 the G.O.C. Anti-Aircraft Command proposed that A.A. guns of the London defences should try to explode the rocket in the air before it crashed. Radar sets on the coast north and south of the normal line of flight, and another set forward in Holland could track the trajectory, and the accuracy of the plotting showed a steady improvement.

By mid-March the radar sets could predict the landing within an area of 2,500 yards square. He proposed to fire 1,200 rounds at each missile, and on the 28th March ordered the guns to be ready to fire; but the last launching site had been overrun, and the last V.2 rocket fired on the previous day, the 27th. On the 30th March the Chiefs of Staff refused permission to fire at rockets.

The idea originated in the belief that the rocket system of propulsion was superior to that of artillery, and the specification for the first experiments in 1930 was for a rocket-propelled missile, carrying one ton of explosive, which would have a range greater than the 70 miles of the "Paris gun" of the 1914/18 War. No clearly defined objective appears to have been in view, such as the bombardment of England or of any other country. Both missiles were developed concurrently; and, owing to their inaccuracy, they were regarded as of no practical value until the spring of 1943 when greater accuracy was obtained. The German Command then decided to use the two inventions as a means of retaliation against England for the destruction of German cities. The account describes the many setbacks which delayed the launchings until the last available weeks.

**The Threat in the Future**
The G.O.C. Anti-Aircraft Command has explained in his despatch that he was convinced the V.2 rocket bomb was the beginning of one of the great defence problems of the future. The solution, he thought, was no more than a further development of the existing methods for "unseen" shooting. Although the science of anti-aircraft gunnery had made prodigious progress during the war he believed that we were still only touching the fringe of future possibilities, and that scientific theory could only advance on the basis of operational shooting. His experiment was to be a means to that end.

The Chiefs of Staff, on the other hand, refused permission to fire for the reason that the scientific background for success was not sufficient to justify the danger to the civil population beneath the barrage. With a hundred to one chance of a hit, permission might have been granted.

A special scientific committee on the subject calculated that about 12,000 rounds would have to be fired to have a chance of hitting one rocket, and the Chiefs of Staff considered the experiment not worth the effort nor the possible adverse effect on civilian morale. In other words, despite the many ingenious inventions available after five years concentration upon defensive weapons of war the country stood defenceless against this new threat. The only remedy was to capture the launching sites, and fortunately the Expeditionary Force advancing northwards through Holland was in a position to do so.

Less than five months later, on the 5th August, 1945, the German V.2 rocket bomb was put into the shade by the atom bomb dropped on Hiroshima by an American aircraft. The single bomb explosion caused 135,000 casualties from blast, burns and injuries, and from the radio-active rays emitted. Nearly half the casualties were deaths; and total destruction resulted over a circle about two miles in diameter below the burst.

That knock-out blow on Japan did more than put out-of-date the war-machine of 1939-45. It carried a great stride further the idea that an aggressor can bring into subjection a neighbouring State by direct action against the civilian population. A single atom bomb would probably have sufficed to deliver the knock-out blow on London in September 1940 which two fleets of German bombers with high explosive and incendiary bombs failed to achieve in two months of sustained air attacks.

Equally, an aggressor can be made to understand that the first use of methods of mass destruction for aggressive purposes would be the signal for the rapid annihilation of his own country. The atom bomb and its subsidiary developments supply that "most terrifying deterrent to aggression" for which the British Cabinet searched in vain in 1934-1939. The United Nations Organization, too, has been given the machinery, which the League of Nations lacked, to implement by force the various international pacts and treaties to outlaw war.

In March 1938 Mr. Neville Chamberlain, as Prime Minister, when deploring the failure of the League of Nations to prevent German aggression into Austria, told the House of Commons of his faith in the future. "The ideals of the League are grand and magnificent, and I will never believe that they are not ultimately attainable." The United Nations organization is a renewed effort to that end.

# Appendices

## List of Appendices

Appendix I

# Air Staff Appreciation of the Possible Scale of Air Attack on Great Britain April 1939

**Germany's Object**

1. Germany's economic difficulties indicate that she could not face with confidence the prospect of a long war. Germany might, however, readily contemplate war against this country if she thought that by the ruthless exercise of air power – combined possibly with naval attack on our seaborne trade – she could obtain an early decision. Moreover, if she could succeed in defeating us there would be no doubt of her ability subsequently to crush France. Further, our defensive preparations must be designed to deal with the worst case. In this paper, therefore, it is assumed that as much as possible of the German air striking force would be directed ruthlessly against us in an attempt to achieve a knock-out blow.

## EXAMINATION OF MAIN FACTORS

**Comparison of Forces**

2. In April, 1939, Germany will have 1,650 first-line long range bombers capable of attacking the United Kingdom from bases in Germany, as compared with 812 British first-line bombers. During the remainder of 1939 and throughout 1940 both forces will increase but the relative numerical proportions will remain approximately the same, although the present disparity in total bomb-lift will be greatly lessened by the increase of heavy bombers in our own force at the expense of medium bombers. In spite of the fact, however, that Germany has, in addition to the bombers mentioned above, a force of short-range bombers which could be used against her neighbours on the Continent, it is extremely unlikely that, even if she decided to concentrate her main air effort against the United Kingdom, she could avoid employing some of her

131

long range bombers against France. Moreover, even in an attempt to knock out Great Britain, Germany would probably be reluctant to use up her air resources – particularly her long range striking force – to an extent which would leave her virtually powerless in face of a subsequent attack by Russia. The assumption is therefore made that not more than four fifths of the effort of her long range bombers would be directed against this country, and if this assumption is correct the relative first-line strengths of the opposing striking forces in April, 1939 would be:

| | |
|---|---|
| Great Britain | 812 |
| Germany | 1,320 |

It should be noted that the French air striking force is omitted from the comparison on the assumption that the French effort in the air would be offset by that of Italy.

3. As regards reserves, it is estimated that German's air striking force will be backed by approximately 100% reserve aircraft in April, 1939, and by a similar amount in April, 1940. Our own reserve aircraft will be approximately 35% of our first-line strength in April, 1939, and 100% in April, 1940. In the matter of reserve flying crews, Germany is considerably superior.

4. It is impossible to compare preparedness in fighter defences by comparing first-line strengths, since the situations facing the two countries differ widely, but general indications are that Germany is not less prepared in this respect than we are.

5. In active ground defences against air attack, and in passive defence measures, Germany's preparations are superior to our own in relation to our respective needs and may remain so during 1940, although our own preparations will by that time show a greatly improved position.

6. In general, therefore, Germany is considerably superior to us in bomber strength and is generally better prepared in defensive measures. In addition, in the early stages of war, she would have a larger productive potential.

**Relative Vulnerability of Great Britain and Germany**
7. The relative vulnerability of the two countries to air attack must be considered in relation to their air strength. Although, if we possessed a striking force equal to that of Germany, it might well be that a determined air offensive against Germany's vulnerable points, such as

the Ruhr, would eventually force Germany on to the defensive and so relieve the scale of attack on this country, or at any rate on our thickly populated centres of industry, the possibility is more remote so long as we are inferior to the extent shown in the previous paragraph. It must also be remembered that Germany, with twice the geographical area of Great Britain, has correspondingly greater opportunities of dispersion, and that a considerable proportion of the aircraft industry in Germany is at very long range for effective air attack, whereas our own aircraft industry is within easier reach of German bombers. Successful attack on our aircraft industry would (in view of the paucity of our reserves) be rapid in its effect on our air strength.

8. Both countries have extremely important areas, namely the Ruhr and London, in the regions where their frontiers are nearest to each other. The Ruhr is of outstanding importance to Germany since it contains practically the whole of the basic heavy industries; but successful attack on that area would not have an immediate effect on Germany's war effort, including her effort in the air (on which she would be mainly relying in her attempt to knock out Great Britain) whereas attack on the heaviest scale against the Greater London area might, if our passive defence measures (including alternative port and distribution facilities) were inadequate, create an immediate and most serious problem for this country.

9. It is thus doubtful, in view of our present inferiority in air strength, whether a counter-offensive, although directed against objectives ultimately vital to Germany's war effort, would cause any great reduction in the scale of German air attack on this country during the early weeks of a war.

**Range and Scale of attack**
10. No part of Great Britain is beyond the reach of long range bombers based in Germany but the intensity of attack would diminish to the westward because of the greater penetration through our defences and the increased fuel needed for the longer ranges. Aircraft attacking Northern Ireland would be operating near their extreme operational range and would carry a considerably reduced bomb load.

11. In the absence of experience of the conditions which would obtain in an air war between two first-class Powers, it is difficult to assess with any expectation of being correct the scale of attack which a bomber force could maintain in the face of modern defences. Our present estimates

may therefore be proved excessive in the event, or possibly the reverse. It is, however, thought that, if Germany employed four-fifths of her long range striking force exclusively against us, the average daily scale of attack on the United Kingdom, in April, 1939 might be some 650 aircraft (700* tons of bombs) during the first week or fortnight at maximum effort, the comparable figures for April, 1940 being 800 aircraft a day (representing 950* tons of bombs).

(*NOTE: The range on which these figures are calculated is that of a mid-point in England (Derby); the possible weight of attack would be greater (because of the shorter range) against objectives further East, and less against objectives further West. It is important also to note that they represent an average daily weight of attack, taking into account such factors as defence, casualties, range, aircraft wastage and serviceability, and also the factor of human endurance of bomber crews. Only a part of the total force directed against this country is assumed to attack each day, and the figures given above for bomb tonnage do not therefore represent the bomb- lift of the whole force. It will also be apparent that, as the figures are averages achieved by part of the total force, they might be considerably exceeded on any one day.)

After this first period at maximum effort, casualties, fatigue, aircraft wastage and possibly supply difficulties would cause a pronounced reduction – possibly 50% – in the average daily scale of attack for a period of several weeks, though periods of attack at maximum intensity might recur from time to time. As was stated in H.D.C. 33-M and endorsed by the Chiefs of Staff in C.O.S. 621: "The weight of attack as a whole which must be anticipated is so great that, even if unlimited money and resources were available, it would be impossible to prevent heavy  casualties and destruction of property; all that can be done is to take whatever steps financial and other considerations may permit, on the one hand to inflict as much damage as possible on the attackers, and on the other hand to minimise the effects of air attack upon the morale of the people and the working of essential services."

## POSSIBLE GERMAN COURSES OF ACTION

12. Germany might employ her striking force initially against our air stations and also possibly our aircraft industry with the preliminary object of crippling our air effort. This is a course which we are preparing to meet and, as our plans mature, such a course would be difficult to achieve in a short time; preparations will not, however, be in an advanced stage during 1939. On the whole, in view of her superior strength in the air and our greater vulnerability to a quick knock-out blow, Germany would

probably be more likely to employ her striking force in the main against objectives other than our air forces from the outset.

13. The other courses open to Germany are:

(a) To deliver unrestricted and sustained attacks on the civil population in the large towns of Great Britain with the object of demoralizing the people and forcing the Government to discontinue the war.

(b) To employ her air forces (in collaboration with her naval forces) in unrestricted attack on our seaborne supplies and against the internal distribution system so as to create a serious shortage of food and raw materials.

(c) To attack our armament factories and other selected objectives so as to reduce our industrial capacity and cripple our war effort.

## Attack Aimed at Demoralization of the Civil Population

14. Air attack might take the form of an attempt to demoralise the will of the people, upon which, more particularly in a democracy, depends the ability of a Government to wage war. In this event the attack would be "unrestricted" in the widest sense of the word. No attempt would be made to confine the damage to any specific area in which objectives of even a semi-military nature, such as centres of government, armament industries, etc., were concentrated. All the crowded centres of population might well be attacked in turn in the hope that widespread damage could be caused to essential services, such as power, water, light, sewerage and transport, in addition to actual casualties. An attempt would also probably be made to exploit the effect of gas and incendiary bombs.

15. The deciding factor in determining whether or not to undertake unrestricted air action of this type might well be that which operated in the early days of submarine warfare, namely, that of time. Information regarding German theories of warfare indicates that it would be quite unsafe to assume that the initial German attack would necessarily be restricted by considerations of humanity; it is far more likely to be dictated mainly by expediency. If they were convinced that widespread air attack would give them a quick decision before our war organisation could get into its stride and before the effects of antagonising neutral opinion (an inevitable outcome of such action) could make themselves felt, then they might undertake it with the utmost ruthlessness and indifference to human suffering.

16. On the other hand, Germany might reflect that this form of action might serve to stiffen the national will to resist, and cause neutral opinion to react unfavourably. Past history gives Germany small grounds for expecting that the people of this country could easily be demoralised into submission, but there is an influential school of thought among the extremist leaders of the Nazi party who at least pretend to believe that the British are decadent. There have, moreover, been recent indications that the views of the German Air Staff are tending to turn in the direction of direct attack on the civil population, and action on these lines is clearly possible and might cause heavy casualties and damage to property, having regard to the weight of attack which the Germans could bring to bear, and the incomplete state of our defences. There can be no doubt that one of the most important factors in deciding them against such a course would be to convince them that the country as a whole is really adequately prepared and organised to meet it and reply to it effectively.

**Attack on our Seaborne Supplies and Distribution System**
17. Great Britain's dependence upon imported food is so well known, and the serious straits to which we were brought by the German submarine campaign in 1917 have been so clearly established, that Germany, by selecting this course, might consider that she had a calculable basis on which to assess her chances of success. It would be a further advantage that Germany's naval forces could co-operate by attacking shipping at sea; and she might satisfy herself, and even persuade certain neutrals, that her attacks were legitimate, since it was partly as a result of measures of economic pressure, notably in regard to food-stuffs and raw materials, that Great Britain forced Germany to submit in 1918.

18. In order to achieve quick success Germany would not only have to destroy existing reserve stocks of food-stuffs, but also prevent the unloading and distribution of supplies reaching this country daily from overseas. German initial attacks would, therefore, probably be directed simultaneously upon our dock areas, which might result in damage to ships in harbour, warehouses, port machinery and clearance facilities, upon key points in our distribution system for important areas, and upon shipping in the narrow seas. In addition, our stocks of oil fuel at the main ports would constitute attractive and vulnerable targets, and the densely populated areas surrounding selected targets would be liable to sustain serious damage either intentionally or as the result of inaccuracy in bombing.

19. Of the objectives which might be attacked if this course of action were adopted, the Port of London, at least in the initial stages of the war, could be regarded as likely to attract most of the enemy's attention, and the points subjected to attack might well include also the power stations, distributing centres and those railways by which an alternative channel of supply in and out of London could be organised.

20. Such action must inevitably result in a considerable loss of civil life and be attended by many of the features to be expected in an attack aiming directly at demoralisation of the civil population. Germany would be well aware of this and the disorganisation of labour in the docks, railways and market areas would contribute appreciably to the general effect of any material damage which might be inflicted. Should, however, the enemy casualties resulting from such action in the face of our strongest defences become excessive, the attack would probably be switched to an increasing extent to our shipping in the estuaries, focal areas and narrow seas, through which it must pass in order to reach port. The attack would probably also tend to become more indiscriminate.

21. Air action on these lines against our seaborne supplies would inevitably affect not only our food, but also the imports of raw materials which are essential to the maintenance of our economic strength and war industry. It must also be expected that such air action would be supplemented to the fullest possible extent by naval attack upon our trade at sea. In these circumstances we should certainly be forced to divert merchant shipping to ports in the west of England, and this would immediately throw a further strain upon a distribution system already subject to air attack.

**Attack on Our War Industrial Organisation**
22. The Allies' war effort would depend largely upon their industrial capacity, and it is clear that French resources would be inadequate for their own requirements. Any considerable reduction in British capacity might therefore have serious results. In particular, by April, 1939 we should have very few reserves of aircraft, and almost from the outset we should have to depend to a large extent upon factory output to maintain our first-line strength.

23. Germany is probably aware of this and would be almost certain to make at least some attempt at the disorganisation of the aircraft industry, whose detailed location would be well known and which,

unlike actual air forces, could not be dispersed or redisposed as a precaution on the outbreak of war. While, however, we could draw on extensive outside sources to replace our own loss of industrial capacity, Germany would be far more limited.

24. Even if Germany did not select this course of action, she would almost certainly submit our industry at least to sporadic attack and the operation of the warning system would in any event cause serious loss of output.

## GERMANY'S PROBABLE SELECTED COURSE

25. The dislocation of our war industry would not produce the most rapid results, and assuming that Germany would be seeking the quickest possible decision it seems unlikely that she would concentrate her attack initially against our industry. It is more probable that Germany would consider that she could defeat us most quickly either by direct attacks on the morale of the civil population or by attacks on our seaborne supplies and distribution system. While it is impossible to say with any degree of certainty which of these two courses Germany would be likely to adopt, it is at least clear that if the latter course were selected (attacks aimed at our food and raw materials) Germany would feel able to base estimates of the probable results of her bombing upon calculable data, whereas the degree of success in ruthless attacks on large centres of population and the time within which such a course could be decisive would be more difficult to predict. On the whole, it seems that Germany's most probable course of action might be to concentrate her air offensive (in conjunction with her naval forces) in unrestricted attack upon our supply and distribution system, including our shipping on the high seas, in narrow waters and in port.

It is, however, possible that, whilst retaining this as her main course, Germany might simultaneously employ a proportion of her air forces in attacks on industrial centres – particularly the aircraft industry – primarily as a means of complicating our defence and internal security problem, and incidentally as a contribution to ultimate success in the war should the knock-out blow fail.

26. So long as Germany was expecting success in her attempt to secure a quick decision, she would be unlikely to concentrate upon sustained attack against our naval forces and establishments. If, however, Germany saw that her attempt to gain a quick decision was failing, she

138

might divert her air effort to deliberate attacks on our war industry as a whole to prevent us from developing our potential for a long war, and might also deliver surprise attacks at great intensity upon our naval forces, including their bases and oil supplies.

A further objective, which might for a time receive the heaviest scale of attack if Germany believed the despatch of the Field Force to be imminent, might be the mobilization centres, communications and ports of embarkation of the Army. If, as might well be possible, Germany were able to replace without delay the casualties and wastage sustained during the opening phase, our naval forces might be attacked by 450 to 500 bombers, dropping about 600 tons of bombs on each series of attacks, and on other occasions a similar weight of attack might be delivered on Army establishments and communications.

## POSSIBLE DISTRIBUTION OF ATTACK

27. It is apparent that, since it is impossible to predict with any confidence which of the courses discussed above would be selected by Germany and also since, whatever course were selected, other attacks not in pursuance of that course, might well be carried out in strength on occasion as diversions, our defensive preparations must be designed to counter all the courses mentioned. It must also be remembered that, in addition to the part which our defences would play in direct interference with the procedure of bomb aiming, further inaccuracy in aim would result if the defences forced the attackers to fly high or to attack more by night. Moreover, effective defences would result in dispersion of the weight of attack over wide areas, not only because of inaccuracies of aim but also because bombers when heavily engaged might drop their bombs without relation to any given objective. Bombing would thus tend to become indiscriminate in effect if not in intention.

28. With these considerations in mind, an attempt has been made in Appendix "A" to indicate the possible distribution of attack by grading the various towns and areas in the United Kingdom according to the likelihood and possible scale of attack. It will, however, be appreciated that such a forecast is based on reasoning rather than on information of German intentions, and that in the absence of practical experience the forecast must be largely conjectural.

29. Whatever objectives were selected, the method of distributing the bombardment might be either:

(a) A sustained attack on objectives in numerous areas, the weight being roughly proportional to their importance; or
(b) the concentration of a heavy scale of attack on a limited number of objectives, followed by a lighter scale to hamper reorganization – the main weight being shifted elsewhere.

The second method of attack would present the more difficult problem in passive defence, in view of the heavy scale of attack for which each place would have to be prepared if complete disorganization were to be avoided, and this, of course, would make such a course more likely to be adopted. In drawing up Appendix "A" therefore, the possible scales of attack on the various areas have been estimated on the assumption that the second method of attack mentioned above would be the one selected.

*Air Staff*
*3rd April, 1939*

*Annex "A" OF Appendix I*

POSSIBLE DISTRIBUTION OF GERMAN AIR ATTACK

1. Taking into account possible German courses of action, together with operational and other relevant factors, an assessment is made below of the likelihood of attack in various areas as a guide in the preparation of passive defence measures. The average daily weight of air attack on the United Kingdom, during the first week or fortnight, might be some 650 aircraft (700 tons of bombs) in April, 1939, the comparable figures for April, 1940, being 800 aircraft a day (representing 950 tons of bombs).

After this first intensive period, various factors would cause a considerable reduction (possibly 50%) in the scale of attack. It will be appreciated that the estimates given below of the possible scales of attack against various areas are based on reasoning rather than on information of German intentions and that they might well be falsified in the event.

**Grade I – London and Thames Area**
2. The outstanding objective in the United Kingdom is that part of the London area, together with certain places along the Thames to the eastward, which surround or contain the majority of London's vital points. This may be defined as:

The County of London, with the addition of:

| | |
|---|---|
| Gravesend | East Ham |
| Tilbury | West Ham |
| Dartford | Leyton |
| Purfleet | Hendon |
| Bexley | Harrow |
| Crayford | Wembley |
| Erith | Willesden |
| Rainham | Acton |
| South Hornchurch | Ealing |
| Dagenham | Brentford |
| Ilford | Chiswick |
| Wanstead | Barnes |
| Barking | Richmond |

3. Objectives in this area might well include the Docks, the City, factories, railway termini and depots, Government offices, power stations, waterworks, oil storage, and important points in the G.P.O. telephone and telegraph system. It is possible that an enemy would feel justified in concentrating temporarily the whole weight of his attack on this area, only small diversionary attacks being made elsewhere during this period in order to embarrass the defences.

## Grade II
4. A list of the towns and areas included in this category is given below. It is unlikely that the whole weight of attack would be concentrated on any one objective in Grade II, and it is felt that the greatest weight which they would be likely to receive, taking into consideration their importance and geographical situation, might be of the order shewn below, expressed as percentages of the total weight of attack on any one day. It should be noted that attacks on the scales envisaged below could be expected to be less frequent on objectives in the West than on those in the Eastern part of the country. It will also be appreciated that the very heavy scale of attack estimated in paragraph 3 above for that part of London included in Grade I would at times spread into other parts of the London area, and that the weight of attack on that part of London shewn below as Grade II would naturally be heaviest in districts immediately adjoining the Grade I area.

London Metropolitan Police Area
outside the limits of Grade I                                    50%
Birmingham–Wolverhampton area including Erdington,

| | |
|---|---:|
| Sutton Coldfield, etc. | 50% |
| Manchester district, including Stockport, Oldham, Bolton, Sheffield, etc. | 50% |
| Liverpool district, including Bootle, Wallasey, Birkenhead, Runcorn and Widness | 50% |
| Coventry | 50% |
| Leeds–Bradford area, including Halifax, Huddersfield, Dewsbury, etc | 33% |
| Sheffield–Rotherham area | 33% |
| Newcastle–Tyneside area, including Sunderland | 33% |
| Middlesbrough and Teeside, including Billingham | 33% |
| Hull area, including Grimsby | 33% |
| Southampton and Portsmouth | 33% |
| Glasgow area | 33% |
| Bristol area, including Avonmouth and Filton | 33% |
| Nottingham and Derby | 25% |
| Chatham–Gillingham area | 25% |
| Crewe | 25% |
| Edinburgh and Rosyth | 20% |
| Stoke-on-Trent | 20% |
| Leicester | 20% |
| Sheerness | 15% |
| Swansea, Barry, Cardiff, and Newport | 15% |
| Belfast | 10% |
| Weymouth | 10% |
| Plymouth | 10% |

**Grade III**

5. Grade III includes towns and urban districts with a population of more than 30/40,000 in which are situated important industries, e.g. Lincoln, Ipswich. Districts in this category would be much less liable to attack than those in Grade II, but the possibility of heavy though not sustained attack must be assumed to exist. Places in Grade III should be prepared to receive up to about 10% of the total weight of attack on any one day.

**Grade IV**

6. This grade includes towns and urban districts which, though of considerable size, are chiefly of a residential character, such as Winchester, Exeter, Cheltenham, Leamington. Districts in this category would be unlikely to be heavily attacked since, if Germany were relying on creating terror and havoc amongst the civil population, she would be more likely to select populous areas in industrial districts and at the

port where success would have an added value. It must, however, be remembered that, in addition to targets which were bombed according to plan, other places would be liable to be bombed by reason of their being mistaken for the intended target or because the attackers, being heavily engaged by the defences, or having been unable to reach their intended objective, might release their bombs without regard to the objective which they had been ordered to attack. Any large town of say, 40,000 or more inhabitants in the eastern half of the country might be so attacked on a number of occasions, but the risk of such fortuitous bombing would be considerably less in the West. Attacks of this kind might be made by a whole wing of 27 aircraft dropping up to as much as 40 tons of bombs, or more.

## Grade V
7. Included in this category are towns of less than about 20,000 inhabitants which do not include any points of outstanding military or war industrial importance. They would not be likely to be attacked deliberately but it is always possible that enemy bombers, unaware of their position at night or in bad visibility, or unwilling to penetrate to their allotted objectives, might drop their bombs anywhere. The attack of places in Grade V would thus be "accidental" and mostly non-recurring. The bomb load of a sub-formation of 9 aircraft (an average of 13 tons) might be dropped on such places in the eastern half of the country but the attack of places in Grade V which lie to the West would be unlikely, though the possibility cannot be ignored.

## Vital Points (Other Than Those in Grades I and II Areas
8. The indications given in paragraphs 4 and 5 above of Grades I and II areas, and also the assessments of the possible weight of attack, take into account the vital points which those areas contain. There are in addition, however, a number of vital points in other parts of the country; some are in Grade III areas, some in comparatively small towns and others in isolated positions away from any centre of population. It would be impossible to compile a list of such points so complete as to exclude other places liable to deliberate attack and, further, any attempt to produce such a list would be highly dangerous in view of the risk of compromising secrecy. It should however be accepted that deliberate attacks would be made from time to time, particularly in the eastern half of the country, on such objectives as important military, naval and air force establishments (including operational aerodromes) and also on factories, oil storage, power stations, etc. of considerable importance in war. It is suggested therefore, that the immediate vicinity of such

potential objectives would not be suitable as reception areas for civilian personnel.

*Air Staff*
*3rd April, 1939*

*Annex "B" OF Appendix I*

## TACTICAL CONSIDERATIONS

**Scale of attack**
1. The German bomber unit ("gruppe") comprises 3 squadrons of 9 aircraft each, plus a "leader-flight" of 3 aircraft, i.e. 30 aircraft in all, and it is likely that, whilst the whole unit of 30 aircraft might be directed against one target, (Note: A "target" means one definite point of aim. Thus, for example, in one particular attack on the Port of London the target might be the King George V Dock impounding station.) squadrons (of 9 aircraft each) would attack the target separately, possibly in quick succession and from different directions. The average weight of bombs which would be dropped by one unit of 30 aircraft may be taken as 30/40 tons and it would be unwise to assume that this would consist of less than 150 bombs.

After several such "gruppe" attacks on any one target (at intervals possibly of 20 minutes or so) it might be that attacks on that particular target would cease until the damage done could be assessed; no reliance, however, could be placed on this, particularly if severe damage to the target selected were regarded as of the highest importance. It should be noted also that, whilst the "gruppe" of 30 bombers is probably the largest number of aircraft which would carry out one attack on any one target, attacks in similar strength might well be carried out simultaneously against other targets in the same area. A big industrial area or a large centre of population could be attacked in this way by several hundred bombers within a few hours.

**Day or Night Attack**
2. It is likely that, at least at the outset, the greatest weight of attack would occur by day, though – since bombers may be expected to operate singly or in small formations of about 3 aircraft by night as compared with formations of 9 aircraft or possible "gruppe" attacks of 30 aircraft by day – the number of raids, even in this initial stage, might not be less by night than by day. It must also be remembered that

although, since good visibility is necessary for accurate bomb aiming, daylight attacks would be chiefly relied on to cause material damage at selected points, the fact that considerable moral effect would result from bombing attacks in darkness and also that such attacks would considerably hamper the work of re-organisation and repair makes it probable that night bombing would be widely used. Further, if enemy bombers suffered heavy casualties when operating by day, an increasing proportion of their attacks would probably be carried out by night.

**Height of Attacks**
3. The height at which attacks might be expected to take place cannot be forecast with any confidence since it would depend on such varying factors as the efficiency of the local defences, the morale of enemy crews, the depth of penetration required through our defence system, the type of target to be attacked, the weather, etc. The choice for the bombers would lie very broadly between the high approach (up to 20,000 feet), the approach at medium height in or above clouds, and the very low approach (down to about 200 feet). Some targets, particularly those which are isolated and easily recognisable from low altitudes, could be most effectively attacked by low flying aircraft. Others, particularly those in densely built areas, might be very difficult to locate from a low flying aeroplane. Approach actually in clouds would handicap the attackers as well as the defence since, apart from the navigational problem, the handling of formations in cloud presents great difficulty and is, in fact, impracticable for anything more than a very small formation. In adverse weather conditions, therefore, the attack might be dispersed to a varying extent in time or space. On the whole, it is probable that the most usual method of attack would be a high approach with, possibly, a reduction in height before the run up to the objective when weather conditions made this necessary for the identification of the target. Steep diving to a low altitude, however, is not practicable with modern long-range bomber aircraft.

**Accuracy of Bombing**
4. The accuracy likely to be achieved by enemy bombers depends again on a number of factors. Very low bombing against a target which is easy to pick up and only lightly defended might be carried out in good weather with an average error of only 50 to 100 yards. The high altitude attacker, on the other hand, would frequently be handicapped by cloud or poor visibility and by difficulty in picking out his target, in addition to which his accuracy of aim would suffer as a result of anti-aircraft fire, fighter attack, and fatigue and strain generally. Thus, even in daylight

the bombing in each series of high altitude attacks on one target might well spread over a considerable area – possibly three quarters of a mile or more in diameter – even though the selected target occupied a small space in the area. There is also the possibility that enemy bombers heavily engaged might unload their bombs without attempting to take accurate aim. If the attacker elected to bomb through clouds (rather than accept the risk of descending below the cloud layer) very great inaccuracy in bombing would be certain to result. Similarly, bombing accuracy would suffer greatly in misty weather and at night.

5. For the foregoing reasons, it would be most unwise to assume that (quite apart from deliberate attacks on the civil population) the risk of serious civilian casualties would be confined to the immediate vicinity of important targets, though the density of bombing would naturally be greatest in areas close to such targets.

**Types of Bombs**
6. It is to be expected that, particularly in the early stages of a war, 75% or more of the <u>weight</u> of bombs dropped on the United Kingdom would be high explosive and up to 25% might be incendiary or gas. The proportions used in individual raids would depend on the type of target and the object of the attack, and some general considerations which would affect the choice of bombs are given below.
(a) <u>High explosive bombs</u>. The smaller types of high explosive bombs would be chiefly used to cause casualties amongst personnel not under cover and would probably therefore not be employed in the bombardment of towns and manufacturing centres; the larger types would be used to cause structural damage as well as casualties. German bombs range in size from the 22 lb. anti-personnel bomb to bombs weighing 1,100 lbs. or more, but bombs of a greater weight than 1,100 lbs. cannot be carried in normal German bombers. It is believed that the German Air Force will have a predominantly large supply of 550 lb. high explosive bombs which would be effective for most destructive purposes, excluding the penetration of armour and subterranean defences. Bombs weighing 110 lbs. and less have been proved suitable for the attack of merchant ships and the German Air Force might also employ marine torpedoes against ships at sea or even against the lock gates of shipping basins, but not in large numbers.
(b) <u>Incendiary bombs</u>. German incendiary bombs are of various sizes from 2.2 lbs. to 66 lbs. Because of their small size, large numbers of incendiary bombs could be carried in modern aircraft, and although a considerable proportion might be expected to fall in roadways or open

spaces, where they would do little or no damage, the reminder might start a number of simultaneous fires. The danger from incendiary bombs would naturally vary in different districts; areas containing big timber storages or large warehouses, or unprotected petrol or oil storage, would be seriously endangered by even the smaller types of incendiary bomb, but substantial buildings, if not previously damaged by high explosive bombardment, would be reasonably safe from attacks with the smallest types though (particularly where inflammable material existed in upper storeys) there would be a serious risk of fire with the larger types. It will be clear that, where a target area could be attacked effectively with the smallest types of bomb, the larger numbers of these which aircraft could carry would increase the chances of hits. Incendiary bombs might be employed simultaneously with high explosive bombs or might be used separately in later attacks carried out by comparatively few aircraft.

(c) <u>Gas bombs and gas spray</u>. Unless a policy of indiscriminate attack were deliberately employed from the outset, the use of gas might well be reserved by Germany as a   measure of desperation. It is, however, known that she has gas bombs of various sizes from 22 lbs. upwards and also apparatus for gas spray from aircraft. If gas were used, the object might be to cause casualties (particularly after high explosive bombs had rendered the more flimsy types of protection ineffective) or to deny normal access to the area attacked, or to hinder the work of reorganisation and repair after a bombardment with high explosive bombs. Mustard gas and Lewisite could be sprayed from containers in aircraft and, although the gas concentration would be considerably less than in the case of gas bombs, the chief danger of such attacks would be that areas might be contaminated without the knowledge of the people on the ground, with the result that casualties might be caused before the presence of the gas had been detected. Gas spray attacks would, however, be more likely against such targets as bodies of troops or against personnel working in the open than against towns. In general, it is probable that the knowledge that adequate precautions had been taken to meet gas attack would to some extent deter an enemy from using gas as a means of causing casualties.

*Annex "C" OF Appendix I*

## MATERIAL EFFECTS OF BOMBING – BARCELONA

1. There is insufficient data on which to assess with any degree of certainty the material effects to be expected from any given weight

of air bombardment against industrial cities, but without some guide as to the possible effect of the great weight of bombs which the German Air Force might drop on this country the tonnage figures given in the appreciation may convey very little. For this reason the following information is given in this appendix regarding the bombardment of Barcelona during the Spanish war. The conditions prevailing in the Spanish war are, of course, very different from those which would obtain in an air war between Great Britain and Germany. The defences of Barcelona have not been comparable with those which would be available for the defence of London, but the scale of attack has been small and the courage and resolution with which these attacks have been delivered have not been of the standard which is to be expected from the German Air Force in attacks on the United Kingdom. Thus offensive action and defence have not been wholly disproportionate.

2. As a capital and a port, Barcelona is in some respects comparable, on a small scale, with London. It is the principal port of Spain and the second largest city, though its population before the war was less than one million. Its industry, railway, fuel and local electric resources are chiefly concentrated along the sea coast on either side of the port and this is to some extent similar to the distribution of London's principal industrial resources along the Thames.

3. Although an official Nationalist target map of Barcelona shows over 200 "military" objectives, most of which are outside the coastal region, by far the greatest proportion of the bombing has been directed against objectives in the coastal region, and particularly against the port.

4. In all, there have been 232 air raids against Barcelona against the following objectives:
    Harbour area
    Other 'military' targets (Principal 'military' targets, apart from the harbour: oil storage, shipyard, power station aero engine works, A.A. batteries.)
    Civil population
    Unclassified

Of these raids, 135 were made by one or other of the three Italian bomber squadrons based in Majorca, and 72 were made by single or at most two German seaplanes from that island. Only 25 raids from

Nationalist aerodromes on the mainland were recorded and some of these were made by German bomber squadrons.

5. In his dispatch dated 25th November, 1938, Mr. Stevenson, British Minister for Republican Spain, wrote:

"The acuteness of the food situation is due in large measure to the air blockade established by the Nationalists. Very effective use has been made of this arm. The port of Barcelona is a wilderness of smashed wharfs, gutted buildings and overturned cranes. An air of desolation and of apprehension hangs over it. What is more sinister is the absence of purposeful activity … Ships are kept in the port as long as four weeks in the case of colliers and never, except in the case of rare munition ships for less than six days. The main reason for this state of affairs is doubtless that so much damage has been caused to the port that practically all unloading has to be done by hand.

"Air bombardments of Barcelona, with the exception of three days indiscriminate bombardment last March have been confined with reasonable accuracy to the port area. Nevertheless the altitude at which the bombing aircraft attack the port, causes indifferent marksmanship at times and the maze of densely crowded streets adjacent to the port suffers. Refuges are not sufficient. But even if this were not so the notice which Barcelona's anti-aircraft defences are able to give is not usually long enough to enable people to take shelter … Often enough the first warning Barcelona has of an air raid is the crash of the bombs themselves.

"The effect of air bombardment on the civil population is difficult to estimate. I am told that during the bombardment of the town itself last March the morale of the inhabitants was very near breaking point. Since then there has been no repetition of indiscriminate bombardment and the demeanour of the people between raids seems quite unconcerned".

6. Although insufficient information is available to make any complete analysis of the effects of the bombardment of Barcelona, the following information is regarded as reliable:

In the 135 raids by the Italians from Majorca 538 tons of bombs were dropped.

In the remainder of the raids it is estimated that a further 190 tons were dropped.

Only 44 tons were dropped during the period of indiscriminate bombing last March, causing the following casualties: Approximately 600 killed, and 700 injured (treated at hospital).

It is probable that less than 500 tons of bombs were dropped in the harbour area. The following effects were achieved by the bombing:

| | |
|---|---:|
| Persons killed | 2,500 |
| Injured persons treated at hospital | over 3,000 |
| Buildings destroyed | over 1,200 |
| Buildings damaged | over 6,000 |
| Ships sunk in harbour | 20 |
| Ships damaged in harbour | 40 |

All mechanical facilities in the harbour destroyed.
All above ground fuel storage completely destroyed.

No reliable information is available regarding damage to factories but it is believed that the power station near the port, although evidently attacked and damaged, was not put out of action permanently.

7. Nearly all the bombing was from high altitudes (approximately 13,000 ft.) and it appears from such photographs as have been inspected in relation to known targets, that the mean error of Italian bombing from that height was of the order of 300 yards. Many of the attacks were made in moonlight, and of the remainder, the majority were made in the morning from the direction of the sun.

# Appreciation by the Chiefs of Staff of The Prospects of Invasion 1937–1939

In accordance with the instruction of the War Cabinet we have re-examined the question of German seaborne or airborne raids on, or invasion of the United Kingdom, and what steps should be taken to meet any risk of such attacks.

2. We attach at Annex I the conclusions we reached in our previous report, prepared in 1937.

3. The threat of invasion is a form of diversion that has been used very freely in the past by our enemies whenever we have been engaged in a war with a Continental Power. The Germans cannot fail to have appreciated the fact that large numbers of troops were retained in England during the last war on this account, and it is a stratagem that they might well think it possible to employ again. We have therefore re-examined the subject at some length.

**General Situation**

4. The German High Command have not yet committed themselves to major land and air operations in France or elsewhere. They should have no difficulty, therefore, in finding the forces necessary for the type of operation we are considering. This factor and the belief that Britain is the mainspring of Allied resistance might conceivably tempt the Germans to raid or invade the United Kingdom, if the operations of their submarines and raiders had succeeded in causing a dispersion of our naval forces away from the North Sea area.

SMALL SCALE SEABORNE OR AIRBORNE LAND ATTACKS

5. Small scale raids might be attempted for the purpose of containing our forces through the threat of invasion, creating demoralisation and the sabotage of vulnerable points.

6. The conclusions of our earlier report, namely that such attacks are possible but that they constitute no serious threat, remain unchanged. Moreover, the strength and dispositions of our home defence garrisons are designed to deal with sabotage by this means, and so long as our naval and air strength is unimpaired, such attacks would not justify the losses likely to be incurred. Our report is therefore confined to consideration of the larger scale of attacks.

## GENERAL EXAMINATION OF LARGE SCALE SEABORNE AND AIRBORNE INVASION

### General

7. We have divided this examination into three sections:
    (a) General remarks on invasion.
    (b) Employment of air forces in overseas invasion.
    (c) Conduct of a seaborne expedition.

8. The large scale overseas invasion of one major Power by another is one of the most hazardous and difficult operations of war that can be attempted. Transporting an army in ships, convoying it through hostile waters, establishing it on the enemy's territory, and then maintaining it by sea communications, all involve certain essential pre-requisites to successful invasion. First of all, the control of the necessary sea routes for the period of the invasion is a vital requirement. Bound up with this is the need to neutralise the defending air forces for an indefinite period. Furthermore to make certain of getting the army ashore, tactical surprise is essential for the first wave of the invaders.

9. A probable preliminary to a German invasion would be to concentrate their air forces in an endeavour to neutralise our fighters and bombers, and, in conjunction with their fleet, to attempt to drive our naval forces from the North Sea. In so doing the Germans would lose strategical surprise, since it would indicate that a major threat to the security of this country was being developed.

10. Assuming for the moment that the Germans achieved sufficient success by these means to give them confidence in their ability to launch an invasion, the latter might take the form of landing advanced troops by air to seize beaches or a port, and aerodromes, the main body being transported by sea under cover of naval and air protection.

11. Recent intelligence reports from Germany suggest that plans of this nature have at least been considered by the enemy, and for this reason we examine their practicability in some detail below.

## EMPLOYMENT OF AIR FORCES IN OVERSEAS INVASION

### Neutralising Defending Air Forces

12. The attempt to neutralise the defending air forces prior to invasion might take the following forms:

(i) Extended operations against our first-line aircraft, operational aerodromes, reserves and aircraft industry.

(ii) A sudden and concentrated offensive in the period immediately prior to the invasion against our first-line fighter and bomber stations.

13. The first type of operation is one of great magnitude and has received close consideration by the Air Staff over a long period. Our air defences have been deployed to meet this threat in particular, though we have recently diverted certain squadrons from that part of the fighter line which covers the Midlands to protect the fleet bases; our fighter strength covering the Midlands is therefore now below the necessary standard of defence. Admittedly the enemy might at first succeed in inflicting considerable damage to our air potential. We should hope, however, that his losses would be so heavy that the intensity of his attacks would be reduced to negligible proportions before he came within reach of neutralisation of our air force.

14. The second form of operation would aim at the complete temporary immobilisation of our fighter defences and our bomber force during the progress of the operations. The effectiveness of attack on first line aircraft dispersed on defended aerodromes is comparatively low, and many aerodromes would escape attack owing to the difficulty of location. We may reasonably expect therefore that the enemy would not succeed in temporarily immobilising our air forces, and even a reduced bomber force could inflict heavy losses on so vulnerable a target as a seaborne expedition.

### Air Action to Secure the Sea Line of Communication

15. Germany's problem would be to achieve control of the sea route to England for the whole period of the invasion. In view of the allied superiority at sea, she would have to rely mainly on air action to secure her sea line of communication. A prolonged period of air operations against our naval forces would be a necessary preliminary to the launching of the expedition. Whatever success such air operations might achieve, we could still harry the German sea communications continuously by our light surface forces, submarines and mines.

Although the requirements of trade protection have greatly reduced our forces immediately available in the North Sea, it is still possible to reinforce than quickly – and to the full extent likely to be required – if so serious a threat as invasion were to develop.

**Parachute Attack**

16. Germany has developed a force of some 4,000 trained parachutists and over 6,000 air infantry for conveyance in air transports. Their composition and functions are given in Annex II to this report.

17. The probable role of this force would be to seize aerodromes and suitable landing beaches or a harbour immediately prior to the arrival of the seaborne expedition. Parachute troops might also be used to put fighter aerodromes out of action.

18. Without air superiority or complete surprise it would be difficult for these forces to achieve their purpose. The organisation for the despatch of a force which, including the bombers and fighters engaged, would run into several thousands of aircraft, is in itself an immense problem. Aircraft could only arrive at their objectives in waves at appreciable intervals of time. If suitable measures are taken for the protection of aerodromes and their rapid reinforcement by troops, the seizure of aerodromes would be a most difficult task.

19. Moreover, it is most unlikely that Germany would attempt to carry out the operation by day. On the other hand, the objectives are extremely hard to identify at night, even in bright moonlight, and it is very doubtful if parachute troops could be dropped in positions which would enable them to concentrate quickly in the dark. Unless they were able to capture a number of aerodromes quickly, only a few German troops would be in England by the time the seaborne expedition arrived. It is questionable whether there would be enough to seize and hold the beaches or harbours required by the main body. In fact the whole project of dropping parachute troops in such a highly populated and well defended country as England can only be regarded as a desperate mission which the participants are unlikely to survive.

**Use of the Low Countries**

20. The violation of the territorial rights of the Low Countries is a necessary adjunct to a German plan for the invasion of this country, because Germany cannot otherwise employ her air transport fleet for the conveyance of the air landing force. Violation would afford her other advantages. She could bring into effective use her short-range dive bomber force, upon which she relies primarily for accurate bombing, and she could employ her fighters on escort duties. She could obtain

these increases in air power by limiting violation to flight over these countries, but invasion would give her advanced bases and enable her to utilise additional fighters.

## CONDUCT OF A SEABORNE EXPEDITION

21. We now consider the general lines on which the Germans might conduct a seaborne expedition against this country, on the assumption that they believed that they had achieved the measure of naval and air control essential to an invasion.

**Size of Expedition and Escort**
22. For the purpose of this examination we assume that the initial forces employed would not be less than 20,000 men conveyed in 20 to 25 ships of about 5,000 tons. A convoy of this size would be extremely vulnerable to attack by our light naval forces and would require a strong naval escort. In any event, in view of our naval superiority, Germany could not depend upon being able to protect this or subsequent convoys by these means.

**Assembly**
23. To preserve secrecy and for administrative reasons the Germans would probably prefer to organise the expedition from their own ports, even if they had invaded Holland and/or Belgium. It would not be necessary for the expedition to assemble in a port, but the whole force would have to take up proper dispositions at sea before dark on the night before the attack was made. A likely area for the naval rendezvous would be inside the southern portion of the German mined area. On the first intimation of German preparations for an expedition special reconnaissances would therefore be required of the area lying between the southern extremity of the enemy minefield and German ports. Also of Dutch ports, if Holland had been invaded.

**Passage and Probable Destination**
24. Disembarkation, which would probably begin at dawn, might take place from boats on a selected beach or at a captured port where sufficient quayage is available. The first alternative is not practicable in winter since the enemy is not in a position to obtain reliable weather reports, and such a landing can be made impossible at all seasons by unsuitable conditions.
25. Most of the East Coast between the Thames and Humber is within 200 miles of the southern point of the German mined area and,

assuming a speed of 15 knots, the expedition would have about 12 to 14 hours steaming. There are good beaches between Flamborough and Spurn Head, and just south of the Humber; but our own mined area extends from Spurn Head northwards to Newcastle. The Humber itself is strongly defended, and from there to Yarmouth, there are shoals and sand-banks through which it would be most difficult to navigate a large convoy at night.

26. The next stretch of coast includes Lowestoft and Southwold, which are within the 200 mile radius mentioned above, and to which there is a clear approach, with no shoal area, from the German minefield. Moreover, it is on this part of the coast that the most suitable beaches are to be found. All the ports and estuaries in this area are, however, inaccessible for transports, except Harwich. While, therefore, Germany might attempt to achieve surprise by sending her seaborne expedition to some unexpected place, it would seem advisable to direct our own preparations against an attack somewhere between Yarmouth and Harwich. At the same time the parachute attack might develop first and indicate the objective of the attack as being elsewhere. These preparations should therefore be sufficiently flexible to permit of adjustment if necessary.

Owing to navigational difficulties and the increased length of voyage it appears to us impracticable for the Germans to attempt to land their expedition in the defended area of the mouth of the Thames.

## Detection and Interception on Passage

27. The chances of even temporary success of any seaborne attack directed against this country would depend to some extent upon how long the convoy could escape detection during its passage. Although air reconnaissance should ensure that any expedition of this size would be detected in reasonable weather, the combination of winter nights and low visibility conditions might enable the invading forces to escape detection. It is desirable therefore that we should be prepared to supplement air reconnaissance with reconnaissance by light naval forces, such as submarines, along the line of probable approach. There can be no certainty of our being able to intercept the expedition with forces adequate to engage the naval escort which the Germans could provide, but the complete protection of a large troop convoy is a difficult task, and we should be able to harass the expedition on passage by light surface forces and submarines, and to affect constant interruption to the passage of subsequent maintenance convoys. Minelaying in the approaches to the port or point of landing

would add considerably to the invaders difficulties, since the conditions for minesweeping close to our coast could be made impossible.

## Air Support to the Expedition

28. In addition to her preparatory measures for achieving air superiority, Germany would undoubtedly provide her transports with a strong escorting force of bombers for attack on surface craft.

29. Assuming that Germany violated Dutch territory, she could also utilise 250 long range fighters (M.E.110) to give local air protection to the convoys. It has been calculated that as many as 50 could patrol during the day over the Lowestoft area, but this force would have no reserves and it would be called upon to protect not only the place of landing but also the transports approaching and leaving our coast. With the use of Dutch bases Germany could also provide fighter escort by short range fighters during part of the voyage.

30. Unless our fighter strength had been drastically reduced by preliminary air attack, we could expect to inflict severe losses on the enemy air escorts in the vicinity of our coast. These operations would, however, require a rapid concentration of fighter squadrons on the East Coast aerodromes and additional facilities in this area may be necessary.

31. Intensive air attack prior to an attempted raid or invasion might result in the dislocation or destruction of rapid means of inter-communication. Arrangements for essential telephone staff to remain at their post during an air raid are therefore necessary and duplication of the more important land lines by radio is advisable.

## Disembarkation and Landing

32. Whatever immunity the expedition might enjoy during passage, its most difficult task awaits it at the point of disembarkation. Complete surprise or air superiority is most improbable. In consequence the expedition may have to effect an opposed landing on a beach or at a partly seized port. The process of disembarkation must occupy not less than 7 hours during which time the transports are vulnerable to air attack and our own troop reinforcements would have concentrated. Any troops disembarked in a shorter period of time must be without guns or transport and could hardly overcome properly constituted defence forces. They could achieve only local successes and their position should rapidly become untenable. Moreover the expedition's line of retreat is threatened both from the air and sea and it is difficult to see how the enemy could extricate his forces without very considerable loss.

## CONCLUSIONS

33. The main conclusions we have reached as to the risks of airborne and seaborne raids on, or invasion of the British Isles can be summarised as under:

(i) We confirm the conclusions in our previous report that small-scale parachute raids or small unescorted seaborne land attacks are possible, but do not constitute a serious threat.

(ii) In certain circumstances it is conceivable that Germany might attempt the invasion of this country by means of a combined airborne and seaborne expedition, but so long as our naval and air forces remain in being and provided the necessary precautions are maintained effectively, such attacks do not constitute a serious threat to our security.

(iii) The risk of such attack does not justify interference with the training of the Field Force in its proper role, or the retention in this country of field formations destined for employment elsewhere. When the bulk of the Field Force has been despatched overseas it should not be difficult to devise some special provision against this risk.

(iv) The violation of Dutch and/or Belgian territory is likely to form a necessary part of a large-scale airborne or seaborne land attack. We cannot rely, however, on a preliminary enemy invasion of the Low Countries as a warning of their intentions.

## RECOMMENDATIONS

34. Although most of these have already been put in hand, we consider it advisable to place on record our views as to the precautionary measures which should be taken against the threat of invasion. These measures are:

(i) The provision of special air and naval reconnaissance to give the earliest possible warning of the assembly and passage of a large seaborne expedition, when such a threat becomes imminent.

(ii) The development of the organisation to give immediate warning to the military authorities of any enemy landing either on our coast or inland.

(iii) The adequate protection of our aerodromes against seizure or sabotage by parachute troops, and arrangements for the rapid move of troops to reinforce aerodrome garrisons.

(iv) The disposition of the requisite light naval forces at ports from where early interception of an enemy expedition can be ensured.

(v) The maintenance of an adequate air striking force in a state of readiness.

(vi) Facilities for concentrating our fighter defences within range of the enemy's most probable areas of disembarkation.

(vii) A suitable proportion of troops should be disposed within easy reach of the East Coast, and plans for their rapid concentration in an emergency should be made.

(viii) The provision of sufficient defences at the East Coast ports in question to afford the necessary delay to any surprise approach.

(ix) The co-ordination of all defence measures to meet this particular threat.

(x) The organisation of communications to ensure rapid inter-communication between all commanders and units concerned and the duplication of essential land lines by point to point radio.

*(Signed) C. L. Newall*
*Dudley Pound*
*Edmund Ironside*
*Central War Room, 18th November, 1939*


*Annex I*

## EXTRACT FROM CONCLUSIONS OF REPORT BY JOINT PLANNING SUB-COMMITTEE DATED JANUARY, 1937

28. "No danger of invasion would exist and the danger to be feared from raids generally would be small. The most important object with which Germany might threaten or even carry out a raid would be to lead us to retain an undue proportion of our forces at home. For us it is therefore most important that the danger of land attack should be seen in its proper proportions, and that disproportionate alarm should not be taken at an enemy operation of which the primary object might be to cause alarm.

**Seaborne Land Attack**
29. We consider a seaborne land attack on a scale which would require a naval escort very improbable. If it were attempted we are confident

that our naval and air forces would defeat it without the help of our land forces. The strength and dispositions of our home defence garrisons should therefore be decided without any consideration of danger from this scale of seaborne attack.

A raid by troops carried in one or two unescorted ships would be possible on the East coast from Caithness to Kent, but is unlikely. Our home defences should be prepared to deal with parties landed to demolish any important point which could not more easily be demolished by air bombardment. They should also be prepared to deal within reasonable time with raiding parties landed on more remote parts of the coast with the object of creating a diversion and holding troops in Great Britain. On all other parts of our coast the maximum scale of landing which need be considered is the strength that could be put ashore from submarines.

### Airborne Land Attack

30. If war occurred at the present time the danger that Germany would attempt an airborne land attack on any considerable scale would be negligible. Small-scale raids landing demolition parties to destroy selected vulnerable points would be feasible and not improbable.

We foresee no development which would modify the foregoing conclusion in the future until Germany has carried out extensive training in landing troops from aircraft by parachute. If this training had been carried out airborne raids on a considerable scale would be possible, but we consider they would remain unlikely because we can at present see no important object of a character likely to justify this form of attack in the eyes of the German Staff.

The strength and dispositions of our home defence garrisons, while designed to deal with sabotage parties landed from the air, need not therefore at present be determined with a view to meeting serious airborne land attack."

*Annex II*

### GERMANY'S AIR LANDING FORCES

1. Germany has developed an air landing force, which comprises units of trained parachutists and air landing battalions, each under its own separate organisation.
2. The estimated strength of the trained parachutists at the beginning of 1939 was between 3,000 and 3,500; the present total probably lies between 3,500 and 4,000. The tactical unit of the parachute force is the

battalion with a strength of 550 men armed with automatic revolvers. Each battalion is also equipped with 12 machine guns, 54 light automatic rifles and a minimum of 7 two-inch mortars. The leap is normally made from a height of between 450 and 600 feet, and personnel being ready for action within 12 to 15 minutes of landing. Although parachutists may be dropped either singly or in small groups, for purposes of sabotage or propaganda, as was done in the war against Poland, their primary object is to seize and hold some locality where aircraft can land and deplane further troops, provisions and armament.

3. The air landing battalions are supplementary to the parachutists, and consist of troops organised for rapid air transport. The total force numbers between 5,000 and 6,000, and is organised into 9 or 10 battalions. The Germans moved a part of this force from Berlin into Czechoslovakia in 300 aircraft during the Sudeten incident.

4. The type of aircraft used by the Germans for both parachuting and air transport is the Ju. 52, of which they possess approximately 980. The Ju. 52 is not a high performance type and would suffer heavy casualties if opposed by modern fighters.

# Appendix III

# List of Defended Ports and Dockyards and Their Armament

## MAJOR DEFENDED PORTS

| PORT (1) | ALLOCATION 1937-39 (2) | IN POSITION MAY 1940 (3) | IN POSTION NOV. 1940 (4) | APPROVED SCALE FEBRUARY 1941 (5) |
|---|---|---|---|---|
| Orkneys (Scapa Flow)* | 4 x 6" (15°) | 6 x 6" | 6 x 6" | 4 x 6" (15°) |
| | 1 x 4.7" | 3 x 4.7" | 3 x 4.7" | 2 x 6" (45°) |
| | | 12 x 12pdr | 3 x 6pdr | 3 x 4.7" |
| | | | 18 x 12pdr | 18 x 12pdr |
| | | | 3 x 6" Naval | 9 x 6pdr |
| Invergordon* | 2 x 6" (45°) | 2 x 6" (45°) | 2 x 6" (45°) | 2 x 6" (45°) |
| | 2 x 6" (15°) | 2 x 6" (15°) | 2 x 6" (15°) | 2 x 6" (15°) |
| | | | 2 x 6" Naval | |
| Aberdeen | | | 2 x 6" (15°) | 2 x 6" (15°) |
| | | | 2 x 6" Naval | |
| Dundee | | 2 x 6" (15°) | 2 x 6" (15°) | 2 x 6" (15°) |
| | | | 2 x 6" Naval | |
| Firth of Forth* | 3 x 9.2" (35°) | 3 x 7.2" | 3 x 9.2" | 4 x 9.2" (35°) |
| | 1 x 9.2" (15°) | 14 x 6" | 2 x 6" Naval | 4 x 6" (45°) |
| | 16 x 6" (15°) | 4 x 12pdr | 14 x 6" (15°) | 12 x 6" (15°) |
| | 6 x 6pdr | | 4 x 12pdr | 4 x 12pdr |
| | | | 6 x 6pdr | 6 x 6pdr |
| Blyth | | 2 x 6" | 2 x 6" (15°) | 2 x 6" (45°) |
| | | | 2 x 6" Naval | 2 x 12pdr |

162

| | | | | |
|---|---|---|---|---|
| Tyne | 2 x 9.2" (35°)<br>4 x 6" (15°) | 1x 9.2"<br>4 x 6" | 1 x 9.2"<br>4 x ^" (15°)<br>2 x 6" Naval<br>2 x 12pdr | 2 x 9.2" (35°)<br>2 x 6" (45°)<br>4 x 6" (15°) |
| Sunderland | | 2 x 6" | 2 x 6" (15°)<br>2 x 6" Naval<br>2 x 12pdr | 2 x 12pdr |
| Tees and Hartlepool* | 2 x 9.2" (35°)<br>4 x 6" (15°) | 1 x 9.2"<br>4 x 6" | 1 x 9.2"<br>4 x 6" (15°)<br>2 x 6" Naval | 2 x 9.2" (35°)<br>2 x 6" (45°)<br>2 x 6" (15°)<br>2 x 12pdr |
| Humber* | 3 x 9.2" (35°)<br>4 x 6" (15°)<br>4 x 6pdr | 2 x 9.2"<br>3 x 6"<br>2 x 4.7"<br>4 x 12pdr<br>2 x 6" Naval<br>2 x 4.7" Naval<br>2 x 4" Naval | 2 x 9.2"<br>4 x 6" (15°)<br>2 x 4.7"<br>6 x 6pdr | 3 x 9.2" (35°)<br>2 x 6" (45°)<br>4 x 6" (15°)<br>6 x 6pdr |
| Yarmouth | | 2 x 6" | 2 x 6" (15°)<br>2 x 6" Naval<br>2 x 12pdr | 2 x 12pdr |
| Lowestoft | | | 2 x 6" (15°)<br>2 x 6" Naval<br>2 x 12pdr | 2 x 6" (15°) |
| Harwich* | 3 x 9.2" (35°)<br>4 x 6" (15°)<br>4 x 6pdr | 2 x 9.2"<br>4 x 6"<br>2 x 12pdr | 2 x 9.2"<br>4 x 6" (15°)<br>3 x 6pdr<br>2 x 12pdr<br>2 x 6" Naval | 3 x 9.2" (35°)<br>2 x 6" (45°)<br>2 x 6" (15°)<br>4 x 6pdr |
| Thames and Medway* | 5 x 9.2" (35°)<br>1 x 6" (75°)<br>10 x 6" (15°)<br>9 x 6pdr | 5 x 9.2"<br>6 x 6"<br>4 x 12pdr<br>2 x 3pdr | 1 x 9.2" (35°)<br>4 x 9.2" (15°)<br>6 x 6" (15°)<br>4 x 6" Naval<br>4 x 5.5" Naval<br>3 x 6pdr<br>2 x 3pdr | 5 x 9.2" (35°)<br>10 x 6" (15°)<br>2 x 12pdr<br>6 x 6pdr |

| | | | | |
|---|---|---|---|---|
| Dover* | 2 x 9.2" (15°)<br>6 x 6" (15°)<br>4 x 6pdr | 2 x 9.2"<br>6 x 6"<br>2 x 12pdr<br>2 x 6pdr | 2 x 9.2"<br>6 x 6" (15°)<br>3 x 6pdr<br>3 x 12pdr<br>3 x 6" (45°)<br>4 x 6" Naval<br>2 x 4" Naval<br>1 x 12"Supercharged | 2 x 15" Naval<br>4 x 9.2" (35°)<br>2 x 9.2" (15°)<br>6 x 8" Naval<br>6 x 6" (45°)<br>6 x 6" (15°)<br>3 x 12pdr<br>3 x 6pdr |
| Newhaven | 2 x 6" (15°) | 2 x 6" | 2 x 6" (15°)<br>2 x 12pdr<br>2 x 6" Naval | 2 x 6" (15°) |
| Portsmouth and Southampton* | 4 x 9.2" (15°)<br>2 x 9.2" (30°)<br>16 x 6" (15°)<br>8 x 12pdr | 2x 9.2"<br>11 x 6"<br>6 x 12pdr | 2 x 9.2" (30°)<br>4 x 9.2" (15°)<br>11 x 6" (15°)<br>3 x 6pdr<br>14 x 12pdr<br>3 x 6" Naval | 2 x 9.2" (30°)<br>4 x 9.2" (15°)<br>14 x 6" (15°)<br>8 x 12pdr<br>8 x 6pdr |
| Portland* | 4 x 9.2" (15°)<br>4 x 6" (15°)<br>4 x 12pdr | 2 x 9.2"<br>4 x 6"<br>4 x 12pdr | 4 x 9.2" (15°)<br>4 x 6" (15°)<br>4 x 12pdr | 4 x 9.2" (15°)<br>4 x 6" (15°)<br>4 x 12pdr |
| Dartmouth | | | 2 x 4.7" Naval | - |
| Plymouth* | 6 x 9.2" (35°)<br>2 x 6" (45°)<br>4 x 6" (15°)<br>11 x 12pdr | 4 x 9.2"<br>9 x 6"<br>9 x 12pdr | 3 x 9.2" (15°)<br>3 x 9.2" (30°)<br>6 x 6" (15°)<br>11 x 12pdr | 6 x 9.2" (35°)<br>2 x 6" (45°)<br>4 x 6" (15°)<br>4 x 12pdr<br>8 x 6pdr |
| Falmouth | 4 x 6" (45°) | 4 x 6" | 2 x 6" (45°)<br>2 x 6" (15°) | 3 x 6" (45°)<br>2 x 6" (15°)<br>2 x 12pdr<br>2 x 6pdr |
| Avonmouth | | | 2 x 6" Naval | |
| Newport | | | | 2 x 12pdr |
| Barry and Cardiff | 2 x 6" (15°) | 2 x 4.7" | 2 x 6" (15°)<br>2 x 6" Naval | 2 x 6" (15°) (Barry)<br>2 x 12pdr (Cardiff) |

| Swansea* | 2 x 6" (15°) | 2 x 6" | 2 x 6" (15°)<br>2 x 4.7" | 2 x 6" (15°)<br>2 x 12pdr |
|---|---|---|---|---|
| Milford Haven* | 4 x 9.2" (15°)<br>4 x 6" (15°) | 4 x 6" | 2 x 9.2" (15°)<br>4 x 6" (15°)<br>2 x 6" Naval | 4 x 9.2" (15°)<br>6 x 6" (15°) |
| Liverpool (Mersey)* | 2 x 6" (45°)<br>2 x 6" (15°) | 4 x 6" | 4 x 6" (15°) | 2 x 6" (45°)<br>2 x 6" (15°) |
| Barrow | 2 x 6" (15°) | 2 x 6" | 2 x 6" (15°)<br>2 x 6" Naval<br>3 x 75mm | 2 x 6" (15°)<br>2 x 6" Naval |
| Clyde* | 4 x 6" (15°) | 4 x 6"<br>2 x 4.7"<br>1 x 12pdr | 4 x 6" (15°)<br>2 x 4.7"<br>1 x 12pdr | 4 x 6" (15°)<br>2 x 4.7"<br>1 x 12pdr |
| Belfast* | 4 x 6" (15°) | 4 x 6" | 4 x 6" (15°)<br>2 x 6" Naval | 4 x 6" (15°) |
| Londonderry (Lough Swilly)* | 2 x 9.2" (35°)<br>2 x 6" (15°) | | 2 x 6" Naval<br>1 x 12pdr | |

# MINOR DEFENDED PORTS

| PORT | ARMAMENT NOVEMBER 1940 (6) |
|---|---|
| Sutton Voe | 2 x 4" Naval |
| Lerwick | 2 x 4" Naval, 2 x 6" Naval |
| Wick | 2 x 6" Naval |
| Peterhead | 2 x 6" Naval |
| Montrose | 2 x 6" Naval |
| Inverness (Fort George) | 2 x 4" Naval |
| Buckie | Nil |
| Berwick | 2 x 6" Naval |

| | |
|---|---|
| Amble | 2 x 6″ Naval |
| Seaham Harbour | 2 x 6″ Naval |
| Whitby | 2 x 6″ Naval |
| Scarborough | 2 x 6″ Naval |
| Boston | 2 x 6″ Naval |
| King's Lynn | 2 x 6″ Naval |
| Brightlingsea (East Mersea) | 2 x 4.7″ Naval |
| Ramsgate | 2 x 6″ Naval, 2 x 12pdr |
| Shoreham | 2 x 6″ Naval |
| Littlehampton | 2 x 6″ Naval |
| Poole | 2 x 6″ Naval |
| Exmouth | 2 x 4.7″ Naval |
| Brixham | 2 x 4.7″ Naval |
| Looe | 2 x 4″ Naval |
| Fowey | 2 x 4.7″ Naval |
| Penzance | 2 x 4″ Naval |
| Padstow | 2 x 4″ Naval |
| Appledore | 2 x 4.7″ Naval |
| Portishead | 2 x 6″ Naval |
| Fishguard | 2 x 6″ Naval |
| Caernarvon | 2 x 4″ Naval |
| Holyhead | 2 x 6″ Naval |

| Preston | 2 x 4" Naval |
| Fleetwood | 2 x 4" Naval |
| Workington | 2 x 4" Naval |
| Stranraer | 2 x 4" Naval |
| Ardrossan | Nil |
| Campbeltown | Nil (Guns required) |
| Oban | Nil (Guns required) |
| Loch Ewe | Nil |
| Stornoway | 2 x 4" Naval (Manned by RN) |
| Lamlash | Nil |
| Kyle of Lochalsh | Nil |
| Larne | 2 x 6" Naval |
| Whitehaven | 4" |
| Fraserburgh | Nil |
| Bridlington | Nil |
| Burnham | 6" (At Foulness) |
| Teignmouth | 4.7" |
| Torquay | 4.7" |
| Salcombe | 4" |
| Llanelly | 4" |

## NOTES:

Category 'A' Ports, marked above with an asterisk, were those at which adequate defences were to be installed in peace-time, to be fully manned before the outbreak of hostilities.

References: C.I.D. 158A (18 Nov. 1927), C.I.D. 266A (29 Oct. 1937), C.I.D. 321A (8 June 1939).

References: G.H.Q. H.F. Bundle 47/9, Paper 26B, 1 May 1940. The guns had the assistance of searchlights (approximately one for each two gun battery) for night firing. Large estuaries such as the Humber and the Thames had no really efficient illuminated area owing to the distances involved. In the Thames estuary the 9.2" guns could not fire by night as they had no fighting lights; and the 6" guns, capable of fighting at 12,000 yards, were reduced to a range of about 4,000 yards which was the range of the lights. The entrance to the Medway was protected by day and night, but the defence of the entrance to the Thames by night was very weak except in clear weather.

Reference: Admiralty L.D. 01566/40, 30 Nov. 1940.

Reference: C.O.S. (41) 89: 12 Feb. The armament in position at some ports exceeded the approved requirement. The extra guns were installed on temporary mountings at the discretion of Commanders-in-Chief.

Reference: Admiralty L.D. 01566/40: 30 Nov. 1940.

Appendix IV

# The Julius Caesar Plan

## Introduction

On the 27th October, 1939, the Commander-in-Chief, Home Forces was called upon to prepare immediate plans to meet an invasion on a large scale, based on a course of enemy action which had previously been ruled out as unlikely. Plans so produced, as it were on the spur of the moment, have necessarily been the subject of considerable modification.

The time had now arrived to set out the outline plan in a compact and handy form, and in as much detail as is necessary for a problem which is likely to be with us for the duration of the war, though as circumstances change the problem may present itself in a somewhat different shape, while the resources with which we meet it will vary considerably.

To facilitate amendment each paragraph and appendix of the plan is typed on a separate sheet and the whole is put together on the loose-leaf system.

## Method of Invasion

No considered appreciation of the scale and form of attack has as yet been issued. The information at the disposal of the Commander-in-Chief, Home Forces, is as follows:

(a) Germany has 4,000 trained parachutists whose action might be to seize an aerodrome or aerodromes on which further troop-carrying aircraft might land.

(b) Germany has 1,000 civil aircraft with the necessary range, each capable of carrying 15 men, though she is only known to possess 6,000 airlanding troops trained as such.

(c) Germany could embark a division in twenty transports of 4,000 to 5,000 tons and the crossing would take 20 hours to the nearest point on the British coast, steaming at 15 knots.

(d) The force would be escorted by 25 to 30 modern destroyers.

(e) A landing in force on a beach is hardly possible during winter weather conditions. A more likely course would be an attempt to enter a port with transports, the port being previously captured by parachute troops.

The most likely ports would be the HUMBER or HARWICH, though the following have also been designated as possible landing places: ABERDEEN, DUNDEE, LOWESTOFT, RAMSGATE.

(f) Were such a method employed, it might be expected that it would be accompanied by a heavy air offensive against the fleet, air force and other objectives in this country. The Germans have 1,750 long range bombers which could operate from Germany. This number could be considerably increased if aerodromes in HOLLAND were used. In order to neutralise the navy, German dive bombers, owing to their short range would have to use Dutch aerodromes.

(g) A landing operation would obviously be much facilitated by the previous capture of HOLLAND.

## Feasibility

It is axiomatic that men landed from the air can bring little with them but rifles, light machine guns and a limited amount of ammunition. They would therefore have little staying power, nor power of manoeuvre, unless quickly supported and maintained from the sea.

The disembarkation of a field force is a very slow and formidable undertaking, even if entirely unopposed, and the rate at which it can be carried out depends largely on the number of ships which can be handled simultaneously, and consequently on the number of quays, wharves, cranes available. For instance it would take several days to land a division at HARWICH complete with transport. Success, therefore, entails the seizure of a considerable port.

If this were attempted by troops landed from the air, these would have to be dropped in an unenclosed area, otherwise they could not collect again, which means some delay in actually getting control of the port. A further delaying factor would be at the time necessary to drive the defence from all grounds covering the docks, anchorage, or entrance to the port before the transports could enter and commence to unload.

Once landing from the air in any form has commenced the point of attack has been disclosed and cannot again be changed. It would be supremely dangerous to attempt seaborne operations until the success of the airlanding operations have been confirmed, so if the initial airlanding operations are a failure, the operation cannot proceed and has definitely failed.

## Action Being Taken by Other Services

Royal Navy — Certain precautionary measures in the North Sea.

R.A.F. — (a) Reconnaissances by day and on moonlight nights to detect concentrations of ships in German harbours or convoys at sea. Reconnaissance is, of course, an uncertain factor depending on moonlight and clear weather.
(b) All available bomber squadrons are maintained in a state of readiness for immediate action.
(c) If an enemy landing were actually effected, arrangements have been made to allot two bomber squadrons for the direct support of the land forces.
(d) No.16 (Army Co-operation) Squadron will be made available for co-operation with any operating Command.
(e) Three communication aircraft have been earmarked to be at the disposal of any operating Command.

## Degree of Readiness to be Maintained

It is estimated that it will be possible to give a minimum of eight hours' notice of any attempted enemy invasion and the plans of General Officers Commanding-in-Chief of Commands will be framed accordingly. Such notice should be sufficient to prevent interference with normal training.

## Command

For the purpose of repelling invasion, all troops (less A.D.G.B.) are under command or operational control of the Commander-in-Chief, Home Forces.

This does not imply that there will be a period of waiting for orders should we be faced by enemy invasion. Immediate action will be taken by the nearest formation to repel the invader, and General Officers Commanding-in-Chief of the Command or Commands involved are responsible for the conduct of the battle in their Command Area.

Steps have been taken to ensure the co-operation of troops of the Anti-Aircraft Command employed in the defence of aerodromes in the event of these being attacked.

## Forces Available by Categories

(a) Troops, the number of which will vary from time to time, are employed in the guarding of vulnerable points including aerodromes in the areas which might be threatened or attacked. These aerodromes also have a number of men belonging to A.D.G.B. or the R.A.F. respectively, who are armed or being armed with small arms weapons.

(b) Divisions in Scotland and on the East Coast of England which have been prepared for active operations by the provision of 1st line of transport, issue of ammunition, etc., portions of them being made quickly mobile by the provision of troop carrying transport.

(c) Divisions in Training Areas in the Aldershot and Southern Commands in a comparatively advanced stage of training are also prepared for active operations as a G.H.Q. Reserve on similar lines to (b) above.

NOTE: The composition of the forces specially prepared for operations, vide (b) and (c) above, their distribution by commands, and the artillery armament     available, are set out in Annex "A".

(d) In addition there are distributed in the areas which might be threatened troops     earmarked as reserves in support of the civil authorities in case of air raids, and troops under training in training centres, from which fighting units could be organised.

**Coast Defences**

(a) A landing at any point protected by Fixed Defences would be impracticable unless those defences had been eliminated or neutralised. Though the former might be carried     out by gun fire or bombing, either would probably be a lengthy procedure.

Neutralisation might be carried out by the fire of infantrymen established to the rear or on the flank of coast defence batteries, these infantry-men having been landed either by parachute or M.T.Bs. Scottish, Northern and Eastern Commands are therefore responsible for providing an efficient local infantry protection for the Fixed Defences in their areas, with particular emphasis on those at THE HUMBER, HARWICH

(b) Scottish Command are responsible for providing an 18-pdr. defence for ABERDEEN and DUNDEE and Eastern Command for LOWESTOFT and RAMSGATE. For similar reasons to those stated above local protection will be provided for the Artillery.

**Main Plan**

The plan of operations in general terms is as follows:

1st Stage     On the assumption that the first enemy attack would be by the troops landing from parachutes and transport aeroplanes, troops in the area will inflict the maximum number of casualties whilst the enemy are actually landing or collecting. There will be no falling back in the face of superior numbers except under orders of formation commanders. Quick action is largely a matter

|            | of warning, dependent on early information which the Fighter Command R.A.F. is prepared to give all formations concerned. |
|------------|---|
| 2nd Stage  | If any landing in force should establish itself, a cordon will be drawn round the area by the troops in the vicinity using all means of mobility provided or capable of improvisation, with the object of immobilising the invader until further troops can be brought up to finish him off. |
| 3rd Stage  | If a landing from the air is affected in YORKSHIRE, LINCOLNSHIRE or EAST ANGLIA, armoured troops or horsed cavalry under the command of the General Officers Commanding-in-Chief Northern or Eastern Command as the case may be, should then be employed to break up the enemy formation whilst they are still endeavouring to concentrate and before they can make the seizure of any port effective. |
|            | Whilst the Heavy Armoured Brigade of the 1st Armoured Division stationed in EAST ANGLIA is in G.H.Q. Reserve, the General Officer Commanding-in-Chief, Eastern Command may regard it as at his immediate disposal, should it be confirmed that the enemy invasion is confined to EAST ANGLIA. |
| 4th Stage  | The larger formations in the Scottish, Northern and Eastern Commands for which troop carrying transport will be provided would then concentrate forward towards the area of operations, if it lay within the boundaries of the Command, moving by road. |
| 5th Stage  | The G.H.Q. Reserve as so designated in Annex "A" would be moved forward by road as circumstances demanded. |

## Code Words to Bring the Plan into Effect

The Code Words to be employed, and action to be taken thereon, are as follows:

(a) Code Word JULIUS – signifying that there are indications that an attack is contemplated. Action:
  • Defence plan will be overhauled and arrangements completed for the obtaining of lifting transport at short notice. Lifting transport will not, however, be collected.
  • All leave will be stopped.
  • The minimum of 8 hours' notice will be curtailed as considered necessary.

- Regional Commissioners will be informed confidentially.
(b) Code Word CAESAR – signifying that invasion is imminent. Action:
  - All transport will be collected ready for action.
  - Ammunition will be distributed.
  - All units will be warned for immediate action.
  - Liaison Officers will take up their posts.
  - Essential telegraph lines for operational purposes will be taken over.
  - Harbour Authorities will be warned to provide standby parties for the immobilization of cranes and harbour facilities on the receipt of more definite information as to the port or ports threatened.

**Reconnaissances**

General Officers Commanding-in-Chief Commands are responsible for the carrying out of the necessary reconnaissances by formations under their Command.

General Officer Commanding-in-Chief, Northern Command for reconnoitring a suitable concentration area for one division from another Command, in the Northern Command Area.

General Officer Commanding-in-Chief, Eastern Command is similarly responsible for reconnoitring concentration areas for two divisions in EAST ANGLIA and one division in the HOME COUNTIES area.

**Transport**

(a) 1st Line Transport. (i) Formations and Units of T.A. Increment, shown in Annex "A" attached, are provided with 1st Line Transport under War Office orders. (ii) In the case of other formations and units shown in Appendix A: 1st Line Transport, required to complete on a basis of effective strength and the numbers of drivers available, is provided by voluntary hiring. Gun-towing vehicles are also provided on a scale of one per gun or howitzer shown in Appendix A.

(b) 2nd Line Transport. If 2nd Line Transport is required, it will be hired when the emergency occurs.

(c) Troop-Carrying Transport. Troop-Carrying Transport will be hired when the emergency occurs.

**Ammunition**

Ammunition for the purposes of the plan is issued to Commands on the following scale:

APPENDIX IV

| Category | 1st Line | 2nd Line | 3rd Line (Command Reserve) |
|---|---|---|---|
| *Artillery Ammunition* | | | |
| 18-pounder | As per W.E. for | 50% of 1st Line | 50% of 1st Line in Scottish and |
| 4.5" Howitzer | the number of | | Northern Commands only |
| 25-pounder | guns shown | | |
| 2-pounder A/T | | | |
| 2-pounder A/T | | | |
| | | | |
| *Small Arms Ammunition* | | | |
| .303-inch for rifles | As per W.E. | | |
| .303-inch for L.M.G.s | As per W.E for | | |
| | number of | 50% of 1st Line | 50% of 1st Line in Scottish and |
| | weapons actually | | Northern Commands only |
| .303-inch for M.G.s | held | | |
| | | | |
| 3" mortar | 25% of W.E. for | Nil | Nil |
| | number of | | |
| | weapons actually | | |
| | held | | |
| A/T (infantry only) | 50% of W.E. for | Nil | Nil |
| | number of | | |
| | weapons actually | | |
| | held | | |
| Hand grenades | 50% of W.E. for | Nil | Nil |
| | number | | |
| Pistols, signal | 50% of W.E. for | Nil | Nil |
| | number | | |

## Air Co-Operation

Arrangements have been made for all reconnaissance reports received by the Coastal Command to be transmitted to G.H.Q. Home Forces. A R.A.F. Liaison Officer has been detailed to G.H.Q. Home Forces. Aerodromes earmarked for R.A.F. co-operation are as follows:

Scottish Command   Grangemouth
Northern Command   York
Eastern Command    Hatfield or Luton

## Liaison With Civil Authorities

General Officers Commanding-in-Chief Commands will consider in conjunction with Regional Commissioners the following problems which would arise out of invasion.

(a) <u>The control of evacuees</u>. In this connection the less the movement of the civil population the easier is the execution of the military plan. The population which is not in any immediate danger should be encouraged to stay in their homes by broadcasts and other means. It is not considered practical or desirable to endeavour to hold up the exodus of the civil population whose lives are in danger, but such movement should be controlled and diverted so that military two-way roads into the theatre of operations are kept clear of all civil traffic.

(b) <u>Liaison with Police</u>. To achieve effective control over the civil population it is desirable that there should be a police liaison office at the Headquarters of every operating Brigade and Division. Normally the Police Staff Officer of the Regional Commissioner or Commissioners concerned will act as the Police Liaison Officer at Command or Advanced Command Headquarters. Close touch with the Regional Commissioner or Commissioners is also essential.

(c) <u>Aid to the Civil Power</u>. For Civil Defence purposes certain troops are earmarked as an immediate aid of the civil power. In the circumstances envisaged by the plan military considerations must predominate, and it lies within the discretion of military commanders to withhold such support, reporting the demand and the reply given to higher authority.

(d) <u>Immobilisation of services of use to the enemy</u>. The circumstances are unlikely to be such as to render desirable or practicable the wholesale destruction of M.T. petrol stocks, public utilities, communications or food stocks, but steps should be taken to prevent M.T. vehicles moving into the area of operations. Cranes and docking facilities could be temporarily immobilised. The severing of certain telephones and telegraph lines should be considered with due forethought to our own reliance on civil communications.

(e) <u>Protection of telephone exchanges</u>. For the same reason protection should be given to civil telephone exchanges in the areas in which our troops are operating to persuade the civil operators to stay at their post.

**Liaison With RAF Sources of Information**
The Air Officer Commanding-in-Chief, Fighter Command is arranging to inform all formations if parachutists land in any of the areas covered by groups of the Observer Corps. This warning can only be given once at the commencement of the invasion.

Army formations should not send liaison detachments to H.Q. of Fighter Groups or Observer Groups as this will tend to hinder their work, and in any case no useful information can be imparted other than that stated above.

## Inter-Communication

(a) Direct Lines exist from G.H.Q. Home Forces, to Coastal Commands, Fighter and Bomber Commands, R.A.F.

(b) G.H.Q. Home Forces is included in the Wireless Net-Work published under W.O. letter No 32/Wireless/565 (S.D.6) of 24th August, 1939, as amended by W.O. letter No 32/Wireless/565 (S.D.6) dated 7th November in Group C.

(c) Formations whose signal organisation is incomplete or insufficiently equipped will rely on civil communications and D.Rs.

(d) Operating formations will give facilities on their communications as so organised for police messages dealing with traffic control or other measures instituted in co-operation with the military authorities.

(e) Three communication aircraft are available. Demand should be made through the R.A.F. Liaison Officer at G.H.Q. Home Forces.

*Annex "A" to Appendix IV*

## SCOTTISH COMMAND

| | |
|---|---|
| 9th Division | 8 x 18-pounders; 0 x 4.5" Howitzers; 0 x 25-pounders, 0 x 2-pounder A/T |
| 15th Division | 0 x 18-pounders; 8 x 4.5" Howitzers; 0 x 25-pounders, 0 x 2-pounder A/T |
| 52nd Division | 16 x 18-pounders; 24 x 4.5" Howitzers; 0 x 25-pounders, 0 x 2-pounder A/T |
| Tanks | n/a |
| Remarks | Elements of these Divisions are employed, The total number of vehicles required to equip these troops with 1st Line Transport is equivalent to that of an Infantry Division. |

## NORTHERN COMMAND

| | |
|---|---|
| 1st Cavalry Division | 12 x 18-pounders; 4 x 4.5" Howitzers; 0 x 25-pounders, 0 x 2-pounder A/T |
| 42nd Division | 14 x 18-pounders; 19 x 4.5" Howitzers; 0 x 25-pounders, 8 x 2-pounder A/T |
| 49th Division | 22 x 18-pounders; 24 x 4.5" Howitzers; 0 x 25-pounders, 6 x 2-pounder A/T |
| 1st Light Armoured Brig | 0 x 18-pounders; 0 x 4.5" Howitzers; 0 x 25-pounders, 0 x 2-pounder A/T |
| 1st/7th R. North Fusiliers | 0 x 18-pounders; 0 x 4.5" Howitzers; 0 x 25-pounders, 0 x 2-pounder A/T |
| Tanks | 77 Light |
| Remarks | 1st Cavalry Division is shortly to be moved to the Middle East. |

## EASTERN COMMAND

| | |
|---|---|
| 18th Division | 16 x 18-pounders; 10 x 4.5" Howitzers; 0 x 25-pounders, 4 x 2-pounder A/T |
| 54th Division | 8 x 18-pounders; 10 x 4.5" Howitzers; 0 x 25-pounders, 2 x 2-pounder A/T |
| 12th Division | 0 x 18-pounders; 0 x 4.5" Howitzers; 0 x 25-pounders, 0 x 2-pounder A/T |
| 1st London Division | 12 x 18-pounders; 12 x 4.5" Howitzers; 0 x 25-pounders, 0 x 2-pounder A/T |
| 1st Armoured Division | 0 x 18-pounders; 0 x 4.5" Howitzers; 0 x 25-pounders, 0 x 2-pounder A/T |

| Tanks | 190 Light, 25 Cruiser; includes the Heavy Armoured Brigade (64 Light Tanks, 25 Cruiser Tanks) in G.H.Q. Reserve |
| Remarks | Vehicles required to equip the troops in this Command with 1st Line Transport are equivalent approximately to the 1st Line Transport of the Infantry of 3 Divisions. |

## ALDERSHOT COMMAND

| 51st Division | 12 x 18-pounders; 24 x 4.5" Howitzers; 0 x 25-pounders, 26 x 2-pounder A/T |
| 60th & 115th Field Regt | 6-8 x 18-pounders; 0 x 4.5" Howitzers; 0 x 25-pounders, 0 x 2-pounder A/T |
| 6th Argyll & Suth High | 0 x 18-pounders; 0 x 4.5" Howitzers; 0 x 25-pounders, 0 x 2-pounder A/T |
| 1st/7th Middlesex | 0 x 18-pounders; 0 x 4.5" Howitzers; 0 x 25-pounders, 0 x 2-pounder A/T |
| Tanks | n/a |
| Remarks | In G.H.Q Reserve. Army Field Regiments are in process of receiving further 18-pounders. |

## SOUTHERN COMMAND

| 48th Division | 16 x 18-pounders; 36 x 4.5" Howitzers; 0 x 25-pounders, 8 x 2-pounder A/T |
| 12th Field Regt | 0 x 18-pounders; 0 x 4.5" Howitzers; 24 x 25-pounders, 0 x 2-pounder A/T |
| 4th Cheshire Regt | 0 x 18-pounders; 0 x 4.5" Howitzers; 0 x 25-pounders, 0 x 2-pounder A/T |
| Tanks | n/a |
| Remarks | In G.H.Q Reserve. 12th Field Regiment (Larkhill) has transport available for one12 gun Bty. |

## WESTERN COMMAND

| 55th Division | 6 x 18-pounders; 8 x 4.5" Howitzers; 0 x 25-pounders, 0 x 2-pounder A/T |
| Tanks | n/a |
| Remarks | This Division will shortly move to Training Area Charnwood Forest (Leicester) where it will be prepared for active operations under G.O.C.-in-C. Northern Command. |

Appendix V

# State of Home Forces 31st May 1941 Memorandum by the Commander-In-Chief Home Forces

With reference to Paper No. C.O.S. (40) 406 of 29th May 1940, I entirely agree that the country should be warned at once and roused to a sense of the imminent danger which faces us and the urgent need to take all possible steps to meet it, whatever the cost may be.

I also consider that Parliament should be re-assembled at once and informed in secret session of this danger, and of the inadequacy of the resources at present available to meet it.

The Army has already been brought to a high degree of alertness and all defences are manned during the hours of darkness, whilst work on defences is being accelerated to the utmost on the Yorkshire, East Anglian, South East and South Coasts.

The composition and strength of the Army at present available for Home Defence, and the state of its armament, are given in the attached Appendix. A large proportion of this force is as yet insufficiently trained and provided with artillery and armoured fighting vehicles to undertake offensive operations, and must therefore act on the defensive in prepared positions. Its dispositions are designed to meet the dual threat of seaborne and airborne attack; of the total of fifteen divisions available eight have the primary role of coast defence with their rear elements disposed to deal with airborne attack. One corps of three divisions is held in G.H.Q. reserve in the area NORTHAMPTON–NORTH LONDON–ALDERSHOT suitably disposed to move rapidly by brigade groups to any threatened area between the WASH and SOUTHAMPTON, a coast li.ne of about 400 miles.

It is necessary, however, to take account of the fact that our West Coast ports, particularly LIVERPOOL and BRISTOL and aerodromes in the West are as exposed to attack by airborne troops as those on the East Coast. It may well be that the enemy will make these ports an objective in order to interfere with essential supplies: I therefore consider that they should have the same priority for defence purposes as those on the East Coast.

It is of vital importance that all possible steps be taken immediately to increase the strength of the forces available for Home Defence. I agree with the Chiefs of Staff that the British Empire is Germany's main enemy, and if she can defeat us, the subsequent capitulation of France follows as a matter of course. It may therefore well be that Germany will launch her next offensive against this country. We are at the present time very ill-prepared to meet such an offensive which may have an initial strength of 20,000 seaborne and 20,000 airborne troops who will be relatively well trained.

I realize that there are bound to be pressing demands from the French for assistance in men and material, but the security of Great Britain must now come first and I cannot be responsible for that security unless all available forces are placed at my disposal.

*(Signed) Edmund Ironside,*
*General,*
*Commander-in-Chief, Home Forces.*

*Annex "A" to Appendix V*

|  | 25-pdr | 18-pdr | 4.5" | 2-pdr A/T | | Bren Carrier | Bren Gun | A/T Rifles |
|---|---|---|---|---|---|---|---|---|
| **DIVISIONAL ESTABLISHMENT** | | | | | | | | |
|  | 72 | - | - | 48 | | 90 | 590 | 307 |
| **SCOTTISH COMMAND** | | | | | | | | |
| 9th Division | - | 4 | 12 | 8 | | - | 590 | 307 |
| 1 Bty. 51st Regt. R.A. | 12 | - | - | - | | - | - | - |
| 151 Field Regt. R.A. | - | 2 | 4 | - | | - | - | - |
| 152 Field Regt. R.A. | - | 2 | 4 | - | | - | - | - |
| 155 Field Regt. R.A. | - | 2 | 2 | - | | - | - | - |
| 156 Field Regt. R.A. | - | 2 | 4 | - | | - | - | - |
| 49 Div. Arty. | 72 | - | - | - | | - | - | - |
| **NORTHERN COMMAND** | | | | | | | | |
| 54th Division | 12 | 6 | 12 | 4 | | 63 | 590 | 154 (a) |
| 66th Division | 12 | 6 | 12 | 2 | | 63 (b) | 590 | 47 (c) |
| One Inf. Bde. 59th Division | - | - | - | - | | - | - | - |

| | | | | | | | |
|---|---|---|---|---|---|---|---|
| 23 & 46 Div. Arty. | - | 6 | 20 | 4 | - | - | - |
| 2 Armoured Div. | - | 4 | 4 | 2 | - | - | - |
| 150 Field Regt. R.A. | - | 2 | 4 | - | - | - | - |
| 153 Field Regt. R.A. | - | 2 | 4 | - | - | - | - |
| 154 Field Regt. R.A. | - | 2 | 4 | - | - | - | - |

**EASTERN COMMAND**

| | | | | | | | |
|---|---|---|---|---|---|---|---|
| 18th Division | - | 4 | 8 | - | - | 407 | 47 (c) |
| 2nd London Division | - | 4 | 8 | 2 | 21 (a) | - | 47 (c) |
| 55th Division | 8 | 4 | 8 | 2 | - | - | 47 (c) |
| 147 Regt. R.M.A. | - | 18 | 4 | - | - | - | - |
| 20 Armoured Bde. | - | - | - | - | - | - | - |
| One Bty. 11th Regt. R.H.A. | 8 | - | - | - | - | - | - |
| 43rd Division | 48 (d) | - | - | 9 (d) | 90 | 590 | 307 |
| 15th Division | - | 6 | 12 | 4 | 63(e) | 590 | 47 (c) |
| 1st London Division | 11 | 4 | 8 | - | 21 (e) | - | 47 (c) |
| 45th Division | 12 | 6 | 12 | 6 | 63 (e) | 590 | 154 (b) |
| 12th Div. Arty. | - | 6 | 12 | - | - | - | - |

**SOUTHERN COMMAND**

| | | | | | | | |
|---|---|---|---|---|---|---|---|
| 52nd Division | 16 | - | - | 12 | 90 | 590 | 307 |
| 12th Field Regt. R.A. | 12 | - | - | 2 | - | - | - |
| 61st Division | - | 6 | 12 | 2 | 21 (e) | - | 47 (c) |
| 143 Field Regt. R.A. | 4 (f) | - | - | - | - | - | - |
| 144 Field Regt. R.A. | 4 (f) | - | - | - | - | - | - |

**ALDERSHOT COMMAND**

| | | | | | | | |
|---|---|---|---|---|---|---|---|
| 1st Canadian Division | 48 | - | - | 48 | 90 | 590 | 307 (d) |
| 11 Canadian Army Field Regt. | 4 (f) | - | - | - | - | - | - |
| 8 Canadian Army Field Regt. | 4 (f) | - | - | - | - | - | - |
| 58 A.T. Regt. (less 2 Btys.) | - | - | - | 24 | - | - | - |

**WESTERN COMMAND**

| | | | | | | | |
|---|---|---|---|---|---|---|---|
| 59th Division | - | 4 | 7 | - | 21 (e) | - | 47 (c) |
| 58th Division | - | 6 | 8 | 2 | - | - | 47 (c) |
| 149 Field Regt. R.A. | - | 2 | 4 | - | - | - | - |
| 137 Army Field Regt. R.A. | - | - | 4 | - | - | - | - |
| 66 A.T. Regt. R.A. | - | - | - | 2 | - | - | - |

## NOTES:

In course of completion to this scale.
In course of completion to this scale.

In course of completion to this scale. Weekly production understood to be 350.
In course of completion up to72x 25-pounders and 48 x 2-pounders.
Completion of Bren carriers to these scales expected within a month.
In course of completion to 24 x 25-pounders.

# Home Forces Operation Instructions Nos. 1 and 3, 5th and 15th June 1940

## G.H.Q. OPERATION INSTRUCTION No.1

### INFORMATION

1. **Enemy Invasion**

To achieve the greatest measure of surprise and the greatest concentration of force, the enemy is likely to use the shortest sea and air route for seaborne and airborne invasion of this country; but the possibility of diversionary or subsidiary operations in the Shetlands, Ireland or North of Scotland cannot be disregarded. It is probable that the enemy will be prepared to accept very heavy losses.

2. Simultaneous attacks at numerous widely dispersed points are probable. At or near each point of attack the enemy is likely to make use of parachutists both to capture landing grounds for the use of troop-carrying aircraft and to disorganize our communications; to take air action by bombers (protected by fighters) against aerodromes, troops, Headquarters and communications; to use Fifth Column to create confusion; and to land seaborne forces including a large number of A.F.V's in the first flights.

3. A seaborne expedition could be transported in surface warships, submarines, transports or flat bottom barges of which there may be a large number capable of carrying 200-300 men below deck. A.F.V's might be carried by ordinary transports relying on port facilities for unloading, by special transports self-contained as regards unloading, by special landing craft and possibly by surface warships.

4. **Probable Area of Attack**

The most favourable area of attack for the enemy is the area in which his fighters and bombers can operate in conjunction and a seaborne expedition can cross from the continent during the hours of darkness.

This area extends from the Wash to Newhaven and may grow to the westward according to his progress in France. A.F.V's can be landed by ordinary transports at a port or by special transports or special landing craft on any open beach from the Wash to Newhaven in fine weather. There are other beaches and ports available to the north of this area, which may be selected, but they would involve a longer sea voyage and would lie outside the area of his maximum air effort.

5. **Probable time of Attack**

It is impossible to forecast the time of attack with certainty, but owing to the comparative inability of fighter aircraft to intercept at night, it seems probable that the enemy will attack at night or at early dawn; and for navigational reasons it is likely that he will attack at high tide.

6. **Warning of Attack**

(a) Coastal Command is carrying out daily dawn and dusk reconnaissances to locate enemy seaborne forces leaving the German, Dutch or Belgian Coasts for the English coast. These reconnaissances should, in clear weather, enable an invading force attacking north of SPURN HEAD to be detected.

(b) Long range reconnaissance is also carried out by submarines. Off-shore reconnaissance is carried out by minesweepers and by as many small craft as can be made available.

7. **Attack on Enemy as he Approaches**

As soon as an enemy force is discovered to be approaching it will be attacked by the Navy and Air Force.

INTENTION

8. To destroy any enemy troops landed in the United Kingdom.

METHOD

9. **Allotment of Troops**

All troops in commands will be under command G.Os. C.-in-C. Commands, with the following exceptions: (a) G.H.Q. Reserve – HQ 4 Corps, 43 Div.; (b) Troops specially earmarked by the War Office.

10. **Role of 4 Corps**

4 Corps will arrange for the reconnaissance of routes to Home Counties, East Anglia, Humber and Lancashire areas. 4 Corps is likely to be employed by Inf. Bde. groups or exceptionally as a Corps. The movement of troops by air will be practised and reconnaissance of aerodromes arranged. The movement of troops by road by day and night will also be practised.

## 11. General Policy for Defence

The general policy governing the defence of the United Kingdom is that there will be no withdrawal and that, should the enemy gain a foothold anywhere, he will be driven out again as quickly as possible. Therefore, demolitions and blocks on communications should be designed to prevent or delay the extension of such a foot-hold without prejudicing offensive operations.

## 12. Demolitions

(a) Bridges both road and rail providing access to and egress from certain specified ports will be prepared for demolition, but the charges on bridges of main communications will NOT be laid.

(b) The destruction of swing or lifting bridges is unnecessary as they can be rendered useless by putting them in the open position and removing a vital part of the mechanism.

(c) All preparations for the demolition of bridges will be made in consultation with the Divisional Road or Railway Engineer concerned and any charges laid will be placed under a guard.

## 13. Construction of Defences

Defences wherever possible will be of concrete construction and provided with overhead cover. All defences will be wired with a fence at least 40 yards from the defended points and if possible another at 60 yards to prevent approach of flame throwers.

## 14. Road Blocks

Road blocks will be constructed only in consultation with the Civil Road Authorities. They will be double blocks and the lateral gap must not be less than 11 ft. 6 inches. The distance between the two blocks must not be less than 50 ft. Commands will submit schemes to G.H.Q. for co-ordination.

## 15. Obstruction of Possible Landing Grounds

The Air Ministry are responsible for the destruction or obstruction of all landing grounds not required by the R.A.F. and all spaces fit for landing within a five mile radius of landing grounds required by the R.A.F. Commands are responsible for the obstruction of all other possible landing grounds: (a) Within a five mile radius of certain specified ports; (b) Within the Metropolitan Area of London; (c) Within five miles of practicable beach landing places; (d) (a) (b) and (c) to include main roads which have a straight run of 600 yards and 90 ft. in width; (e) The general method of immobilizing possible landing grounds will be by trenches dug on a chequer board pattern with 150 yards sides. Crops will NOT be disturbed; (f) Roads within the above areas should be blocked by wire ropes suspended 20 ft. from the ground at 300 yard intervals. Under no circumstances will the obstruction interfere with road traffic. Concrete blocks or pillars down the centre of the road are on no account to be erected. They may, however, be placed on alternate edges of the road at 150 yd. intervals.

16. **Beach Defences**

(a) Beaches selected for defence will be protected with wire above high water mark and defended by L.M.G's in pill boxes. Anti-tank obstacles such as concrete blocks will be constructed.

(b) Exits from the beach will be mined with A.Tk. Mines and protected by pill boxes.

(c) Certain selected beaches where egress from the beach is unobstructed will be mined above high water mark.

(d) The position of all mines will be accurately charted with a view to their subsequent recovery.

17. **Action of Troops on receipt of Code Word**

On receipt of Code word "CROMWELL" troops will take up battle stations, telegraph lines essential for operational purposes will be taken over and all liaison officers will take up their duties.

18. **Action of Troops on Attack Taking Place**

(a) Troops (including Local Defence Volunteers) in the area of a seaborne or airborne landing will inflict the maximum number of casualties on the enemy while he is landing.

(b) Should the enemy succeed in landing, the area held by him will be piquetted by a cordon of such troops as can be made quickly available to give time for stronger forces to concentrate and attack the enemy. Commands will organize small mobile columns ready to move quickly to the area where landings have been effected. The tasks of Local Defence Volunteers will be to hold their observation posts, in certain cases to man road blocks, to prevent the enemy from debouching from the area, and to send information of any movement to the nearest military commander. Certain A.A. mobile detachments come under command of G.Os C.-in-C. Commands as soon as Operations against parachutists commence.

(c) Subsequently larger formations will be moved by Commands as necessary to attack the enemy.

(d) Finally G.H.Q. reserve will be employed as necessary either remaining under command of G.H.Q. or a part or the whole being decentralized to Commands.

19. **A.A. Protection**

A.A. Regiments or Brigades, if available, will be placed under command Eastern and Northern Commands from the time they reach RV arranged between A.A. Command and Command concerned.

20. **R.A.F.**

(a) Bombers. Two bomber squadrons No.2 Bomber Group R.A.F. (H.Q. CASTLE HILL HOUSE, HUNTINGDON) will be under command G.H.Q. and will be allotted as necessary.

(b) A.C. Following A.C. Squadrons will be under command of Commands:

| | |
|---|---|
| Eastern Command | 2 and 26 A.C. Sqns. |
| Northern Command | 4 A.C. Sqn. |
| Western Command | 13 A.C. Sqn. |
| Scottish Command | 614 A.C. Sqn. |

Inter-communication to be arranged direct between Commands and squadrons. Squadrons remain under 22 Group R.A.F. for administration. A.C. arrangements for Northern Ireland District will be made later.

21. **Administrative Instructions**

To be issued later.

22. **Intercommunication**

(a) Reports. Observer Corps are reporting parachute descents through the normal channels.

(b) A.A. Divs. are giving Commands information by direct line, and lower formations and units can make arrangements to obtain information direct from A.A. formations, units or sub-units.

23. (a) Civil communications will be used to supplement military signal resources.

(b) Wireless. No restriction beyond normal signal security is placed on the use of mobile wireless sets for training or operational purposes. Stations of the Home Defence wireless organisation are limited to 5 minutes transmission in any half hour. In the event of complete breakdown of the telephone and telegraphic means of communication during active operations transmission will not be so restricted but will be limited to urgent operational and intelligence messages.

(c) Line. In the event of partial breakdown of the telegraph or telephone service special attention must be paid to the restriction of traffic. Lines must be kept clear for really urgent messages.

24. H.Q's._(a) Alternative sites will be prepared by all H.Q's. (b) All H.Q's will be prepared for all round defence and garrisons will be detailed.

*B. Paget, Lt.-Gen., C.G.S.*

## G.H.Q. OPERATION INSTRUCTION No.3

## G.H.Q. POLICY FOR HOME DEFENCE

### OBJECT
1. To defeat the enemy landing or when landed in the British Isles.

### FACTORS
2. <u>Naval and Air Protection</u>. With the present Naval and Air Forces at our disposal, immunity from invasion cannot be guaranteed. But once the enemy has committed himself, naval and air forces should be able seriously to interrupt his lines of communications.

The role of the Royal Navy is to obtain information of the approach of a seaborne expedition by means of submarine and surface patrols and when the expedition is located, to attack with all forces available. If the initial expedition is successful the role is to prevent the arrival of reinforcements.

The principal roles of the R.A.F. in the prevention of invasion are the defence of vital areas against attacks by air, reconnaissance to obtain earliest information of assembly and dispatch of invading forces, and thirdly co-operation in the attack of convoys and surface craft as they approach the British coast and of any enemy forces establishing themselves in the country.

3. <u>The Scale and Nature of an Enemy Attack</u>. To achieve the greatest measure of surprise and the greatest concentration of force, the enemy is likely to use the shortest sea and air route for his main effort of seaborne and airborne invasion of this country. But the possibility of diversionary or subsidiary operations in the Shetlands, Ireland or the North of Scotland cannot be disregarded. It may be accepted that the enemy will be prepared to accept very heavy losses.

A seaborne expedition could be transported in motor boats, motor landing craft, warships, submarines, transports and flat-bottomed barges, of which there are reported to be a large number capable of carrying 200-300 men below deck. A.F.V's might be carried by ordinary transports relying on port facilities for unloading, by special transports self-contained as regards unloading, by special landing craft and by air. Simultaneous attacks at numerous widely-scattered points are probable. These points are likely to include ports, the capture of which would facilitate the rapid disembarkation of A.F.V's transport and troops, since speed is an essential factor in his plan. At or near each point of attack the enemy is likely to make use of parachute troops,

Above: The German Blitzkrieg underway. A German self-propelled gun is pictured on the move through Cambrai during the invasion of France and the Low Countries in 1940. According to the original album the image was taken from, the unit is Panzerjäger SFL Pz.Jg. I. (Historic Military Press)

Below: Throughout 1940 and 1941 building of anti-invasion defences continued apace throughout the UK. 'Concrete barriers are ready on the roads, blockhouses have been built, barbed wire barricades are waiting' notes the original caption to this picture, dated 22 August 1940, of a soldier on duty by a pillbox. (Historic Military Press)

Above: A camouflaged defensive position constructed in the north wall of Pevensey Castle, East Sussex, during the Second World War. One report states: 'At the time of the construction of the defence works in the walls of Pevensey Castle, from late July 1940 through August and September, the infantry regiment at Pevensey had been the 4th Bn. Duke of Cornwall's Light Infantry, and the commander of this battalion, Lt. Col. Harrowing, appears to have been responsible for the siting of the machine gun emplacements, and for organising the strengthening of various of the dungeons and towers of the medieval castle to serve as headquarters buildings. This work was carried out by 562nd Field Company Royal Engineers.' (Historic Military Press)

Above: Soldiers from the Royal Scots lay barbed wire defences during the summer of 1940. (Historic Military Press)

Above: The British Army on exercise during 1940. Here we can see a Morris Commercial CDSW 6x4 Field Artillery Tractor towing an 18/25-pounder on a Mk.1 Carriage. The sheer scale of the losses of both men and equipment during the fall of France and the subsequent evacuation from Dunkirk meant that, in the summer of 1940, the British Army was frequently lacking in artillery pieces such as these. (Historic Military Press)

Below: Members of the Home Guard manning an improvised road block in the summer of 1940. (Historic Military Press)

Above: Throughout the summer of 1940, the British Army watched and waited for any sign of the invasion. (Historic Military Press)

Below: A picture of the flame barrage demonstration held in (or on) the waters of Studland Bay, Dorset, on 1 February 1941. As the patches of oil on the surface of the sea merge into one another to form a continuous strip, the strip is ignited at several points, and the oil begins to burn.(Historic Military Press)

Above: Members of the 1st Northumberland (Berwick) Battalion, Home Guard, the so-called 'Fishermen's Home Guard', take 'a well-warned rest during a Sunday morning's manoeuvres on their island home', 30 June 1942. A handwritten note on the rear states the image was taken at Lindisfarne. Second from the left is Corporal John Tough, a fisherman by profession. (Historic Military Press)

Left: A member of the RAF Regiment at a machine-gun post, part of the defences of an un-named airfield in the UK. (US Library of Congress)

Above: Personnel of the Auxiliary Territorial Service at a heavy anti-aircraft gun site in the UK, February 1943. Note the winter clothing they are wearing. (US Library of Congress)

Below: A photograph of Spitfires of 65 Squadron at RAF Westhampnett between October and December 1941. (Mark Hillier Collection)

Above: RAF personnel raise a balloon barrage during the Second World War. Barrage balloon units played an important part in the UK's defence against German aircraft and then, later in the war, the flying bomb menace. (Historic Military Press)

Above: The scene in the Aldwych, London, caused by the explosion of a V-1 flying bomb, March 1944. (Historic Military Press)

Left: The moment that a German V-2 rocket is test-fired. The first test launch of a V-2 occurred on 13 June 1942. The first V-2 strike against the UK took place on 8 September 1944. (Historic Military Press)

Below: Evidence of Britain's wartime defences can be seen throughout the country. This pillbox, for example, is located in High Wood near Christ's Hospital, Horsham, in West Sussex. (Historic Military Press)

both to capture landing grounds for the use of troop-carrying aircraft, and to disorganise our communications. He will most probably precede any landing by very intensive air action by bombers protected by fighters, against our aerodromes, troops, headquarters and communications. The possible scale of airborne invasion is ten to fifteen thousand men landed in one day in the South Eastern Counties, provided that the enemy can gain temporary local air superiority. In addition, he will rely on such elements of the Fifth Column as exist in this country to create confusion.

There is no reason to suppose that his tactics on land to be employed against the United Kingdom will differ materially from those he is now using in France, and therefore we must expect him to push on widely scattered columns without consideration of support or protection of flanks. This method of attack should therefore allow us, if properly equipped and organised, to deal with these columns in detail. It can be assumed that, whereas the enemy will land on open beaches a considerable number of A.F.V's capable of operating as units at once, it is unlikely that he can land sufficient transport to make his infantry and guns adequately mobile, until he succeeds in capturing a port with sufficient off-loading facilities. It therefore follows that, generally speaking, the larger threat to be countered is that from enemy A.F.V's.

4. <u>Probable Area of Attack</u>. The most favourable area of attack for the enemy is that in which his fighters and bombers can operate and to which a seaborne expedition can cross from the Continent during the hours of darkness. This area at present extends from the Wash to Newhaven, and may grow to the West, according to his progress in France. At a later date, however, the possibility of attack from Ireland on the West Coast of England and Wales may have to be considered. Taking the more immediate threat only into consideration, protection in order of priority is from the Wash to Newhaven, from the Wash to Newcastle-upon-Tyne and from Newhaven towards Land's End. It is considered that an attack on Scotland would be outside the protection which can be afforded by his Air Force and, as it is in close proximity to our naval bases, such an attack would be intended only as a diversion, designed primarily to draw off the British Naval forces from the area of his main effort, to one in which enemy submarines can operate in force.

5. <u>Beaches</u>. Reconnaissance reports shew that the coastline from Newcastle-upon-Tyne down the East Coast and South Coast contains a very great number of beaches suitable for the landing of both troops and A.F.V's and a strong defence of all of them is impracticable. We must therefore accept the possibility of the enemy being able to land in certain selected spots unopposed.

6. <u>Fixed Defences</u>. We already have a number of Fixed Defences which will act as deterrents and so limit the number of beaches on which the enemy can land unopposed. But such Fixed Defences must be adequately guarded by other troops, if they are not to be quickly overwhelmed by land attack.

7. <u>Ports</u>. There are many ports capable of affording the enemy sufficient harbour facilities from which to land comparatively large columns.

8. <u>Roads</u>. As in France, a large majority of the main roads converge on the main towns. There are few main roads running parallel to one another. It is understood that in France the leading elements of A.F.V's nearly always kept to the roads. Provided, therefore, we manage to hold the focal points where roads converge, we shall go a long way to limit enemy concerted action.

9. <u>Air Fields</u>. Generally speaking, there are a very large number of places, both near to and at a distance from the coast, on which the enemy may be able to land troop-carrying aircraft. Furthermore, it is understood that the enemy has been trying to develop gliders which can pancake in a very small place. This latter form of attack may not at present assume large proportions, but it is a factor which it would be well not to ignore. Account must also be taken of the possibility of the enemy landing aircraft on inland stretches of water including reservoirs. The best method of dealing with enemy parachutists and troops landed from aircraft is by immediate offensive action to prevent assembly and the execution of the enemy's pre-conceived plan.

## ENEMY OBJECTIVES

10. The enemy's undoubted object is to defeat the United Kingdom and thereby to destroy the British Empire. His main objectives will be the Centre of Government in London and the Centres of Production and Supply, coupled with mining off the coasts and heavy air attack on overseas supplies approaching the United Kingdom. Thus, it is necessary to ensure protection for London, the industrial areas of the Midlands and North, and the main ports for supplies.

## CONCLUSIONS

11. The fact that the initiative rests with the enemy, imposes on us a strategical defensive, but it is necessary to emphasize the difference between an active and a passive defence. The first object is to prevent or limit an enemy landing by Sea or Air, and the capture of any port or area which will facilitate the development of the invasion.

The second object is, by means of offensive mobile columns, to deal swiftly and adequately with the enemy's widely scattered forces before these have established themselves, and to prevent their reinforcement.

The third object is to prevent the enemy from interrupting or destroying vital resources of the country.

## COMMAND AND PLAN OF DEFENCE

12. *Command*.
(a)  Command is exercised by the Commander-in-Chief Home Forces acting through Staff Officers of the Navy, Army, Air Force and Civil Services.
(b)  *Navy*. The requirements of the Commander-in-Chief will be conveyed by his Naval Staff Officer to the Vice Chief of the Naval Staff.
(c)  *Army*.
(i)  For the purpose of repelling invasion all troops including L.D.V's but less A.A. Command (except as in paragraph 3(b) below) are under command or operational control of the Commander-in-Chief, Home Forces. Immediate action will be taken by the nearest formation to repel the invader and General Officers Commanding-in-Chief of the Commands concerned are responsible for the conduct of the battle in their Command areas.
(ii)  G.H.Q. Reserve. The Commander-in-Chief may place formations of the G.H.Q. reserve under command of General Officers Commanding-in-Chief Commands, or may retain command of these formations although they are working in Command areas.
(iii)  Units of the A.A. Command and Balloon Command are co-operating with Home Forces in the measures taken for ground defence. Local military commanders belonging to Home Forces are responsible for co-ordinating these ground defence schemes, but they will not issue orders to units of the A.A. or Balloon Commands unless and until enemy action necessitates some units of these Commands undertaking ground defence, when they will come under the operational control of the local military Commander.
(d)  *Air Force*
(i)  The requirements of the Commander-in-Chief will be conveyed by his Air Staff Officer to the Deputy Chief of the Air Staff.
(ii)  The Commander-in-Chief, Home Forces exercises direct executive control of certain Bomber Squadrons, and of certain A.C. Squadrons. Operational control of some of these A.C. Squadrons has been decentralized to Commands.
(e)  *Civil*. The requirements of the Commander-in-Chief will be conveyed by the Chief Civil Staff Officer to the Civil Ministries concerned.

(f)   *Regional Commissioners.*

(i)   <u>Normal Conditions</u> The Regional Commissioners work direct to the Minister of Home Security. Their functions are mainly of a co-ordinating nature, though they have a direct responsibility for the efficiency of Civil Defence arrangements in their area. They have attached to them in a consultative capacity local representatives of Government Departments. These representatives work direct, however, to their own Ministries.

In regard to police and fire, the Regional Commissioner has certain operational responsibilities for the movement of reinforcements. At his Headquarters he has a Regional Police Staff Officer and a Regional Fire Inspector to operate their respective services. Hospital arrangements are dealt with centrally by the Ministry of Health through their Regional Hospital Officer, the Regional Commissioner having no direct responsibility.

Local controllers of scheme making authorities, i.e. County Councils, County Borough Councils and certain specified non-county boroughs are under the operational control of the Regional Commissioner. Counties are split up into a number of areas, each having sub-controllers, but these work direct to County Council main control.

At the Ministry of Home Security there is a Chief of Staff for Operations, who works direct with Regional Commissioners for this purpose, and is directly responsible to the Minister.

In all other matters, administration, finance, etc., Regional Commissioners deal with the administrative side, the head of which has also responsibility for the co-ordination of the various Government Departments concerned in civil defence. Regional Commissioners have very limited financial powers.

(ii)  <u>In state of acute emergency</u>. Against the contingency in which communications have broken down, or a state of acute emergency has arisen, the Minister has conferred on Regional Commissioners a suspended authority of a kind which would normally only be exercised by a Minister of the Crown. Such powers can be of the widest possible character, and would, in effect, give the Regional Commissioner more or less complete power in so far as the exercise of Civil Defence and Civil Government in his Region are concerned. The representatives of other Government Departments have conferred certain powers on their local representatives, and they will in general be responsible to the Regional Commissioner.

In certain cases of Central Government Services, which it is impossible in any case to control effectively on a local basis, the

Regional Commissioner cannot act without reference to some Central Authority. As an example, diversion of shipping from one port to another cannot be ordered by a Regional Commissioner. The Regional Commissioner has in no circumstances any authority over any of the Armed Forces of the Crown. The main difference between a case of acute emergency and that of ordinary circumstances is that in the former the Regional Commissioner assumes administrative and financial in addition to operational control; and in the latter, he has operational control but only general co-ordinating functions as regards general administration.

(iii) Commands will in both cases convey their requirements to the civil population or to civil organizations through the Regional Commissioners.

## PLAN OF DEFENCE

13. The general plan of defence is a combination of mobile columns and static defence by means of strong points and "stops". As static defence only provides limited protection of the most vulnerable points, it must be supplemented by the action of mobile columns. However mobile such columns may be they cannot be expected to operate immediately over the whole area in which it is possible for the enemy to attempt invasion by sea or air. It is, therefore, necessary to adopt measures for confining his action until such time as mobile columns can arrive to deal with him. This will be done by means of "stops" and strong points prepared for all round defence at aerodromes which are necessary to prevent the enemy obtaining air superiority, at the main centres of communication, and distributed in depth over a wide area covering London and the centres of production and supply. This system of "stops" and strong points will prevent the enemy from running riot and tearing the guts out of the country as has happened in France and Belgium.

14. *Coastal Area.* This should be regarded as an outpost zone, to give warning of, to delay and break up the initial attack. Attempts to approach the Ports and Beaches in transports, and the disembarkation therefrom, will be hampered by the Fixed Defences, but these defences will require to be supplemented by other defence weapons, such as lighter artillery, small arms, mines etc. for their local protection.

Since our resources will not permit the occupation of defensive positions to cover all possible landing beaches with fire, the defence of the latter will be confined to those which lend themselves to a landing in force with A.F.V's, particularly those which give access to important ports, or objectives inland.

These beach defences will be reinforced by strong points in rear, designed primarily to hold up enemy A.F.V's, and giving facilities for all round defence. Similarly, ports will be protected by all round defence.

The principle must be to obtain early information and to hold mobile Reserves ready to move to the threatened points and to attack the enemy.

15. *Ports*. Specified ports will be made capable of all round defence as laid down in G.H.Q. Operation Instruction No. 2 dated 11th June.

16. *Beaches*. Defence of selected beaches will be organised by the construction of self-contained strong points at the 6" Naval guns mounted at various points on the foreshore and portions of the beach which may be considered especially vulnerable, particularly from the point of view of tank exits. The 6" Naval guns are mounted in sites selected in accordance with the requirements of the Royal Navy, and their task is to deal with transports which are attempting to land troops. The gun detachments are not capable of local defence without interference with their main role.

The task of these strong points will be to stop the enemy's A.F.V's and other troops at all costs and from them there must be no withdrawal.

In those strong points, which cover particularly suitable tank exits, it may be desirable to include one or more of the improvised static anti-tank guns (6 pdr. or 4") but the dissipation of a too great proportion of the limited number of guns in isolated points will result in a dangerous weakness in the main defensive system.

The necessary defence against tanks may be provided by anti-tank mines which, to be fully effective, must always be under the fire of the defence.

The remainder of the beaches will be covered by patrolling. Greatest attention will be paid to obtaining early information bicycle and motor bicycle patrols being especially useful for this purpose.

The provision of wire is necessary for all strong points. If Dannert wire is used on tank stops it should be loosely fixed in ten or more belts.

17. *Inland Area*. The inland area will be divided into zones consisting of a series of "stops", culminating in a zone selected to cover London and important industrial centres. This zone will be selected by G.H.Q. Although it may not at the present time be possible to garrison all "stops" they should all be prepared immediately and provided with necessary defensive weapons such as anti-tank obstacles, pill boxes, wire, static anti-tank guns and, where suitable, mines. The major proportion of the limited number of static anti-tank weapons at present available will be sited in

these "stops", the remainder being used for beach defence. Guns with sufficient mobility will be included in mobile columns. A.A. defence will also be fitted into the general framework of the zones and its use against A.F.V's as a secondary role will be considered.

18. *G.H.Q. Reserve.* A G.H.Q. Reserve will be formed, probably consisting in the first instance of one Armoured Division, less "I" tanks, one Bn. R.T.R. and two Infantry Divisions. One portion of this Reserve will be located North of the Thames and one portion South of the Thames. It will be made as mobile as possible and will not be used for static defence.

19. *G.H.Q. Zone of "Stops".* The normal principles in F.S.R. apply but the long frontages and the shortage of artillery necessitate certain modifications in the application of the principles until these difficulties have been met.

20. *Stops.* "Stops" fall into two categories:

(a) A waterway or other efficient tank obstacle, such as steep hills. These portions must under the present circumstances be lightly held in order to provide sufficient troops, especially artillery, for the remainder. It is essential that the fullest use of waterways should be made. In order to make efficient demolition belts, successive lines of bridge demolitions, and cratering of important road junctions are essential. Waterways at right angles to the general line of the front are of great value as they hinder lateral movement of the attack; they will always be included in the demolition scheme.

(b) In the remainder of the zone where no natural tank obstacle exists, static defence will be provided by the construction of "stops" distributed in great depth covered by an artificial tank obstacle (ditches and mines) and concrete pill boxes, utilising the improvised anti-tank guns as well as those available in the formations. It cannot be too strongly emphasised that great depth in the anti-tank defence is of primary importance. The determined advance of a few tanks deep into the position is intended to create alarm and confusion; the effect of such penetration can be prevented by a resolute defence to avoid any widening of the gap.

21. *Inundations.* In view of the fact that the defence is based on mobile columns, the use of inundations must be very carefully controlled. The completion of an inundation is generally a matter of a week or more and is dependent on the weather and possibly the tides. No inundations will be initiated without reference to G.H.Q.

22. *Canals as Tank Obstacles.* Canals in England are seldom part of the main drainage of the country. The retention of water in the canals is

therefore entirely dependent on the maintenance of lock gates. Lock gates will always form a possible crossing place for infantry and if the retention of the canal line as an obstacle is considered necessary, the local defence of the locks must be undertaken.

23. *Vulnerable Points.* A list of vulnerable points including aerodromes which have to be guarded is in possession of G.Os C.-in-C. Commands. No deletion from this list will be made without reference to G.H.Q. and no additions will be made without the authority of G.Os. C.-in-C. Commands. The bulk of the garrisons for these V.Ps. is found by Holding Battalions and it is hoped in the near future to find the balance from similar units, thus setting free all troops of the Field Force. An instruction dealing with the responsibilities of the various units allotted to the defence of aerodromes will be issued shortly.

24. *Local Defence Volunteers.* The guards for other V.Ps. not included in the list referred to above and of a lower category will be found by L.D.Vs. The personnel for these guards will be found by the Ministries, Authorities and Undertakings concerned and will be armed and equipped under G.H.Q. arrangements.The other duties performed by L.D.Vs include:

(a) Provision of observation posts in conjunction with A.A. defence for the purpose of detecting and dealing with enemy parachutists in the immediate vicinity of their posts.

(b) Manning of road blocks under the orders of military Commanders.

(c) Keeping a check on the activities of possible Fifth Columnists in their neighbourhood.

The action of L.D.Vs will be co-ordinated throughout by the local Military Commander in whose area they are operating.

25. *A.A. Defences.* In addition to their primary role of defence against aircraft, the organization of the A.A. defensive system provides valuable assistance to the general scheme.

There is a belt 40 miles wide running from Edinburgh, along the East Coast to Portland in which are distributed Searchlights every 6,000 yards or less and many gun positions. There are telephone communications everywhere as far as sections, and in certain areas down to individual lights. These telephones are connected through Companies to R.A.F. Section A Operation Rooms and should be invaluable sources of information.

Each Searchlight detachment is equipped with a Lewis Gun and rifles. At every Company Headquarters, the relief section is organised into a mobile column with rifles and Lewis guns, ready to proceed at once to any threatened point. All A.A. personnel have been ordered, if they see parachutists (a) to inform the nearest higher authority at once, (b) to send back a messenger at once when they are located, (c) to engage them and to place themselves under the local Infantry Commander as soon as he arrives and to ask his permission to withdraw back to their Searchlights as soon as he can spare them.

Should Searchlight positions be over-run they will place themselves under the nearest body of troops.

Similarly an anti-parachute party is being organised in every gun position.

26. *Balloon Command*. The Balloon Command which provides a static defence against enemy aircraft has a strength of 40,000 men of which 9,000 are armed. The personnel are trained in the use of arms and being located round the most important industrial areas can give valuable assistance in their local defence. Liaison between them, the Observer Corps and L.D.V. is established.

## COMMUNICATIONS

27. *Roads*. Road communications are required for: (a) Military operational traffic. (b) Essential civil service of food supply. (c) Production of war material. (d) Refugees from areas in which active operations are impending or in progress. Maps shewing Roads allocated for these purposes have been issued.

The destruction or restriction of road communications will form an essential part of the defence. A co-ordinated scheme is necessary to balance the conflicting requirements of movement and restriction of movement. If it is found that a bridge on an essential road is considered a necessary tank stop, the obstacle must be made by artillery defence and not by demolition.

In all areas, schemes for blocking roads and demolishing bridges, where necessary, will be prepared forthwith.

In specially vulnerable areas specified by G.H.Q., such as certain ports, selected aerodromes, etc. preparations which involve a certain measure of restriction of traffic may be carried out, but no demolitions will be executed without written orders from Command Headquarters, or under the immediate threat of capture by the enemy. In all other areas, only such preparations will be made as do not interfere with traffic.

28. *Railways*. The maintenance of the Railway System is essential to the economic life of the country. Its use by an invading force will be denied by the removal of rolling stock.

No railway bridges, tunnels or ancillary services will be destroyed except where a railway bridge affords an effective crossing of a waterway selected as an A.F.V. "stop". Railway repair material will not be removed for other purposes.

In cases where the destruction of a railway bridge is considered necessary, all preparations will be made which do not interfere with traffic but no demolitions will be carried out except on the receipt of a written order from G.H.Q., or under the immediate threat of capture by the enemy.

29. *Cable.* The main system of Army Signals is based on the use of the cables provided by the G.P.O. and is used for telephony and telegraphy by teleprinter. A system of large switching centres connected on a grid is the basis of both systems and when completed will provide means of obtaining communications through several channels and will thus reduce the possibilities of breakdown due to enemy action.

30. *Wireless.* Wireless stations give communication between G.H.Q., the various Command H.Q., the Regional Commissioners and certain Area H.Q. The wireless system is carried to lower formations by the use of the field wireless sets in Signal units.

31. *Command Broadcasting Arrangements.* Another wireless system is in being by which information of enemy invasion reported to any Service is transmitted to Command H.Q., which can broadcast the information by wireless over an area of a radius of 100 miles. Formation H.Qs. and battalion H.Q. are provided with listening sets to receive the information. Special arrangements are made to assure listeners that the messages are official and not bogus.

32. *Liaison Officers: Despatch Riders.* A service of liaison officers and contact officers will be maintained by all formations.

## MISCELLANEOUS

33. *Evacuation.* The general policy is to prevent indiscriminate evacuation, though the controlled evacuation of women and children is in progress. In addition, at certain selected ports considered especially vulnerable, a 60% evacuation may possibly be undertaken, though it is likely to be ineffective as it is voluntary. There will be a residual population even in areas where active operations are in progress and in such event it is hoped that they will remain.

34. *Public Utility Services.* These include water supply, electric light and power and gas undertakings.

The "nuisance" value to a hostile force, achieved by a destruction of these facilities, is negligible compared with the hardships which would be imposed on our own people. No provision will therefore be made to demolish or destroy these undertakings.

Purely local demolition schemes, such as for example putting out of action electrically operated cranes and machinery in a port will however be prepared for execution should the necessity arise.

The responsibility for the immobilisation of ports has already been laid down.

35. *Local Resources.* These include food in depots, retailers' stocks and live-stock, oil and petrol both in bulk and retail and possibly supplies of defence stores.

Owing to the possibility of hostile attacks on our overseas supplies, it is a matter of the greatest importance to maintain stocks of all imported stocks at the highest possible level. The residual population in any area of operations will need food; it must therefore be accepted that complete destruction in such areas is not feasible even though the enemy will also make use of it. Large quantities of food have, however, been removed from vulnerable areas by the Ministry of Food. Specially valuable and surplus livestock will be removed, but a complete disruption of the food distribution organization and the farming industry would produce greater damage to ourselves than to the enemy. Bulk oil and petrol stores will be destroyed, if necessary, under arrangements made by the Petroleum Board. The policy to be followed in this connection has been issued separately to Commands and the Civil Government Departments concerned.

Retail petrol stocks are being reduced to the minimum in the especially vulnerable areas. Defence preparations will include schemes for the destruction of the remaining stock, if and when it is clear that they are about to fall into the enemy's hands. Experience of the last war and the present one has clearly proved that any quick removal or destruction of engineer defence stores is not feasible. The accumulation of large stocks is unnecessary owing to the quick delivery possible, and is therefore forbidden.

## CONCLUSION

36. Finally it must be emphasized that the defeat of the enemy, should he succeed in landing in the British Isles, will depend on a carefully co-ordinated scheme of defence, making full use of the many resources available, backed up by the most energetic action on the part of mobile columns and resolute determination on the part of the troops allotted to static defence.

*A. I. Macdougall, D.C.G.S., for Lt.-Gen., C.G.S.*

Appendix VII

# Chiefs of Staff Review of the Prospects of Invasion After the Fall of France

The object of this paper is to investigate the means whereby we could continue to fight single-handed if French resistance were to collapse completely, involving the loss of a substantial proportion of the British Expeditionary Force, and the French Government were to make terms with Germany. The assumptions we have made are contained in Appendix A of the Annex. Of these the two most important are that:

(i) United States of America is willing to give us full economic and financial support, without which we do not think we could continue the war with any chance of success.

(ii) Italy has intervened against us.

2. In particular we have asked ourselves two questions: (a) Could the United Kingdom hold out until assistance from the Empire and America made itself felt? And (b) Could we ultimately bring sufficient economic pressure to bear on Germany to ensure her defeat?

We summarise our conclusions and recommendations below. As regards the latter there are a large number of measures which we consider should be carried out at once irrespective of whether a French collapse is or is not likely.

## CONCLUSIONS

3. There are three ways in which Germany might break down the resistance of the United Kingdom – unrestricted air attack aimed at breaking public morale, starvation of the country by attack on shipping and ports, and occupation by invasion.

*Air Factor*

4. The vital fact is that our ability to avoid defeat will depend on three factors:

(a) Whether the morale of our people will withstand the strain of air bombardment;

(b) Whether it will be possible to import the absolute essential of commodities necessary to sustain life and to keep our war industries in action;

(c) Our capacity to resist invasion.

All of these depend primarily on whether our fighter defences will be able to reduce the scale of attack to reasonable bounds. This will necessarily mean the replacement of casualties in personnel and aircraft on a substantial scale. Our capacity to resist invasion may, however, depend also to a great extent on the maintenance of an effective air striking force.

These factors cannot be assessed with certainty, and it is impossible to say whether or not the United Kingdom could hold out in all circumstances. We think there are good grounds for the belief that the British people will endure the greatest strain, if they realise – as they are beginning to do – that the existence of the Empire is at stake. We must concentrate our energies primarily on the production of fighter aircraft and crews, and the defence of those factories essential to fighter production should have priority. At the same time it is clear that we cannot afford to neglect our bomber force or to expend it on operations that are not of first importance.

*Civil Defence*

5. As long as the present quasi-peacetime organisation continues, it is unlikely that this country can hold out.

The present Home Security Organisation was constituted to deal with air attack only by aircraft operating from bases in Germany; it is not sufficient to grapple with the problems which would arise as a result of a combination of heavy air attack from bases on a semi-circle from Trondheim to Brest, invasion, and internal attack by the "Fifth Column."

*Land Forces*

6. Germany has ample forces to invade and occupy this country. Should the enemy succeed in establishing a force, with its vehicles, firmly ashore – the Army in the United Kingdom, which is very short of equipment, has not got the offensive power to drive it out.

*Naval Forces*

7. Our first naval task is to secure the United Kingdom and its seaborne supplies against naval attack. We have sufficient Naval forces to deal with those that the enemy can bring against us in Home Waters, and we can provide naval security for our seaborne supplies. Our ability to

defeat at sea a seaborne attack on this country is dependent on the extent to which our Naval forces can operate in the face of heavy air attack on both ships and bases, and it is of the greatest importance to strengthen our systems of intelligence and reconnaissance to ensure early and accurate warning of enemy intentions is obtained.

*Seaborne Supplies*

8. We have adequate shipping to meet our requirements, but again the provision of air security is the main problem. We may have to abandon our ports on the South and East Coasts for trade purposes, and our ability to carry on the war will then depend on West Coast ports entirely. These, therefore, must be adequately defended. All unimportant imports must be eliminated. If we can maintain 60 per cent. of our present imports we can obtain enough food for the population and raw materials to continue essential armament production.

*Overseas*

9. On a long-term view, Germany, in concert with Italy, will strive to overthrow our position in Egypt and the Middle East.

10. The immediate effect of a French collapse would be the loss of naval control in the Western Mediterranean. Italy would be able to concentrate all her strength against Malta, Gibraltar and Egypt. Malta could probably withstand one serious assault. We could continue to use Gibraltar as a naval base until Spain became hostile. Even then Gibraltar should hold out for 60 days.

11. To contain the Italian Fleet and secure Egypt a capital ship fleet should be based on Alexandria. In due course a heavy scale of attack could be mounted on Egypt from Libya, and we might have to withdraw the Fleet through the Suez Canal to Aden and block the Canal. Preparations to do this should be undertaken as soon as the contingency considered in this paper arises.

12. The retention of Singapore is very important for economic control, particularly of rubber and tin. To counter Japanese action in the Far East, a fleet, adequately supported by air forces, is necessary at Singapore. It is most improbable that we could send any naval forces there, and reliance would have to be placed upon the United States to safeguard our interests.

13. We should endeavour to maintain our position in all our overseas possessions.

*Ability to Defeat Germany*

14. Germany might still be defeated by economic pressure, by a combination of air attack on economic objectives in Germany and on German morale and the creation of widespread revolt in her conquered territories.

15. We are advised in the following sense by the Ministry of Economic Warfare. We cannot emphasise too strongly the importance of the substantial accuracy of this forecast, since upon the economic factor depends our only hope of bringing about the downfall of Germany.

16. In spite of immediate economic gains obtained from her conquests, Germany will still be very short of food, natural fibres, tin, rubber, nickel and cobalt. Above all, even with Romanian supplies, she will still have insufficient oil.

17. Given full Pan-American co-operation, we should be able to control all deficiency commodities at source. There will be no neutrals except Japan and Russia.

18. The effect of a continued denial of overseas supplies to Germany will be:

    (a) By the winter of 1940-41, widespread shortage of food in many European industrial areas, including parts of Germany.

    (b) By the winter of 1940-41, shortage of oil will force Germany to weaken her military control in Europe.

    (c) By the middle of 1941, Germany will have difficulty in replacing military equipments. A large part of the industrial plant of Europe will stand still, throwing upon the German administration an immense unemployment problem to handle.

19. Air attacks on Germany's oil centres will be an important contribution to the enemy's defeat and to the reduction of the intensity of his air offensive. The pressure we could exert by air action will be extremely limited for some time owing to the effects of the enemy's attacks and the need to conserve our striking power to deal with the contingency of invasion.

20. The territories occupied by Germany are likely to prove a fruitful ground for sowing the seeds of revolt, particularly when economic conditions deteriorate.

21. Finally, we emphasise once more that these conclusions as to our ability to bring the war to a successful conclusion depend entirely upon full Pan-American economic and financial co-operation.

22. In view of our terms of reference and the speculative nature of the problem, we have not considered whether the Empire can continue the war if the United Kingdom were defeated.

## RECOMMENDATIONS

23. The following recommendations were drafted before the Bill conferring on the Government complete power of control over persons and property for the prosecution of the war was passed. We have not

had the opportunity of studying the details of this Bill, so some of our recommendations are no doubt covered by its provisions.

We recommend that the following measures should be carried out NOW, irrespective of events in France. These measures are confined to those which we consider necessary for the security of this country against attack during the critical period that may arise in the next few months:

(i) We should do our utmost to persuade the United States of America to provide aircraft, particularly fighters, as soon as possible and in large numbers, including those from stocks now held by the United States Army and Navy.

(ii) Measures should be taken to ensure the strictest economy in A.A. ammunition expenditure.

(iii) The most ruthless action should be taken to eliminate any chances of "Fifth Column" activities. Internment of all enemy aliens and all members of subversive organisations, which latter should be proscribed.

(iv) Alien refugees are a most dangerous source of subversive activity. We recommend that the number of refugees admitted to this country should be cut to the minimum and that those admitted should be kept under the closest surveillance.

(v) In order to ensure the necessary co-operation between the Civil and Military Authorities, operational control of all Civil Defence Forces, including county and borough police, &c., should be vested in the Ministry of Home Security and exercised through Regional Commissioners.

(vi) Any evacuation which the Government intends to carry out in emergency should be carried out now. We recommend that a modification of the scheme for reception areas, in view of the dangers of invasion, should be carried out.

(vii) Immediate steps to be taken to obtain destroyers and M.T.Bs. from the United States of America.

(viii) Every possible measure should be directed to obtaining the active support of Eire, particularly with a view to the immediate use of Berehaven.

(ix) Our intelligence system to be strengthened with a view to getting early warning of German preparations for invasion of this country.

(x) Dispersal of stocks of raw materials to free our West Coast ports to deal with the heavy increase in imports should now be made.

(xi) So far as is practicable distribution of food reserves throughout the country with a view to meeting the disorganisation of transport which may occur.

(xii) Bunkering facilities and other arrangements necessary to deal with a heavy volume of merchant shipping in West Coast and Irish ports should be organised.

(xiii) All unimportant and luxury imports to be cut out.

(xiv) Finally we consider that the time has come to inform the public of the true dangers that confront us and to educate them on what they are required to do and what NOT to do, if the country is invaded.

*(Signed) C.L.N. Netwall, Dudley Pound, A.E. Percival A.C.I.G.S. (for C.I.G.S.).*
*Richmond Terrace, S.W.1.*

*Annex*

## BRITISH STRATEGY IN A CERTAIN EVENTUALITY

## APPRECIATION

**Object**

The object of this paper is to investigate the means whereby we could continue to fight single-handed if French resistance were to collapse completely involving the loss of a substantial proportion of the British Expeditionary Force, and the French Government were to make terms with Germany.

2. We have based our investigation on certain assumptions which we have set out in Appendix A. Of these, we would draw particular attention to the assumption that we could count on the full economic and financial support of the United States of America, without which we do not consider we could continue the war with any chance of success. Briefly, the general strategic situation which would arise under these assumptions is as follows:

**Strategical and Political Situation**

3. From the first few weeks of a French collapse the United Kingdom and its sea approaches will be exposed at short range to the concentrated attack of the whole of the German Naval and Air forces operating from bases extending from Norway to the North-West of France. The threat of invasion will be ever present. Italy will be in the war, and the Mediterranean – except for the Eastern end and possibly, to a limited extent, the North African coast – will be closed to us.

4. As time goes on – over a period of some months – our enemies will be able to extend their economic and military control to Spain, Portugal and North Africa in the West and to the Balkans, except Turkey, in the East. This will somewhat improve their economic situation, will provide additional bases for attack on British trade in the Atlantic, and enable a heavy scale of attack to be prepared in Libya against Egypt. On the other hand, we have assumed that we can count on the full economic and financial support of the United States, possibly extending to active participation. Japan we see as purely opportunist – prepared to exploit the situation but with a watchful eye on the United States of America. Russia, through fear of Germany's growing domination, may come to an understanding with Sweden and Turkey.

**Probable enemy action**

5. The defeat of France will not free Germany from the risks of economic strangulation and air attack. The main objective in German policy must therefore be the rapid elimination of resistance in the United Kingdom.

6. There are three broad methods by which Germany might achieve this end:

   (a) Unrestricted air attack aimed at breaking down public morale;
   (b) Starvation of this country by attack on shipping and ports;
   (c) Occupation of the United Kingdom by invasion.

In all of these the primary factor would be full-scale use of air forces.

7. On a longer term view, in concert with Italy, German strategy will strive ultimately to overthrow our position in Egypt and the Middle East and to open a trade route through the Red Sea.

OUR ABILITY TO WITHSTAND ATTACK

**Attack on the United Kingdom and its Approaches**

8. To withstand German attack on the United Kingdom and its approaches we must be able to defeat invasion, to maintain a large proportion of our seaborne supplies, to keep factories working and to sustain the morale of the people of this country.

**Air Forces**

9. The crux of the whole problem is the air defence of this country. The following are the main factors affecting the enemy scale of attack: The Germans will be free to concentrate the whole of their air force against this country. Its numerical strength at the present time is shown in Appendix B. The area which this force could cover in the situation assumed is as follows: The long-range bomber force could operate over the entire British Isles and the approaches to all West coast ports, including Irish and Scottish ports. The dive-bomber force and long-range fighters could reach an area in southern and central England

extending as far as a line drawn between Cardiff and Grimsby, while the short-range fighters could reach South-East England.

10. The Germans will thus be able to concentrate a very heavy weight of long and short-range bomber attack over a large area of this country, including our vital areas in the Midlands and over all probable areas for enemy landings on our coast. The fact that they would be able to escort this force with fighters creates a threat, the seriousness of which cannot be overstressed, since it will involve a very much higher wastage rate in fighters than we have previously estimated. Should they succeed in obtaining a high degree of air superiority, they could deal comparatively unhindered, except by A.A. gunfire, with any objectives they might select. This would enormously increase our difficulties in maintaining the normal life of the country and in meeting invasion.

11. We have, on the other hand, the following factors in our favour: A proportion of the German air force will be operating from aerodromes far removed from their main organisation and supplies and in unfriendly country. The German casualties have been extremely high and will continue, though perhaps at not quite such a high rate. Although the enemy is still able to replace aircraft from reserves and production, the replacement of his most highly trained crews will seriously affect the efficiency of his Air Force. There is no doubt that the morale of the flying personnel also has suffered, and that it will deteriorate further, so long as our fighter defences remain effective. It is therefore open to doubt whether attacks will be pressed home whole-heartedly, particularly by day, and whether the enemy air force is capable of sustaining a large-scale offensive so long as such opposition exists.

12. The capacity of the German Air Force to reduce the effectiveness of our air defence depends to a considerable extent upon his ability to destroy our aerodromes, aircraft on the ground and our aircraft industry. We have a well-dispersed system of aerodromes and satellite landing grounds. The enemy will certainly have to employ large forces with determination before he begins to inflict serious losses to our first-line strength by attack on aerodromes. During this time his own losses from fighter and A.A. gunfire will be heavy, but protection of aerodromes will absorb a proportion of our fighter strength which would be available for the defence of other vital areas. In our aircraft industry the dangerous weakness is the concentration of the whole of our engine production for the fighter force in two factories. Under a sustained rate of attack it is extremely doubtful if we could expect to receive more than a fraction of our present production figure. Our first-line strength may, therefore, diminish rapidly both because of a high

rate of wastage and a low rate of replacement. It will accordingly be of extreme importance to do everything to obtain quantities of aircraft from America and to keep open our sea routes across the Atlantic.

13. Ability to protect both our aerodromes and aircraft industry depends to an overwhelming extent upon the maintenance of a force of fighter aircraft. Its completely dominating position in an Air Defence organisation has been clearly shown during the last few weeks. Including naval forces and fleet bases our fighter organisation has immense areas to cover. Ability to concentrate at decisive places would be of the greatest value in economising fighters, and any steps that can be taken to reduce the vital areas to be defended should be adopted.

14. The second factor in Air Defence is the gun. There are at present of the approved numbers for A.D.G.B. only 44 per cent. of heavy and 18 per cent. of light equipments available. These meagre resources must also clearly be concentrated in the most vital areas only, and the maximum number extricated from France. It is equally important to economise ammunition and to ensure that plans and preparations are made to modify tactical dispositions to meet successive stages of the enemy's attack.

15. We cannot resist invasion by fighter aircraft alone. An air striking force is necessary not only to meet the seaborne expedition, but also to bring direct pressure to bear upon Germany by attacking objectives in that country.

16. The fighter and bomber forces, which we have available in this country at the present date are shown in Appendix C. The strength of this force will no doubt be further reduced before the situation under consideration arises.

It will be noted that our reserves have reached dangerously low totals, and that we are therefore vitally dependent on a continued flow of production. The aircraft for operational units due to reach us from the United States of America and Canada are given in Appendix D. The present orders are totally inadequate to replace wastage if our own production ceases. Further orders for fighters now under consideration should be given a very high order of priority, and we should persuade the United States Government to release aircraft from their first line strengths.

**Civil Defence**

17. There can be no doubt that, in the circumstances we are considering, the morale of the country will be subjected to a heavier strain than ever before. Not only will the physical damage and demoralisation of continued and heavy bombing attacks sap the nation's courage but

these attacks will be directed at important objectives with a view not only to destroying the objective but driving away labour. Furthermore, propaganda and "Fifth Column" activities will play a dangerous part in demoralising the country.

18. As long as the present quasi-peacetime organisation continues there is no guarantee that this country could hold out. The present Home Security Organisation was constituted to deal with air attack only and the volume of such attack was estimated on the basis that the enemy aircraft would be operating from Germany. It does not take into account the new problems arising from a combination of heavy air attack, invasion and "Fifth Column" activities such as has been experienced by the countries already subjected to attack by Germany, and to which we are now liable. An attack of this character may now be regarded as probably based on the channel ports.

We believe that, with proper organisation, this country could hold out, but if we are to survive total war, it is essential to organise the country as a fortress on totalitarian lines.

We are satisfied that the country is ready to accept whole-heartedly any steps that may be considered necessary provided that clear direction is given. At the same time immediate steps must be taken to bring home to the nation the gravity of the problem and the need for individual self-sacrifice in the interests of the Empire.

19. To this end we consider that the following steps, inter alia, should be taken to implement this recommendation.

(a) That the operational control of all civil defence forces, including County and Borough Police, should no longer be exercised by local authorities but should be vested in the Ministry of Home Security and exercised through the Regional Commissioners.

(b) That all enemy aliens and persons known to be members of subversive organisations should be incarcerated.

(c) That no evacuation or movement of refugees should be allowed, in order not to hamper essential movements. The evacuation problem is thus restricted to one of local "panic" conditions. (It should be noted that the corollary of this is that any evacuation considered necessary should have been carried out before the emergency arises.)

**Land Forces**

20. Germany would have ample troops (70 divisions or more) for the invasion of this country, even after providing for the occupation of conquered territory, including France, and for limited operations in South-East Europe. The troops available in this country during the next two or three months will be:

| Trained, equipped and mobilise | 3½ divisions |
| Partly trained, mainly equipped except for artillery | 3 divisions, 2 motor divisions |
| Relatively untrained, little equipment | 5 divisions |

and two armoured divisions, of which the equivalent of about two brigades could be mobilised.

In addition, there are 57 Home Defence Battalions employed on the defence of vulnerable points and many men in holding units, training centres, &c. It is unlikely that more than a small portion of the British Expeditionary Force could be extricated from France. Most of its equipment and ammunition is likely to be lost. On the other hand, additional Dominion Forces, which are not fully trained or equipped, are en route to the United Kingdom.

21. The major weakness of our Home Defence Forces is lack of equipment, artillery and ammunition. Should the Germans succeed in establishing a force with its vehicles in this country, our army forces have not got the offensive power to drive it out. The maintenance of the lines of communication of such a force would, however, be a difficult problem for the enemy.

**Naval Forces**

22. The first and vital task of our naval forces is to ensure the security of the United Kingdom and its essential supplies against seaborne attack. All other naval commitments are secondary to this; and, if our naval forces at home become depleted through loss or damage, we must at all costs maintain their strength by drawing on outlying stations.

23. It is also important to retain our position in the Eastern Mediterranean, and for this a capital ship force to contain the Italian Fleet will be essential. After providing for this, it will still be possible to match the German Fleet in Home Waters and to provide for ocean convoy escorts. In this we may be helped by any French Naval forces that may not have capitulated.

24. Whatever the strength of our Naval forces in Home Waters, our ability to exercise command of the North Sea and Channel will depend on our ability to operate surface forces within close range of enemy air bases. Whether we shall be able to maintain effective naval forces in bases on the East and South Coasts in the face of a very heavy scale air attack is uncertain; if we cannot do so, the chance of intercepting enemy forces before they reach our shores will clearly be less. Finally, whether we shall be able to operate surface forces in strength in the southern part of the North Sea and the Channel at all is also uncertain. At the best, we may be able to continue using our present bases and to operate

surface forces in adequate strength off our South and East Coasts without prohibitive loss or damage; at the worst, we may have to face the fact that we cannot do so. All that we can say at the moment is that it would be imprudent to count upon being able to do so.

25. With Germany in possession of ports in Norway, Holland, Belgium and France our Naval dispositions must be planned to meet the threat of seaborne invasion on either the East or South Coasts of the United Kingdom. In such an operation Germany would probably employ the whole of her Naval forces and we must therefore base a capital ship Fleet to intercept German heavy forces. Rosyth is the most suitable base in the North Sea for this purpose, but air attack may make it untenable, in which circumstances, Scapa is the next best base.

26. The problem in the Channel is more difficult, as with enemy naval forces operating from French ports, the cover provided by a Fleet in the north is not adequate, and capital ships might have to be based on West Coast or Irish ports. The use of Berehaven as an operational base would be of the greatest importance for this and for our light forces, which will be covering the approaches to the West Coast ports. In this connection, we point out that it will be even more important to prevent Germany from making use of naval or air refuelling bases in Eire, and we consider that the strongest representations should be made to the Government of Eire in this respect.

27. We cannot stress too strongly the importance of strengthening our intelligence systems and reconnaissance patrols to get the earliest possible warning of the preparation of invasion.

28. Our ability to control the North Sea and Channel depends on the number of light forces that we can dispose in these waters and operate there in the face of air attack. We are short of destroyers, and it is essential that every effort should be made to obtain reinforcements from Canada and the United States. Withdrawal from Narvik would make additional destroyers available.

29. Minelaying operations in the Straits of Dover to prevent movement of shipping southward to French ports and the laying of a south-coast barrage should be planned, and minelaying off enemy ports intensified.

30. Apart from defensive methods, operations to destroy enemy shipping concentrations in port must be undertaken, if opportunity offers, to strike directly at the enemy's ability to carry a seaborne expedition.

**Seaborne Supplies**

31. We have adequate shipping resources at present to meet our requirements, although we must assume that enemy naval attacks, both on our trade and Naval forces, in Home Waters and overseas, will be intensified.

32. The provision of air security is, however, the real problem in Home Waters. If the enemy launches a full-scale offensive against the United Kingdom, a very heavy scale of air attack will be developed on our ports on the south and east coasts, and we may have to abandon them altogether for trade purposes.

33. Plans have already been prepared to divert all shipping to West Coast ports and, provided we can maintain approximately 60 per cent. of our present imports, we believe that we should be able to obtain enough food to support the population and sufficient raw materials to continue our essential armament production, although at a reduced rate. We again draw attention to the importance of reducing now the unimportant imports (such as bananas and children's toys), so that the maximum import of important raw materials may be available to increase our stocks of these essentials. Moreover, even if our imports were reduced to a mere trickle; we should still be able to tide over a critical period of a few weeks by drawing on our reserve stocks, which have been accumulated to meet a crisis of this nature. To increase our ability to hold out in a critical period, we should now put into operation plans for drastic rationing and distribution of stocks. Nevertheless, our ability to carry on the war is absolutely dependent upon the eventual maintenance of supplies through the West Coast ports, and we would point out that this will raise major problems of labour transference. Moreover, the West Coast ports themselves will be subjected to air attack, although possibly on a lesser scale to that on the East and South Coasts.

**The Influence of the Air Factor in our Ability to Withstand Attack**

34. The vital fact is that our ability to avoid defeat will depend on three factors:

(a) Whether the morale of our people will withstand the strain of air bombardment;

(b) Whether it will be possible to import the absolute essential minimum of commodities necessary to sustain life and to keep our war industries in action;

(c) Our capacity to resist invasion.

All of these depend primarily on whether our fighter defences will be able to reduce the scale of attack to reasonable bounds. This will necessarily mean the replacement of casualties in personnel and aircraft on a substantial scale. Our capacity to resist invasion may, however, depend also to a great extent on the maintenance of an effective air striking force.

These factors cannot be assessed with certainty and it is impossible to say whether or not the United Kingdom could hold out in all circumstances. We think there are good grounds for the belief that the British people will endure the greatest strain, if they realise – as they are beginning to do – that the existence of the Empire is at stake. We must concentrate our energies primarily on the production of fighter aircraft and crews, and the defence of these factories essential to fighter production should have priority. At the same time it is clear that we cannot afford to neglect our bomber force or to expend it on operations that are not of first importance.

## ENEMY ACTION AGAINST OUR OVERSEAS POSSESSIONS AND INTERESTS

**Naval Forces**
35. The immediate effect of a French collapse on the Mediterranean and Middle East situation would be the loss of naval control in the Western Mediterranean. This would leave Italy free to concentrate the whole of her strength against Malta, Gibraltar, Egypt and our interests in the Near East.
36. Malta has six months' food reserve for the population and garrison, but A.A. guns and ammunition are short, and the island is not likely to withstand more than one serious seaborne assault, nor could it be used as a Naval base.
37. Gibraltar, provided it was not attacked by gas, could hold out for 60 days against a hostile Spain, and it is even probable that supplies could be made available to extend this period. It would be possible to continue using Gibraltar as a naval base until Spain became hostile.
38. It would be impossible, with the forces at our disposal, to control sea communications in the Western as well as in the Eastern Mediterranean. We should, however, retain light forces in the Atlantic approaches with a view to intercepting raiders, coastwise shipping and blockade runners. In the event of Gibraltar becoming unusable, we might occupy Casablanca, failing which the nearest bases are Dakar and Freetown, both of which are too far away to be of much value. It would be important to prevent enemy forces using the Azores, Canary Islands and Cape Verde Islands as bases, and, should we be unable to use Casablanca, we might require to base naval forces on these islands ourselves.
39. The only naval bases left in the Mediterranean would be Alexandria and Haifa in the Eastern basin, and so important is it to hold our position in Egypt in order to maintain economic pressure that we consider a capital ship fleet should be based on Alexandria.

40. We estimate that sufficient force could be made available to contain the Italian fleet and still leave us sufficient Naval units for operations at Home and elsewhere. Supply by the Red Sea route would be subject to attack from Italian East Africa, and the Fleet itself would operate continuously within range of enemy bomber forces. In spite of this, we believe it should be retained there as long as possible for the security of Egypt and as a stabilizing influence on Turkey and the countries of the Middle East. Furthermore, it would, by its presence, contain a large proportion of Italian Naval forces from making sorties into the Western Mediterranean and Atlantic.

**Land and Air Forces**

41. In the early stages the situation in Egypt would not be greatly altered from that already envisaged in the event of war with Italy. Our land forces are strong enough to meet Italian attack in that area and equipment and ammunition reserves are sufficient for 90 days at full wastage rates. There is, however, a serious shortage of aircraft and anti-aircraft guns and the air defence problem is a serious one even in the scale of attack at present envisaged. The problem of further maintenance would be acute with a closed Mediterranean and hazardous Red Sea. The scale of attack in the Red Sea would, however, gradually diminish, as the enemy would find difficulty in maintaining his air effort in Abyssinia.

42. After a period of some months the Germans and Italians would no doubt gain military and economic control of the whole of the Balkans, except Turkey, of Spain and of French North Africa. The scale of attacks mounted from Libya would be greatly increased and in the meantime the internal security problem in the Middle East would have grown. Eventually, after a period of months, a heavy attack supported by considerable air forces could be launched from Libya, in which case it is doubtful whether we can maintain our position in Egypt. If we could not, it will be necessary to withdraw the fleet to Aden and block the Canal. Preparations for this should be put in hand as soon as the contingency considered in this paper materialises. Unless previous to this it were possible to increase the scale of air defence in Egypt, it is doubtful whether the garrison could hold out.

43. The situation in Iraq depends chiefly on the maintenance of internal security in that country. No immediate deterioration might follow the French collapse. After some months, however, our position up country might become untenable, in which case it would be necessary to withdraw to a position at Habbaniya to protect Basra and the Anglo-Iranian Oilfields. A division could be provided from India for this purpose.

44. There will be no direct military threat to India, but we could not rely on being able to withdraw any British troops from India.

**The Far East**

45. A threat to our interests in the Far East can only arise in the event of a hostile Japan. With America actively on our side Japan would be unlikely to make a direct attack on British territory; though she would no doubt exploit any opportunity that offered. The retention of Singapore is extremely important from the point of view of our economic control – particularly of rubber and tin.

46. To counter Japanese action in the Far East, a fleet, adequately supported by Air Forces, is necessary at Singapore. What forces we can send can only be judged in the light of the situation at the time. It is most improbable that we can send any naval forces to the Far East. Therefore we must rely on the United States of America to safeguard our interests in the Far East.

47. Australia should be asked to consider a reinforcement of the garrison in Singapore.

**Other Overseas Garrisons**

48. We should endeavour to maintain our position in all our overseas possessions. In view of the necessity for concentration of all British resources at vital points, it is for consideration whether responsibilities for isolated garrisons might not be taken over by the Dominions, e.g., Canada might be asked to take over the defence of the West Indies and of Iceland.

## ABILITY TO DEFEAT GERMANY

49. The defeat of Germany might be achieved by a combination of economic pressure, air attack on economic objectives in Germany and on German morale and the creation of widespread revolt in the conquered territories.

**Economic Pressure**

50. The following general conclusions which we have reached on this wide economic problem have been arrived at after consultation with a representative of the Ministry of Economic Warfare.

51. German control of the resources of Western Europe and a part of Northern Africa will secure for her a number of immediate economic assets. Nevertheless Germany and the area under her control will still depend on outside sources for certain essential commodities, particularly natural fibres for clothing and footwear, rubber, tin, nickel and cobalt. Moreover the occupied territories of Western Europe will aggravate the food shortage which is already a serious problem in the

Reich; and the whole oil output of Romania, Poland and Germany together with such supplies as are likely to be available from Russia will not suffice to maintain German and Italian stocks, which would have to be drawn on from the outset.

52. With genuine and extensive Pan-American co-operation and with the Dutch, Belgian and French Empires at our disposal, we shall be in a strong position to control all deficiency commodities at source, as except for Japan and Russia and a few isolated territories, there will be no neutrals. It will no longer be practicable by normal contraband control methods involving visit and search.

Our ability to apply economic pressure of this nature will depend primarily upon American co-operation. On this assumption, and provided that we can maintain control over the Allied Overseas Empires and naval control of the wider oceans and focal points leading to the blockaded area, the trickle of supplies reaching Germany by blockade running will be negligible.

53. The effect of the denial of overseas supplies to Germany will manifest itself in the following ways: Firstly, food shortage. Dependent upon the yield of the harvests in 1940, which are expected to be low, German-controlled Europe will be somewhat short of bread-stuffs. There will also be a widespread scarcity of essential fats and fruits. Life will be sustained for a period by the heavy slaughtering of immature animals. This will be necessary because, after the end of the grazing season, there will be a dearth of feeding-stuffs. It will probably be only a matter of months before hoarding by the peasant population creates a really acute shortage of food in the industrial areas, including parts of Germany herself.

54. Secondly, Germany's war potential itself must be expected to decline through deficiency in oil. The whole of her own and of Italian stocks of petrol plus the whole output of Romania and small supplies from Russia will nearly suffice to provide the lubricants and petrol needed to maintain orderly administration and the minimum industrial activity in the Continent as a whole. As soon as the initial stocks are exhausted, and if synthetic plants can be destroyed, the German garrisons would be largely immobilised and her striking power cumulatively decreased.

55. A third effect will be on the quality of Germany's war equipment. It is impossible to estimate the amount of war material that the German fighting forces will have to consume under the conditions postulated. But it is certain that deprived of all imports of certain essential non-ferrous metals, alloys, rubber and cotton and wool, Germany will not be able to maintain a high rate of replacement, and the quality of her war

equipment, including aeroplanes, must be expected to decline. Even with practically no consumption of war equipment a large part of the industrial plant of Europe will stand still, throwing upon the German administration an immense unemployment problem to handle.

56. With regard to the time factor, effective denial of these supplies is, we are advised, likely to produce widespread starvation in many of the industrial areas, including parts of Germany, before the winter of 1940 (assuming an early French collapse). By the same date the depletion of oil stocks will force Germany to weaken her military control in Europe or to immobilise her armed forces. By the middle of 1941, Germany will find it hard to replace her military equipments. This process of exhaustion would be somewhat hastened by destruction of Germany's synthetic oil plants and of Romanian wells, by blockage of the Danube and the diversion of Russian oil supplies.

**Air Attack on Economic Objectives in Germany**

57. Economic factors have shown that the primary objective for our air attack should be the enemy's oil resources and focal points in his transport system. We have already made progress in the systematic elimination of the key objectives (the effect of which have not been allowed for the estimate of supplies above) and if we can maintain these attacks, even on a light scale, an important contribution will be made towards the enemy's defeat. Moreover, shortage of lubricating oils and petrol may have a very important effect on the intensity of the air offensive against this country in the ensuing months.

58. The pressure we could exert by air action would, for some time, be extremely limited, owing to the effects of the enemy's offensive and the need for conserving a proportion of our striking power to deal with the contingency of invasion. We could not expect to do more than maintain a very limited scale of attack until we could obtain additional resources from the Dominions and from the United States. In the course of time we could hope to bring a heavier scale of attack on Germany by developing the United Kingdom as an advanced base for the operation of large long-range bombers flown from production centres across the Atlantic.

**Subversive Action**

59. The only other method of bringing about the downfall of Germany is by stimulating the seeds of revolt within the conquered territories. The occupied countries are likely to prove a fruitful ground for these operations, particularly when economic conditions begin to deteriorate.

In the circumstances envisaged, we regard this form of activity as of the very highest importance. A special organisation will be required and plans to put these operations into effect should be prepared, and all the necessary preparations and training should be proceeded with as a matter of urgency.

**Political Aspects of Economic Pressure**

60. The political and moral issues involved in imposing on the mass of Europe the severe effects of economic pressure may present serious difficulties. It will be necessary to realise, however, that it is only by this pressure that we can ensure the defeat of Germany, and that by holding out we shall remain as a nucleus on which the rebuilding of European civilisation may be attempted.

If, on the other hand, we do not persevere, the economic collapse of Europe and the United Kingdom under a corrupt Nazi administration would only be postponed for a short while, and we should have no chance of contributing to Europe's reconstruction.

*Annex A*

ASSUMPTIONS AS TO THE POLITICAL BACKGROUND

1. The precise political situation cannot be foretold, but we consider the most likely assumptions that we can make are:
(a)   Italy will be hostile.
(b)   All French European and North African territory will be accessible to enemy forces in course of time, and will be treated as hostile territory. French armed forces in Europe and North Africa will cease to fight. Parts of the fleet and certain land and air forces in outlying parts of the French Empire will continue to assist in the war.
(c)   Spain, Portugal and all the Balkan States (excluding Turkey), together with their resources, will eventually fall under German or Italian military and economic domination.
(d)   Our prestige in the Middle East generally will suffer a great set-back, which is likely to involve us in serious internal security problems in Egypt, Palestine and Iraq. The extent of our trouble will be largely conditioned by the attitude of Turkey, who may not remain as an active Ally in the circumstances envisaged.
(e)   Japan will exploit the situation to her advantage in the Far East, though whether she would go to the length of a direct attack on British territory will depend on the attitude of the United States.
2.   On the other hand, we assume that:
(a)   The whole Empire, with the possible exception of Eire, would increase their efforts in support of the United Kingdom. The attitude of India might, however, be doubtful and would be largely

influenced by the situation in the Middle East and the extent of our difficulties at home.

(b)  We could count on the full economic and financial support of the United States of America, possibly extending to active participation on our side. This example is likely to be followed by the remainder of the American States. The degree to which American forces might assist us would depend on the extent to which America became involved with Japan.

(c)  Russia will be really frightened of the increasing might of Germany. She will try to improve her position vis-à-vis Germany if she can do so without becoming involved in a major military commitment. To this end she might come to an understanding with Turkey and Sweden.

*Annex B*

## STATEMENT OF GERMAN AIRCRAFT POSITION

| | 10 May 1940 | | Lost in period | Produced | Balance | Reserves at |
|---|---|---|---|---|---|---|
| | 1st Line | Reserve | 10.5.40 to 24.5.40 | Over Period | | 24.5.40 |
| L.R. bombers | | | | | | |
| Bomber Recce | 2,600 | 3,300 | 1,000 (100 | 500 | -500 | 7,000 (less |
| Dive bombers | 500 | 1,200 | slightly | | | 100 slightly |
| Fighters | 1,500 | 2,500 | damaged) | | | damaged) |
| Army Co-Op | 400 | 200 | | | | |
| Coastal | 350 | 300 | | | | |
| *Total* | *5,350* | *7,500* | | | | |
| | | | | | | |
| Bomber Transport | | | | | | |
| Ju.52 | 500 | 300 | 400 | | 25 | -375 -75 |
| Ju.86 | 100 | ... | | | | |

Notes:

B.A.F.F., French and Dutch reports of German aircraft losses have not given details of types. It is therefore not possible to state the losses of the individual categories.

Reserve trained crews are estimated at 100 per cent. of 1st line crews.

*Annex C1*

## STRENGTH OF THE HOME BASED AIR FORCE ON MAY 17, 1940, EXCLUDING ALL AIRCRAFT BASED IN FRANCE

## OPERATIONAL STRENGTH
Including ALL 1st line aircraft in operational squadrons serviceable within 7 days

| | |
|---|---|
| Heavy Bombers | 316 (Inc. Reserve Sqns which can operate if necessary) |
| Medium Bombers | |
| Blenheim | 84 |
| Battle | - |
| Fighters | |
| Hurricane, Spitfire, Defiant | 491 |
| Blenheim | 145 |
| Gladiator | 3 |
| Army Co-Operation | - |
| Coastal | |
| General Recon and Torpedo Bombers Land-planes | 184 |
| Flying boats | 33 |

## RESERVE OF OPERATIONAL AIRCRAFT IMMEDIATELY AVAILABLE TO FLY
Including (i) serviceable reserve aircraft in squadrons; (ii) aircraft in operational training units and non-operational squadrons; (iii) serviceable aircraft stored

| | |
|---|---|
| Heavy Bombers | 148 |
| Medium Bombers | |
| Blenheim | 98 |
| Battle | 103 |
| Fighters | |
| Hurricane, Spitfire, Defiant | 134 |
| Blenheim | 63 |
| Gladiator | 27 |
| Army Co-Operation | 134 |
| Coastal | |
| General Recon and Torpedo Bombers Land-planes | 221 |
| Flying boats | 13 |

## RESERVE OF OPERATIONAL AIRCRAFT NOT IMMEDIATELY AVAILABLE TO FLY
Including (i) aircraft repairable in units; (ii) stored aircraft short of equipment; (iii) aircraft of service types in Training and Reserve Commands, some percentage of which may be fully equipped

| | |
|---|---|
| Heavy Bombers | 445 |
| Medium Bombers | |
|     Blenheim | 264 |
|     Battle | 753 |
| Fighters | |
|     Hurricane, Spitfire, Defiant | 528 |
|     Blenheim | 157 |
|     Gladiator | 50 |
| Army Co-Operation | 200 |
| Coastal | |
|     General Recon and Torpedo | |
|     Bombers Land-planes | 820 (including 643 Ansons) |
|     Flying boats | 20 |

NOTES

(a) Above return does <u>not</u> include aircraft crashed beyond the capacity of units to repair or aircraft without engines.

(b) Total operational strength differs from past statements in that it takes account of serviceability.

(c) Losses since May 16 amount to 114.

*Annex C2*

BRITISH AIR FORCES, NOT INCLUDED IN TABLE OF HOME-BASED UNITS, WHICH HAVE BEEN OR ARE EMPLOYED IN FRANCE

| | |
|---|---|
| A.A.S.F. in France on May 22 | |
|     Battle | 52 |
|     Hurricane | 38 |
|     Blenheim – | |
|     Returned to United Kingdom | number unknown |
| Air Component returned to United Kingdom: | |
|     Blenheims | number unknown |
|     Hurricane | 45 Reported |
|     Gladiator | 15 Reported |
|     Lysander | number unknown |

Detachment from Fighter Command returned to United Kingdom on May 21:

| | |
|---|---|
|     Hurricane | possibly 30-40 |
| *Total of above* | |
|     Blenheim | unknown |

| | |
|---|---|
| Battle | 52 |
| Hurricane | 120 approximately |
| Gladiator | 15 |
| Lysander | unknown |
| Norway | |
| Hurricane – returning | 18 |
| Gladiator | 16 |

*Annex D*

## FORECAST OF HOME (AND DOMINIONS) PRODUCTION OF AIRCRAFT
### May – October 1940

About 90 per cent. of these aircraft will be delivered to Air Storage Units to await certain items of equipment. Some of the May production is probably included in the Reserves shown in Annex C.

NOTE. – It has recently been decided to concentrate on the production of existing models at the expense of the long-term production of new types. This may make some alteration in the figures given.

*Annex E*

## COMPARISON OF NAVAL FORCES

| | Great Britain | Germany | Italy |
|---|---|---|---|
| Capital ships | 13 (plus 1 in September) | 2 (plus 1 during September) | 2 (plus 4 more possibly in June) |
| Aircraft carriers | 6 (plus 1 in May) | 1 | - |
| Armoured ships | - | 2 | - |
| 8-in. cruisers | 14 | 2 (plus 1 in Autumn) | 7 |
| 6-in. cruisers | 24 (plus 5 during Summer) | 4 | 12 |
| Old cruisers | 15 | - | 4 |
| A.A. cruisers | 6 | - | - |
| Destroyers | 170 (plus 14 during Summer) | 9 to 15 | 67 |

| | | | |
|---|---|---|---|
| Torpedo boats | - | - | 55 |
| Submarines | 67 (plus 6 during Summer) | 45 to 50 (plus 25 to 30 in summer) | 155 |
| M.T.B's. | 18 (plus 12 approximately during summer) | 30 to 40 | 100 |

Notes:

(a) Ships undergoing long refits or damage repairs and not likely to be available within the next three months not included.

(b) Japanese forces not shown, as we should hope that any Japanese threat would be countered by the American fleet.

(c) Our own position would be correspondingly improved if American destroyers become available by purchase.

Appendix VIII

# Air Staff Memorandum on Invasion 30th July 1940

It is impossible to forecast with any certainty or precision the form in which Germany may attempt to carry out an invasion of this country. It is, however, possible to predict the broad courses of action open to her and their relative importance. Thus, it is possible to define the role of our air forces in the face of various forms and scales of attacks as they develop, irrespective of the order in which they come.

2. The general view, arrived at after a series of appreciations of the problem, is that the most likely form and order of Germany's major operations in the invasion of this country would be somewhat as follows.

3. In order to attempt and sustain a major invasion of the British Isles, it is essential for Germany to secure her sea communications between the coast of the Continent and this country. In view of our predominance at sea, it would not have been possible for Germany to have attempted this before the rise of air power. On account of the narrow waters between the opposing coasts and the fact that the whole of the German air force can now be concentrated against this country, Germany must rely upon her bomber and fighter forces to secure her lines of sea communication by clearing the air of our fighting aircraft, and thus securing her ability to use her bomber aircraft freely against our naval forces.

4. Until Germany has defeated our fighter force, invasion by sea is not a practical operation of war. In consequence, it is held that her first act must be to attempt, at least in the vital area, to establish virtual air supremacy. To do this it will be necessary for her to dispose of our fighter force, not only by the destruction of our fighters in the air but by large-scale attacks on our aircraft factories and aerodromes. Consequently, the first phase of the invasion of this country is likely to be a large-scale air offensive against the fighter defence, i.e., fighters in

the air, fighter aerodromes and organisation and the aircraft industry.

5. In this phase of operations,

(a) the task of the Fighter Force is to meet the attack on its own organisation and the aircraft industry and defeat it;

(b) the task of the Bomber Force is to reduce the scale of attack by continuing to strike at suitable objectives in Germany, the objectives being specially selected as those which will most directly affect the maintenance of her air effort. Attacks will also be directed against concentrations of aircraft at enemy aerodromes and of shipping in enemy ports, should these be revealed by reconnaissance or other sources of intelligence, inmaccordance with existing instructions;

(c) Coastal Command squadrons will continue with their primary task of reconnaissance to give early warning of enemy troop concentrations in the vicinity of ports, and the movements of ships or concentrations of shipping which may indicate an enemy invasion following on her air offensive.

6. The enemy, however, still may not risk a seaborne invasion until he has at least seriously weakened our naval forces. Another preliminary stage, simultaneous with that outlined above, may therefore be a heavy air attack on our naval forces and their bases, particularly those on the East and South-East coasts but possibly extending to Scapa. It is not possible to lay down in advance any order of priority for fighter action as between this and the attack on our air power. The situation will have to be dealt with on its merits, and the Commander-in-Chief, Fighter Command, must be left to deal with the enemy as effectively as his resources will permit according to the situation as it develops. It is recognised, however, that it is of vital importance that our naval forces should not be destroyed while in harbour.

7. During recent operations on the Continent, Germany obtained marked success by the use of airborne troops, and she is still capable of transporting a large body of parachute troops, landing troops, light artillery and possibly small tanks by air. It is clear that this is a course of action Germany may well adopt in the ensuing phase of operations. Such an attack may take the form of a raid on the more remote and less defended areas in the British Isles, (e.g., Northern Scotland or Southern Ireland); or, alternatively, it may be undertaken with a view to seizing a port of disembarkation for a seaborne expedition.

8. Should this threat develop

(a) the task of the Fighter Force is to destroy enemy tank-carrying aircraft (should they materialise), troop-carrying aircraft, bombers and fighters, in this order of priority. Should a seaborne expedition approach simultaneously with an airborne attack, the Commander-in-Chief, Fighter Command, will be guided by the principle that the protection of our naval forces at sea will rank equally with the destruction of airborne landings in the vicinity of important ports; and that both these tasks will take precedence over airborne landings taking place elsewhere;

(b) the task of the Bomber Force is to continue operations with the object of reducing the scale of air attack, being prepared immediately to divert the effort to the attack of enemy concentrations of ships, should these materialise;

(c) the task of Coastal Command is to continue their anti-invasion reconnaissance.

9. The enemy may well conclude that the complete defeat of this country cannot be ensured without seaborne invasion. If this occurs, there are bound to be three principle phases:

    I.   The concentration of shipping and troops at points of departure.

    II.  The voyage from the Continental coasts to our own.

    III. The establishment of a bridge-head in this country.

10. When it is clear that Phase I has begun –

(a) The Fighter Force is to provide such protection as is possible within the limit of range, for our counter-offensive aircraft bombing the points of departure while continuing to destroy such hostile aircraft as approach or cross our coasts;

(b) The Bomber Force is to attack the ports where the expedition is assembling with the object of destroying troop-carrying vessels;

(c) Coastal Command is to continue their reconnaissance and to undertake bombing or torpedo operations against concentrations of enemy transports and naval vessels at their points of departure.

11. During Phase II (viz., the voyage from the Continental coasts to our own) –

(a) the primary task of Fighter Command must be to afford protection to our naval forces engaged in destroying the enemy transports and war vessels, and secondarily to afford as much security as is possible for our bomber aircraft engaged in the attack of the seaborne expedition. In carrying out these tasks, the Fighter Force must have particular regard to the destruction of enemy dive bombers which are a major threat to our own surface forces;

(b) Bomber Command will attack the enemy transports with bombs and machine-gun fire;

(c) Coastal Command will provide protection with long-range fighters for our naval forces engaged in destroying enemy transports, particularly where these are out of range of the short-range fighters. They should also undertake bombing and torpedo operations against the enemy expedition and naval vessels as well as continuing their anti-invasion reconnaissance to give warning of and to shadow any additional expeditions which may be deploying against our coasts.

12. As regards Phase III, it is considered that, in order successfully to establish a bridgehead, Germany's best course of action would be, simultaneously with a seaborne invasion, to launch an airborne attack, probably on aerodromes in the vicinity of the point of seaborne landing with the object of gaining a port at which transport, tanks and heavy equipment could be landed and subsequently maintained.

13. In any event the close approach of the expedition to our coast and the attempt at landing a force by air pre-supposes an effort by the G.A.F. to establish virtual air superiority over the area. This would localise the air operations of all three Commands and would become the decisive point of action. In this situation –

(a) the task of Fighter Command will be to destroy the elements of the G.A.F. engaged in this operation. At first sight the primary objective would seem to be the destruction of enemy troop or tank-carrying aircraft. It has been pointed out, however, that for the invasion to be effective a seaborne expedition must he landed and maintained. This cannot be done unless the enemy can neutralise our surface naval forces. The order of priority for the destruction of enemy aircraft will therefore be as follows:

(i) Dive bombers operating against our naval forces.

(ii) Tank-carrying aircraft.

(iii) Troop-carrying aircraft.

(iv) Bombers.

(v) Fighters.

(b) the task of Bomber Command will be to attack with bombs and machine-gun fire enemy transports approaching our coasts and at a later stage enemy concentrations of troops or equipment that have been landed;

(c) the task of Coastal Command will be to continue reconnaissance and to attack with bombs or torpedoes enemy transports and war vessels in this order.

14. It should be noted that the order in which the major operations, or indeed a major diversion, may take place in a German attempt to overwhelm this country cannot be predicted with certainty, and therefore our air forces must be prepared to take action in the event of two or more of these major operations taking place concurrently.

15. Of all these possible courses of action, a seaborne invasion, if successful, will be most dangerous, since not only would our naval bases be captured but our industrial areas and aircraft factories would also be liable to seizure by the enemy. Our ability to sustain war would be thereby removed. Accordingly, the predominant and first task of the armed forces must always be to concentrate their attack upon the seaborne invasion.

16. Next in importance is the necessity to ensure the security of the fighter force by preventing the destruction of our aircraft industry and fighter organisation; and the third in importance is to dispose of the airborne invasion.

17. In the event of major operations taking place concurrently Commanders-in-Chief should adjust the action of their forces in accordance with the general instructions laid down above.

*Air Ministry,*
*30/7/1940.*

Appendix IX

# Re-distribution of the Anti-Aircraft Defences, August 1940

Memorandum by the Sub-Committee on the Allocation of Active Air Defence

Part I
GENERAL OBSERVATIONS

1. Three main factors necessitate the review of A.D.G.B.:
    (1) The defeat of France, which opens up the West and North-west of the United Kingdom to a higher scale of attack than has hitherto been possible. Furthermore, hostile bombers escorted by fighter aircraft can now attack a large proportion of the country.
    (2) The possibility of Eire being used as a base for air attack on this country.
    (3) The anticipated increase in German air strength (see paragraph 3), with the likelihood that this may be reinforced by Italian air forces.
2. The broad conclusions to be derived from the above considerations are as follows:
    (1) A higher scale of defence is necessary over large areas of country and to cover the Irish Sea and the approaches thereto, which had previously been regarded as relatively immune from air attack.
    (2) Considerable extensions of the searchlight zones will have to be made.
    (3) The existing gun and searchlight zones are not susceptible to any decreases. In fact, the paramount necessity for maintaining our industrial effort and the rapid growth of industry itself calls for certain increases in defences, quite apart from the new areas open to increased scale of attack.

## Part II
## INCREASES IN FIGHTER SQUADRONS AND BALLOON BARRAGES

*Fighter Aircraft*

3. The present first line strength of the German Air Force is assessed at approximately 5,400 aircraft. This includes 1,550 fighters of which 500 are long range fighters. The German long range bomber and bomber reconnaissance force comprises some 3,107 aircraft. It is anticipated that the first line strength will rise to approximately 6,500 aircraft by the 1st August, 1941. Of these, 1,870 would be fighters while the bomber strength would be 3,670. In addition, the possibility of the employment of Italian air forces against this country must be taken into account.

4. In order to provide an adequate scale of defence in terms of first line fighter aircraft to enable us to match the enemy bomber and fighter strength in the new strategic situation, a large increase in the number of fighter squadrons is necessary.

5. Immediate increases are clearly necessary and it has been found practicable to increase the fighter force by the equivalent of 10 additional fighter squadrons. In addition, a further three foreign squadrons have been formed. The latter should be operationally fit in the course of a few weeks. This brings the strength of the fighter defence to 76 squadrons or 1,216 first line fighters, and includes the equivalent of 5 long range fighter squadrons under Coastal Command. Further it is intended to form an additional 4 squadrons as soon as circumstances permit. It should be appreciated however that this increase has been obtained by adding an extra section of aircraft to certain fighter squadrons. It is the intention to withdraw these and amalgamate them into squadrons as soon as circumstances permit and until this is done the increase in first line strength will not be fully effective.

6. The full number of squadrons required to meet the potential scale of attack cannot be reached for some considerable time, nor indeed is it possible to estimate with any accuracy the optimum scale of fighter defence necessary until we have had more experience of the effect of intensive attack on the air defence system as a whole and of our counter air offensive.

7. In order to deploy these new resources to the best advantage, having regard to the new areas open to the increased scale of attack, new sectors will be required in the following areas:

North-East coast of Scotland
Ayrshire
Cumberland
Westmorland
Lancashire
Shropshire

Warwickshire
South Wales
Devon
Cornwall

Work on the provision of those sector stations and communications has already begun on a high priority.

8. As regards the provision of R.D.F. observation in the new areas and the Observer Corps, the R.D.F. screen is now being extended to cover the Western coast of Great Britain and appropriate extensions to the Observer Corps are being made.

9. If Ireland is invaded and we go to her aid, it is proposed to establish sector stations in the vicinity of Dublin and Wexford (to enable interception to be made from both sides of the Irish Sea) together with the necessary R.D.F. stations. Preparatory arrangements on these lines have already been undertaken. It will be realised, however, that such facilities take time to organise and until sector stations and intelligence resources have been developed the air defence based on the East Coast of Eire will not be fully effective.

*Balloons*

10. As regards balloon defence, not only are new barrages necessary in certain vulnerable areas, formerly reasonably secure from heavy scale attack, but extensions to existing barrages require consideration. An examination of these suggests that 6 new barrages will be required, i.e. at Falmouth, Pembroke, Ardeer, Yeovil, Newport and Belfast, while extensions to existing barrages will be necessary at Liverpool, Runcorn, Manchester, Bristol, Hull, Swansea, Port Talbot, Cardiff, Barry Docks and Clyde.

11. Moreover, on account of the greatly increased scale of minelaying now being undertaken by Germany the necessity of providing anti-mine laying barrages at our major ports on the South and West coasts can no longer be ignored. The proposed provision of new barrages and the extension of existing barrages are shown at Appendix B. From this it will be noted that a total of 436 first line balloons will be required. In addition it is recommended that a further 164 balloons should be provided to meet unforeseen requirements. The authorised establishment of Balloon Command has therefore been raised from 2,000 to 2,600 first line balloons with 100% reserve, and production has been increased accordingly.

## Part III
## A.A. SEARCHLIGHTS

*Searchlight Zones and Requirements*

12. The existing searchlight zones and the proposed new extensions are

231

shown on the sketch map attached at [missing from file – handwritten comment states to be brought to meeting]. The requirements of searchlights are defined at Appendix D. The calculations for these requirements have been made on the basis of wide spacing (6,000 yards) for general area defences, and close spacing (3,500 yards) for the more important gun zones, both existing and new. It will be noted from Appendix D that the total new searchlight requirements are estimated to be as follows – (exact requirements can be arrived at only by reconnaissance).

| Role | No. of Batteries | No. of Lights |
|---|---|---|
| (i) To cover new areas of wide spacing | 87 | 2,088 |
| (ii) To thicken up gun zones | 60 | 1,440 |
| (iii) Mobile reserves (see para. 14) | 12 | 288 |
| *Total* | *159* | *3,816* |

It is considered that these lights should be provided on a scale of one A.R.C. light to two hand controlled equipments.

*New Areas and Gun Zone Lights*

13. First priority should be given to the completion of the A.F.Z. (87 batteries); the thickening up of the gun zones (60 batteries) can be relegated to a later phase. In fact the employment of G.L.II as a means of engaging the unseen target by gunfire may render unnecessary the close spacing of searchlights in gun zones. Furthermore, there are the requirements of the Field Force. These initially amount to 60 batteries, to be followed by an additional 36 to correspond to possible future expansion of the Field Force. The requirements of the Field Force are not an immediate commitment. It will be convenient, therefore, at this stage to merge the Field Force's initial requirement (60 batteries) into that of the batteries wanted for thickening up gun zones in A.D.G.B. (60 batteries).

*Mobile Reserves*

14. No allowance has yet been made for extra searchlights to be placed round specially selected vital points in order to ensure that attacking aircraft are dazzled on approach, and therefore unable to pick out the exact location of the target. For this purpose it is considered that 12 batteries should be provided which would allow of 24 specially selected places being covered by these lights. It is not possible at this stage to allocate these lights to definite objectives. They are therefore included under the heading of the Mobile Reserves.

15. Production forecasts suggest the possibility of supplementing the searchlight programme as follows. By January 1st, 1941, 36 batteries and thereafter 16 batteries per month.

The requirements of the expansion of the A.F.Z. (87 batteries) could thus be met by April, 1941, and thereafter provision could be made at a rapid rate to meet any future expansions of A.D.G.B., to thicken up gun zones, and to meet Field Force requirements.

The production problem is thus satisfactory and the position as regards further orders can be reviewed later on.

16. Detailed priorities within the first phase, i.e. the completion of the expanded A.F.Z. must depend on a number of factors which require further examination, but from an operational standpoint it is suggested that a start should be made as follows:

(i) Completion of present authorised zones (6 batteries).

(ii) The Devon – Cornwall extension (19 batteries).

(iii) South Wales coast (5 batteries).

(iv) Edinburgh – Tyne corridor (8 batteries).

(v) Northern Ireland (7 batteries).

In addition the organization for the other zones should be started forthwith and developed so that units can be fitted in smoothly as desired. It follows that latitude must be given to the completion of (i) to (v) above if smooth development elsewhere should demand it.

## Part IV
## INCREASES IN HEAVY A.A. GUNS AND LONG-RANGE U.P. WEAPONS

*Heavy A.A. Guns*

17. Increases in Heavy A.A. gun defences over the scales of defence authorised in C.I.D. paper No.319 i.e. 2,232 guns are required for the following reasons:

(i) Certain localities, already allotted gun defences, are now open to a heavier scale of attack.

(ii) Certain localities, for which no gun defences have hitherto been allotted, have now assumed a higher degree of importance by virtue of the expansion of industry.

(iii) The experience of this campaign indicates that there is a marked difference between the efficacy of enemy attacks when heavy A.A. gun defences exist and when there is nothing of this nature to deter him. Furthermore, fire against the unseen target, the technique of which is a relatively new development, is an essential element of air defence as a whole. When flying in clouds, etc. the enemy should be subjected to this form of fire as often as possible.

(iv) The possibilities of sea or airborne invasion of this country render it necessary to be able to allocate heavy A.A. defences to cover the operations of our land forces in this country.

(v) Morale of the civil population.

It is essential that any enemy, who has penetrated the main defences, should be fired on. The mere presence of a few A.A. guns will suffice to avoid considerable loss of industrial output and dislocation of normal life.

Broadly speaking, apart from the obvious necessity of reinforcing certain existing defences, the problem is to provide a measure of defence for all communities of any size engaged on industrial work of national importance and to hold a reserve to meet unforeseen requirements and to cover the operations of land forces at home.

The details of the proposed increases in Heavy A.A. guns are shown in Appendix E from which it will be seen that they amount to 1,512 guns.

It is desirable that 50% of the guns should also be mobile, but a higher proportion of static guns would be acceptable if a marked increase in rate of production would thereby be obtained. Should, however, it be necessary to accept a higher proportion of statics every effort should be made to make these transportable by the provision of extra transporters and holdfasts.

*Ammunition*

18. The Ministry of Supply have been recently asked to increase the rate of production of Heavy A.A. gun ammunition to 500,000 rounds per month, a rate which can be dropped to 400,000 per month on completion of the gun programmes.

The ammunition programme is based on the conception of building up a 'capital' allocation to each equipment of 1,200 rounds with an overall monthly wastage requirement, which up till now has been assessed at 350,000 rounds per month. In order to smooth out the production problem the average figure stated above of 500,000 rounds per month has been accepted.

It is considered that this large ammunition figure for the equipment programme already authorized will suffice to absorb the increased ammunition requirements arising out of the proposed increases in guns (1,512 equipments).

*The 3" U.P. Weapon as a Supplement to Long-Range Heavy A.A. Defence*

19. With a view to increasing the density of fire against massed aircraft targets the provision of a 24 barrel projector is under examination. The production of suitable multi-barrel projectors is not likely to present insuperable difficulties. The limiting factor is the large supplies of special cordite involved. This aspect of the problem is being examined and it seems that we should be justified in introducing about 160 multiple barrel projectors into A.D.G.B. These would be distributed in the more important gun zones to provide an additional 24-48 barrel density.

*Defence against low flying attack*

*Light A.A. Guns.*

20. The authorized scale of Light A.A. defence in A.D.G.B. is 1,860 barrels, corresponding to the defence of about 300 vital points. The number of Vital Points which now require Light A.A. protection has greatly increased. These may conveniently be divided into two headings – industrial and service requirements. A comprehensive survey of

industry is now available in the lists of Category 1 Vital Points summarized in Secret Document KP/DI. A study of this document suggests the need for protection of a further 200 points. Service requirements, for the most part new operational aerodromes, amounts to a further 150 points.

21. Furthermore war experience indicates the necessity for light A.A. weapons for the following additional purposes:

(i) Anti-mine laying aircraft.

(ii) To cover balloon barrages – there is evidence to show that the enemy regards the destruction of balloon barrages as an essential preliminary to major scale air attack.

These may be said to be the equivalent of a further 75 Vital Points, making a total of 425 additional points to be provided with Light A.A. defences.

22. The average number of equipments to cover a vital point on the present scale of defence is six. It is arguable that a higher scale of defence is desirable, but it is considered that such reinforcements as are necessary can largely be obtained in terms of the U.P. weapon (see para. 23 below). Accepting, therefore, the average requirement of 40 mm. equipments to be six per vital point, the extra 425 vital points indicated above will call for 2,550 equipments. The total figure required for A.D.G.B. thus becomes 4,410.

*U.P. Weapon*

23. 8,000 3-inch U.P. projectors have been ordered with the specific object of defence against low-flying attack. 5,000 of these will be single and the reminder it is hoped will be twin barrel projectors. These are being organized in troops each of 16 projectors i.e. 500 troops in all.

*Summary*

24. The increases recommended in this paper may be summarised as follows:

*Royal Air Force*

(i) Fighter Squadrons 17 of which 13 have already been formed (para. 5).

(ii) Balloons. From an operational strength of 2,000 to 2,600 with 100% reserve (para. 11).

*Army*

A.A. Searchlights

(i) Phase I: To extend A.F.2. 87 Batteries (para. 12).

(ii) Phase II (problematical): To thicken up gun zones. 60 batteries (paras. 12 and 13).

(iii) Mobile Reserve 12 batteries (para. 14).

A.A. Guns

(iv) Heavy A.A. Guns, 189 batteries (para. 17 and. Appx. E).

(v) Light A.A. equipments, 212 batteries (para. 22).

U.P. Weapons

(vi) Single or Twin U.P., 125 batteries (para. 23).

(vii) Multi barrel U.P. weapon, 160 equipments (para. 19).

It should be noted that the acceptance of the above recommendations will involve appropriate increases in ancillary services and in the holding of reserve equipments on the authorized scales.

25. Higher Organisation.

The above increases, which amount to between 170 and 180 regiments will call for a corresponding increase in brigades, divisions, and also in the creation of some intermediate formations such as A.A. corps, between the A.A. higher command and the divisions. The exact requirements in the above respects calls for more detailed examination. At this stage, therefore, it will suffice to indicate that there are two cardinal principles which must govern the new organisation.

(i) A.O.C.-in-C., Fighter Command must have a single A.A. Commander to deal with.

(ii) The location and boundaries of A.A. corps and divisions must be largely dictated by the necessity for close co-operation with Royal Air Force Groups.

Although the production of A.A. heavy and light artillery equipments has still considerable leeway to make in order to complete authorised programmes, nevertheless much preliminary work, reconnaissance, etc., for the new defences has to be done and should accordingly be initiated as soon as possible. With regard to A.A. searchlights, the expansion will begin almost at once.

The Committee are, therefore, of opinion that the details of the new organisation should be a matter for early examination and the necessary new formations and their staffs set up without delay.

26. The Deputy Chiefs of Staff are therefore asked –

(i) To take note of the increases in Fighter Squadrons and Balloon barrages indicated in paragraphs 5, 10 and 11 i.e. 17 more squadrons, 6 new balloon barrages and increases to existing balloon barrages. Further to note that increases beyond the above figures may prove necessary but that the assessment of these requirements must be deferred until more experience is obtained both of the effects of enemy attacks and of our counter offensive.

(ii) To approve the suggested increases in A.A. defences as follows:

(a) *Searchlights*:

(i) Stage I., 87 batteries to complete the extensions of the A.F.Z.

(ii) Stage II., 60 batteries to thicken up gun zones. This stage to be undertaken only if necessary should the developments of G.L.II as an adequate means of directing gun fire prove unsuccessful.

(iii) The provision of a mobile reserve of 12 batteries.

(b) *Heavy A.A. guns*: 1,512 guns making a total of 3,744 H.A.A. guns for A.D.G.B.
(c) *Light A.A. guns*: 2,550 equipments making a total for A.D.G.B. of 4,410
(d) *Single or twin barrel U.P.*: 500 troops i.e. 8,000 projectors.
(e) *Multi barrel U.P. weapon*: 160 equipments.
(iii) They are further asked to endorse the view expressed in paragraph 25 that the higher organisation necessitated by the above increases, should be examined by the War Office as a matter of urgent priority and that the new organisation arising from this examination should be implemented forthwith.

> *(Signed) D.F. Stevenson,*
> *Chairman, on behalf of the Sub-Committee.*
> *Richmond Terrace, S.W.1.*
> *16th August, 1940.*

## Annex B

### PROPOSED INCREASES IN BALLOON BARRAGE DEFENCES

New Land Borne Barrages

| | |
|---|---|
| Pembroke | 48 (to cover Convoy Assembly Anchorage, mine-filling depot and oil tanks). |
| Falmouth | 24 |
| Ardeer | 48 (to cover I.C.I. and R.O.F.) |
| Yeovil | 24 |
| Newport | 40 (to cover Docks; industrial plants of town, G.W.R. Bridge and Lysaghts Steel Works). |
| Belfast | 40 (exact number dependent on reconnaissance). |
| *Total* | 224 |

Extensions to Existing Barrages

| *Location* | *Additional* | *New Total Establishment* |
|---|---|---|
| Cardiff | 16 | 32 |
| Barry | 8 | 16 |
| Swansea | 24 (to cover Llandarcy) | 32 |
| Port Talbot | 8 | 16 |
| *Totals* | *56* | *96* |

Anti-Mine Laying Barrages

| | |
|---|---|
| Clyde (Greenock) | 6 land borne (excluding water-borne V.L.A.) |

| | |
|---|---|
| Mersey | 8 in outer barrage + 4 in inner all water-borne |
| Bristol Channel | 10 water-borne (above Barry to Avonmouth) |
| Plymouth | 2 land-borne + 6 water-borne |
| Portsmouth | } |
| (Spithead to Nab.) | } |
| Milford Haven | } |
| Poole | } |
| Portland | } |
| Barrow | } |
| Humber | } 10 each (subject to reconnaissance) |
| Hartlepool | } |
| Tyne | } |
| Blythe | } |
| Falmouth | } |
| Swansea | } |
| Belfast | } |

*Annex D*

## DETAILED A.A. SEARCHLIGHT REQUIREMENTS
### For (a) Extensions of the A.F.Z. and (b) Thickening up Gun Zones

| Locations | No. of batteries to cover area at wide spacing | No. of batteries required to thicken up gun zones | Total |
|---|---|---|---|
| To complete authorised zones | 6 | 14 | 20 |
| To close gap in cente of England | 25 | 6 | 31 |
| Devon – Cornwall extension | 19 | 3 | 22 |
| South Wales Coast | 5 | 3 | 8 |
| North Wales fringe and Snowden area | 2 | - | 2 |
| North Lancashire extension | 3 | 5 | 8 |
| Glasgow extension | 4 | 3 | 7 |
| Edinburgh – Tyne Corridor | 8 | - | 8 |
| Northern Ireland District | 7 | 1 | 8 |
| Aberdeen. | 1 | 1 | 2 |
| Inverness. | 2 | 1 | 3 |
| Anglesey | 1 | - | 1 |
| Stranraer. | 1 | - | 1 |
| Carlisle Area. | 3 | 2 | 5 |
| To provide close spacing for gun defended areas in existing lighted zones | - | 21 | 21 |
| | 87 | 60 | 147 |

| Mobile Reserve | - | - | 12 |
|---|---|---|---|
| *Totals* | | | |
| | *87* | *60* | *159* |
| *Number of Lights* | *2,088* | *1,440* | *3,816* |

## Annex E

## PROPOSED INCREASES IN HEAVY A.A. DEFENCE

### 1. Increase to defences authorised under C.I.D. 319.

| Location | Authorised at present | Increases Required | Total | Remarks on increases |
|---|---|---|---|---|
| Clyde Area | 80 | 40 | 120 | Ardeer Irvine 16 |
| | | | | East Glasgow 24 |
| Belfast | 24 | 24 | 48 | Strengthening defence |
| Bristol-Avonmouth | 56 | 24 | 80 | Strengthening defence |
| South Wales Area | 80 | 128 | 208 | |
| Derby | 24 | 16 | 40 | |
| Harwich | 16 | 8 | 24 | |
| Dover | 16 | 8 | 24 | |
| Bradford-Huddersfield Area | 64 | 16 | 80 | |
| *Totals* | *360* | *264* | *624* | |

### 2. Defences authorised since C.I.D. 319 and suggested increases.

| Location | Authorised at present | Increases Required Total | Total |
|---|---|---|---|
| Aberdeen | 8 | 8 | 16 |
| Kyle of Lochalsh | 8 | - | 8 |
| Shetlands | 12 | 4 | 16 |
| Scunthorpe | 24 | - | 24 |
| Barrow | 16 | 8 | 24 |
| Scapa | 64 | - | 64 |
| Dundee | 4 | 12 | 16 |
| Langley Slough & Hounslow | 32 | - | 32 |
| Chesterfield | 16 | - | 16 |
| Leighton Buzzard | 4 | 4 | 8 |
| Daventry | 4 | 4 | 8 |
| Crewe | 8 | 8 | 16 |
| Bramley | 8 | - | 8 |
| Falmouth | 8 | 16 | 24 |
| Caerwent | 8 | 8 | 16 |
| Brockworth | 40 | - | 40 |
| Brooklands | 16 | - | 16 |
| Blyth | 8 | - | 8 |
| Stanton | 8 | - | 8 |

| | | | |
|---|---|---|---|
| Stanley | 16 | - | 16 |
| Broughton Moor | 16 | - | 16 |
| *Totals* | *328* | *72* | *400* |

Under C.I.D. 319-168, guns were authorised to meet new requirements. The above can, therefore, be satisfied by provision of a further 232 guns i.e. (400-168).

## 3. New Defences Recommended

| Location | Number of Guns | Total | Industrial Importance |
|---|---|---|---|
| 1. Carlisle – Longtown | 24 | 24 | Ammunition Depot – Carlisle Railway Junction. |
| 2. Anglesey | 8 | 8 | Port and communication. |
| 3. Lancashire Area | 104 | 104 | General industrial war, to include particularly: |
| Warrington | | | |
| Salford | | | |
| Southport | | | Chemicals I.C.I. |
| Wigan | | | Aircraft Factories |
| Bolton | | | Ordnance Factories |
| Rochdale | | | Glass |
| Bury | | | Copper |
| Chorley | | | British Aluminium |
| Preston | | | |
| Blackburn | | | |
| Blackpool | | | |
| Fleetwood | | | |
| Lancaster | | | |
| 4. Chester Area | 48 | 48 | |
| Chester | 12 | | Aircraft and Rly. Junction |
| Mold | 8 | | I.C.I. |
| Wrexham | 12 | | Magazine Iron & Steel Works |
| Overton Area | 8 | | Hydro Electrics |
| 5. Stoke Area | 24 | 24 | |
| Stoke, Swynnerton | 8 | | Marshalling yard, shell filling, copper works |
| Lyme | 8 | | Aircraft, aluminium |
| Stafford | 8 | | Abrasive wheels |
| 6. West Country | 72 | 72 | |
| Gloucester | 12 | | Aircraft |
| Cheltenham | 8 | | Air screws |
| Hereford | 12 | | Shell filling and R.O.F. |
| Worcester | 8 | | Shell filling and testing machine tools |
| Kidderminster | 8 | | Aero components, Food storage |
| Redditch | 12 | | High duty alloys – B.S.A. – Tubes |
| Shrewsbury | 12 | | Gun factory & R.O.F. |

| | | | |
|---|---|---|---|
| 7. <u>Fishguard Area</u> | | 16 | 16 |
| Fishguard | 8 | | Port and communications |
| Trecwn | 8 | | Ammunition depot |
| 8. <u>Swindon Area</u> | 32 | 32 | |
| Swindon | 16 | | Engineering & Railway Works |
| Malmesbury | 8 | | Aircraft and instruments |
| Chippenham | 8 | | Engineering |
| 9. Redruth Area | 16 | 16 | |
| Redruth | 8 | | I.C.I. and communication |
| Dartmouth | 8 | | Shipbuilding |
| 10. Shoreham by Sea | 8 | 8 | Electric power and oil research works |
| 11. <u>Reading Area</u> | 24 | 24 | |
| Reading | 8 | | Aircraft |
| Aldershot | 16 | 24 | Military camp |
| 12. <u>East Coast Area</u> | 216 | | 216 |
| Ipswich | 12 | | Docks – mills – shipbuilding and repairs |
| Norwich | 12 | | Instruments and range finders |
| Yarmouth | 8 | | Docks, shipbuilding and repairs |
| Lowestoft | 8 | | Docks, shipbuilding. Armament and ammunition |
| Colchester | 8 | | Ordnance Depot and garrison |
| Cambridge | 8 | | Instruments |
| Luton | 12 | | Ball bearings, lorry output, engineering |
| Peterborough | 12 | | Armament firms – bombs R.O. Depot |
| Northampton | 12 | | Machine tools and Fighting Equipment |
| Leicester | 12 | | Engineering Works and Iron Works, Aircraft, Napiers |
| Corby | 8 | | Steel Works |
| Rugby | 12 | | Dynamos – KLG plugs, W/T Station |
| Newark | 8 | | Ball bearings |
| Lincoln | 8 | | Armoured vehicles |
| Beeston (Notts.) | 16 | | Chemicals – Medical |
| York | 8 | | Instrument makers |
| Barnsley | 16 | | Coke ovens |
| Doncaster | 12 | | Railway works |
| Darlington | 16 | | Heavy steel works |
| Selby | 8 | | Food stores – magazine |
| 13. <u>Durham Area</u> | 24 | 24 | |
| Chester le Street | 24 | | Ordnance – oxygen |
| 14. Workington | 8 | 8 | Heavy steel and coke ovens |
| 15. <u>Scotland</u> | 56 | 56 | |
| Inverness | 8 | | Aluminium |
| Bishoptown | 8 | | Ordnance Factories |
| Caledonian Canal | 8 | | Aluminium and Electric power |

| | | | |
|---|---|---|---|
| Stranraer | 8 | | Port |
| Oban | 8 | | Port |
| Wick | 8 | | |
| Campbeltown | 8 | | W/T station and communication |
| *Total* | | *672* | |

## 4. Aerodromes

Under C.I.D. 319-128 A.A. guns were authorised for the defence of 32 aerodromes. There are now 100 operational aerodromes (including aerodromes of the Fleet Air Arm co-operational Training Units and Aircraft-storage units) located within 20 miles of the coast. It is considered that H.A.A. defences should be allocated for these aerodromes on a scale of 4 per aerodrome. The total commitment will thus be 400 of which 128 are already provided for. An extra 272 guns will thus be required. Total 272

## 5. Reserve

C.I.D. Paper 319 authorised a mobile reserve of 168 guns. In view of the need for covering land forces operating in this country and for meeting a new tactical situation it is recommended that this reserve should be retained. (No extra provision over that of C.I.D. 319 is therefore required for the mobile reserve). In addition a new requirements reserve should be provided to take the place of the reserve provided under the Ideal Scheme and which has now been absorbed. It is recommended that in view of the increased defences provided under this paper that this new requirement should be limited to 72 guns.

6. The total increases thus recommended are:

(i) To increase defences authorised under C.I.D. 319 (para. 1) – 264
(ii) To provide for defences authorised together with their increases since C.I.D. 319 (para. 2) – 232
(iii) To create new defences (para. 3) – 672
(iv) For aerodrome defence (para. 4) – 272
(v) To create a fresh new Reserve (para. 5) – 72
*Total: 1,512*

# Appendix X

# Relative Vulnerability of the Coastal Sectors

MINUTE BY THE PRIME MINISTER AND MINISTER OF DEFENCE

Bearing in mind the immense cost in war-energy and disadvantage of attempting to defend the whole west coast of Great Britain, and the dangers of being unduly committed to systems of passive defence, I should be glad if the following notes could be borne in mind:

1. Our first line of defence against invasion must be as ever the enemy's ports. Air reconnaissance, submarine watching, and other means of obtaining information should be followed by resolute attacks with all our forces available and suitable upon any concentrations of enemy shipping.
2. Our second line of defence is the vigilant patrolling of the sea to intercept any invading expedition, and to destroy it in transit.
3. Our third line is the counter-attack upon the enemy when he makes any land fall, and particularly while he is engaged in the act of landing. This attack which has long been ready from the sea, must be reinforced by Air action; and both sea and air attacks must be continued so that it becomes impossible for the invader to nourish his lodgments.
4. The land defences and the home Army are maintained primarily for the purpose of making the enemy come in such large numbers as to afford a proper target to the sea and air forces above mentioned, and to make hostile preparations and movements noticeable to Air and other forms of reconnaissance.
5. However, should the enemy succeed in landing at various points, he should be made to suffer as much as possible by local resistance on the beaches, combined with the aforesaid attack from the sea and the air. This forces him to use up his ammunition, and confines him to a limited area. The defence of any part of the coast must be measured not by the

forces on the coast, but by the number of hours within which strong counter attacks by mobile troops can be brought to bear upon the landing places. Such attacks should be hurled with the utmost speed and fury upon the enemy at his weakest moment, which is not, as is sometimes suggested, when actually getting out of his boats, but when sprawled upon the shore with his communications cut and his supplies running short. It ought to be possible to concentrate 10,000 men fully equipped within six hours and 20,000 men within twelve hours, upon any point where a serious lodgment has been effected. The withholding of the reserves until the full gravity of the attack is known, is a nice problem for the Home Command.

6. It must be admitted that the task of the Navy and Air Force to prevent invasion becomes more difficult in the narrow seas, namely: from the Wash to Dover. This sector of the coast front is also nearest to the supreme enemy objective, London. The sector from Dover to Lands End is far less menaced because the Navy and Air Force must make sure that no mass of shipping, still less protecting warships, can be passed into the French Channel ports. At present the scale of attack on this wide front is estimated by the Admiralty at no more than 5,000 men. Doubling this for greater security, it should be possible to make good arrangements for speedy counter-attack in superior numbers, and at the same time to achieve large economies of force on this southern sector in which the beach troops should be at their minimum and the mobile reserves at their maximum. These mobile reserves must be available to move to the south-eastern sectors at short notice. Evidently this situation can only be judged from week to week.

7. When we come to the west coast of Britain, a new set of conditions rules. The enemy must commit himself to the broad seas, and there will be plenty of time, if his approach is detected, to attack him with cruisers and flotillas. The Admiralty dispositions still conform to this need. The enemy has at present no warships to escort him. Should we, for instance, care to send 12,000 men unescorted in merchant ships to land on the Norwegian coast, or in the Skagerrak and Kattegat, in face of superior sea power and air power? It would be thought madness.

8. However, to make assurance triply sure, the Admiralty should pursue their plan of laying a strong minefield from Cornwall to Ireland, covering the Bristol Channel and the Irish Sea from southward attack. This minefield is all the more necessary now that by the adoption of the North-about route for commerce we have transferred a large part of our patrolling craft from the Western Approaches which have become permanently more empty and unwatched.

9. The establishment of this minefield will simplify and mitigate all questions of local defence north of its point of contact with Cornwall. We must consider this sector from Cornwall to the Mull of Kintyre as the least

vulnerable to seaborne invasion. Here the works of defence should be confined to guarding by a few guns or land torpedo tubes the principal harbours, and giving a moderate scale of protection to their gorges. It is not admissible to lavish our limited resources upon this sector.

10. North of the Mull of Kintyre to Scapa Flow, the Shetlands and the Faroes lie in the orbit of the main Fleet. The voyage of an expedition from the Norwegian coast would be very hazardous, and its arrival anywhere right round to the Firth of Forth would not raise immediately decisive issues. The enemy, who is now crouched, would then be sprawled. His advance would lie in difficult and sparsely-inhabited country. He could be contained until sufficient forces were brought to bear, and his communications immediately cut from the sea. This would make his position all the more difficult, as the distances to any important objective are much longer and he would require considerable wheeled transport. Scapa is the main naval base. Cromarty Firth and Invergordon are fortified. The Firth of Forth is a very strong fortress. Flotillas are available in all these bases. It would be impossible to fortify all landing points in this sector, and it would be a waste of energy to attempt to do so. A much longer period may be allowed for counter-attack than in the south-east opposite London.

11. From the Forth to the Wash is the second-most important sector, ranking next after the Wash to Dover. Here, however, all the harbours and inlets are defended, both from the sea and from the rear, and it should be possible to counter-attack in superior force within twenty-four hours. The Tyne must be regarded as the second major objective after London, for here (and to a lesser extent at the Tees) grievous damage could be done by an invader or large scale raider in a short time. On the other hand, the sea and air conditions are more favourable to us than to the southward.

12. The combined Staffs should endeavour to assign to all these sectors their relative scales of vulnerability and defence, both in the number of men employed in the local defence of beaches and of harbours, and also in the number of days or hours within which heavy counter-attacks should be possible. As an indication of these relative scales of attack and defence, I set down for consideration the following:

| | |
|---|---|
| Forth to Wash inclusive | 3 |
| Wash to Dover promontory | 5 |
| Dover promontory to Lands End, and round to start of minefield | 1½ |
| Start of the minefield to the Mull of Kintyre | ¼ |
| Mull of Kintyre Northabout to the Firth of Forth | ½ |

*(Initialled) W.S.C., 5th August, 1940*
*Richmond Terrace, S.W.1.*

Appendix XI

# Admiralty Appreciation of Invasion in May 1940

## (Admiralty M.010329: 29 May 1940)

**Foreword**

In order to achieve the greatest measure of surprise it is likely that the enemy will use the shortest sea route to his objective, but the possibility of diversion or subsidiary operations in the Shetlands, Ireland or North of Scotland must be borne in mind in making out dispositions. This paper deals only with the Naval side of Invasion.

**Enemy's Action**

2. It is probable that the enemy will employ his maximum scale of effort and will accept almost catastrophic losses.

3. Wide dispersion of the points of attack is likely and simultaneous attacks at numerous points probable. At each point of attack the best possible use will be made of air, 5th Column and armoured vehicles in the first wave. Success or failure of the first wave will decide whether the enterprise ever reaches the scale of an invasion.

4. There are many forms of air action the enemy may take, and these are discussed in other papers, but the object of our naval forces being to prevent seaborne attack, this paper is confined to the consideration of this point only.

5. Seaborne attack may be delivered by:

> (a) Ordinary transports of orthodox type, relying on port facilities for unloading.
> (b) Transports of a special type, self-contained as regards unloading.
> (c) Special Landing Craft.
> (d) Surface Warships.
> (e) Submarines.

6. It appears from the deliberations of the Home Defence Executive that the most formidable threat to this country would be the landing of armoured vehicles. It is therefore proposed to deal with this first.

7. These vehicles could be carried by ordinary transports relying on port facilities for unloading, by transports of a special type self-contained as regards unloading, by special landing craft, and possibly by surface warships. We must expect every available fighting ship to be used in the best way to secure the sea passage.

8. The enemy may be expected to assemble his expedition in the shortest possible time before it is launched, and he may attempt to evade our reconnaissance by assembling at numerous points, large transports being distant, while smaller craft would be collected in the numerous canals and estuaries closer to our coasts. The expedition may debouch from many points on the coast, each unit proceeding independently to its point of attack.

9. Owing to the necessity for synchronising the air and seaborne efforts and the comparative inability of fighter aircraft to intercept at night, it is probable that the attack will be made on a dark night or at early dawn and at high tide. This cannot, however, be relied upon.

10. The most favourable area for this operation will be that which provides the optimum conditions for landing the first wave. This is within the area where his fighters and bombers can operate in conjunction. It extends at present from the Wash to Newhaven, and will grow to the westward according to his progress in France.

11. The greatest threat is from armoured vehicles, and these can be landed by ordinary transports or warships only at an established port, or by transports of a special type or special landing craft on any open beach in fine weather from the Wash to Newhaven. There are other beaches and ports available to the northward of this area which may be selected, but this would involve a longer sea voyage and lie outside the area of his maximum air effort.

**Methods he may Employ to Support the Expedition**

12. (a) *Strategical*. This may take the form of:

(1) An attempt by surface ships to draw our surface forces away from his selected invasion area or by heavy attacks on trade by submarines in secondary theatres to draw off our destroyers and light craft.

(2) Mining either defensively in the area of his operations or offensively against our Fleet bases.

(3) Interception of our forces by a suitable disposition of submarines.

(b) *Tactical*

(1) Close escort by destroyers and M.T.Bs.

(2) Support by cruisers or other large surface forces, but at present he may well hesitate to risk his battle cruisers in the southern part of the North Sea.

(3) Cover by his heavy ships and submarines.

**Our Counter-measures**
13. As the best disposition of our forces and/or arrangement of our patrols and also the action taken at our ports are dependent upon the amount of warning we can get, it is vital to our interests that every means should be employed to give the earliest possible indication of the assembly and the movement of the expedition.
14. We can attack the expedition:
 (a) Before departure;
 (b) During passage;
 (c) At its points of arrival.

**Attack before Departure**
15. To attack before departure, which is the most effective method, we must have early indication of assembly by means of our intelligence and reconnaissance. We can then attack by air, mine the approaches to the points of assembly and possibly bombard these from seaward.
16. Since any attack on the expedition on passage must primarily depend upon adequate and accurate reconnaissance (which may not in the event be available) it is considered that our main dispositions should be designed to deal with attack at the points of arrival, whilst retaining sufficient flexibility to deal with attack during passage if the necessary information is available.
17. It is therefore proposed to deal with the attack at the points of arrival first, and then to adjust, if necessary, our dispositions in accordance with the possibility of attack during passage, whilst bearing in mind that his heavy ship force which may be employed to support the expedition or to create a diversion must be engaged by our own heavy forces.

**Attack at Point of Arrival**
18. Any attempt to forecast the exact positions of the points of arrival would be fruitless, since it is anticipated that he would accept risks from his own and our own mines, and navigational difficulties are not insuperable on any part of the coast, especially if special landing craft are used. Our forces must therefore be so disposed as to cover the area Wash to Newhaven as a whole.
19. Reconnaissance must be as complete as possible. This should be achieved by:
 (a) Long range reconnaissance provided by the Coastal Command and by submarines.
 (b) Medium reconnaissance provided by the Fleet Air Arm shore-based aircraft.
 (c) Offshore reconnaissance by small craft, such as minesweepers and as many smallcraft as can be made available.
 (d) Coast watching.

20. For the inshore work entailed in the attack and destruction of the enemy expedition at its points of arrival, striking forces of destroyers and M.T.Bs. aided by smaller craft, are most suitable. The area of operations is so large that the number of these craft required will greatly exceed those immediately available without weakening the forces in other areas.

21. The enemy heavy ship force which we have to consider is shown in Appendix C. We must therefore be prepared to operate not less than five heavy ships and one aircraft carrier with a minimum of two flotillas of destroyers. The proposed disposition of our heavy force is dealt with in paras. 32 and 33.

22. The only suitable places for basing striking forces in or near the area Wash to Newhaven are: Dover, Sheerness, Harwich, Humber, Portsmouth. It is considered that not less than four flotillas of destroyers should be based on these ports, Portsmouth being an alternative to Dover.

23. Minesweeping forces should be employed in maintaining the searched channels. When not so employed a proportion of them could be used to seaward of the channels for offshore reconnaissance.

24. The maximum number of craft, such as destroyers (ex-Escort Vessels D), Corvettes, etc., as can be spared from escort duties should be allotted to the area. A/S Striking Forces within the area must be prepared to act as gunboats. Numbers of small motor yachts and other comparatively insignificant craft should be collected immediately for watching close inshore and hampering the enemy's operations. Even if unarmed, these craft would be most valuable for giving warning.

25. The exact allocation of these numerous smaller craft to the various Flag Officers' Commands should be investigated immediately.

26. It is necessary to provide support for the four striking destroyer flotillas and the most suitable bases for such supporting forces are Sheerness, Harwich and the Humber. These supporting forces should be ARETHUSA-class cruisers, A/A cruisers and sloops, as it is desirable to leave the heavier 6-inch cruisers for operations with the Main Fleet.

27. The employment of submarines inside the East Coast barrier is not advocated.

28. The F.A.A. T.S.R. Squadrons now disembarked and operating under Coastal Command would add greatly to our striking effort, and should be prepared to use the torpedo in the first instance.

29. The minelaying destroyers (20th D.F.) should be employed from now onwards in mining off energy ports or in strengthening existing fields. At the time of the approach of the expedition they may therefore be in varying stages of readiness for minelaying. If empty of mines they

should be employed to strengthen our striking forces, using their gun armaments. An attempt to lay a tactical minefield is not advocated.

**Attack During Passage**

30. It remains to examine whether the above dispositions to defeat the attack on its arrival are sufficiently flexible to compete with the happy possibility that our reconnaissance might enable us to intercept the expedition on passage.

31. The enemy may employ his heavier surface forces as a diversion or as cover to his main expedition. The diversion to be effective must be to the northward of our Fleet base and threaten some interest valuable to us, such as the Northern Patrol, our forces at Narvik, or the ocean trade routes, or Eire.

32. His battle cruisers are likely units to be used in the northern diversion which, with the present situation at Narvik and of the Northern Patrol, must be countered. He also has adequate strength to operate as many as two 8-inch cruisers, three 6-inch cruisers and possibly two old battleships in the southern part of the North Sea. It is therefore necessary for us to provide a sufficient force of heavy ships, with reconnaissance and screening forces to counter both these possibilities.

33. The forces to operate against the expedition on passage should be the four striking flotillas with such cruiser support as is available.

34. No useful purpose would be served by the sloops and smaller craft stationed to the westward of the mined barrier being drawn to seaward. These weak units should remain inshore to engage those enemy units that escape interception by our four striking flotillas and supporting cruisers.

35. The striking and supporting forces are so stationed that they can operate against the expedition at the point of arrival or on passage if adequate warning is given.

**Attack in the English Channel**

36. It may be that the enemy will attempt to force the Straits of Dover and land on the South Coast. This would be rendered easier if he succeeds in capturing the Channel ports. If he succeeds in establishing himself in the Channel ports a re-appreciation will be necessary.

37. In the meantime, should he break through to the westward of Dover, the Striking Flotilla based on Dover or Portsmouth and the South Coast submarines are well placed to attack, but the former lacks support. To make good this deficiency such "R"-class battleships as can be made available should be based at Plymouth and operate in support of the striking forces in the Channel, with such escorts as Commander-in-Chief, Western Approaches, can make available.

**Subsidiary Landings**

38. The Shetlands are within cover of the forces based at Scapa. A trawler patrol in the vicinity of the Shetlands is necessary for warning.

**Ireland**

39. Owing to the very small quantity of trade being conducted with the northern Norwegian, Finnish and Russian ports, it is uneconomical to maintain our Northern Patrol, but the A.M.Cs. as disposed for that patrol are well placed to give warning of the approach of any expedition from Norway to Ireland.

**Future Considerations: Mining**

40. The possibility of enemy occupation of the Channel ports should be kept in mind, and to be prepared for such an eventuality certain mining projects should be examined forthwith.

41. The Dover Barrage should be made as heavy and complete a block in the Straits as possible and plans should be made for a mined barrier off the South Coast similar to that now laid off the East Coast. Immediate consideration should be given to the possibility of using the mines earmarked for Operation SN for this purpose if found necessary.

Appendix XII

# Home Fleet Dispositions
# June 1940

(Admiralty Signal 1958: 7 June 1940)

"It appears that, during the next few weeks, the Fleet should be disposed to deal with four possible eventualities, viz:

(1) Invasion on the East Coast.

(2) Break-out of German ships to the northward as a diversion.

(3) Attack on Ireland.

(4) Break through into the Channel to cover an invasion of the South Coast Channel ports.

The best dispositions to deal with these situations appear to be:

(a) At Sheerness: GALATEA, ARETHUSA. The latter will return to Sheerness from Gibraltar as soon as a relief at the latter place can be found for her.

(b) Four flotillas under the C.-in-C., Nore.

(c) SOUTHAMPTON-class at the Humber.

(d) At Rosyth: NELSON, RODNEY and 2 flotillas. Also any additional 6-inch cruisers of the SOUTHAMPTON-Class that are available.

(e) At Scapa: HOOD, RENOWN, GLORIOUS and 1½ flotillas.

(f) In the Clyde: All available 8-inch cruisers, one of which would always be at sea.

(g) ARK ROYAL and one 8-inch cruiser always at sea, except when refuelling, working to the westward of a line joining Iceland and the West Coast of Ireland ......

(h) At Plymouth: VALIANT, REPULSE. C.-in-C., Western Approaches, providing the necessary destroyer escorts.

The advantages of the above appear to be:

(1) We should use our best protected ships (NELSON and RODNEY) for proceeding south to deal with invasion.

(2) The 8-inch cruisers, owing to their vulnerability in air attack, would be kept out of the southern part of the North Sea.
(3) Full use will be made of ARK ROYAL's long endurance.
(4) With the 8-inch cruisers at the Clyde, and VALIANT and REPULSE at Plymouth, ships would be as well disposed as possible to deal with an invasion of Ireland."

# Operation J.F. October 1940

## Anti-Invasion Operations
### (Short title – Operation JF)

**Operation JF**

It is possible that the enemy may attempt a raid by landing forces by any, or all, of:

(a) Ships, probably small ones which can be beached, and barges.

(b) Troop-carrying land or seaplanes.

(c) Parachutes.

(d) Fast motor boats.

(e) Tanks in self-propelled lighters.

**Object**

2. To destroy enemy before landing; or if landed to destroy him on the shore.

**Preliminary dispositions**

3. (a) Submarine patrols may be established in the Channel in accordance with Portsmouth Command War Order No. 8.

(b) Outer offshore and inshore patrols are established along the South Coast, to give early warning of enemy movements.

(c) All available armed vessels will be placed at short notice to go to the threatened area.

**Offshore patrols**

4. Offshore patrols are established as follows:

| | | | |
|---|---|---|---|
| C | From 50° 25′ N., 01° 18′ W | to | 50° 26′ N., 01° 58′ W |
| D1 | From 50° 32′ N., 02° 03′ W | to | 50° 26′ N., 02° 20′ W |
| D2 | From 50° 26′ N., 02° 20′ W | to | 50° 29½′ N., 02° 40′ W |
| E | From 50° 29½′N., 02° 40′ W | to | 50° 32½′N., 02° 57′ W |
| F, G, H | see Appendix IV | | |
| L | From 50° 33′ N., 0° 26′ W | to | 50° 29′ N., 0° 52′ W |
| M | From 50° 29′ N., 0° 52′ W | to | 50° 25′ N., 01° 18′ W |

5. These patrols will be detailed from the available yachts, A/S and M/S trawlers. During daylight and in good visibility patrols are to withdraw as follows:

A and B to Newhaven.

D and E as ordered by Flag Officer-in-Charge, Portland.

C, L and M as ordered by Extended Defence Officer (East).

In thick weather patrols are to be continuous.

**Outer Patrols**

6. (a) Outer patrols are established as follows:

| | | | |
|---|---|---|---|
| A | From 50° 38′ N., 0° 47′ E | to | 50° 31′ N., 0° 00′ |
| B | From 50° 31′ N., 0° 00′ E | to | 50° 25′ N., 0° 41′ W |
| J | From 50° 25′ N., 0° 41′ W | to | 50° 20′ N., 1° 57′ W |
| K | From 50° 20′ N., 1° 57′ W | to | 50° 09′ N. 3° 00′ W |

J and K are sub-divided into J1, J2, K1, K2, at longitudes 1° 19′ W. and 2° 30′ W. respectively, the lower number to the eastward.

(b) When orders are given to occupy the outer patrol lines, vessels which are detailed for F, G and H patrols are to patrol A and B as one line; L, M and C are to patrol J; D1, D2, and E are to patrol K. Special orders will be given should it be required to occupy sub-divisions of the outer patrol line.

(c) Vessels on outer patrol are to proceed in company using the highest cruising speed. They are to open fire at once on sighting strange vessels unless they have been warned that friendly vessels may be in their area, in which case the challenge must be made. To avoid encounter with adjacent patrols they are to turn 2 miles short of the ends of their patrol lines.

**Submarine Patrols**

7. Submarines may be ordered to patrol in areas adjacent to certain of the patrol lines given in paragraph 4. Outer and offshore patrols will be warned of this and the limitations of attack given below will then be in force.

**Limitations of Attack when Submarines are Operating**

8. (a) Destroyers and aircraft are warned that when these operations are put into force it may not be possible to notify surface and air patrols of the areas in which friendly submarines are operating. After the danger has passed, some hours will probably elapse before all friendly submarines have returned to harbour or resumed their normal patrol areas.

(b) Surface vessels are not to attack submarines unless undoubtedly hostile in any areas in which friendly submarines may be operating or on passage.

(c) Aircraft are not to attack submarines unless undoubtedly hostile.

(d) Submarines are similarly warned that it may not be possible to notify them that friendly surface vessels and submarines may pass through the areas in which they are operating and they are not to attack unless certain that the targets are hostile.

**Inshore Patrols**

9. Organisation. Inshore patrol craft are organised in groups of 6 boats. Each group is commanded by a lieutenant or sub-lieutenant R.N.V.R., and is distinguished by the letters of the patrol area for which the group is responsible.

| Group letters | Patrol Area | Base | Responsible Naval Officer |
|---|---|---|---|
| NP | St. Leonards to Eastbourne | Newhaven | N.O.I.C., Newhaven |
| NQ | Beachy Head to Newhaven | Newhaven | N.O.I.C., Newhaven |
| NR | Newhaven to Shoreham | Newhaven | N.O.I.C., Newhaven |
| NS | Shoreham to Littlehampton | Littlehampton | R.N.O., Littlehampton |
| NT | Littlehampton to Selsey | Littlehampton | R.N.O., Littlehampton |
| QU | Needles to Hengistbury Head | Yarmouth* | X.D.O. (west) |
| QV | Hengistbury Head to Durlstone Head Poole | | R.N.O., Poole |
| WW | 3′ W.S.W. of St: Albans to 2′ S. of Whitenose | Portland | F.O.I.C., Portland |
| WX | 2° 30′ W. to 2° 44′ W. | Bridport | F.O.I.C., Portland |
| WY | 2° 44′ W. to 2° 58′ W. | Bridport | F.O.I.C., Portland |

*Repair base at Hamble*

10. Motor boats are to patrol in pairs at a distance of up to five miles from the shore, depending on the visibility. Whenever weather permits there is to be at least one pair of boats on patrol in each area. If considerations of repairs and maintenance allow, a second pair of motor boats in each group is invariably to be kept at short notice in order to reinforce the pair on patrol, in the event of warning being received that enemy forces are approaching the English coast.

11. Patrols are to be disposed so as to maintain a constant watch on the lines of approach to the most likely landing places.

**Information to be Given to Patrols**

12. Patrol craft are to be given instructions on the following points:

(a) The positions of friendly sloops, yachts or trawlers patrolling to seaward of them. (See paragraph 4).

(b) The positions of any batteries in their particular area. (See Appendix II). When proceeding to attack the enemy, these positions should not be approached directly until the batteries have obviously identified and are engaging the enemy.

(c) Details of the War Watching Organisation in so far as it affects their particular area.

*Note*: It must be impressed upon patrol craft that should there be any doubt as to whether an alarm signal has been seen, the nearest watching station or battery must be closed at full speed and the signal repeated.

### Action to be Taken on Threat of Enemy Landing

13. If the first indication of a landing is received by the Commander-in-Chief, a signal will be made to ships required: "Stand by Operation JF". On receipt of this all ships and small craft addressed are to raise steam for full speed and vessels larger than M.T.B's are to proceed to anchor at Spithead at immediate notice.

14. If an area is attached or threatened, the signal will be made: "Operation JF – (locality)" and all vessels addressed are to proceed with all despatch to the locality indicated. The locality is to be given by naming the nearest town, headland, etc., or by giving distance and bearing therefrom.

### Portland and Newhaven

15. Flag Officer-in-Charge, Portland and Naval Officer-in-Charge, Newhaven, are authorised to make the executive signal should an area in their sub-commands be threatened or attacked.

### Reporting Enemy Vessels Encountered

16. It is desired to emphasise the paramount importance of making a report of suspicious or enemy forces at the first possible moment. Arrangements are made to ensure that reports reach the local military and air authorities concerned.

### Attacking the Eenemy

17. Primary object._The primary object of outer inshore and offshore patrols, subsequent to reporting the presence of the enemy, is to prevent enemy transport craft from effecting a landing. Enemy WARSHIPS should only be engaged in so far as they interfere with the primary object. It is possible that the enemy may make a feint with empty transport craft in order to draw our forces into dive-bombing attacks before the real landing develops. Every effort must therefore be made to distinguish between troop and vehicle carrying vessels and those that may be empty.

### Action at Close Range

18. The paramount importance of action at the CLOSEST range must be impressed upon all concerned and the following is as true today as when it was originally written: "No captain can do very wrong if he places his ship alongside that of an enemy".

The use of depth charges from chutes and throwers dropped among enemy troop carriers, particularly if of slow type and massed together, should receive consideration.

**Destroyer Patrols**

19. Destroyer patrols may be operating to the southward of the inshore and offshore patrol lines and may be met.

**Forces from Portland**

20. Forces from Portland are to co-operate as above and Flag Officer-in-Charge, Portland, is to make arrangements accordingly.

**Attacking on Sight – Without Challenge**

21. Ships operating ALONE in a definite area or on a patrol line may be given special orders to attack any vessel sighted WITHOUT CHALLENGE.

**Code-word**

22. The code-word CAT will be used for this, followed by any limits of area.

**Example**

23. The following signal to a ship on patrol "B": "CAT south of 50° 32′ N. Acknowledge".

Will mean that she may engage without challenging any vessel met south of 50° 32′ N., and between the longitudes of 0° 41′ W. and 0° 00°.

*W.M. James, Admiral.*

*Annex 1*

OPERATION JF
(Portsmouth Memorandum No. 0115G/83 of 1st October, 1940)

COMMUNICATIONS

**Codes**

The following code words are to be used for making first reports of enemy invasion. The code words marked with an asterisk are applicable to Navy, Army and Air Force, and are designed primarily for use of Coastal Forces in Home Waters employed on coast watching against invasion, and by Shore Authorities for the rapid conveyance of information essential to the three services. The code words may also be used for this purpose by other ships and aircraft when their use would be more appropriate than the normal methods of reporting the enemy.

| *Code word* | *Meaning* |
|---|---|
| BLACKBIRD* | I have sighted enemy invading forces on the sea. N.B.: The following pyrotechnic signal is also to be fired when enemy invading forces on the sea are encountered: "3 or more illuminating rockets type M2 which give a bright white light for about seven |

seconds fired in rapid succession at 3 second intervals". This signal will be replaced by green flares throwing out stars when the flares are available.

BISHOP* — I have sighted suspicious vessels which I think are probably enemy but I am not sure.

APPLES* — I have sighted a large number of aircraft believed enemy, flying towards the shore.

GALLIPOLI* — Enemy landing from ships or boats at "..............."

CATERPILLARS* — Enemy landing tanks at "..............."

PARASOLS* — Enemy parachutists (number indicated) landing at "..............."

STARLINGS* — Enemy aircraft landing at "..............."

PEPPER AIR — I am being attacked by aircraft.

PEPPER LIGHT — I am being attacked by light forces.

PEPPER HEAVY — I am being attacked by heavy forces.

FINISH — It is no longer possible for me to maintain my patrol.

PHONE — Return to harbour arriving at the time indicated by the four figure number following the code word. N.B.: Exact hour and half-hours will not be used in order to avoid calling attention to the fact that a time is being signalled e.g. "Hallo, Patrol G, George calling, Phone 1453".

JACKDAW — Friendly M.T.B's will be passing your patrol position within the next half-hour or at the time indicated. N.B.: It must be realised that it will probably only be feasible to give this information when M.T.B's are outward bound from their base.

Positions at sea are to be indicated by normal methods. Positions ashore are to be indicated by plain language place names.

Messages are to be prefixed "Emergency".

For reports other than code words given above, or other than the P/L amplifying report in accordance with para.6 (b), normal naval codes are to be used.

**Pyrotechnic Signals**
(a) In addition to the signal given in para. for BLACKBIRD above, the following pyrotechnic signal is in use by coastguards, coast defence units and civil authorities – Red flares throwing out stars: I have sighted enemy forces on the land.
(b) Coastguards and coastwatchers may also use the green flares vide BLACKBIRD above, if they sight enemy invading forces on the sea.

## Use of W/T or R/T
W/T or R/T is only to be used:

(i) To report enemy surface forces, submarines, or large numbers of aircraft

(ii) To report distress.

(iii) To report any suspicious occurrences.

(iv) Give any other information which might be of vital interest to the Commander-in-Chief.

On no account is W/T to be used for non-essential signals.

## Wave Frequency
Ships on patrol lines L. M and C. 2450 kc/s R/T continuous watch working with Culver. Ships on patrol lines F, G and H, or A and B. 2450 kc/s R/T continuous watch working with Newhaven (or with Culver when west of Selsey Bill, proceeding to or from patrol).

## Call Signs
(a) When making enemy reports, ships on patrol are to use the single letter denoting their patrol as their call sign.

(b) When making other signals in naval codes, ships normal W/T or R/T call sign is to be used.

(c) Collective R/T call sign of all ships on patrol keeping watch on 2450 kc/s is "Harry".

(d) The call sign for Culver is "Mabel". Call sign for Newhaven is "George".

## ENEMY REPORTS
### Offshore Patrols
When making enemy reports the first message should consist of the appropriate code words vide para. above, e.g., "Hallo George (or Mabel), Hallo George (or Mabel), Patrol G calling, Patrol G calling, Blackbird, Blackbird". When the word Blackbird is used the appropriate firework signal is to be fired.

After this signal has been passed an amplifying report in P/L may be made but this must be kept as short as possible. It should give the number and type of enemy sighted and any other important information, e.g., "Hallo George, Patrol G calling, 4 transports sighted, course N.E., my position 160 Beachy Head 15".

### Inshore Patrols
As these vessels are not fitted with W/T or R/T their only method of reporting is by firing the appropriate firework signal (vide para. above). Each motor boat of the inshore patrol is to carry the following pyrotechnic stores:

    Illuminating rockets type M2 – 1 box (12).
    Wooden uprights, firing – 4 in number.

Firework signals are only to be made by ships which sight the enemy. They are not to be repeated by ships who sight a firework only.

Certain vessels of the inshore patrol may be supplied with an R/T broadcast receiver. Instructions as to the wave length on which this is to be used, the hours of watch, and the call sign of the transmitter to be received will be issued by the Flag or Naval Officer-in-charge of the area.

This is known as the "Beetle" system and in addition to the normal instructions for watch-keeping, sets are to be switched on at once if enemy activity becomes known (e.g. by sighting another vessel's firework), and they are to be left on until it is known that the alarm was false. Sets are on no account to be used for other purposes since this will exhaust the batteries unnecessarily.

Every opportunity is to be taken when in harbour to charge the accumulator and check the H.T. battery of the "Beetle" receiver.

Any ship fitted with wireless sighting one of the firework alarm signals (vide para. above), is to report the fact by W/T stating the direction in which it was sighted e.g. "Hello George, Patrol G calling, have sighted white illuminating rockets S.W. of me".

**Recognition Signals**

Auxiliary patrol vessels will be supplied with the minor war vessels single letter challenge and reply which is to be used to identify themselves to other patrol vessels and to H.M. ships. For entry into defended ports in the Portsmouth Command and to identify themselves to coast defence batteries the local recognition signal promulgated in C.P.G.O's is to be hoisted.

When on patrol at night, A/P craft should not normally approach the shore nearer than visibility distance, or within 5 miles whichever is the less. In cases of doubt the military forces ashore may fire two rifle shots or a burst of Lewis gun fire as a challenge, in the direction of the craft sighted. If this is done the A/P craft is to reply immediately with 4 flashes from a torch, which is to be kept in instant readiness. In the event of a craft not replying to the challenge within a reasonable period, or putting to see without answering, she will be fired at.

*Annex 2*

POSITION OF SHORE BATTERIES

| | | |
|---|---|---|
| Eastbourne | 49° 45' 36" N., | 00° 17' 00" E. |
| Seaford | 50° 46' 00" N., | 00° 17' 30" E. |
| Brighton | 50° 48' 48" N., | 00° 06' 06" W. |
| Shoreham | 50° 49' 36" N., | 00° 14' 54" W. |

| Worthing | 50° 48′ 18″ N., | 00° 23′ 24″ W. |
| Littlehampton | 50° 48′ 06″ N., | 00° 32′ 06″ W. |
| Poole | 50° 41′ 15″ N., | 01° 57′ 30″ W. |
| Swanage | 50° 36′ 24″ N., | 01° 56′ 42″ W. |
| Abbotsbury | 50° 39′ 24″ N., | 02° 37′ 06″ W. |
| Lyme Regis | 50° 44′ 06″ N., | 02° 55′ 30″ W. |

Note: The above batteries are supplementary to the fixed defences at Newhaven, Portsmouth and Portland.

*Annex 3*

## AIRCRAFT PATROL

Lysander aircraft will carry out dusk and dawn anti-invasion patrols along the coast of Sheerness to Selsey Bill. There will be five separate patrols of one aircraft each. Aircraft will operate up to 6,000 feet depending upon visibility and will not proceed more than 15 miles from the coast. Dawn patrols will be for two hours from first light. Dusk patrols will be for two hours before sunset.

Anti E-boat patrols may be carried out on moonlight nights. Aircraft will leave Thorney so as to arrive in positions 50° 10′ N., 0° 40′ W. and 50° 10′ N., 01° 00′ W., one hour before the moon's meridian passage. They will patrol for two hours along lines 60 miles long, 072° and 270° respectively from the above positions.

*Annex 4*

## ORDERS FOR MINESWEEPING TRAWLERS

**Information**
The enemy may lay moored mines in the Channel with the object of preventing the free passage of our forces east and west.
**Object**
2. To carry out a search for mines during the day if ordered and maintain an observation patrol in the searched channel during the night.
**Method of Execution**
3. M/S trawlers based at Portsmouth carry out a nightly patrol of searched channel QZS. 125 and westward towards Portsmouth western channel. Patrol lines –

| F | from 50° 46′ N., 0° 50′ E | to | 50° 38′ N. 0° 26′ E |
| G | from 50° 38′ N., 0° 26′ E | to | 50° 35′ N. 0° 00′ |
| H | from 50° 35′ N., 0° 00′ | to | 50° 33′ N. 0° 26′ W |

4. Six trawlers will generally be on patrol at any time. *Note:* Minesweeping trawlers from Dover carry out a nightly patrol of QZS. 105.

5. In good visibility after a daylight sweep in the channel, patrols are to withdraw close inshore. In thick weather patrols are to be continuous.

**Action to be Taken if Mines are Found**

6. The position is to be danned and a report prefixed "Immediate" is to be made to the Commander-in-Chief. Search is then to be made to find a clear passage to the southward of the channel.

**Action to be Taken if Enemy is Sighted**

As for other patrols.

*Annex 5*

IDENTIFICATION MARKS

At 0001 G.M.T. on 18th July, 1940, identification marks were brought into force as follows:

| Reference letter | Identification mark to a/c | ID mark to surface vessels and shore batteries |
| --- | --- | --- |
| J | Single large red spot | Triangle point up |
| K | Two large red spots | Triangle point down |
| L | Single red bar fore and aft | Two triangles base to base |
| M | Two red bars fore and aft | Two triangles point to point |

2. Each pair of identification marks remain in force for a period of 24 hours and continues in force in the sequence J, K, L, M, J, K, L, M, and so on until further orders. Thus identification marks came into force in the following sequence, at 0001 G.M.T. 20th September, marks J, at 0001 G.M.T. 21st September, marks K, at 0001 G.M.T. 22nd September, marks L, and so on.

**Secrecy**

3. It is essential that the secrecy of these marks should be preserved and they are not to be displayed by ships unless engaged in operations in connection with an invasion. GREAT CARE IS TO BE TAKEN THAT THEY ARE NOT VISIBLE IN HARBOUR.

**Ensigns**

4. As additional safeguard under these circumstances maximum number of largest ensigns should be flown in pairs, one superior to the other in each hoist.

**Vessels Acting Suspiciously**

Should a vessel showing these signals act in a suspicious or hostile manner it may indicate signals have been compromised. There should be NO hesitation in treating her as hostile and the circumstances should be reported by signal at earliest opportunity to enable other units to be warned and identification marks withdrawn if evidence proves this necessary.

*Annex 6*

SHORT APPRECIATION AND FIGHTING INSTRUCTIONS

The following general instructions, which are supplementary to the orders contained in Operation JF, are intended to act as a guide to all Commanding Officers of ships in the Portsmouth Command which may take part in repelling an invasion of England.

**Enemy Intelligence**

2. The following is a list of some of the types of vessels that might be used by the enemy for the transport of an expeditionary force.

(a) Train ferries – 20 knots.

(b) Barges, towed or self propelled.

(c) Fast motor boats.

(d) Shallow draught motor vessels.

(e) Fishing craft.

(f) Sealers (7 - 12 knots).

(g) Ships with masts and funnels cut down, guns mounted for and aft and ports cut in side and stem.

Merchant vessels may also be used as mine bumpers.

3. In France and the Low Countries barges are dispersed in practically all the ports from Flushing to Havre, and it is estimated that the number of small craft available is sufficient to transport a force of at least 150,000 men. There are also concentrations of merchant shipping at Rotterdam, Antwerp and Havre and to a lesser extent at Cherbourg, Brest, Lorient and Nantes. Whatever form of transport were adopted, the invading force would undoubtedly be well provided with A.F.V.'s and artillery.

4. There is a considerable number of "E" boats, "R" boats and other small craft in the Channel ports, a few T.B.'s and 6 or 7 large destroyers. Ten U-boats were recently reported at Lorient.

**The Enemy's Plan**

5. It is dangerous to attempt to lay down the law regarding what the enemy will do. The chief factor in the success of all the operations undertaken by the Germans since September, 1939, has been that of surprise.

6. The superiority in numbers of the G.A.F. points to the extensive use of aircraft for the escort of his convoys should the enemy decide upon

a day crossing. Dive bombers might be used for attacking our shore batteries (See Operation JF, App. II). A wide range of cloud and visibility conditions would be suitable for such operations.

7. Powerful batteries have been erected on the French coast between Calais and Etaples. These might be used to support a landing on the Kentish coast, though their value by night would probably be low.

8. Convoys crossing by night would probably be escorted by "E" boats, T.B.'s and destroyers. A night crossing would have many advantages for the enemy, though the G.A.F. would be able to give little support until dawn broke.

9. If the enemy were determined to stake all upon the success of an invasion, the possibility that cruisers and/or heavy ships might be sent into the Channel cannot be ruled out. Cherbourg and harbours on the French Atlantic coast are available to them.

10. The invasion forces would probably be split up into several parts, some of which would be merely diversionary. To distract our attention, landings might be attempted in Ireland, the Shetlands or Iceland, but the main blow is expected to fall at some point between Cromer and Portland.

**Our Forces**

*Naval*

11. A list of the striking forces at Portsmouth is shown in C.P.G.O. 2596, to which must be added H.M. Ships Despatch and Dunedin.

12. The offshore and inshore patrols watching the coast are described in Operation JF.

13. Two submarine patrols are maintained off the French coast in the vicinity of Havre and Cherbourg respectively. The primary object of these submarines is to report the sailing of an expedition and secondarily to attack.

*Military*

14. It is the intention of the army to stop the enemy on the beaches, but in order to do so it is essential that the army commanders should receive early information of the approach of the enemy, and thus be able to concentrate their mobile reserves near the threatened point. Lightly armed auxiliary patrol craft may not be able to do great damage to the enemy, but they will have performed a vital service for the country if they have succeeded in warning the authorities ashore that an expedition is on its way.

*R.A.F.*

15. Information regarding the progress of the enemy's invasion preparations is mainly dependent upon air reconnaissance. When an invasion has been launched the tasks of the R.A.F. will be as follows:

| Coastal Command | Reconnaissance and attacks upon enemy convoys. |
| Bomber Command | Attacks upon enemy convoys. |
| Fighter Command | Protection of vital points and our surface forces. |

The R.N. Air Service will co-operate with the R.A.F. in carrying out the above tasks.

**Our Plan**

16. An overseas expedition is most vulnerable during the critical period between the final approach to the enemy's coast and the establishment of a bridgehead ashore. It is the intention of the Commander-in-Chief to reserve the main force of the naval counter-attack in the Portsmouth Command until this critical period, for the enemy, is reached.

17. The enemy may precede an invasion by dive-bombing attacks on ships in harbour and mine-laying in the approaches to our ports. On the whole the advantage is considered to lie in keeping our striking forces in harbour as long as possible where they will be under the protection of the shore A.A. guns and the balloon barrage. This will also give more time for sweeping the searched channels. The movements of our destroyers are however governed largely by the probable necessity for reinforcing the Dover Command.

18. The principal danger to our naval striking forces is to be apprehended from attack by the enemy's dive-bombers. On an average, our fighters can give protection up to thirty miles from the coast. By day our forces should endeavour to work within this distance of the shore, though this instruction should not be allowed to hinder Commanding Officers when in contact with the enemy. By night greater latitude can be allowed in the choice of areas in which to attack the enemy.

19. When striking forces have been despatched to any given area (See Operation JF, para. 14) it is the general intention that H.M. Ships Despatch and Dunedin and destroyers should operate to seaward say between 10 – 30 miles from the coast and the smaller vessels up to 10 miles from the coast, except for M.T.B.'s and M.A./S.B.'s which should have complete freedom of action owing to their comparative immunity from enemy air attacks.

20. It is the primary object of all striking forces to stop or disable the greatest number of enemy transports. Ships that have been disabled can be mopped up subsequently. Enemy warships should only be attacked if they are preventing the achievement of the primary object.

21. Economy in the use of ammunition should be practised, ships closing if possible to short or point-blank range. In the case of merchant

vessels the engine and boiler rooms near the waterline are vulnerable points to attack. If the barges are in tow, the tug should first be sunk or disabled. Raking shots will inflict the greatest damage on unarmed vessels. At very short ranges, quarters firing may be preferable to director firing because director salvoes are liable to miss due to uncorrected dip. Vessels carrying A.F.V.'s are important targets.

22. Ships with strong bows should seize any opportunity for ramming barges or other small craft. Destroyers should not ram.

23. Destroyers should use their torpedoes with discretion. If cruisers or heavy ships have been reported in the Channel it may be essential to attack them in order to clear the ground for attack on the transports by our smaller craft. Otherwise torpedoes may be used against transports, set to run at high speed and shallow depth.

24. If opportunity arises, depth charges set to 50 or 100 feet should be dropped close ahead of enemy vessels.

25. Enemy troops ashore should not be fired at as long as any suitable targets remain afloat and then only if fire is definitely asked for by the military authorities. Small craft should avoid operating within 6,000 yards of our shore batteries. If firing at landing craft or transports close to the shore it is desirable if possible to enfilade the area of sea near the beaches. (If fire is opened at right angles to the shore, the "overs" are liable to injure our own troops).

**Enemy Reports**

26. It is of the greatest importance that ships making contact with the enemy should inform the Commander-in-Chief of the enemy's position, course and speed and any available details regarding his composition. Brief situation reports should be signalled by W/T as the action develops, but care should be taken not to congest the W/T lines with unimportant details or duplicated reports.

*14th October, 1940*

## Appendix XIV

# VII Corps Operation Instruction No.3

### 3rd August 1940

1. Canadian Force Operation Order No. 10 of 17 Jul. 1940, is cancelled with effect from 1800 hrs., 4 Aug. 1940.
2. Formations under Comd.:
    1 Armd. Div.
    1 Army Tk. Bde.
    1 Cdn. Div.
    2 N.Z. Div. (incomplete)
    Corps Tps.
3. Task. 7 Corps is in G.H.Q. Reserve. Its primary task is to counter-attack and destroy any enemy forces invading the counties of SURREY – KENT – SUSSEX – HAMPSHIRE which are NOT destroyed by the troops of Eastern and Southern Commands.
4. Degree of Readiness. All troops in the Corps are at 8 hours' notice to move.
5. Zones of Operations. The area of probable operations can be divided into three zones:
    (a) KENT and East SUSSEX, from SHEERNESS R 39 to BEACHY HEAD R 01.
    (b) The SOUTH DOWNS from BEACHY HEAD to LITTLEHAMPTON.
    (c) The PORTSMOUTH area from LITTLEHAMPTON to WINCHESTER.
6. For the purpose of dealing with an enemy force in zone (a) a position of readiness has been selected in the area TONBRIDGE R 06 – STAPLEHURST R 26 – HAWKHURST R 14 – HARTFIELD Q 95, (See Appendix "A"), and it is possible that the Corps will concentrate in this area before offensive operations are undertaken.

7. To deal with an enemy force in zones (b) and (c) the Corps will probably deploy direct from its present area.

8. But whether the Corps moves to a concentration area prior to taking the offensive, or whether it deploys direct from its present area, contact with the enemy will be preceded by a road move, and all plans must be made for this opening phase to be carried out quickly and without confusion.

9. Routes. Routes have been selected for a move into the three zones of operations:

    Zone (a) <u>EAST</u> Routes A, B, C, D
    Zone (b) <u>SOUTH</u> Routes E, F, G, H, J, K
    Zone (c) <u>SOUTH-WEST</u> Routes L, M, N, O, P, Q

It be seen that switches are possible in most of these routes, and formations must be prepared to vary them as the situation demands. It is the intention that each of the three Divs. shall advance on two roads, and that 1 Army Tk. Bde. (road party), Corps Arty., and Corps Engineers shall each move on one road. Plans will be made on this assumption.

10. Starting Points. To co-ordinate movement of colns. on parallel routes, the 7 Corps executive order for the move will specify the time at which heads of colns. will cross a given line. The line will be as shown below routes in Appendices "B", "C" and "D". Formations will select their own S.P's for each route on which they may have to move.

11. Speed and Density:

| | |
|---|---|
| a) 1 Cdn. Div., 2 N.Z. Div, Corps Troops | Speed 12½ m.i.h. by day. Variable by night, dependent on weather conditions. It will be laid down by Corps. Density 15, 30 or 45 v.t.m. as ordered by Corps. |
| b) 1 Armd. Div. | Speed as for (a). Density normal 20 v.t.m. by day; 40 v.t.m. by night. |
| c) 1 Army Tk. Bde. | Speed, I Tanks 4 Bn. 8 m.i.h. by day, I Tanks 8 Bn. 3 m.i.h. Density normal 20 v.t.m. Other vehicles both bns. – as for (a) |

12. Rail Moves. In the event of it being possible to move I Tanks of 1 Army Tk. Bde. by rail, they will entrain at the stations listed.

13. Traffic Control. Traffic Control for rd. moves falls under two heads: (a) Keeping the rds. selected for the move clear of civilian traffic. This is the responsibility of the Commands and Corps through whose area the move takes place, and is carried out by Traffic Control Coys., assisted by the civil police. At the same time formations must be prepared to assist in this work, if the necessity arises.

(b) Guiding the coln. from S.P. to Dispersal Pt. This is the responsibility of the formation using the route. The formation will withdraw its traffic control personnel with the tail of its coln.

14. A.A. Defence. Is the responsibility of each formation on its own routes.

15. Reconnaissance. Reconnaissances will be carried out forthwith to enable all units in the Corps to be thoroughly conversant with their task in the opening phase of operations.

Appendix XV

# The German Plan for Invasion (Operation Sealion)

Directive No.16: Preparations for the Invasion of England

As England, in spite of the hopelessness of her military position, has so far shown herself unwilling to come to any compromise, I have therefore decided to begin to prepare for, and if necessary to carry out an invasion of England.

This operation is dictated by the necessity of eliminating Great Britain as a base from which the war against Germany can be fought; and if necessary the island will be occupied. I therefore issue the following orders:

1. The landing operation must be a surprise crossing on a broad front extending approximately from Ramsgate to a point West of the Isle of Wight. Elements of the Air Force will do the work of the artillery and elements of the Navy the work of engineers. I ask each of the fighting services to consider the advantage from their respective point of view of preliminary operations such as the occupation of the Isle of Wight or the Duchy of Cornwall prior to the full scale invasion, and to inform me of the result of their deliberations. I shall be responsible for the final decision. The preparations for the large scale invasion must be concluded by the middle of August.

2. The following preparations must be undertaken to make a landing in England possible:

(a) The British Air Force must be eliminated to such an extent that it will be incapable of putting up any substantial opposition to the invading troops.

(b) The sea routes must be cleared of mines.

(c) Both flanks of the Straits of Dover and the Western approaches to the Channel, approximately on a line from Alderney to Portland, must be so heavily mined as to be completely inaccessible.

(d) Heavy coastal guns must dominate and protect the entire coastal front area.

(e) It is desirable that the English fleets both in the North Sea and in the Mediterranean should be pinned down, (by the Italians in the latter instance), shortly before the crossing takes place; with this aim in view, the naval forces at present in British harbours and coastal waters, should be attacked from the air and by torpedoes.

3. Organization of Commands and of the Preparations.

The Commanders-in-Chief of the respective branches of the Armed Forces will lead their forces, under my orders. The Army, Navy and Air Force General Staffs should be within an area of no more than 50 kms. from my Headquarters (Ziegenberg) by the 1st August. I suggest that the Army and Naval General Staffs establish their Headquarters at Giessen.

The C.-in-C. of the Army will nominate one Army Group to lead the invasion forces.

The invasion will be referred to by the code name 'Sea Lion'.

During the period of preparation and execution of the landings, the armed forces will carry out the following measures:

(a) Army:

Will draft a plan for the crossing and operations of the first wave of the invading force. The necessary anti-aircraft batteries will remain under the command of the individual army units until such time as their tasks can be divided into the following groups: support and protection of the land troops, protection of the disembarkation ports, and protection after their occupation of air bases. The Army will allocate landing craft to the individual units and determine, in conjunction with the Navy, the points at which the embarkation and the landings will take place.

(b) Navy:

Will provide and safeguard the invasion fleet and direct it to the individual points of embarkation. As far as possible, ships belonging to defeated nations are to be used.

Together with aircraft patrols, the Navy will provide adequate protection on both flanks during the entire Channel crossing. An order on the allocation of the commands during the crossing will follow in due course. The Navy will further supervise the establishment of coastal batteries, and will be responsible for the organisation of all coastal guns.

The largest possible number of heavy guns must be installed as soon as possible to safeguard the crossing and to cover both flanks against enemy interference from the sea. For this purpose, A.A. guns mounted on railway bogies (supplemented by all available captured guns) with railway turn-tables will be used. The Todt Organization will be entrusted with the technical side of the organization.

(c) <u>The Air Force</u>

Will prevent all enemy air attacks, and will destroy coastal defences covering the landing points, break the initial resistance of the enemy land forces, and annihilate reserves behind the front. The accomplishment of these tasks will require the closest co-operation between all individual units of the Air Force and the invading Army units. In addition, roads used for troop movements will be attacked and approaching enemy naval vessels engaged before they can reach the embarkation and landing points.

I invite suggestions concerning the use of parachute and airborne troops, and in particular as to whether it would be advisable to keep the parachute and airborne troops in reserve for use only in case of necessity.

4. The necessary preparations for the installation of signals communications between France and England are being undertaken by the Signals Corps. The armoured under-sea cables are to be laid in co-operation with the Navy.

5. I hereby order the Commanders-in-Chief to provide me with the following information:

(a) The plans drawn up by the Navy and Air Force for providing the above basic conditions necessary for the Channel crossing (see (2)).

(b) A detailed survey of the location of the Naval coastal batteries.

(c) An estimate of the shipping space necessary and of the methods of preparation and equipment. Will civilian authorities be asked to co-operate? (Navy).

(d) The organization of air defence in the areas in which the invading troops and vehicles are concentrated. (Air Force).

(e) The plan for the Army crossing and operations; the organization and equipment of the first wave.

(f) Details of measures planned by the Navy and Air Force for the execution of the crossing itself, its protection, and the support of the landing operations.

(g) Suggestions concerning the use of parachute and airborne troops, and the organization of the anti-aircraft artillery, once the spearhead troops have advanced sufficiently on English soil to permit their use. (Air Force).

(h) Location of Army and Naval Headquarters.

(i) Are the Army, Navy and Air Force Commanders of the opinion that the invasion should be preceded by a preliminary small-scale landing?

*(Signed) Hitler*
*(Initialled) Keitel and Jold*

273

Appendix XVI

# Directive for the German 9th and 16th Armies

On the 17 July '40 HALDER issued a warning order in which he announced HITLER's decision to embark on a large scale invasion of ENGLAND. Two Armies, 16 and 9, were to make landings on the South coast of ENGLAND from FOLKESTONE to WORTHING, and a third Army, 6 Army, was to land in the area WEYMOUTH.

All inland waterway transport in the areas of 4, 6, 7, 9 and 16 Armies was to be requisitioned and removed to the coastal areas from which the invasion forces were to embark, i.e. from ROTTERDAM to CAEN, and the CHERBOURG peninsula.

On the 29 July orders were issued to commence training. It was stressed that such an operation was an entirely new task, that plans were to allow for the maximum of elasticity in their operation and that individual initiative should be in every way encouraged. The invasion date would necessarily depend on a number of factors, the chief being the time required to gain air superiority and to prepare sea transport, weather conditions, and the political situation. In any event the army must be ready for action from 25 August. (This date was later altered to 20 September).

The security problem was solved by accepting the fact that the preparation for invasion could scarcely be concealed from the enemy, but that the extent and time of the operation must be concealed. Deception measures were to take the form of threats of landings on the East coast from NORWAY and HOLLAND, and in IRELAND from the West of FRANCE.

On the 30 August BRAUCHITSCH issued a general directive on SEELOWE (the cover name for the invasion).

The object of the invasion was to eliminate BRITAIN as a possible base for operations against Germany, and if necessary to occupy it completely.

274

The <u>Army</u>, while maintaining forces in FRANCE and other fronts, was to effect a large scale landing in the South of ENGLAND, defeat the British Army, and occupy LONDON, and, if necessary, other areas of ENGLAND.

The German <u>Air Force</u> was to destroy the Royal Air Force and its supply bases, thus ensuring air superiority. In addition the German Air Force was responsible for reconnaissance of South ENGLAND, mining of South coast ports occupied by British Naval units, air cover of the invasion fleets and close support of the land forces. Luftflotten 2 and 3 were placed in support of 16 and 9 Armies respectively.

The German <u>Navy</u> was made responsible for the sea transport and the actual crossing. In the narrow Straits of Dover this was to take the form of a river crossing operation. 9 Army's crossing from LE HAVRE would take the form of a landing operation. A mine-free lane must be prepared, the flanks of which would be protected by mines, fast surface craft and U-boats. In addition the command of the heavy artillery covering the crossing from the shore was a navy responsibility.

**Invasion Plan as at 14 September '40**
Army Group 'A' composed of 16 and 9 Armies, was entrusted with the main invasion task, while Army Group 'B' (6 Army reinforced) was to stand by to carry out a second landing in the area of WEYMOUTH if the situation justified this step.

The general plan was that the specially equipped divisions of the first wave should win local bridgeheads, which were immediately to be extended to a connected landing area with unity of command. Immediate measures must be taken for defence of this area against the inevitable bitter British counter attacks. Port facilities must be seized as soon as possible. The divisions of the second wave, which included all the armour, should begin landing by the fourth day.

As soon as sufficient forces were available, probably 8 days after the initial landing, the German forces would go over to the offensive, their first objective being the line THAMES Estuary – hills South of LONDON – PORTSMOUTH. Sufficient forces must then be built up to continue the offensive, smash the remaining British forces in the SOUTH, occupy LONDON and reach the second objective, namely the general line MALDON (NE of LONDON) – SEVERN Estuary.

**Particular Tasks**
<u>16 Army</u>, consisting of 15 divisions in three waves, would load in the invasion ports from ROTTERDAM to CALAIS. Its landing was to be effected on a broad front from FOLKESTONE to HASTINGS. Simultaneously a paratroop regiment, was to be dropped on the hills

North of DOVER. As speedily as possible troops of the main landing force were to link up with the paratroops, capture DOVER from the landward side and take the important landing area RAMSGATE – DEAL, which offered particular difficulties to sea attack. The initial bridgehead, sufficient to cover successive landings, would be up to the line CANTERBURY – ASHFORD – TENTERDEN – ETCHINGHAM.

The next stage would be the advance to the first objective (see general plan above), and as soon as this was gained motorised elements must be pushed forward to the area West of LONDON to cut the capital off from South and West, and seize the THAMES crossings preparatory to advancing towards the line WATFORD – SWINDON.

9 Army, with 10 divisions in three waves, was to land between BEXHILL and WORTHING, but only the first echelons of 3 of the 5 divisions in the first wave could be shipped direct from LE HAVRE, the remaining echelons and waves would cross from BOULOGNE, under the screen cover of 16 Army's crossing, and disembark EAST and WEST of EASTBOURNE. Two paratroop regiments would be dropped to seize the important hills North of BEACHY HEAD (later the German Air Force withdrew the use of this force, and landing forces were allotted the task). The initial bridgehead should extend to the line HADLOW DOWN – BURGESS HILL – Westwards of STORRINGTON.

Army Gp. 'B'. It was decided that Army Group 'B' should play no part in the first landings. In the event of a favourable development of the sea situation, however, the group might be employed later from the CHERBOURG area in an air and sea landing in LYME REGIS Bay and seize WEYMOUTH and the hills to the North. It would then move towards BRISTOL. Its final task might be the occupation of DEVON and CORNWALL.

The embarkation ports allotted to the invasion forces were:

16 Army   ROTTERDAM & ANTWERP For motorised and armoured forces, ANTWERP, OSTEND, DUNKIRK, CALAIS
9 Army    BOULOGNE, LE HAVRE

Forces to be employed:

### Army Group 'A', 16 Army

| First Wave | Second Wave | Third Wave |
|---|---|---|
| 13 Corps: 17 Div., 35 Div | 5 Corps: 30 Div., 12 Dvi | 42 Corps: 45 Div., 164 Div |
| 7 Corps: 7 Div. | 41 Corps: 8 Armd. Div., | 4 Corps: 24 Div., 58 Div |

1 Mtn. Div,
10 Armd. Div.,
29 Mot. Div.,
Adolf Hitler fmn.,
1 Regt. G.D.

Army Group 'A', 9 Army

| *First Wave* | *Second Wave* | *Third Wave* |
| --- | --- | --- |
| 38 Corps: 26 Div., 34 Div. | 15 Corps: | 24 Corps: |
| | 4 & 7 Armd. Div. | 15 Div., |
| | | 78 Div.,20 |
| | | Mot. Div. |
| | 8 Corps: 8 Div., 28 Div. | |
| | 10 Corps: 6 Mtn. Div. | |

Army Group 'B', 6 Army
2 Corps: 6 Div., 356 Div, 87 Div.

The shipping space available consisted of: 150 steamships, 1,939 barges, 422 tugs, 994 motor boats, 100 motor coasters.

At the beginning of October a decision was being considered as to whether the invasion should be postponed for the winter months, and by the end of October it had apparently become tacitly accepted that the invasion was 'off' till the following spring, an OKH order stating that "the coming months must be employed to perfect preparations for SEELOWE".

*M.I.4/14(j)*
*30 Oct. '45*

277

# Appendix XVII

# Time Table for Operation Sea Lion

**ITEM 1**

| | |
|---|---|
| Date | Present time (3.9) |
| Order | Preparation directives and orders |
| ARMY | Movements to ports so that 1st Wave (11 Div.) is ready for embarkation. Further waves can get ready. |
| NAVY | (a) Preparation of transports in invasion ports; (b) M/S crossing lanes; (c) Minelaying in hoofden. |
| LUFTWAFFE | Air war against England. |
| Deception | The fact that a landing is being prepared is not to be concealed. Through preparations being spread over a wide area enemy can be made uncertain of landing points. 'Herbstreise' in preparation. |
| Remarks | - |

**ITEM 2**

| | |
|---|---|
| Date | D-10 (earliest) 11.9 |
| Order | Begin Operation S. Orders issued. |
| ARMY | Embarkation begins (material etc.); troops to wait. |
| NAVY | Embarkation begins (material etc.); troops to wait. U-boats proceed (mine barriers to be laid on flanks). |
| LUFTWAFFE | Embarkation begins (material etc.); troops to wait. Measures referring to Paratroops will be reported later. |
| Deception | HIPPER proceeds on D-9 for 'Herbstreise'. |
| Remarks | Operational H.Q. manned. |

**ITEM 3**

| | |
|---|---|
| Date | D-3 (forenoon) (earliest) 18.9 |
| Order | Decision on D-Day and H-hour |

278

| ARMY | Embarkation of troops. |
|---|---|
| NAVY | Embarkation of troops. |
| LUFTWAFFE | Embarkation of troops. |
| Deception | HIPPER off Iceland. 'Herbstreise II' ships from Norway to S. of North Sea. |
| Remarks | (a) H-hour to be 2 hours after high water a.m. on D-Day; (b) C-in-C Army gives 72 hours' warning before H-hour. |

**ITEM 4**

| Date | D-2 (earliest) 19.9 |
|---|---|
| Order | - |
| ARMY | - |
| NAVY | Deception. |
| LUFTWAFFE | - |
| Deception | Deception operation from Germany and Norway against English E. coast. |
| Remarks | - |

**ITEM 5**

| Date | D-24 hours |
|---|---|
| Order | Last moment for stopping operation. |
| ARMY | Maintain present operations or disperse until a new preparation date. |
| NAVY | Maintain present operations or disperse until a new preparation date. |
| LUFTWAFFE | Maintain present operations or disperse until a new preparation date. |
| Deception | If the operation is called off the enemy is not to know it. |
| Remarks | Preparations can be maintained from day to day until 27.9. |

**ITEM 6**

| Date | D-1 (earliest) 20.9 |
|---|---|
| Order | - |
| ARMY | Transport fleets proceed. |
| NAVY | Transport fleets proceed. |
| LUFTWAFFE | Transport fleets proceed. |
| Deception | Deception orders awaited. |
| Remarks | - |

**ITEM 7**

| Date | D-Day |
|---|---|

| | |
|---|---|
| Orders | - |
| ARMY | Begin landing. |
| NAVY | Begin landing. |
| LUFTWAFFE | Begin landing. Support landings. |
| Deception | - |
| Remarks | - |

## Appendix XVIII

# Air Raid Warning Organization

### Memorandum by the Home Secretary

1. It may be convenient to the Committee to have a description of the working of the Air Raid Warning System.

2. The responsibility for initiating all air raid messages for the general warning system is vested in the Air Officer Commanding-in-Chief, Fighter Command (C.I.D. Minute 9 of 301st meeting, 18th November, 1937). Fighter Command receive indications of the appearance and course of hostile aircraft from the various parts of the detector system. This information is filtered and transferred to a map in the Operations Room, and upon his reading of the situation the Air Officer Commanding-in-Chief decides whether an air raid message shall be sent. The Air Officer Commanding-in-Chief possesses, and uses, the widest possible measure of personal discretion in his decision.

3. The whole country is divided into 111 Warning Districts. The air raid message is directed to, and reaches, one Warning District at a time, so as to avoid unnecessary dislocation of industry. The districts to receive the message are defined by the use of a protractor, with the centre of its base at the reported position of the hostile aircraft. The protractor follows the course of the raid and the warnings advance correspondingly.

4. There are two distinct warnings – the Preliminary Caution or Yellow Message, and the Action Warning or Red Warning.

The Preliminary Caution is given as the outer lines of the protractor touch a Warning District, and the Red Warning as the inner lines touch it. The Preliminary Caution represents 22 minutes flying time, and the Red Warning 12 minutes flying time.

"Green" is given when the raiders have passed out of a Warning District, and "White" when all preparations can be relaxed.

5. The Warning Messages are sent out through three Trunk Exchanges, London, Liverpool and Glasgow. Each of these Exchanges in turn serves about six Group Exchanges and these Group Exchanges link up with the local Exchanges who work the warning system. On the average, the time required from the instructions of Fighter Command to the last receipt of the warning by persons on the Warning List is five minutes.

6. The Yellow Caution is given on an order of priority to Government Departments, Naval and Military and Air Force Establishments, A.R.P. Headquarters, major Police Stations, Fire Stations, certain A.R.P. Services, public utility services, explosive factories, certain factories of national importance, large oil installations and works, e.g. blast furnaces, with industrial processes involving external glare which can be reduced if prior warning is given.

It is a confidential message. Those who receive it are instructed to take whatever preparatory action is absolutely necessary, but in as unobtrusive manner as possible, in order that the public may not be troubled by the receipt of the Caution. This is essential because it by no means follows that a Yellow Message will be succeeded by a Red Warning. The attack may be beaten off or may turn its course, and experience during the last week has shown that many parts of the country can be under Yellow Caution without the Red Warning supervening.

7. The Red Warning List follows the same priority as the Yellow Caution, though it goes out to a larger number of recipients.

8. The public warning system is based on the authority of the police. It consists either of sirens controlled entirely by the police, i.e. on police boxes, or in most cases outside London by a combination of such sirens and factory sirens and hooters, under arrangements made between the police and the establishment by which the telephone for the receipt of instructions at the establishment shall be manned continuously. The use of sirens and hooters except in connection with air raid warnings has been prohibited in all parts of the country; and in some areas arrangements have been made by which other sirens, are sounded when the official sirens are heard.

9. The warning system is based on the personal appreciation by the Air Officer Commanding-in-Chief, Fighter Command (or a Senior Officer to whom he has delegated his discretion), of reports which are often confusing. He has had some difficulty initially in identifying hostile and friendly aircraft, but the equipment for enabling friendly aircraft to be identified is being fitted as rapidly as possible. This process will not be

completed for a few months. He has also to distinguish between a reconnaissance flight of hostile aircraft which will probably not make an attack on any area, and a bombing attack, and may have on occasion to distinguish between the possibility of attack upon a general objective, such as an industrial area, and a specific objective within that area, such as ships at anchor in the harbour.

Unless he is automatically to release the warning system, with its consequent dislocation of production and disturbance to popular morale, every time a hostile aircraft, even if it is a single aircraft, is approaching the coast, he must make the best judgment possible of the probable intentions of hostile aircraft. It is inevitable that he may on occasion make what will be described as a mistake and either withhold a warning, (for example, of the approach of a single aircraft which appears to be on a reconnaissance flight, but does, in fact, subsequently drop bombs) or give a warning of an attack which does not develop. But the sensible working of the warning system depends so much upon the study of the behaviour of the enemy that he has been assured that it is wished that he should exercise this personal responsibility.

10. If the general warning system is to work satisfactorily it is essential to maintain the decision of the Committee of Imperial Defence that the warning system originates only from the A.O.C.-in-C., Fighter Command. In recent days other agencies have been injecting warnings into the general warning system, with considerable local confusion.

11. It is almost equally important that the distinction should be maintained between the Yellow Cautionary Message and the Action Warning. It may not be possible to prevent some of the things that are done, and properly done, upon receipt of the Yellow Caution, from being observed, but it should be possible to prevent a loose dissemination of the receipt of the Yellow Caution, especially as in certain cases it is wrongly described as a warning. Steps are being taken to tighten up this side of the warning system.

12. There were special circumstances affecting the warnings for the raid on the Firth of Forth, but in any case it is quite certain that occasionally a solitary raider, or perhaps two or three planes, whose behaviour has led the Air Officer Commanding-in-Chief to conclude that they are on reconnaissance work, may attack some objective; and that, as the area concerned has not been given Red Warning, the public sirens will not be sounded.

It has been suggested that if the raid actually develops before instructions have been received to give the public warning, somebody in the locality should be authorised to sound the sirens immediately. This is not so easy as it looks. In the first place, the sirens disturb sound location systems, and the Air Officer Commanding-in-Chief has already called attention to this in connection with the extended periods during which air raid warnings sounded in the first week of the war. At night the interference of the sirens can be more serious, for a sound location system is related to the searchlights, which would become less effective just at the time when they might be most useful to the anti-aircraft guns.

Moreover, the "authority" for sounding the sirens must, for reasons indicated above, be jealously guarded. For the area must not only be warned, but also cleared from the warning.

If, for example, the local police, either because they see an air attack in progress or because they think they hear guns and believe that the guns are near and that they are connected with an air raid, sound the local sirens, they have, for the purposes of the warning system, put that area under Red Warning. The fact has not been notified to Fighter Command, and it is more than doubtful whether arrangements could be made for Fighter Command to receive notice of local action of this kind until many minutes had elapsed.

The local police sergeant is, however, in much more serious difficulty in expressing a judgment whether the raiders have passed. He may not be able to see them or to hear them any longer, but he does not know what they are doing, for he is not linked automatically to any system of reporting.

The Air Officer Commanding-in-Chief, on the other hand, from the reports that reach him and from the deductions he can make as to the course the hostile aircraft are taking, can know with some definiteness that the Warning District can be made Green. But at that stage he may not have learnt that it had ever been Red, and it is the essence of the Warning System that, once the Air Officer Commanding-in-Chief has given his personal decision whether a warning shall or shall not be given, the rest of the process shall be as automatic as possible and interfered with at no stage by any personal judgments.

13. I have discussed the matter with the Secretary of State for Air and we propose to advise the War Cabinet on the following lines:

(1) The right of the Air Officer Commanding-in-Chief at Fighter Command to exercise his judgment on the situation as he sees it should be affirmed.

(2) The public should be advised that occasionally a single raider, which has been diagnosed is probably upon reconnaissance, may make an attack, or that two or three planes similarly regarded as likely to be on reconnaissance work, may prove to be a bombing squadron, and that it is to be recognised that the area affected will not necessarily in all such cases have been put under Red Warning.

If an area is to be put under Red Warning every time hostile aircraft are approaching it, the interruption of vital production and the disturbance to the life of the people will be out of proportion to the risks that might be run by leaving the aircraft unheralded. The absence of a public warning, as was shown in the Firth of Forth, does not mean that hostile aircraft would not be engaged promptly by the defending forces.

(3) No permission can be given to any local authority, police or otherwise, to sound the sirens unless they have received instructions originating from Fighter Command Headquarters. Unless this is accepted the warning system would come immediately into confusion.

(4) If an unheralded attack develops on an area persons should take cover as though the warning sirens had been sounded. The Air Officer Commanding-in-Chief, Fighter Command, will at once receive notification of the attack and will, if he thinks right, give the instructions for the sirens to be sounded and will subsequently give the signal when the raiders have passed.

J.A.
Home Office, 21st October, 1939.

# Appendix XIX

# States of Readiness for the Three Defence Services

The Admiralty had three degrees of readiness. The first implied that invasion was imminent and attack likely to occur within the next 12 hours; the second implied that the enemy was prepared to invade and might attack within three days; the third that the enemy was preparing for invasion but that the attack was not expected in the next three days. The Admiralty 'Standstill' order to shipping was an operational order to ships caught at sea after invasion had begun.

The Royal Air Force also had three degrees of readiness – "Invasion Alert I, II and III (see section 60)". The implications were the same as the three degrees of readiness for the Royal Navy.

From the 19th September 1940 (see Section 58) Home Forces had two states of readiness: "Stand-to" implying conditions particularly favourable for an invasion, and "Action Stations" indicating the immediate threat of invasion.

These signals were to be issued to the Commands immediately concerned for action, and to be repeated to other Commands and formations for information. The Chief Civil Staff Officer at G.H.Q. Home Forces was to issue both signals to the Civil Departments, making clear to which areas the signal had been issued for action on the military side; and the Ministry of Home Security was to issue the messages to Regional Commissioners by whom they would be distributed to Chief Constables, A.R.P. Controllers, and Regional representatives of Government Departments.

The steps to be taken by Home Forces when either of those states of readiness were ordered are described in the Note below.

A NOTE ON THE STEPS TO BE TAKEN WHEN THE STATE OF
IMMINENCE OF INVASION IS DECLARED

1. There are two conditions of readiness, one in which the Army at home has been held pending the receipt of the Code Word declaring the imminence of invasion, the second one of complete readiness which is reached on receipt of this Code Word.

2. In the first stage conditions are generally as follows:

(a) Defences are manned to a degree considered necessary by Corps Commanders, which is generally 33% by day with men sleeping within a few minutes of their posts by night; a small proportion of Home Guard man posts under local arrangements.

(b) All troops stand to, dusk and dawn.

(c) Road blocks not manned.

(d) Battalions and brigades rely mainly on the normal civil telephone system.

(e) Courses are in progress.

(f) Leave, including week-end and normal up to a total of 7½, is allowed.

(g) Certain transport for the carriage of A.A. ammunition and railhead use is hired from day to day.

(h) The normal hospital routine is followed and no special steps are taken to evacuate beds in coastal areas.

3. When a state of imminence of invasion is declared the finishing touches are put to preparations and a state of instant readiness is maintained.

Measures taken are shown in Annex "A", and opposite each is an estimate of the time which must elapse before each can be effective. These times have been shown, as on them depends the decision as to what steps can be left until the threat materialises.

It should be realised that to maintain the complete state of readiness aimed at is to produce a situation in which all are tuned to concert pitch, a state of affairs which can be maintained for short periods but not indefinitely.

To bring the Army to its highest state of efficiency at the required moment demands the relaxation of certain of the precautions given, and it is suggested that measures, effect to which can be given within 6 hours, should be temporarily relaxed, as should other measures which take up to 12 hours, whose effect will not immediately be required.

Other measures which require longer notice should be adopted now.

Based on these principles I recommend that, if it is necessary for civil reasons to institute a state of sustained imminence, the following should be relaxed and modified measures taken:

(a) 100% manning of defences by troops and Home Guards should be relaxed at the discretion of Corps Commanders.

(b) Road blocks need not be manned.

(c) Leave should be stopped, but men on leave should not be recalled.

(d) Universal confinement of troops to barracks should be relaxed at the discretion of Corps Commanders.

(e) Men on Courses should remain unless the men in question are key men, in which case they should rejoin their units.

(f) Traffic personnel should not be required to man their posts unless to do so takes more than 6 hours.

(g) Personnel to man refugee car parks should not take post unless to do so takes more than 6 hours.

4. The following Military measures should be taken at once:

(a) Civil lines should be taken up.

(b) Hospitals in threatened areas should be evacuated.

(c) M.I.5 measures should be taken.

(d) Emergency labels should not be issued and refugee routes should not be marked.

5. To bring the Army to a state of instant readiness an additional Code Word is required which it is suggested might be "ACTION STATIONS". On this:

(a) Defences are manned 100% by troops and Home Guards.

(b) Road blocks are manned.

(c) Traffic personnel take post.

(d) Men on leave are recalled.

(e) All troops are confined to barracks.

(f) Emergency labels are issued.

(g) Refugee car parks are established.

(h) Routes are marked.

(i) Men on courses report to nearest Military Unit for orders.

(j) Take up extra transport.

*8th September, 1940.*

*Annex A*

## MEASURES TO BE TAKEN ON RECEIPT OF CODE WORD ORDERING INSTANT READINESS AND TIME TAKEN TO GIVE EFFECT TO THEM

1. 100% manning of defences by troops and Home Guards.     6 hrs.
2. Road blocks manned.     6 hrs.
3. Traffic personnel take post.     6 hrs.

| | |
|---|---:|
| 4. Refugee car parks established. | 6 hrs. |
| 5. Transport taken up for A.A. amn. | 6 hrs. |
| 6. Civil lines taken up. | 24-36 hrs. |
| 7. Refugee routes marked. | 12 hrs. |
| 8. Emergency labels issued. | 12 hrs. |
| 9. Hospitals evacuated. | 24-48 hrs. |
| 10. Men on Courses return to Units or join the nearest Unit. | 24-48 hrs. |
| 11. All leave stopped and men on leave recalled. | 24-48 hrs. |

# Note on the "Invasion Imminent" Signal 7th September 1940

On the 7th September the Chiefs of Staff considered a report by the Joint Intelligence Committee on possible German action against the United Kingdom. The main features of this report were:

(a) the westerly and southerly movement of barges and small ships to ports between Ostend and Havre suggesting a very early date for invasion, since such craft would not be moved unnecessarily early to ports so exposed to bombing attacks;

(b) the increase of the striking strength of the German air force, disposed between Amsterdam and Brest, by the transfer of 160 long-range bomber aircraft from Norway; and the re-disposition of short-range dive-bomber units to forward aerodromes in the Pas de Calais area, presumably in preparation for employment against this country;

(c) four Germans recently captured landing on the south-east coast from a rowing boat had confessed to being spies, and had said that they were to be ready at any time during the next fortnight to report the movement of British reserve formations in the area Oxford – Ipswich – London – Reading;

(d) moon and tide conditions during the period 8/10 September were most favourable for a seaborne invasion on the south-east coast.

The report indicated that German preparations for invasion were so advanced that it could be attempted at any time. Taking into account the German air attacks, which were then being concentrated against aerodromes and aircraft factories, the Chiefs of Staff agreed that the possibility of invasion had become imminent, and that the defence forces should stand by at immediate notice.

On enquiry into the state of readiness of the Defence Services the Chiefs of Staff were told that:

(1) the Navy had already put all small craft, including cruisers, at immediate notice;

(2) the Royal Air Force was Alert II, i.e., invasion within three days, at which state 24 medium bombers were at 30 minutes notice for close action with Home Forces, and 50 per cent. of the remainder were ear-marked for anti-invasion tasks;

(3) Home Forces were at 8 hours' notice to move, and the troops 'stood to' at dawn and at dusk; and

(4) the Civil Departments had not received any special warning.

At G.H.Q. Home Forces, there was no machinery by which the existing 8 hours' notice for readiness could be adjusted to a state of readiness for "immediate action" by intermediate stages. The code word "Cromwell" signifying "invasion imminent", was therefore issued by G.H.Q. Home Forces that evening (8 p.m. 7th September) to the Eastern and Southern Commands, and implied "action stations" for the forward (coastal) divisions; also to all formations in the London area and to the 4th and 7th Corps in G.H.Q. Reserve, implying a state of readiness at short notice. The code-word was repeated for information to all other Commands in the United Kingdom. (N.B.: The code-word Cromwell for "invasion imminent" had replaced the code-word Caesar on the 5th June when the occupation of France and Belgium transformed the Home Defence plan. The code-word Julius indicating that an invasion was impending had been ordered on the 10th May, the day Holland was invaded, and it had remained in force.)

In some parts of the country certain Home Guard Commanders, acting on their own initiative, called out the Home Guard by the ringing of church bells. This action gave rise to rumours that enemy parachutists were landing. There were also various reports, subsequently proved to be incorrect, that parachute landings had actually occurred, and that German E-boats were approaching the coast.

On the following morning, (8th Sept.), G.H.Q. Home Forces gave instructions that it was not intended that the Home Guard should be permanently called out on receipt of the code-word "Cromwell" except for special tasks; also, that church bells were to be rung only by order of a Home Guard who had himself seen not less than 25 parachutists landing, and not because other bells had been heard, or for any other reason. The danger was that airmen baling out from damaged aircraft might be mistaken for enemy parachutists.

# Chiefs of Staff Review of the Dispositions To Meet Invasion, 1941

We have thought it right to carry out a thorough examination of the possibilities of invasion of the British Isles, and to review the organisation and dispositions to meet it. Our report is attached, and is divided into two parts. Part I deals with the likelihood of invasion, and Part II with our dispositions.

2. During the course of a lengthy examination of this question, the situation has undergone some change.

3. The question as to whether invasion of this country will, or will not, take place in the near future is clearly a matter of speculation, but, in view of the continued detachment of German forces to the Balkan and Middle East area, and taking into account the progressive increase in our own army and air strength in the United Kingdom, the possibility of Germany attempting the invasion of this country in the near future has, in our view, become less likely. The growing intensity of the Battle of the Atlantic aiming rather at the "strangulation" of the Great Britain lends colour to our view.

4. Nevertheless, the enemy undoubtedly designs to hold the invasion threat against us with a view to pinning us down in this country, and, if we allow this threat to keep us pinned, we shall only be playing his game.

5. We must therefore accept the fact that the impact of events may make it necessary to send forces overseas which, if the invasion threat alone were regarded as paramount, we should like to keep in this country. At the same time we must recognise that the Germans, with their aerodromes already established in North-West Europe and with a highly developed system of roads and railways, could always concentrate for an invasion far more quickly than troops despatched overseas could be brought back to this country to meet the threat.

6. Our commitments in the Balkans and Middle East will absorb all the forces which we can spare from the United Kingdom, taking into account reinforcements from the Dominions. This leads us to the conclusion that any other major overseas commitment cannot be accepted in the present circumstances.

*(Signed) Dudley Pound, C. Portal, R.H. Haining, (V.C.I.G.S.).*
*Great George Street, S.W.1., March 27, 1941.*

## PART I
## LIKELIHOOD OF INVASION AND MOST PROBABLE DATE

### Likelihood

Everything points to the most strenuous endeavours by Germany to win the war in 1941. Economic evidence, in particular, supports the view that Germany hopes for a short war.

2. Successful invasion of this country would end the war, but, in our opinion, invasion is bound to be so much a gambler's throw that the Germans are likely to try all other means of defeating us before embarking on it.

3. We think that Germany will do everything possible to intensify her attacks on our trade, industry and morale and to stretch our naval and shipping resources to the maximum extent by pressure through Spain, from Italy or in the Balkans before playing the last card of invasion, possibly in the autumn of 1941.

4. If, on the other hand, she could succeed in bringing in Japan, without the United States coming in on our side, she would have hopes of success without having to attempt invasion; in these circumstances she might postpone invasion until 1942. We do not consider, however, that there is any likelihood of the United States remaining neutral if Japan enters the war.

5. In any event, Germany must fear America's entry into the war. Moreover, by the end of 1941, with the full effects of the U.S.A. assistance, we shall be so strong that Germany will be faced with the prospect of defeat, or at best stalemate. And, again, if the United States should enter the war, Germany's only hope of success would be to invade this country before American military aid becomes effective.

6. We must, therefore, be ready for invasion. We do not think that the Germans have yet taken the final decision to invade, but they will perfect and maintain their preparations, and will be ready to launch an invasion as soon as the weather allows and when they think that there

are reasonable conditions for success. This state of uncertainty might continue throughout 1941.

**Date**

7. An essential requirement for invasion is a protracted calm spell. We have examined the meteorological evidence and consider that the danger period for invasion can hardly arise before the 1st April.

**Warning**

8. The Germans could not mount the invasion without giving a number of indications of the final preparations. Starting from the position at the present moment, we feel that we are bound to obtain these indications during the period of about three weeks prior to the earliest date at which the expedition could be launched. It must be emphasised, however, that the fact that an invasion is mounted does not necessarily signify when it will be launched or even that it will be launched at all. It might be kept mounted for a considerable period during which it could start at any time, subject to the fact that the assembled ships and craft would be exposed to our air attacks.

9. At the present time we cannot rely on obtaining warning of the exact date or hour of the setting out of the expedition. This is a grave handicap. We might reasonably expect to receive, at least from enemy-occupied territories, news of the embarkation of troops and of the sailing of large numbers of ships; but this is not the case. We recommend that S.I.S. should take every possible step to remedy this extremely unsatisfactory state of affairs.

## PROBABLE FORM AND SCALE OF ATTACK

**Immediate Prelude**

10. Operations which are likely to take place immediately before or simultaneously with an invasion are:

   (i) Intensified minelaying.

   (ii) Attacks on R.D.F. Stations; Fighter Aerodromes; including attacks by parachutist troops and airborne tanks; Communications in the area to be attacked; The seat of Government; The Fleet.

   (iii) Attempts to create panic, e.g., by driving the civilian population on to the roads by the use of gas.

   (iv) Diversions to draw off our naval forces.

Some of the above operations, such as attempts to neutralise fighter aerodromes, might be carried on as an attrition process by night as well as by day for weeks before invasion. The majority, however, would probably be at the last possible moment to ensure surprise.

**Main Attack, Form and Scale: Land Forces**

11. Having decided to play their last card, the Germans will concentrate

the maximum possible effort. They will use all the troops they can transport, and will be prepared to accept very heavy casualties.

12 It is impossible accurately to assess the scale of this attack, but a reasonable estimate of the size of the invading force might be 6 armoured, 4 airborne and 26 infantry divisions. It is probable that the Germans will make their initial assault with the largest possible number of armoured formations, for which they will have built large numbers of special lending craft.

## Airborne Troops

13. The Germans are likely to make the fullest use of airborne troops to attack the beach defences in rear, to intercept the movement of our reserve, to capture aerodromes or to create alarm over as wide an area as possible.

## Naval Forces

14. Germany's weakest feature is her navy, but it is probable that she will use all her naval forces in support of invasion or as a feint. It is also conceivable that Hitler might persuade Italy to attempt to send their fleet into the Atlantic to assist with invasion or to act as a diversion; and our coast defences and the present naval strength at Gibraltar could not prevent this. We think it is most unlikely that the Italians would agree, but it would undoubtedly be correct strategy if our enemies had decided to risk everything. It would be unsafe, therefore, to rule out this possibility.

## Air Forces

15. The Joint Intelligence Sub-Committee have estimated that the Germans might employ the following numbers of aircraft against this country:

| | |
|---|---|
| Long-range bombers | 1,540 |
| Dive-bombers | 560 |
| Fighters | 1,520 |
| Transport Aircraft | 1,000 |

Based on the above figures, it is estimated that the Germans could launch 2 airborne divisions with a few tanks in the "first wave" and 4 such divisions in all during the first three or four days.

16. It is conceivable, however, that Germany might make use of the whole of her air forces. It has been computed that these might amount to about 14,000 aircraft including 1,360 transport aeroplanes. Sufficient aerodromes for operating this number of aircraft are available. This unnaturally inflated force would be relatively inefficient though its morale might be very high at first. Germany, however, would be realising all her capital for a huge gamble. If it failed, she might find

herself almost bankrupt in air power in the very near future. It is reasonable to assume that we would be certain to get indications of Germany's preparations for such an operation.

**Supply**

17. The success of the invasion must stand or fall on the ability of the Germans to maintain their forces after the initial landing of supplies has been exhausted. It is clear that their difficulties in this respect will be very considerable.

**The Kent Area**

18. Apart from the problem of landing supplies, a secure line of communications would be essential. But it appears to us that there is only one area where there is any real chance of Germany obtaining this, namely, the Dover Strait area. If the Germans could succeed in capturing the Kent coast and mounting guns on it, or by capturing our guns, they could hope to deny the Straits to our naval forces, as they would then have guns on both sides of the Straits. They would frustrate our air force by making the maximum use of the dark hours. If invasion is launched, we feel certain that the Germans will make a determined effort to seize this vital area and to isolate it from the rest of the country by airborne troops, and possibly gas. It is the only area in which we can visualise their establishing a reasonable supply line for nourishing their lodgement. It is possible that attempts may be made to move on to London by a pincer movement with armoured forces landed in East Anglia and in Sussex.

**Diversions**

19. We consider that the main attack would be accompanied by a number of diversions. As already mentioned, naval diversion, possibly including action by the Italian Fleet, would be made with the object of drawing off our ships, while military diversions might be of the following order:

(a) Some 3 infantry divisions from Norway and a further 3 divisions from the Baltic directed on one or more of the following: Northern Scotland, the North-East Coast of England, Orkneys and Shetlands, the Faroes, Iceland, or possibly Northern Ireland.

(b) Up to 5 divisions from French Westerly or North-Westerly ports against Eire, and Devon and Cornwall. This operation may not only be a diversion but may be a move to establish air and submarine bases from which to attack our shipping.

**Conclusions**

20. An attempt to invade this country would be so much of a gambler's throw that Germany is likely to try all other means of defeating us before embarking on it.

21. We ought to obtain timely indications of German preparations to mount an invasion, but these will not tell us when it is to be launched, or even if it is to be launched at all.

22. At present we cannot rely on getting any warning of the exact date of an invasion. This is a grave defect in our intelligence arrangements, and should be remedied by every possible means.

23. The danger period for invasion can hardly arise before the 1st April.

24. We do not think that a final decision to invade has yet been taken, but we regard it as almost certain that an invasion will be mounted and be kept mounted.

25. If invasion comes, the Germans are certain to use all the troops they can transport. They are likely to employ large numbers of armoured formations and airborne troops.

26. The difficulties facing an invader, particularly those of supply, are great. The Germans may under-rate them, however, and decide to take risks.

27. Particular importance attaches to the Kent area. If the Germans succeeded in capturing the Kent coast and mounting guns on it, they might obtain a reasonably secure supply line for their forces in that area. This is the only area in which we can visualise them obtaining such a line.

28. An invasion of Eire through the comparatively undefended Irish ports might be attempted not merely as a diversion, but in order to establish air and submarine bases for attack against our shipping.

29. Finally, there is every inducement for the Germans to attempt invasion in 1941.

## PART II
### ORGANISATION AND DISPOSITIONS TO MEET A GERMAN INVASION

30. We have examined in general the organisation and dispositions of our Naval, Army and Air Forces to meet invasion. We consider that the various Commanders-in-Chief have made the most suitable dispositions and arrangements for their forces the resources that are at their disposal. In the course of our examination a number of points have emerged to which we wish to draw attention.

### NAVY
**Withdrawal of Naval Forces from the N.W. Approaches**

31. We have already stated that the Germans may well mount an invasion some considerable time before the actual invasion is launched. In view, however, of the scale of attack on our trade to-day and the vital

need for imports, we consider that a premature redistribution of our forces from trade to anti-invasion duties would be unsound.

32. To complete our concentration of surface ships in the invasion area would take between 5 and 7 days. It is hoped, however, that we should obtain such information as would enable us to commence transferring destroyers from trade protection to anti-invasion duties before the invasion is actually launched. In this case considerable reinforcements for our permanent East Coast Naval forces should arrive in time to assist in intercepting the German seaborne attacks before their arrival on our coasts.

## ARMY

### The Kent Area

33. In view of the importance which we attach to this area we examined in detail the dispositions which the Commander-in-Chief, Home Forces, had made in South-East England. The number of armoured formations in that area is not as great as we should like, but, taking into consideration the general dispositions of our forces throughout the country, we are unable to suggest any alteration. We are strongly of the opinion that no armoured formations should be despatched overseas for the present.

### Vulnerable Points

34. We have not attempted to review this organisation in detail, but we have had it outlined to us by the Vulnerable Points Adviser. There are a large number of men locked up in guarding Vulnerable Points. General Barker has, however, effected a considerable saving in the numbers of guards required and the formation of the Special Service Police force will in time release more soldiers. We are satisfied that General Barker is fully alive to the need to conserve man-power and, under his present policy, he is doing all he can to this effect.

### Ireland

35. The Germans may attempt a landing in Eire to seize bases to increase their scale of air attack on our shipping. If they were to do so the present striking force in Northern Ireland is not sufficient to drive them out, particularly as it includes no armoured units in that country. We emphasize the importance of destroying any German forces which have landed before they can establish themselves and seize aerodromes from which to maintain themselves by air. The existing striking force could do no more than secure Dublin and its aerodromes. Already a delay in reaching the enemy is imposed on our forces through having to wait for a German invasion before they can cross the border. A further delay in providing the division from England even under the accelerated

reinforcement plan cannot, in our view, be accepted if our forces are to be in a position to attack the enemy before he is established.

We therefore recommend that our forces should be strengthened by moving the 5th Division to Northern Ireland, and that this should be done forthwith.

**Forces Available for Despatch Overseas**

36. At the present time two infantry divisions are earmarked for the Middle East and one for Northern Ireland; in addition, one corps of two divisions is earmarked as a possible expeditionary force.

37. The forces in Great Britain are none too big to deal with a determined attempt at invasion. A large percentage of the available man-power of the army is allocated to tasks which are not directly related to measures for dealing with invasion. For instance, the army is now providing men for what may be termed "ancillary tasks", such as firefighting, smoke production, clearing of debris and for the protection of merchant shipping. These commitments, together with the protection of vulnerable points and aerodromes, will bring the number to about 105,000 in about 6 weeks, and demands for these ancillary tasks will inevitably increase.

Accordingly, the despatch overseas of any armoured forces, or indeed of any divisions over and above those earmarked for the Middle East and Northern Ireland respectively, would constitute a risk which would require careful assessment in the light of the moment. It seems almost inevitable, nevertheless, that we shall have to reinforce the Middle East and Greece. It is therefore all the more important that we should avoid any other major overseas commitment.

AIR FORCE

38. It is probable that the effect of our bomber effort on the nearer invasion ports, such as Dunkirk, Calais or Boulogne, would be very considerable and would cause the greatest disorganisation. On the other hand, the larger ports, such as Antwerp and Rotterdam, where there are more facilities for dispersion, present a more difficult problem and no great disorganisation can be expected, unless we concentrate on them at the expense of others. At our maximum effort, we could not deal simultaneously with more than six ports in the Low Countries and Northern France or two in Norway and Denmark.

39. We consider that the policy for the employment of the Royal Air Force laid down in the Chief of the Air Staff's Memorandum (see Appendix 8) dated the 30th July, 1940, is sound, and that this Memorandum should continue in force as the approved directive on our air effort during the invasion period.

**Airborne Troops**

40. The probability that the Germans will use airborne troops must be taken into account. Their attack may take the form of gliders, tank and troop-carrying aircraft, or parachute troops. We do not regard either gliders or troop-carrying aircraft as a very serious menace, since we are confident that our fighters would inflict heavy casualties upon them. But parachute troops are a more difficult problem. They might be used in two ways:

   (a) As a preliminary to invasion, in order to knock out our aircraft industry;

   (b) Simultaneously with invasion, to secure positions behind the main landings and to neutralise our fighter squadrons.

The Commander-in-Chief, Home Forces, is alive to these dangers and, as far as possible, is making dispositions to meet them.

**Gas**

41. Gas would not be used to resist invasion without special authority from the War Cabinet, even if the Germans were to use it first.

42. The use of low spray by day is likely to cause us aircraft casualties out of all proportion to the effect produced. Gas bombs are more effective than high spray. A proportion of high spray, however, on embarkation ports might interfere with the movement of reinforcements and might complicate supply arrangements.

43. If the enemy uses gas it may not necessarily be to our advantage to retaliate with spray. Although no notice beyond the three hours for normal preparations is required for arming up bombers with gas bombs, at least eighteen hours is required to fit spray equipment, with a consequent reduction in our bombing effort, unless it is done when the crews are resting.

44. Therefore, in view of the importance of maintaining our maximum bombing effort, we should not undertake retaliatory measures, using spray, without careful consideration of the relevant factors.

*Great George Street, S.W.1,*
*March 27, 1941.*

# Appendix XXII

# Appreciation by C.-In-C. Home Forces for the Spring Of 1942

1 August, 1941

## INTRODUCTION

**Object**

1. The object of this appreciation is to determine what military forces are the minimum necessary for the defence of this country by 1st April 1942.

## SCALE OF ATTACK

**Seaborne Invasion**

2. There are ample troops available to carry out invasion. The limiting factors are shipping, and the number of craft which can issue from the suitable ports at one time. The J.I.C.in their paper (41) 302 of July 1941 suggest that the scale of attack might be as follows:

(a) A "first wave" of 3 armoured and 4 infantry divisions, carried in light craft, and some merchant vessels converted for running ashore and landing direct on to the beach.

(b) The above to be followed as quickly as possible by a further 2 armoured and 3 infantry divisions, in light craft.

(c) A "main body" of 4 armoured and 16 infantry divisions, carried in merchant vessels, to arrive as soon as arrangements had been made for their reception.

3. This gives a total threat of 9 armoured and 23 infantry divisions, to which must be added some 11 infantry divisions for use as diversions. Any diversion to EIRE is likely to include a proportion of tanks.

**Airborne Invasion**

4. The J.I.C. estimate that airborne descents might amount to 55,000

troops and equipment. Some 3,600 airborne troops might descend on LONDON by night.

**Conclusion**

5. Since 27th November, 1940, the estimated scale of enemy attack has increased by 3 armoured divisions and 4 airborne divisions. There has been a decrease of 8 infantry divisions.

## INFLUENCE OF OTHER ARMS

6. Interdependence of Services. The defence of the United Kingdom against invasion is a combined operation on a large scale. No one service can prevent the GERMANS landing. The requirements of the Anny in this country were, up to the autumn of 1940; based upon two assumptions:

(a) that sufficient naval forces are retained in home waters to afford a good prospect of intercepting a hostile expedition on passage; and to ensure that, outside the narrow waters at least, the enemy is unable to maintain by sea any forces he succeeds in landing; and

(b) that the Royal Air Force is strong enough to render untenable any landing outside the limit of enemy fighter cover, and precarious within that limit.

It is necessary to examine whether these assumptions are still sound.

**Royal Navy**

7. In the summer and early autumn of 1940, 30 to 40 destroyers were based at ports in East and South ENGLAND as an Anti-Invasion Striking Force.

8. The necessity to provide as many destroyers as possible to escort Ocean convoys has forced the Admiralty to reduce drastically the Anti-Invasion Striking Force. The number of cruisers required to cover convoys to the MIDDLE EAST and elsewhere has led to a reduction in the available cruiser strength of the Home Fleet. The Admiralty have therefore stated that it may now be as much as 5 to 7 days after the invasion has started before the Navy in home waters can be fully deployed in an anti-invasion role against the GERMAN lines of sea communication with this country.

9. With modern armoured forces, 5 to 7 days is a long time, within which it would be perfectly possible to lose this country and the War, unless the Army is of sufficient strength to deal with the enemy armoured formations. Armoured forces are the best answer to armoured attack. A high scale of armoured formations in this country is therefore now essential.

**Royal Air Force**

10. The Air Staff believe that until GERMANY can defeat our fighter forces and gain air supremacy, invasion by sea or air is not a practical operation because:

(a) In order to sustain a major invasion, GERMANY must maintain sea communications between the Continent and this country.

(b) With BRITISH predominance at sea this would not have been possible before the rise of air power.

(c) GERMANY must rely upon her fighter and bomber forces to secure her lines of communication by clearing the air of our fighter forces and thus enable her bombers to operate freely against our naval forces.

Consequently, until GERMANY has defeated our fighter force, invasion by sea or air is impracticable.

11. The Air Staff are undoubtedly correct in stating that the struggle for air supremacy will affect the whole course of invasion, but the defeat of our fighter force is not necessary before GERMANY can land troops in this country. Insufficient consideration seems to have been given to the following factors:

(a) Approach under cover of darkness, fog or smoke.

(b) Except in narrow waters, it is doubtful whether the enemy would rely upon securing sea communications for more than a short period, and he might not rely upon capturing a port.

(c) The period of 5 to 7 days during which our naval opposition will not be fully available.

(d) The degree of risk which the enemy will be prepared to accept. The longer the war the more will this increase.

12. Neither side seems likely to gain such a degree of air superiority that on the one hand invasion would be a comparatively simple operation, or on the other that it would be virtually impossible. It would be dangerous to make any other assumption.

13. Our fighter force will be engaged upon:

(a) Meeting the attack on its own organization.

(b) Taking toll of airborne invasion.

(c) Protecting our naval forces.

(d) Providing, within the limits of range, cover for our bombers.

14. Interference with seaborne invasion will therefore depend upon our bombers being able to deal in turn with:

(a) The ports of embarkation.

(b) Craft on passage.

(c) GERMAN troops on our beaches.

15. This ability will be hampered by the following factors:

(a) Enemy fighters. The assembly of the GERMAN force will be given the maximum fighter cover, and, while our fighter force is engaged in protecting its own organization from GERMAN bombers, our bombers will have to face heavy opposition from GERMAN fighters.

(b) The enemy's possession of the Seaboard from NORWAY to BREST including the BALTIC, will enable him to assemble his invasion force outside the limits of our main bomber effort.

(c) The effort of any bomber force has limitations, and the task of disorganizing and disintegrating a force of some 40 divisions before it sails must be accepted as beyond the power of our bomber force.

This also applies to the craft on passage or enemy landed on our beaches by which time the bomber forces will have suffered losses and be operating at reduced efficiency.

16. The withdrawals from DUNKIRK, GREECE and CRETE were undertaken with a varying degree of fighter cover in the face of heavy bombing, and must lead to the conclusion that the Royal Air Force could not prevent a large GERMAN force being landed in this country. Every replacement of merchant shipping by T.L.C. capacity will assist the GERMANS in avoiding the effects of air bombardment.

**Conclusion**

17. Thus, while taking into account the casualties which may be inflicted by the Royal Navy and Royal Air Force, the Army must be strong enough to deliver a decisive blow against the maximum enemy force which can be transported to this country.

## PROBABLE NATURE OF ATTACK

18. Enemy alternatives. It is open to the enemy:

(a) To launch an airborne invasion. This is improbable, since it could not by itself be decisive, or supplied for any length of time unless followed up by a seaborne invasion. Airborne attack is therefore only likely as a subsidiary to seaborne attack.

(b) To attack by sea in foggy weather, without preliminary air action, with the intention of fighting out the air battle subsequently. Attack in these circumstances demands most exact timing, and will deny to the enemy the extensive air reconnaissance and air support which have so far been a feature of all his assaults. This is therefore a possible, though not a probable alternative.

(c) Preliminary air action directed at obtaining temporary air superiority, followed by seaborne and airborne attack.

(d) To invade by sea and air in fine weather, without preliminary air action, relying on surprise, speed and mass of T.L.Cs. and light craft.

19. If the invasion threatened last autumn be excepted, Germany has never yet in her many campaigns disclosed the imminence of attack by preliminary air bombardment, nor are the Germans likely to repeat the air campaign of last autumn. Further, it must be known to the Germans that there is of necessity a time lag of some days before the weight of our naval power can become effective in Home Waters. The Germans cannot afford to waste one hour of that time.

That the enemy will act in two phases, first an attack to gain temporary air superiority, and second an air and seaborne invasion, is a less probable assumption than that these two phases will follow each other so closely as to merge into one concentrated attack, using every resource of land, sea and air to secure a quick issue by surprise, speed and sheer weight of attack. Of courses (c) and (d), (d) is therefore considered the more probable.

**Seaborne Invasion**

20. The main features of seaborne invasion are likely to be:

(a) A main attack between the WASH and WEYMOUTH. The need for a quick sea passage, a short maintenance route, and adequate fighter cover, make it unlikely that the main effort will come North or West of the above places respectively.

(b) Diversions aimed at ICELAND (c) and EIRE, and at points on the SCOTTISH Coast and in N.E. and S.W. ENGLAND.

(c) In the main effort, we must prepare for 60/70 ton tanks landed from T.L.Cs. each capable of carrying 4/5 tanks, and with a speed of 10 – 15 knots.

**Airborne Attack**

21. As invasion becomes imminent, there will be a change in the character of the enemy's bombing. It is at present employed against civilian morale and on blockade. As invasion approaches, heavy bombing is to be expected on:

(a) Our fighter organization.

(b) Ports on which Fleet counter-action effort will be based; and

(c) Headquarters, roads, railways and communications, with the object of hindering the movement of reserves.

22. The airborne effort, which may be composed of parachutists, glider troops, or troops in troop carrying aircraft, may be employed in four directions:

(a) A concentrated attack on Fighter Command and its associated R.D.F. stations. If successful, this would have the effect of allowing the enemy's air attack to develop unhindered, and would largely cripple our own air counter offensive.

(b) In the rear of beach defences. To assist the seaborne attack. This must be met by all round defence and mobile local reserves.

(c) On the main approaches for reserves. These may be on the main approaches to the beaches with the object of stopping the arrival of reserves, upon which the success of the battle may depend.

(d) On LONDON itself. The GERMANS might attempt to put down a small force by night with the object of putting out of action Government offices and centres of communication.

Of the above, (a) and (b) constitute the greatest threats. It is not possible to state which is the more likely, as this must depend on the enemy plan. It is probable that there will be a combination of the two, with descents on the most important aerodromes as well as behind the beaches near the vital bridgeheads. Less important aerodromes are likely to be dealt with by air bombardment.

## DEDUCTIONS

**Main deductions**

23. Consideration of the probable scale of attack, of the influence which will be exercised by the other Services, and of the probable nature of attack, makes it possible to draw certain main deductions as to how the defence of this country must be organized.

24. The enemy may attack anywhere between SHETLAND and LANDS END. The resources at the disposal of this country are limited, and it is impossible to think of holding so wide a front in strength. Equally, the number of suitable objectives in the shape of fighter aerodromes, R.D.F. stations, road defiles, etc. for airborne attack, make it impossible to be strong everywhere. It follows, therefore, that there must in this country be a minimum of troops on the coast to deal with seaborne attack, and a minimum inland to deal with airborne attack. Behind these there must be sufficient reserves capable of a rapid counter-offensive against both infantry and armoured formations. It follows that these reserves must include an adequate proportion of armoured formations, and must in all cases be 100% mobile.

**Detailed deductions**

25. It is also possible to draw certain detailed deductions:

*Troops on the coast*

(a) The likelihood that the main enemy attacks will arise between the WASH and WEYMOUTH demands that the outpost lines in Eastern and South-Eastern Commands, and in that part of Southern Command which lies EAST of WEYMOUTH, must be in greater strength than elsewhere.

(b) The increase in the period before relief to 5 to 7 days, coupled with the increased threat from armoured forces, which the enemy will attempt to land early, demands that the outpost line have at its disposal infantry tanks for immediate counter attack.

*Troops inland*

(c) The probability of concentrated attack both by bombing and by airborne troops on Fighter Command and its associated R.D.F. stations demands that special protection should be afforded to those aerodromes and their satellites which are considered essential for Fighter Command to continue in the air, and so afford protection to all the others.

(d) The increased airborne threat to Eastern, South Eastern and Southern Commands demands special measures for covering such places as the approaches through the FENS,and through the SOUTH DOWNS, and SALISBUY PLAIN. For such purposes light tanks or carriers are required.

*Counter-attack troops on the coast*

(e) Behind the troops on the coast must be disposed Corps and Army Reserves containing, a sufficient armoured element to deal with a possible armoured threat in the area, and sufficient infantry to provide support for our tanks and to deal with airborne descents in rear of the beaches.

*Counter-attack troops inland*

(f) The size of tanks that can be landed by aircraft is limited, and consequently the main threat inland is confined to airborne descents or landings and to certain Commands. For this purpose, infantry are required.

*G.H.Q. Reserves*

(g) Behind the Corps and Army Reserves, the following will be required as G.H.Q. strategic reserves:

(i) A high proportion of armoured divisions.

(ii) A low proportion of infantry divisions.

(iii) Parachutists with which to assist the counter-attack on such places as the ISLE OF WIGHT or THANET.

Before proceeding to examine the requirements of each Command in turn, it is desirable to apply the above conclusions to the present situation in order to decide whether the present degree of protection can be reduced or should be increased and whether the present organization is suitable.

## APPLICATION OF THESE DEDUCTIONS TO PRESENT SITUATION

**Troops on the coast**

26. A cross-section has been taken of representative parts of the coastline in order to decide whether the present degree of protection can be reduced or should be increased. The cross-sections selected are:

(a) The mainland of SCOTLAND.

(b) The coast between NORTH BERWICK and ALNWICK.

(c) The coast between incl. RYE and excl. PORTSMOUTH.

(d) The coast between excl. EXMOUTH Westabout to incl. LYNTON.

The results of a detailed examination of these cross-sections may be summarised briefly as follows:

(a) That on SCOTLAND there is a gap in the defence line on the coast extending from DUNBAR to BERWICK-ON-TWEED, which in view of a possible German attempt to separate ENGLAND and SCOTLAND is undesirable.

(b) That the coast between RYE and PORTSMOUTH is held by two divisions each with three brigades up, the average frontages held being:

| | |
|---|---|
| brigades | 14 miles |
| battalions | 5½ miles |
| companies | 2¼ miles |

(c) That the whole coastline between EXMOUTH and LYNTON is held by one county division, the average frontages held being:

| | |
|---|---|
| brigades | 121 miles |
| battalions | 33 miles |
| companies | 11 miles |

27. Examination of the frontages held makes it apparent that no reduction in the number of infantry divisions and brigades required to hold the coastline can be contemplated, unless they are to become merely watchmen. On the other hand, the increased period before relief, and increased armoured threat, demand that this crust should be stiffened by the provision of additional army tank brigades.

28. As regards organization, there is no particular reason why the protection of the coast should not be wholly undertaken by county divisions. It is, however, essential that divisions in the KENT and SUSSEX salient should have a higher proportion of supporting arms. This is the main reason for placing field army divisions on the coast.

**Troops Inland**

29. The existing scale of aerodrome defence allows for garrisons of

varying size, from one platoon to a company. These garrisons are, wherever possible, supported by arrangements for a relief column equivalent to one infantry battalion and a counter-attack force equivalent to one brigade, to be available within one hour and two or three hours respectively.

In addition, it has lately been considered necessary to station light tank or Beaverette troops at a number of aerodromes, and in addition to detach and station within one mile of some 36 essential fighter aerodromes a complete infantry battalion or its equivalent.

These arrangements have only been possible owing to the number of infantry formations at present available, and even then it has been necessary to employ battalions of infantry or squadrons of tanks from formations in G.H.Q. Army and Corps Reserve.

30. It follows, therefore, that any reduction in the number of infantry formations available in the interior of the country will create a situation in which it will be necessary to have a number of independent battalions, sufficient to take on this task in the face of the increased airborne threat to the Commands in question. This may only be possible at the expense of aerodrome garrisons in other Commands.

**Counter-Attack Troops for the Coast**

31. The enemy may elect to employ the full weight of his armoured strength against, in order of priority,

Eastern and South Eastern Commands

Southern and Northern Commands.

To meet this threat it is necessary to dispose armoured formations for immediate counter-attack in these Commands as there will not be time to move them from one Command to another.

This measure of dispersion in defence which is forced upon us makes it essential that our armoured strength shall be greater than that which the enemy can employ against us.

Additional army tank brigades will, therefore, be required for this role.

**Counter-attack Troops Inland**

32. The increased threat of airborne attack in Eastern, South-Eastern and Southern Commands now demands special measures. It is possible that the Germans may employ eight airborne divisions in this area.

33. The defence against this form of attack at present relies upon mobile columns organized from area troops, and upon the cover which the presence of mobile armoured and infantry divisions in the interior of the country automatically gives. It follows, therefore, that sufficient of these formations must be available in the vulnerable Commands to counter this threat.

34. Under the present dispositions there are five armoured and seventeen infantry divisions disposed as Corps, Army and G.H.Q. reserves. Under F.F.C.36 there will be eight armoured but only twelve infantry divisions of which four must be stationed on the coast, leaving only eight for disposal in reserve. This reduction from a total of twenty two armoured divisions to a total of sixteen is likely, on examination of the situation by Commands, to prove too great.

**G.H.Q. Reserves**

35. These at present consist of armoured and infantry divisions in approximately equal proportions. They must be sufficient in number, to turn the scale against any superiority in numbers which the Germans may mount against any particular Command. Armoured formations are most suitable for this purpose and a reduction in infantry can therefore be accepted in G.H.Q. reserve.

## EXAMINATION OF REQUIREMENTS BY COMMANDS

### Possible Scale of Attack in Each Command

36. Detailed notes on each Command are attached as Appendices 'F' to 'M'.

37. The probable scales of attack on the main Commands may be summarised as shown in the following table:

SCOTTISH COMMAND

| | |
|---|---|
| Anticipated Scale of Attack Up To: | 2 seaborne divisions; small airborne parties |
| Points of Departure for Enemy Seaborne Forces: | Bergen, Stavanger |
| Method: | Fast convoy |
| Length of Passage: | 280 miles |
| Time of Transit (Approx.) | 20 hours |

NORTHERN COMMAND

| | |
|---|---|
| Anticipated Scale of Attack Up To: | 3 seaborne divisions; 1 airborne regiment |
| Points of Departure for Enemy Seaborne Forces: | Cuxhaven, Wilhelmshaven or Norwegian ports |
| Method: | Fast convoy |
| Length of Passage: | 300-350 miles |
| Time of Transit (Approx.) | 24 hours |

EASTERN COMMAND

| | |
|---|---|
| Anticipated Scale of Attack Up To: | 3 armoured divisions; 9 infantry divisions; 8 airborne divisions |
| Points of Departure for Enemy Seaborne Forces: | Scheldt, Ostend |
| Method: | Fast convoy and barges |

| | |
|---|---|
| Length of Passage: | 100 miles |
| Time of Transit (Approx.) | 7-14 hours barges, 4-7 hours fast convoy |

SOUTH-EASTERN COMMAND

| | |
|---|---|
| Anticipated Scale of Attack Up To: | 4 armoured divisions; 11 infantry divisions; 8 airborne divisions |
| Points of Departure for Enemy Seaborne Forces: | Calais, Boulogne |
| Method: | Fast convoy and barges |
| Length of Passage: | 20-50 miles |
| Time of Transit (Approx.) | 3-6 hours barges, 1-4 hours fast convoy |

SOUTHERN COMMAND

| | |
|---|---|
| Anticipated Scale of Attack EAST OF WEYMOUTH: | 2 armoured divisions; 3 infantry divisions; 8 airborne divisions |
| Anticipated Scale of Attack WEST OF WEYMOUTH: | 2 seaborne divisions; small airborne parties |
| Points of Departure for Enemy Seaborne Forces: | Havre, Cherbourg, St. Malo, Brest |
| Method: | Fast convoy and barges |
| Length of Passage: | 70-120 miles |
| Time of Transit (Approx.) | 10-16 hours barges, 5-8 hours fast convoy |

## 38-40. Analysis of Army Scales.

### Summary of Minimum Additional Requirements

41. The additional requirements of each Command are given in Appendices 'F' to 'M'.

42. They may be summarised as follows:

(a) Organization of 108 county battalions into 12 county divisions of 3 brigades of 3 battalions, as opposed to 9 county divisions of 3 brigades of 4 battalions. This number of formations, which will be allotted to Northern, Eastern and Southern Commands, is considered to be the minimum necessary for the control of the long length of coastline in those Commands.

(b) An additional 4 army tank brigades are required over and above the 6 now allowed for.

(c) London District require 3 independent infantry brigades and 10 holding or training battalions. If these are provided, it will release the 1 full scale infantry division which would otherwise have to be allotted.

(d) Scottish Command require an additional independent infantry brigade for the defence of CAITHNESS. In addition, 6 independent infantry battalions are required for OSDEF. (e) Northern Command require 1 full scale infantry division in place of 1 independent infantry brigade group now allotted. If this were done, the 1

311

independent infantry brigade group already allotted could be released.

(f) Western Command require troops for both NORTH WALES and SOUTH WALES. The release of 1 independent brigade group from Northern Command will provide this brigade group for SOUTH WALES. 1 additional battalion is required for the ISLE OF MAN.

(g) The situation of Eastern Command can otherwise be accepted. See (a) above.

(h) South-Eastern Command require the 2 independent brigades which at present form the garrisons of DOVER and FOLKESTONE for the defence of this most vulnerable area. These 2 extra independent infantry brigades are therefore required.

(i) Southern Command require 1 independent infantry battalion for the SCILLY ISLES.

## G.H.Q. REQUIREMENTS

**Types of Requirements**

44. In addition to the needs of individual Commands, there are the following G.H.Q. requirements:

(a) Aerodromes – calculated to include construction programme up to end of 1942.

| | |
|---|---|
| As garrisons | 118 Battalions |
| As independent battalions | 24 Battalions |
| As Light Tank troops | 38 Troops |

Details are given below.

(b) V.Ps. – The total estimated military requirements for protection of V.Ps. calculated with reference to the end of 1942, are: 25 Battalions Home Defence Troops; C.M.P.(V.P.) 12,000 men. Details are given below.

(c) Coast Artillery – The total number of men required up to 1 April 1942 is 43,224, of which 38,110 are now available. Details are given below.

(d) Reserves – No additional G.H.Q. reserves are required beyond those allowed for … namely 1 full scale and 4 armoured divisions, except that 1 airborne brigade is required to assist counter-attacks against such objectives as the ISLE OF WIGHT, the SCILLY ISLES or the ISLE OF THANET.

(e) Home Guard – As the number of infantry formations is reduced, the Home Guard will become an increasingly essential adjunct to the Field Army. Their role is the breaking up of local airborne attack, and also of seaborne attack by the defence of nodal points. In addition, on the coast they can assist by reinforcing the troops already there. Now that their training is advancing they must be asked to provide from their younger men more mobile detachments using bicycles, motor-cycles and motor-cars, with which they would be able to get quickly about inland to deal with airborne attack.

(f) 1st reinforcements – It is to be assumed that, in the event of invasion, all formations will be engaged simultaneously, and will be called on to fight a series of major actions within a fortnight or three weeks. Heavy casualties must be expected, especially in the opening action; it will be essential that reinforcements are available to bring formations up to fighting strength. The following is therefore considered the minimum:

| | |
|---|---|
| R.A.C. | 15% |
| R.A. | 7.5% |
| R.E. | 5% |
| Signals | 5% |
| Infantry | 15% |

with a slightly higher proportion of officers in each case.

## CONCLUSION

### Total Revised Minimum Requirement

45. The minimum requirements of this country are therefore:

1 Airborne brigade.

OSDEF (6 independent battalions).

5 independent infantry brigades.

3 independent infantry brigade groups.

12 county divisions of 3 brigades of 3 battalions.

14 full scale divisions.

8 armoured divisions.

10 army tank brigades.

188 battalions (Young Soldier or Home Defence) as aerodrome garrisons.

300 light tank troops as aerodrome garrisons.

24 independent battalions as external protection to essential fighter aerodromes.

2 independent battalions for the ISLE OF MAN and SCILLY ISLES.

11 holding or training battalions for London District.

25 battalions of Home Defence Troops for V.Ps.

12,000 C.M.P.(V.P.) for V.Ps.

43,224 men to man coast artillery batteries.

A greater measure of mobility for the Home Guard.

1st reinforcements on the scale of:

| | |
|---|---|
| R.A.C. | 15% |
| R.A. | 7.5% |

| R.E. | 5% |
|------|-----|
| Signals | 5% |
| Infantry | 15% |

with a slightly higher proportion of officers in each case.

## SCOTTISH COMMAND

**General**

1. An enemy seaborne expedition against Scotland would for geographical reasons probably be launched either from Norway (BERGEN and STAVANGER) or via the Skagerrak from German Baltic ports. Owing in the one case to the broken nature of the Norwegian coast, in the other to distance, we could not be sure of obtaining warning of the preparation of an expedition.

2. The distance from BERGEN to KINNAIRDS HEAD is 280 miles; from the western exit of the Skagerrak somewhat longer. For a small force the enemy might use a 16 – 18 knot convoy capable of completing the passage in 16 – 20 hours. During the winter much, if not all, of this passage could be accomplished in darkness, and it would be unwise to rely on any but the briefest warning of attack. On the other hand the hours of light in summer much reduce the likelihood of seaborne attack in these latitudes, and greater risks would be justifiable.

3. Similarly an enemy airborne attack, based on Norwegian or on the main continental aerodromes, could be launched without warning.

**Possible enemy objectives**

4. The order of importance of the more likely objectives is thought to be:

| | |
|---|---|
| (a) SCAPA FLOW (Y 92) | Naval base. |
| (b) CAITHNESS | For operation against SCAPA FLOW. |
| (c) FIRTH OF FORTH | Fleet anchorage, Naval and R.A.F. installations, port of Leith, and gateway to (d). |
| (d) GLASGOW – CLYDE | Industrial and shipping area. |
| (e) INVERGORDON (J 29) | Fleet anchorage. |
| (f) Coast of MORAY and BANFF | As a base for air operations. |
| (g) ABERDEEN | For diversionary purposes. |

5. As regards these objectives the reinforcement for the ORKNEYS or SHETLANDS is dependent upon the availability of a seaborne reserve in the CLYDE which can be moved in good time to SCAPA. It is assumed that this force will now always be maintained.

314

6. The county of CAITHNESS is extremely isolated and requires a permanent garrison. An additional Infantry Brigade is therefore required.

7. The loss of the GLASGOW – CLYDE area would in time probably be decisive. Its defence and that of the FIRTH OF FORTH which leads directly to it are therefore of first importance. They are virtually a single problem. The Polish Forces provide a minimum defence for the north of the FORTH. A gap, however, exists south of the FORTH which cannot be covered except by the provision of one Field Army Division in reserve.

8. The defence of INVERGORDON and the Coast of MORAY and BANFF must be self-contained, since poor communications will prevent any rapid reinforcement from southern Scotland. One full scale Field Army Division is required.

9. ABERDEEN is of little real importance.

10. Finally it is possible that the enemy might make use of the good road exits S.W. from BERWICK to direct forces landed on the inter-Command boundary against CARLISLE with the ultimate aim of isolating SCOTLAND from ENGLAND.

**Likelihood and Scale of Enemy Attack**

11. The threat of seaborne attack must be rated as small for the following reasons:

    (a) Lack of an objective such as London, the capture of which might be decisive quickly;

    (b) relatively long sea voyage through very dangerous waters, making subsequent maintenance, if not the original passage, of an expedition most hazardous; and

    (c) difficulty of providing fighter cover.

The threat of airborne attack must be rated as very small. The main continental aerodromes are far distant; Norwegian aerodromes are limited in number. From neither could any sustained fighter cover be given.

In this connection it is understood that the enemy could not, by airborne invasion alone, use Scottish aerodromes as bases for attacking the fleet at Scapa Flow; since he could not, at the distance, supply his aircraft in Scotland in the face of opposition. Any such attack would, therefore, either have to be launched from Norwegian aerodromes or the enemy would have to keep open a line of communication by sea to Scotland.

12. The most that is to be expected therefore is a raid, probably for diversionary purposes and not exceeding up to 2 seaborne divisions, and small airborne parties.

Even if the enemy succeeded in putting such forces ashore, his effort could only be of short duration since he would have the greatest difficulty in maintaining them. It is on this basis that defence requirements must be estimated.

**Total Requirements**

O.S.D.E.F. (incl. 6 independent battalions)

Polish Forces

2 full scale divisions

1 independent infantry brigade

## NORTHERN COMMAND

**General**

1. An enemy seaborne expedition against Northern Command might be launched from the Low Countries, in which case the actual passage (Scheldt – Humber about 200 miles) could be completed at night during the winter months. It is far more likely, however, that the enemy would decide to launch his main attack on south-eastern England, for which purpose he would need Dutch, Belgian and French harbours, and that only a diversionary raid would be launched against Northern England from the Elbe or via the Skagerrak from Baltic ports. In this event the sailing of the northern convoys might well he observed in fair weather, although it would be unsafe to rely on any but the briefest warning of attack.

2. A seaborne expedition against Northern Command would suffer from much the same disadvantages as an expedition against Scotland, i.e. –

(a) Relatively long sea passage, not lending itself to the use of barges and specialised small craft.

(b) Eventual serious interference from the Royal Navy, at least as far south as the Humber.

3. Enemy airborne attack based on the main continental aerodromes could be launched with little warning. At present such an attack would suffer from the inability of most of the enemy's fighter aircraft to cover the operation. It would also be difficult for the enemy to nourish an airborne expedition in this part of England.

**Possible Enemy Objectives**

4. In order of importance these are:

(a) The HUMBER leading directly to the LEEDS – BRADFORD industrial area.

(b) The TYNE.

(c) The TEES, leading directly to MIDDLESBROUGH – DARLINGTON and a possible route for a flank attack on the LEEDS area.

The loss of the main industrial area of the Midlands, i.e. LEEDS – BRADFORD – MANCHESTER would in time be decisive; the nearest approach is by the HUMBER, where the coast is generally more suitable for landing than elsewhere. The defence of the Humber area is therefore of first importance.

**Likelihood and Scale of Enemy Attack**

5. For the reasons given in paras. 3 and 4, nothing more than a large scale raid for diversionary purposes is to be expected. Its scale might be up to 3 seaborne divisions [and] 1 regiment of airborne troops

6 and 7. Allotment.

8. The long coast line and corps organization of Northern Command make it essential that instead of 3 county divisions of 3 brigades of 4 battalions, it be allotted 4 county divisions of 3 brigades of 3 battalions with the corresponding increase in supporting arms which this will imply. 1 additional army tank brigade is also required.

9. The reserves available are too small in proportion to the length of frontage held and the possible scale of attack. 1 additional full scale infantry division is required, instead of the 1 brigade group.

**Minimum Requirements**

10.    4 county divisions of 36 battalions
       1 armoured division
       1 full scale division
       2 army tank brigades

## EASTERN COMMAND

**General**

1.    The salient factors which affect the defence of Eastern Command are:
      (a) the wide range of ports available to the enemy for the preparation and launching of a seaborne expedition; these include German Baltic ports, and ports of the Low Countries,
      (b) the Command lies within effective range of all the enemy's fighter forces, short range and long range,
      (c) the short sea passage favours the use of barges and other specially prepared small craft from which direct landings can be made on beaches,
      (d) the narrow seas are the one area in which our naval superiority, particularly in heavy ships, is likely to be least effective and longest delayed.

**Enemy Objectives**

2. There is only one real objective – LONDON. The capture of LONDON would automatically include the destruction of the organization of A.D.G.B. the loss of which would deprive us of effective fighter protection. The capture of fighter aerodromes and R.D.F. stations would probably be included amongst the enemy's initial objectives.

**Likelihood and Scale of Attack**

3. A major attack on this part of England must be regarded as possible at any time and in any season. The most probable plan would be a pincer movement directed on LONDON or to the west of it from East Anglia on the one hand and Kent and Sussex on the other, with defensive flanks thrown out as necessary. The scale of seaborne attack is estimated at: 3 armoured and 9 infantry divisions.

4. As regards airborne attack the enemy could land up to:8 divisions.

5 and 6. Allotment.

7. The Corps organization of Eastern Command would permit of 3 county divisions consisting of 12 battalions, but in the general interest of uniformity 4 divisions of 9 battalions are preferred. The force available can be accepted subject to:

(a) the need explained elsewhere for additional army tank brigades;

(b) the increase in supporting arms which the proposed reorganization of county divisions will imply.

**Minimum Requirements**

8. These are therefore:

4 county divisions of 36 battalions

2 full scale divisions

1 armoured division

3 army tank brigades

## LONDON DISTRICT

**General**

1. LONDON lies in the area over which the enemy can obtain maximum fighter cover and to which he has the shortest sea passage from the continent. It is, moreover, certain to be the objective of any enemy attack in south east England.

**Likelihood and Scale of Enemy Attack**

2. The security of LONDON is the essence of the defence problem in Eastern and South Eastern Commands. There are, however, two possibilities, defence against which is the primary responsibility of London District. They are an attempted coup-de-main against the capital by either:

(a) large scale parachutist and airborne attack; and/or

(b) a direct assault by shallow draught craft up the Thames Estuary. Projects such as these might well appeal to the enemy. Their object would be to paralyse the machinery of government at the very time it was most needed.

3. The number of parachutists who might theoretically be landed has been estimated as about 3,600.

4. So long as our fighter aircraft continued to operate from aerodromes in south east England, however, troop carrying aircraft of all sorts would suffer very heavy casualties by day and it is unlikely that the number of parachutists who could land simultaneously, or within a short period, would be enough to isolate LONDON. A small descent by night might, however, be used in an attempt to disorganize the Government and communications at a critical time. The possibility of gliders being used on the outskirts of LONDON cannot be overlooked.

**Resources of LONDON**

5. Before estimating the troops required in London District, it may be observed that:

(a) the Thames Estuary is covered by fixed defences and by light naval forces at HARWICH and CHATHAM;

(b) the narrower waters inside the estuary are covered by M.G. defences and armed river craft;

(c) the Home Guard total nearly a quarter of a million men;

(d) the presence of the balloon barrage and of strong A.A. defences provide armed detachments of considerable value.

**Internal Security**

6. Internal security was always a heavy commitment in the London District in peace, and it was anticipated that the commitment would become heavier in war. In fact, there has up to the present been no demand for troops for internal security, but it is not sound to assume that no such demand will be made. War conditions, with continued bombing and enemy propaganda, may yet lower civilian morale.

There are, however, over 20,000 police in LONDON and several military depots capable of turning out small columns. It is therefore not considered necessary to make specific provision for internal security in addition to the field force recommended below.

**Field Force**

7. As explained in paragraph 2, the main battle for LONDON must be fought by formations in South Eastern and Eastern Commands. Locally, the entrances to LONDON should be held by Home Guards. What is required of the field forces in the District is ability to deal with surprise incursion and to restore a situation by delivering a counter-attack. For

this it is estimated that 1 full scale division or the equivalent is sufficient.
8. Allotment.
**Minimum Requirements**
9. It is, however, difficult to employ artillery etc. in LONDON, and it is considered that the following could be accepted:

1 brigade group
2 brigades
10 holding or training battalions

exclusive of the requirements of the Royal Household and of the Cabinet.
10. The provision of these would release one full scale division for employment elsewhere, e.g., NORTHERN COMMAND.

## SOUTH-EASTERN COMMAND

**General**
1. The salient factors which affect the defence of South Eastern Command are:

(a) The wide range of ports available to the enemy for the preparation and launching of seaborne attack.

(b) The Command lies within the effective range of all the enemy's fighter forces – short range and long range.

(c) The short sea passage favours the use of barges and other specially prepared small craft from which direct landings can be made on beaches; a particularly dangerous area in this respect being between the NORTH FORELAND and DUNGENESS. It also rules out the possibility of relying on even short warning that an expedition has sailed.

(d) The narrow seas are the one area in which our naval superiority, particularly in heavy ships, is likely to be ineffective. The enemy can command at least half the beaches of the Channel with the heavy coast artillery which he has mounted. He can well hope to cover the rest of the passage with dive bombers. Here, if anywhere, the German can put down his head and charge like a bull.

(e) The lack of depth between the coast and LONDON, which makes it essential that the enemy should be stopped on or near the beaches. All usable beaches must be held, and held in some strength.

**Enemy Objectives**
2. There is only one real objective – LONDON, the capture of which would mean the loss of the centralised fighter control. The capture of fighter aerodromes and R.D.F. stations would probably be included amongst the enemy's initial objectives.

**Likelihood of Scale of Attack**

3. A major attack on this part of England must be regarded as possible at any time and in any season. The most probable plan would be a pincer movement directed on LONDON, or to the west of it from East Anglia on the one hand and Kent and Sussex on the other, with defensive flanks thrown out as necessary. The scale of seaborne attack is estimated at 4 armoured and 11 infantry divisions.

4. As regards airborne attack, the enemy could land 8 divisions. Airborne landings would be easier to cover in Kent and Sussex than anywhere else in England.

5. Allotment.

6. It is essential that on this part of the coast all usable beaches and ports should be adequately covered. This cannot be done without the 2 additional brigades which are at present located at DOVER and FOLKESTONE.

**Minimum Requirements**

7. Minimum requirements are therefore:

> 2 brigades
> 6 full scale divisions
> 1 armoured division
> 3 army tank brigades

## SOUTHERN COMMAND

**General**

1. An enemy seaborne expedition against the Southern Command would probably be launched from northern or north western France. There should be some warning of the preparation of this expedition but, in conditions of poor visibility, it might be launched unobserved. The approximate distance between assembly ports and ports of the south coast are:

| | |
|---|---|
| CHERBOURG to ISLE OF WIGHT | 70 miles |
| CHERBOURG to PORTLAND | 75 miles |
| HAVRE to ISLE OF WIGHT | 95 miles |
| ST. MALO to LYME REGIS | 157 miles |
| BREST to PLYMOUTH | 180 miles |
| L'ORIENT to FALMOUTH | 250 miles |

It would, therefore, be possible for 15 knot ships, and in winter probably barges and T.L.Cs. also, to reach ISLE OF WIGHT – LYME REGIS during the hours of darkness from CHERBOURG or HAVRE. Ships from ST. MALO might make the crossing in darkness during the winter, but ships from BREST or L'ORIENT would have to start or complete the crossing in daylight.

2. An airborne attack from aerodromes in northern France could take place with little warning.

**Likely Enemy Objectives**

3. There appear to be two distinct objects which the enemy might have in view in attacking the Southern Command, and each gives rise to a distinct defence problem:

(a) an attack on the Southern or south-western areas to create a diversion and draw off reserves in that direction;

(b) an attack on the Hampshire area with a view to forming a defensive flank facing west to cover his main operations in Kent and Sussex.

Either is likely to be accompanied by airborne landings in the Salisbury Plain – Berkshire Downs area.

4. or the two it is thought that (b) is the more likely, because the chances of maintaining the expedition by sea would be greater. Moreover, this course would have a more direct influence on the main attack in Kent and Sussex. Any such operation is likely to be accompanied by an attack on the ISLE OF WIGHT. As regards (a) a possible plan would be an attempt to cut off Devon and Cornwall, and the cables to America and the Dominions by seizing the narrow neck of land LYME REGIS – TAUNTON – BRIDGWATER BAY.

**Likelihood and Scale of Attack**

5. While the launching of the main attack against this part of England does not hold out sufficient prospects of a quick decision to be attractive to the enemy, subsidiary operations must be regarded as probable.

6. Their scale of attack is estimated at up to 2 armoured, 3 infantry and 8 airborne divisions east of WEYMOUTH as a diversion; 2 seaborne divisions and small airborne parties west of WEYMOUTH.

7 and 8. Allotment.

9. Only one Corps Headquarters will be available to Southern Command. In these circumstances it is desirable that county divisional commanders should have a less unwieldy front to handle, which will ease the increased responsibility which they will have to accept, and facilitate the action of reserves. 4 county divisions of 3 brigades of 3 battalions are therefore required. The scale of defence can therefore be accepted, subject to:

(a) the need explained elsewhere for additional army tank brigades;

(b) the increase in supporting arms which the proposed reorganization of the county divisions will imply, and

(c) 1 independent battalion for the SCILLY ISLES.

**Minimum Requirements**

10. These are therefore:

4 county divisions of 3 brigades of 3 battalions
1 full scale division
1 brigade group
1 armoured division
2 army tank brigades
1 independent battalion.

## WESTERN COMMAND

**General**

1. An enemy seaborne expedition against the Western Command would under present conditions have to be launched from the north-west or west coast of France. We should obtain warning of its approach except perhaps in foggy weather, although we certainly might not have warning of its preparation.

A seaborne expedition would have to run the gauntlet of the minefield between CORNWALL and EIRE, and would be liable to attack by submarines and light craft as well as by aircraft. The initial passage would be hazardous and, it is most improbable that the enemy would be able to maintain any forces he succeeded in landing.

2. It is unlikely that the enemy would attack EIRE as a prelude to the invasion of Western Command. His objects in attacking EIRE would almost certainly be:

(a) to obtain a decision by blockade;

(b) to divert forces from the United Kingdom preparatory to an attack on south eastern England;

Indeed an enemy attack on EIRE would increase the threat to South Eastern and Eastern, rather than to Western Command.

3. Despite the paucity of our fighter defences in the west, and particularly in the narrow neck of land LYME BAY – TAUNTON which forms the direct route for aircraft to Wales, an airborne attack on the Western Command other than for sabotage purposes is unlikely because:

(a) it could only be supported by a seaborne expedition with great difficulty;

(b) most of the Command lies outside the limit of the enemy's short range fighters.

4. To sum up – the threat to Western Command is at present not great.

The threat from seaborne attack is unlikely to be substantially increased even after a successful enemy occupation of EIRE.

**Possible Enemy Objectives**

5. These are:

    (a) The area MERTHYR-TYDFIL (0 52) – NEWPORT (0 70) – CARDIFF – SWANSEA (0 11)

    (b) MANCHESTER – LIVERPOOL – BIRKENHEAD

    (c) WOLVERHAMPTON (K 31) – BIRMINGHAM – COVENTRY

    (d) BARROW-IN-FURNESS (D 69) and ports in the vicinity.

**Likelihood and Scale of Enemy Attack**

6. For the reasons given in paragraphs 1 – 4 above, the most that need be anticipated is a small seaborne raid of the tip and run type and small airborne raids for purposes of sabotage. As a basis for assessing defence requirements the following appears reasonable:

    Seaborne        1 to 3 brigades

    Airborne         1 or 2 battalions

7. Allotment.

**Minimum Requirements**

8. It is only possible to give Western Command one full scale division. The possible internal security problem at the Western Ports and in South Wales, and the geographical features of the Command demand troops in both North and South Wales. In addition the one division may have to be withdrawn from Western Command as G.H.Q. is forced to reconstitute its reserves during battle. One additional infantry brigade group is necessary, together with 1 battalion for the ISLE OF MAN. These are therefore:

    1 full scale division;

    1 brigade group;

    1 independent battalion.

The two first formations are likely to be required as G.H.Q. Reserves as the battle develops.

## AERODROMES

1. The requirements of aerodrome defence fall under two heads:

    (a) A permanent garrison

    (b) External forces equivalent to 1 infantry battalion for vital Fighter aerodromes.

2. In addition to the above, there are on all aerodromes personnel who are normally concerned with the administration and maintenance of the aircraft at the station, but who are available, assuming that they are armed and trained to take their part in the defence of the aerodrome when the battle is joined.

3. Under the present organization, personnel for the permanent garrison (para. 45(a)) are found partly by the Army and partly by the R.A.F. For purposes of calculation it is assumed that all these personnel will in future be found by the Anny.

4. External forces (para. 45(b)) are at present found from Field Force formations in Corps, Army, or G.H.Q. Reserve. In view of the greatly decreased numbers of infantry formations which will, under the new dispositions, be available, it will no longer be possible to find all these battalions from that source. New arrangements will be required, and can only be found by the provision of additional independent battalions.

5. There are at present 459 aerodromes; it is anticipated that by the end of 1942 there will be 755 aerodromes. It is unlikely that this number will ever be greatly increased, as there is a limit to the flat ground available in this country.

In addition, there are now 85 R.D.F. Stations; it is anticipated that there will be 170 by the end of 1942.

Personnel (including R.A.F. ground defence personnel) at present available for the defence of aerodromes and R.D.F. Stations, or already asked for and approved by the Chiefs of Staff, totals 126,800 men, say 127 battalions.

Troops required up to the end of 1942 are:

|  |  |
|---|---|
| (a) As garrisons | 188 battalions |
| (b) As independent battalions | 24 battalions |
| (c) As light tanks or beaverette troops | 300 troops. |

If, however, the R.A.F. retain responsibility for Class 'C' aerodromes for finding A.A. L.M.G. personnel on all aerodromes and for finding personnel to man Beaverette Troops, the above figures will be reduced to:

|  |  |
|---|---|
| (a) As garrisons | 118 battalions |
| (b) As independent battalions | 24 battalions |
| (c) As light tank troops | 38 troops. |

## V.Ps.

1. The attached table shows the total estimated military requirements for the protection of V.Ps., calculated with reference to the end of 1942. These are:

25 battalions Home Defence troops

C.M.P. (V.P.) 12,000 men.

2. It will only be possible to reduce the Home Defence troops to 25 battalions by providing them with a high scale of mobility.

## ESTIMATED V.P. REQUIREMENTS TO END OF 1942

| | V.P.1 | Mil V.P.s | V.P.2 | V.P.3 | V.P.4 | Docks | Totals |
|---|---|---|---|---|---|---|---|
| *Military* | | | | | | | |
| Nos. | 108 | 110 | 499 | 1,200 | 3,650 | - | 5,567 |
| Static gd. | 11,000 | 4,000 | - | - | - | - | 15,000 |
| Mobile col, | - | - | 10,000 | - | - | - | 10,000 |
| CMP (VP) | - | - | 8,000 | - | - | 4,000 | 12,000 |
| *Civil and Other Services* | | | | | | | |
| H.G. | - | - | - | - | 520,000 | - | 520,000 |
| Dock Police | - | - | - | - | - | 1,400 | 1,400 |
| Civil Police | - | - | - | 5,000 | - | - | 5,000 |
| W.D.C. | - | - | 6,300 | - | - | - | 6,300 |
| Air Ministry Wardens | - | - | 2,500 | - | - | - | 2,500 |
| Royal Marine Police | - | - | 2,500 | - | - | - | 2,500 |
| Air Ministry Civil Police | - | - | 850 | - | - | - | 850 |

| | |
|---|---|
| Total Military Personnel Required | 25,000 or 25 Btns |
| C.M.P. (VP) | 12,000 |
| *Total* | 37,000 (inc. overheads) |

## COAST ARTILLERY

1. The requirement for coast artillery personnel up to 1 April 1942 is 43,224, of which 38,110 are now available.

2. The local protection of coast artillery batteries is in many cases insufficient, by reason of the fact that the outpost line on the coast cannot always cover these batteries, and coast artillery war establishments make no provision for personnel for this purpose.

3. Each coast battery in the ORKNEYS and SHETLANDS and from WICK to LANDS END requires such protection. Of these, some are covered by existing defended localities; others are isolated. Overall infantry on the scale of 1 platoon per battery is required.

4. On this basis a total of 18 battalions of static troops would be necessary for affiliation as required to county and field formations on the coast. The need, however, for the utmost economy of troops imposes the necessity of doing without these battalions and accepting the risk.

# Admiralty Anti-Invasion Programme, Spring 1942

This table shows the light forces available for anti-invasion duties on an average day and the probable increase in these forces on the following assumptions:

**Day 1**
Admiralty (a) Order the 3rd Degree of Readiness for Invasion (ships in dockyard hands capable of being made efficient in the time to be given utmost priority).
(b) Recall destroyers lent to N.F.E.F. on completion of current escort duties.
(c) Withdraw from trade protection the corvettes fitted for mine-sweeping        duties.
(d) Commence re-adjusting Coastal and Minesweeping forces as necessary.

**Day 17**
Admiralty (a) Order 2nd Degree of Readiness for Invasion.
(b) Complete re-adjustment of Coastal forces.
(c) Recall all destroyers on Atlantic Trade Routes.

**Day 20**
Admiralty order 1st Degree of Readiness for Invasion.

LIGHT FORES AVAILABLE IN HOME WATERS FOR ANTI-INVASION

| | CRUISERS | | DESTROYERS | SLOOPS | CORVETTES | | COASTAL FORCES | | |
|---|---|---|---|---|---|---|---|---|---|
| | 6″ | A/A | | | Ducks | M/S | ML | MGB | MTB |
| DAY | | | | | | | | | |
| 1 | 1 | 1 | 63 | 9 | 5 | 4 | 56 | 34 | 26 |
| 2 | | | 64 | | | | | | |
| 3 | | | 66 | | | | | | |
| 4 | | | 69 | | | 6 | | | |
| 5 | | | 73 | | | | | | |
| 6 | | | 74 | | | | | | |
| 7 | | 2 | 76 | | | | | | |
| 8 | | | 78 | | | | | | |
| 9 | | | 79 | | | | | | |
| 10 | | | 80 | | | 8 | 84 | 51 | 39 |
| 11 | | | 81 | | | | | | |
| 12 | | | 82 | | | | | | |
| 13 | | | 83 | | | | | | |
| 14 | | | | | | | | | |
| 15 | | | | | 6 | 11 | | | |
| 16 | | | | | | | | | |
| 17 | | | | | | | | | |
| 18 | | 3 | 87 | 11 | | | | | |
| 19 | | | 92 | | | | | | |
| 20 | 1 | 3 | 97 | 11 | 6 | 11 | 114 | 51 | 39 |

Note 1: Home Fleet is not included and no vessels have been recalled from Foreign Stations.

Note 2: The 97 destroyers shown as available on Day 20 are approximately two-thirds of the total number of destroyers in the Home Commands on that day.

Note 3: The Coastal forces shown on Day 1 are 50% of the total stationed between Falmouth and Rosyth South about. The final figures given for Day 20 are 75% of the total available in the United Kingdom.

328

Appendix XXIV

# Instructions for the Coast Defence Artillery

G.H.Q. Operation Instruction No.34

**Application**

1. This Instruction applies to all coast artillery.

**Composition of Coast Artillery under command G.H.Q.**

2. The coast artillery under command of G.H.Q. comprises:

(a) Coast Artillery in major defended ports consisting of:

(i) Permanent and war permanent batteries equipped with Land Service guns.

(ii) Naval equipments installed to increase or extend the defences.

(b) Land and Naval service equipments installed at minor defended ports.

(c) Naval equipments installed for the defence of landing beaches.

(d) Radiolocation stations.

**Defended Ports**

3. A list of major and minor defended ports is given below.

**Tasks**

4. The tasks of coast artillery, in order of priority, are,

(a) Guns covering major defended ports

(i) Engagement of enemy warships.

(ii) Engagement of enemy transports and landing craft.

(iii) Engagement of targets on or adjacent to landing beaches in the vicinity of the port.

(b) Guns covering minor defended ports and landing beaches

(i) Engagement of enemy transports and landing craft.

(ii) Engagement of enemy warships.

(iii) Engagement of targets on or adjacent to landing beaches.

5. In addition at both major and minor defended ports the coast artillery will support the examination service where it is in force.

**Operational Control**

6. Operational control of coast artillery is vested in corps, with the following exceptions:

(a) Coast artillery in Scottish Command, except ORKNEY and SHETLANDS, and in Western Command, will be directly under Command Headquarters.

(b) Coast Artillery in ORKNEYS and SHETLANDS will be under Commander, ORKNEY and SHETLAND Defences.

(c) Coast Artillery of the THAMES and MEDWAY Defences will be directly under South Eastern Command.

7. Coast Artillery will NOT be placed under the command of divisions or other formations below Corps, except that on ACTION STATIONS all troops in a sector of the coast may be put under the command of the commander of the sector. This commander will not, however, interfere with the normal tasks of the coast artillery so long as these tasks can be carried out.

8. Except in Canadian Corps, Commanders Corps Coast Artillery will be under the Commanders Corps Royal Artillery concerned, and will be responsible to them for all matters connected with coast artillery in the corps area.

In Canadian Corps, the responsibility of the Commander Corps Coast Artillery to Headquarters South Eastern Command and to Commander Corps Royal Artillery, Canadian Corps, respectively, will be in accordance with the policy given in War Office letter 112/Misc/2787(S.D.1) dated 18th October, 1941. Exact details will be arranged by Headquarters, South Eastern Command.

9. At most major defended ports, an Army Plotting Room has been, or is being, established from which the Commander, Corps Coast Artillery or Commander, Fixed Defences, will exercise operational control either through the Fire Commander or through Commanders of Special Coast Regiments.

**Opening of Fire**

10. Major Defended Ports. Fire will be opened in accordance with the instructions contained in Coast Artillery Training Volume III, except that naval equipments will be bound by the conditions of paragraph 11.

11. Minor defended ports and batteries on beaches. Fire will be opened as early as is compatible with the probability of scoring direct hits with the opening rounds. Though this will rarely be the case at ranges greater

than 6,000 yards, Battery Commanders should not hesitate to engage a ship which commits a hostile act, provided that:

(a) The engagement of more important targets, e.g. transports and landing craft, approaching the beaches is not prejudiced.

(b) There is a prospect that hits can be obtained.

**Radiolocation**

12. The fullest use should be made of radiolocation methods to engage both seen and unseen targets.

**Landward Firing and Targets on Beaches**

13. Such targets as can be engaged within the limit of gun arcs will be selected, registered if possible, and recorded; and arrangements will be made for observation of fire. Targets which can be equally well engaged by mobile artillery should not, as a rule, be selected if others are available.

14. The ability of coast artillery to engage such targets is limited by the number of landward firing shell provided. Armour piercing and C.P. type shell, and H.E. shell fuzed 45P are NOT suitable for use against personnel, and should only be used against Armoured Fighting Vehicles. Within these limitations, it is the duty of all coast batteries, in addition to their anti-ship role, to engage land or beach targets within their arcs of fire. Where possible arrangements will be made for indirect fire to be controlled from other coast artillery observation posts and observation posts of heavy and super heavy batteries.

Unobserved Fire

15. (a) Unobserved fire will be restricted to targets on beaches, which have been previously registered either by shooting or by silent registration. These targets will only be engaged on orders from the local military commander.

(b) Schemes for unobserved fire seawards may be arranged in accordance with Coast Artillery Training Volume III pamphlet 8 section 4, provided a sufficient volume of fire can be brought to bear on the selected areas without dangerously depleting the ammunition held in the batteries concerned.

The engagement of unseen targets by radiolocation methods will NOT be classified as unobserved fire.

**Coast Artillery Searchlights**

16. The policy for the exposure of coast artillery searchlights will be based on the following requirements:

(a) That no hostile vessel or low flying aircraft is able to approach within range without being illuminated.

(b) That the safety of friendly vessels is not jeopardised by their being illuminated.

Coast artillery searchlights will therefore NOT be exposed without permission of the responsible Naval officer unless the fire commanders and battery commanders have reason to suspect the presence of a hostile vessel or low flying aircraft, in which case they will expose their searchlights on their own initiative.

17. When exposed, searchlights must NOT illuminate beach or land defences held by our own troops. Screens will therefore, be arranged in emplacements to prevent the illumination of beach or land defences held by our own troops. These screens should be removable, so that full use can be made of the arc of each light in an emergency.

**States of Readiness**

18. Policy. The policy regarding states of readiness will be as follows:

(a) The state of readiness of coast batteries forming the key defences of all major defended ports and selected minor defended ports will be governed by the visibility.

(b) The state of readiness of all other coast batteries will be governed by the strategic situation.

19. Definition. The definition of the various states of readiness will be as follows:

| | | |
|---|---|---|
| Immediate | Up to 30 secs. | Duty watch may NOT sleep. |
| Short | 30 secs. to 2 mins. | Duty watch may sleep. |
| Long | Any time over 2 mins. | Duty watch may sleep. |

20. Application of Policy:

(a) Examination Batteries

(i) Full time Examination Batteries:

Pre-stand-to. One gun always at immediate readiness. The second gun at short readiness under night conditions.

Stand-to. One gun always at immediate readiness. The second gun may be brought to immediate readiness.

(ii) Part Time Examination Batteries. Part time Examination Batteries which also form part of the key defences of a port will normally be at the same state of readiness as batteries in sub-paragraph (b). Part time Examination Batteries which are NOT included in key defences will normally be at the same state of readiness as batteries in sub-paragraph (c). All Part Time Examination Batteries may, however, be brought to immediate readiness for short periods for a specific task at the request of the Naval Authorities.

(b) Close Defence Batteries forming the key defences of major defended Ports.

Pre-stand-to. One gun always at short readiness under night

332

conditions. Remaining guns at 5 mins. readiness under night conditions.

Stand to. All guns may be brought to immediate readiness.

(c) All other Batteries with a Close Defence Role only.

(i) Pre-Stand to. The state of readiness will be governed by intelligence reports of the movements of enemy or unidentified suspicious shipping. This information will normally be issued by Army Plotting Rooms. In cases where there are no Army Plotting Rooms, the information will be obtained from local Naval authorities.

(ii) Stand to. The state of readiness will correspond to that of local Field Army Troops.

(d) 6-pdr. twin and 12-pdr. A/M.T.B. Batteries. All such batteries, except CALSHOT, BUNGALOW, MOUNTBATTEN and WESTERN KINGS (12 and 6-pdrs.) will be at immediate readiness under night conditions. CALSHOT and BUNGALOW will normally be at 5 minutes under night conditions. MOUNTBATTEN and WESTERN KINGS will normally be at two minutes under night conditions.

(e) Counter Bombardment Batteries.

(i) The state of readiness of batteries which have a day role only will be governed by intelligence reports of movements of enemy shipping.

(ii) The state of readiness of whose which also have a close defence role will be that given in (b) above.

Batteries in these categories are listed below.

21. Look Outs. All batteries, whatever their role or state of readiness will post observation post look-outs under day conditions and gun and observation post look-outs under night conditions.

22. Manning.

(i) Guns at immediate readiness. Sufficient men must be ready in the immediate vicinity of the guns to open fire immediately and maintain it until the complete manning detail arrives.

(ii) Guns at short readiness or five minutes. Sufficient men must be ready in the vicinity of the guns to open fire within two minutes or five minutes of the alarm, and maintain it until the complete manning detail arrives.

(iii) Guns at lower states of readiness. During official night, one watch must be near enough to the guns and the battery observation post to open fire within five minutes of the alarm, and maintain it until the remainder of the manning detail arrives.

23. Night Conditions. The expression "Night Conditions", where used in this instruction, means either "Official night" or "Conditions when visibility is 5,000 yards or less". Action to be taken under night conditions may, at the discretion of the local Commander, be modified in accordance with weather conditions.

24. Control of Shipping and Entry into Defended Ports. Details are contained in Admiralty Publications C.B 01618(Q) (41) and C.B. 01618(R) (41), and in the Manual of Coast Defence, Chapter VII.

25. A list of ports where either a full or improvised examination service is in force is at below, and examination batteries, either full or part time, will only be established at the ports detailed below.

**Liaison with Royal Navy**

26. Liaison between the Royal Navy and the coast artillery is of the greatest importance if the coast artillery is to carry out its tasks to the best advantage. Coast Artillery Commanders will therefore maintain the closest touch with the responsible naval officers at major and minor defended ports and will consult them on all subjects of common interest to the two Services.

**Ammunition**

27. Use of various types. Details of the most suitable types of ammunition and fuzes for use by land and naval service equipments against different targets are contained in War Office letters 43/Artillery/1773 (C.A.1.b) dated 19th March, 1941, and 30th September, 1941 respectively.

28. Replenishment of ammunition during operations.

(a) Commands will report their bulk requirements to G.H.Q. under the following headings:

(i) Nature of ammunition.

(ii) Quantity required.

(iii) Command A.D. for consignment.

(iv) Any special requirements or priorities.

(b) Reports will be submitted as ammunition is required, and will be franked "Emergency Operations".

(c) Priority of replenishment between Army Commands will be decided by G.H.Q.

(d) Replenishment will be made either from available stocks, or by transfers between Army Commands.

29. G.H.Q. Coast Artillery Operation Instructions Nos. 1 and 2. G.H.Q. Coast Artillery Operation Instructions Nos. 1 and 2 are cancelled and all copies will be destroyed by burning.

*Lt-Gen., C.G.S.*

*Annex 'A'*

## ISSUED WITH G.H.Q. OPERATION INSTRUCTION No.34 DATED 16 MAR. '42

### Major Ports

Orkneys
Invergordon
Aberdeen
Dundee
Forth
Blyth
Tyne
Sunderland
Tees and Hartlepool
Humber
Yarmouth
Lowestoft
Harwich
Thames and Medway
Dover
Newhaven
Portsmouth, Isle of Wight
Southampton
Londonderry

Portland
Dartmouth
Plymouth
Falmouth
Avonmouth (Portishead)
Bristol Channel (Lavernock)
    (Flatholm)
    (Steepholme)
    (Brean Down)
Newport
Cardiff
Barry
Swansea
lford Haven
Mersey
Barrow
Clyde
Belfast

### Minor Ports

Sullom Voe
Lerwick
Scalloway
Wick
Montrose
Inverness
Berwick
Amble
Seaham Harbour
Whitby
Scarborough
Boston
Kings Lynn
Brightlingsea
Burnham

Ramsgate
Shoreham
Littlehampton
Poole
Exmouth
Torquay
Brixham
Salcombe
Looe
Fowey
Penzance
Padstow
Appledore
Llanelly
Fishguard

Caernarvon
Holyhead
Preston
Fleetwood
Whitehaven
Workington
Stranraer
Ardrossan
Campbeltown
Oban
Loch Ewe
Stornoway
Lamlash
Kyle of Lochalsh
Larne

APPENDIX XXIV

*Annex 'B'*

ISSUED WITH G.H.Q. OPERATION INSTRUCTION No.34 DATED
16 MAR. '42

**Examination Batteries**

FULL-TIME EXAMINATION BATTERIES

|  | *Battery* | *Location* |
|---|---|---|
| *Scottish Command* | Greenhead | Shetlands |
|  | Ness of Sound | Shetlands |
|  | Stromness | Orkneys |
|  | Stanger | Orkneys |
|  | Rerwick | Orkneys |
|  | Galtness (4.7) | Orkneys |
|  | South Sutor | Cromarty |
|  | Torry Point | Aberdeen |
|  | Salthouse | Peterhead |
|  | Broughty | Dundee |
|  | Kincraig | Forth |
|  | Kinghorn | Forth |
|  | Inchkeith North | Forth |
|  | Toward | Clyde |
|  | Loch Ewe | Loch Ewe |
| *Northern Command* | Seaton | Blyth |
|  | Castle (6-inch) | Tyne |
|  | Roker | Sunderland |
|  | South Gare | Tees |
|  | Spurn (6-inch) | Humber |
| *Eastern Command* | Links | Yarmouth |
|  | North Denes | Yarmouth |
|  | Lowestoft | Lowestoft |
|  | Landguard | Harwich |
| *South Eastern Com.* | Langdon | Dover |
|  | Newhaven Fort | Newhaven |
| *Southern Command* | Nodes (6-inch) | Isle of Wight |
|  | Nomansland | Portsmouth |
|  | Bouldnor | Isle of Wight |
|  | Breakwater | Portland |
|  | Drakes (6-inch) | Plymouth |
|  | Picklecombe | Plymouth |

336

|                  |                     |                         |
|------------------|---------------------|-------------------------|
|                  | Half Moon           | Falmouth                |
| *Western Command*| Nells Point         | Barry                   |
|                  | Mumbles Island      | Swansea                 |
|                  | West Blockhouse     | Milford Haven           |
|                  | Soldiers Rock       | Milford Haven (Note 1)  |
|                  | Crosby              | Liverpool               |
|                  | Holyhead            | Holyhead                |
|                  | Fleetwood           | Fleetwood               |
|                  | Workington          | Workington              |

*Note:* SOLDIER'S ROCK MILFORD HAVEN will only be at the state of readiness of a full time examination battery when actually carrying out examination duties. At other times it will be at the state of readiness of a "Key" battery.

## PART-TIME EXAMINATION BATTERIES

|                      | *Battery*                 | *Location*     |
|----------------------|---------------------------|----------------|
| *Scottish Command*   | Sullom Voe                | Shetlands      |
|                      | Scalloway                 | Shetlands      |
|                      | Wick                      | Wick           |
|                      | Montrose                  | Montrose       |
|                      | Finnart                   | Stranraer      |
|                      | Ardhallow (Key)           | Clyde          |
| *Northern Command*   | Bull Sand Fort 6" (Key)   | Humber         |
|                      | Heugh (Key)               | Hartlepool     |
|                      | Gibraltar Point           | Skegness       |
|                      | Spurn (4-inch)            | Humber         |
| *Eastern Command*    | Mersea East               | Brightlingsea  |
| *South Eastern Com._*| Shoreham                  | Shoreham       |
|                      | Littlehampton             | Littlehampton  |
| *Southern Command*   | Brownsea                  | Poole          |
|                      | Dartmouth (4.7-inch)      | Dartmouth      |
|                      | Brixham                   | Brixham        |
|                      | Fowey                     | Fowey          |
|                      | Appledore (4.7)           | Barnstaple     |
|                      | Hayle                     | Hayle          |
|                      | Penzance                  | Penzance       |
| *Western Command*    | Old Lighthouse            | Port Talbot    |
|                      | Fishguard                 | Fishguard      |
|                      | Perch Rock (Key)          | Liverpool      |
|                      | Lytham                    | Preston        |
|                      | Hilpsford (Key)           | Barrow         |
|                      | Whitehaven                | Whitehaven     |

*Annex 'C'*

ISSUED WITH G.H.Q. OPERATION INSTRUCTION No.34 DATED
16 MAR. '42

## Close Defence Batteries Forming the Key Defences of Major Defended Ports

|  | *Battery* | *Location* |
|---|---|---|
| *Scottish Command* | Hoxa | Orkneys |
|  | Inchkeith South | Forth |
|  | Leith Docks | Forth |
|  | Cloch Point | Clyde |
| *Northern Command* | Spanish | Tynemouth |
| *Eastern Command* | Grand | Lowestoft |
|  | Beacon Bill | Harwich |
| *South Eastern Com.* | Grain | Thames and Medway |
|  | Garrison Point | Thames and Medway |
|  | Canvey | Thames and Medway |
|  | South Breakwater | Dover |
|  | Pier Turret | Dover |
|  | Knuckle | Dover |
| *Southern Command* | Cliff End | Isle of Wight |
|  | Horse Sand | Portsmouth |
|  | Spit Sand | Portsmouth |
|  | Nothe | Portland |
|  | Dartmouth (6-inch) | Dartmouth |
|  | Watchhouse | Plymouth |
|  | St. Anthonys | Falmouth (until Roselands is in action) |
| *Western Command* | Lavernock Point | Severn Defences |
|  | Flatholm North | Severn Defences |
|  | Flatholm South | Severn Defences |
|  | Steepholme North | Severn Defences |
|  | Steepholme South | Severn Defences |
|  | Brean Down | Severn Defences |
|  | Mumbles Hill | Swansea |

*Note 1.* All full time and some part time examination batteries form part of the key defences of major defended ports. They are detailed in Appendix 'B' and are NOT repeated in this list.

*Note 2.* Counter Bombardment batteries with a close defence role also form part of the key defences. They are detailed in Appendix 'E' paragraph 2 and are NOT repeated in this list.

*Annex 'D'*

## ISSUED WITH G.H.Q. OPERATION INSTRUCTION No.34 DATED 16 MAR. '42

|  | *Battery* | *Location* |
|---|---|---|
| *Scottish Command* | Wellington | Orkneys |
|  | Nigg | Invergordon |
|  | Fort George | Inverness |
|  | Innes Links | Lossiemouth |
|  | Girdleness | Aberdeen |
|  | Stannergate | Dundee |
|  | Inchkeith West | Forth |
|  | Pettycur | Forth |
|  | Fidra | Forth |
| *Northern Command* | Amble | Amble |
|  | Druridge Bay | Widdrington |
|  | Gloucester | Blyth |
|  | Park | South Shields |
|  | Whitburn | Sunderland |
|  | Seaham | Seaham |
|  | Seaton Carew | Hartlepool |
|  | Whitby | Whitby |
|  | Scarborough | Scarborough |
|  | Filey | Filey |
|  | Hornsea | Hornsea |
|  | Sunk Island | Humber |
|  | Stallingborough | Humber |
|  | Grimsby | Humber |
|  | Mablethorpe | Mablethorpe |
|  | Jacksons Corner | Skegness |
|  | Boston | Boston |
|  | Berwick | Berwick |
| *Eastern Command* | Kings Lynn | Kings Lynn |
|  | Hunstanton | Hunstanton |
|  | Brancaster Bay | Brancaster Bay |
|  | High Cape | Wells Next The Sea |
|  | Cley Eye | Cley Next The Sea |
|  | Sheringham | Sheringham |

| | |
|---|---|
| Cromer | Cromer |
| Mundesley | Mundesley |
| Happisburgh | Happisburgh |
| Winterton | Winterton |
| Hopton | Yarmouth |
| Pakefield | Lowestoft |
| Kessingland | Kessingland |
| Easton Wood | Covehithe |
| Southwold | Southwold |
| Dunwich | Dunwich |
| Minsmere | Minsmere |
| Sizewell | Thorpeness |
| Aldeburgh | Aldeburgh |
| Bawdsey | Bawdsey |
| Felixstowe | Felixstowe |
| Frinton | Frinton |
| Clacton | Clacton |
| Mersea West | Mersea Island |
| Foulness | Foulness |
| Shoeburyness | Shoeburyness |
| Coalhouse | Thames |
| Shornmead | Thames |
| No.1 Bastion | Sheerness |
| Shellness | Shellness |
| Herne Bay | Herne Bay |
| Margate | Margate |
| Kingsgate | Broadstairs |
| Dumpton Point | Broadstairs |
| Ramsgate | Ramsgate |
| Bethlehem | Pegwell Bay |
| Sandwich Bay | Sandwich Bay |
| Sandown Castle | Deal |
| Deal | Deal |
| Kingsdown | Walmer |
| Western Heights | Dover |
| Folkestone East | Folkestone |
| Folkestone West | Folkestone |
| Hythe | Hythe |
| Grand Redoubt | Hythe |
| Dymchurch | Dymchurch |
| Greatstone | Greatstone |
| Dungeness 6-inch | Dungeness |

*South Eastern Com.*

340

|  | | |
|---|---|---|
|  | Dungeness 4.7-inch | Dungeness |
|  | Jurys Gut | Dungeness |
|  | Winchelsea | Winchelsea |
|  | Pett | Rye |
|  | Hastings | Hastings |
|  | Bexhill | Bexhill |
|  | Cooden | Cooden |
|  | Normans Bay | Pevensey |
|  | Pevensey | Pevensey |
|  | Eastbourne | Eastbourne |
|  | Seaford | Seaford |
|  | Brighton | Brighton |
|  | Worthing | Worthing |
|  | Angmering | Angmering |
|  | Bognor | Bognor |
| *Southern Command* | Stone Point | Southampton Water |
|  | Southbourne | Christchurch |
|  | Mudeford | Christchurch |
|  | Swanage | Swanage |
|  | Upton | Weymouth |
|  | Abbotsbury | Abbotsbury |
|  | West Bay | Bridport |
|  | Lyme Regis | Lyme Regis |
|  | Seaton | Seaton |
|  | Sidmouth | Sidmouth |
|  | Exmouth | Exmouth |
|  | Dawlish | Dawlish |
|  | Shaldon | Teignmouth |
|  | Corbyns Head | Torquay |
|  | Salcombe | Salcombe |
|  | Looe | Looe |
|  | Par | Par |
|  | Helford | Helford River |
|  | Newquay | Newquay |
|  | Padstow | Padstow |
|  | Instow | Barnstaple |
|  | Ilfracombe | Ilfracombe |
|  | Harbour | Minehead |
| *Western Command* | Portishead | Portishead |
|  | Burry Point | Llanelly |
|  | Belan | Caernarvon |
|  | Walney | Barrow |

*Annex 'E'*

ISSUED WITH G.H.Q. OPERATION INSTRUCTION No.34 DATED
16 MAR. '42

## Counter Bombardment Batteries: Day Role Only

| | Battery | Location |
|---|---|---|
| *Scottish Command* | Nil | - |
| *Northern Command* | Godwin | Humber |
| *Eastern Command* | Nil | |
| *South Eastern Com.* | Fletcher | Thames and Medway |
| | Wanstone | Dover |
| *Southern Command* | Culver Down | I. o. W. |
| | Needles | I. o. W. |
| | Blacknor | Portland |
| *Western Command* | Nil | |

## Counter Bombardment Batteries: With Additional Close Defence Role

| | Battery | Location |
|---|---|---|
| *Scottish Command* | Inchkeith | Forth |
| | North Sutor | Cromarty |
| | Kincraig | Forth (when equipped with 6-inch 45° guns. Is also full time examination battery and will be at state of readiness for such batteries). |
| *Northern Command* | Castle (9.2-inch) | Tyne |
| | Frenchmans | Tyne |
| | Heugh | Hartlepool (when equipped with 6-inch 45° guns). |
| | Pasley | Tees |
| | Ringborough | Humber |
| *Eastern Command* | Brackenbury | Harwich |
| | Landguard | Harwich (when equipped with 6-inch 45° guns. Is also full |

| | | |
|---|---|---|
| | | time examination battery and will be at state of readiness for such batteries). |
| *South Eastern Com.* | Joss Bay | Broadstairs |
| | St. Margarets | Nr. Dover |
| | South Foreland | Dover |
| | Fan Hole | Dover |
| | Citadel | Dover |
| | Lyddon Spout | Dover |
| | Capel | Dover |
| | Hougham | Dover |
| | Mill Point | Folkestone |
| | Newhaven Fort | Newhaven (when equipped with 6-inch 45° guns. Is also full time examination battery and will be at state of readiness for such batteries). |
| *Southern Command* | Nodes (9.2-inch) | I. o. W. |
| | East Weare | Portland |
| | Renny | Plymouth |
| | Peniee | Plymouth |
| | Roselands | Falmouth |
| | Half Moon | Falmouth (is also a full time battery and will be at state of readiness for such batteries). |
| *Western Command* | East Blockhouse | Milford Haven |

*Annex 'F'*

ISSUED WITH G.H.Q. OPERATION INSTRUCTION No.34 DATED
16 MAR. '42

**Ports with an Examination Service**

List A.   Search Ports (i.e. Full Examination with extra personnel for special search duties).

List B.   Non-search ports with full Examination Service.

List C.   Non-search with improvised Examination Service.

| List A | List B | List C |
|---|---|---|
| Falmouth | Plymouth | Newhaven |
| Portland and Weymouth | Brixham | Poole |
| Portsmouth and | Newlyn | Penzance |
| Southampton | Shoreham | Littlehampton |
| Kirkwall | Thames and Medway | Appledore |
| Thurso | Brightlingsea | Padstow |
| Loch Ewe | Harwich | St. Ives and Hayle |
| Oban | Lowestoft | Mevagissey |
| Rothesay | Yarmouth | Pentewan |
| Brodick | Humber | Charlestown |
| Belfast | Hartlepool – Tees | Par |
| Workington | Sunderland and Tyne | Fowey |
| Fleetwood | Blyth | Looe |
| Holyhead | Firth of Forth | Salcombe |
| Fishguard | Montrose | Dartmouth |
| Milford Haven | Aberdeen | Torquay |
| | Peterhead | Teignmouth |
| | Invergordon and | Exmouth |
| | Inverness | Dover |
| | Londonderry | Ramsgate |
| | Stranraer | Skegness |
| | Liverpool | Burnham-on-Crouch |
| | Dee Estuary | Scarborough |
| | Barrow | Whitby |
| | Preston | Amble |
| | Menai Straits | Berwick |
| | Swansea | Dundee |
| | Scapa | Fraserburgh |
| | Wick | Macduff |
| | Lerwick | Buckle |
| | | Lossiemouth |
| | | Sullom Voe |
| | | Loch Alsh |
| | | Stornoway |
| | | Whitehaven |
| | | Larne |
| | | Llanelly |
| | | Port Talbot |

Note: All Examination at The Nore takes place near the boom which is beyond the range at which the coast guns can give effective assistance to the examination vessel.

*Annex 'G'*

FIRING OF PREDICTED CONCENTRATIONS ON R.D.F.
INFORMATION
G.H.Q. Operation Instruction No.34

1. Predicted concentrations based on R.D.F. information will be fired by all batteries except 138 mm., 5.5", 4.7", 4" and 12-pdrs., with the following restrictions:

(a) No battery holding less than 150 r.p.g. of all types of equipment ammunition will fire on R.D.F. concentration.

(b) No target is to be engaged at greater ranges than as under:

| | |
|---|---|
| 10,000$^x$ | by a 6" emergency battery. |
| 13,000$^x$ | by a 6" (15°) L.S. battery. |
| 20,000$^x$ | by a 6" (45°) L.S. battery. |
| 18,000$^x$ | by a 7.5" L.S. battery. |

Max. Range by all 9.2" batteries.

(c) The Fire Commander or Regimental Commander of the batteries concerned will be in communication with the Army Plotting Room, and with his batteries throughout the shoot, and will only fire on orders from the Army Plotting Room.

(d) Not more than 6 r.p.g. (4 in the case of 7.5") will normally be fired on each target, but Cs.C.C.A., Commanders Fixed Defences or Regimental Commanders i/c of A.P.Rs retain the right to continue if the enemy craft approach the shore and a landing raid or similar operation appears to be developing.

(e) Not more than 2 salvoes from 6" and one from larger calibre equipments should be fired at any single prediction.

(f) In the case of the 6-pdr. twin, where R.D.F. sets are capable of following targets at short ranges, concentrations of 5 rounds per barrel may be fired on each prediction below 4,000$^x$. Ammunition expenditure must depend on the action of the hostile vessel and on the chance of its engagement by visual methods; normally not more than 30 r.p.b. should be fired on each target.

2. The following is a suggested procedure for application to batteries whose guns are fitted with bearing arcs and, in the case of N.S. batteries, with bubbles or Elevation indicators to enable them to lay for range:

(a) An unidentified plot is thought to be coming within the ranges shown in para. 2(b) of a coast battery or batteries.

(b) Communication is established from the A.P.R. to the Regimental Commander or F.C. of the batteries concerned.

(c) Communication is established between the Regimental

Commander or F.C., and the batteries he considers may be required, and they are brought to an "Immediate" state of readiness.

(d) The track proves hostile and after consultation with the Navy engagement appears probable. The alarm is passed to the batteries concerned together with a first estimate of time and position of engagement.

(e) A point is estimated at which the target will be in say 3 minutes time (times will very and can only be found by actual trial). The co-ordinates are sent to the batteries concerned, are converted by them to bearing and range and the guns are laid.

(f) Batteries report "Ready".

(g) The A.P.R. duty officer orders 2 salvoes shoot (1 in the case of 7.5" and above) together with a fresh prediction if necessary; these are fired at the time given less the time of flight, the second salvo being fired as soon as possible after the first.

(h) The procedure from (c) to (g) is repeated up to a total of 6 r.p.g. (4 r.p.g. in the case of 7.5" and above) provided the target remains within the ranges laid down in para. 2 (b).

3. The procedure given in para. 2 may need modification or variation to suit local conditions. It is essential, however, that Regiments or Fire Commanders should always be in communication with A.P.Rs and with their batteries, so that orders to open fire or stop can be given at an moment.

4. Nothing in the foregoing paragraphs is to be interpreted to limit the powers of Cs.C.C.A., Cs.F.D. and Regimental Commanders from engaging and continuing to engage a raid, or invasion landing. Under these circumstances all equipments will fire by any means within limitations laid down in paras. 10 and 11 of the Operation Instruction.

## Location of Sqns. of G.H.Q. Liaison Regt.

| | |
|---|---|
| HQ | Althorp Park, Nr. Northampton. East Haddon 232 |
| "A" | Stonehead House, MERE, Wilts. |
| "B" | Althorp Park, Nr. NORTHAMPTON. |
| "C" | RICHMOND. |
| "D" | RICHMOND. |
| "E" | BARHAM, Ipswich. |
| "F" | LISBURN, B.T.N.I. |
| "G" | M.E. |
| "H" | RICHMOND. |
| "J" | WINCHESTER |

# 12 Corps' Plan to Defeat Invasion

## ROLE OF 12 CORPS

1. Acting under command South-Eastern Command, 12 Corps is responsible for defeating invasion in Kent.

## SCALE AND NATURE OF ATTACK

2. From the German point of view, Kent provides the most attractive area in which to stage the main effort of an invasion for the following reasons:

(a) He can concentrate a larger sustained fighter effort over East Kent than over any other part of England.

(b) Communications from the Continent to East Kent are much the shortest and therefore most easily kept secure.

(c) East Kent coast has two reasonably good ports in DOVER and FOLKESTONE, and two indifferent but useful harbours in RAMSGATE and MARGATE.

3. East Kent will therefore probably be the scene of the enemy's main effort, which would be both seaborne (including armoured formations) and airborne.

## 12 CORPS PLAN IN OUTLINE

4. In order to defeat invasion 12 Corps plan will be based on the following:

(a) The holding of the beaches by strong, well wired platoon or company localities, capable of all-round defence and of holding out until our reserves get into action.

(b) Offensive action by reserves of forward Bns., Bdes. and Divs. for the purpose of taking immediate and energetic action against any enemy penetration of beach defences or against enemy airborne landings in rear of the beach defences.

(c) Offensive action by Corps and Army reserves in an area in which certain vital "fortresses" will hold firm indefinitely.

## FORTRESSES

5. (a) The most serious menace in Kent would be the presence of an enemy force, armoured or otherwise, which had penetrated or overcome the forward defences. In order that such a force may be destroyed by our reserves, it is necessary to have certain strong "FORTRESSES" to act as "hinges", or pivots of manoeuvre, in the area where these reserves will operate.

(b) The vital "fortresses" will be as follows. On the coast: the defended areas of FOLKESTONE and DOVER, each held by one Independent Inf. Bde. Inland: the towns of CANTERBURY, ASHFORD, MAIDSTONE and TONBRIDGE, each held by a special garrison.

(c) The importance of these six places is immense; as long as they hold out, and remain intact, East Kent cannot be lost. They must, therefore, hold out, and will do so.

## 12 CORPS' PLAN – IN DETAIL

6. The "invasion battle" in the coastal belt will be fought by the two forward Divs. of 12 Corps.

Each Division has one Ind. Inf. Bde. under command holding the "fortresses" of FOLKESTONE and DOVER respectively. Each Division has one Inf. Bde. in reserve. Right forward Div. has one Army Tank Bn. under command: Left forward Div. has an Army Tank Bde. (less one Bn.) under command. MAIDSTONE Sub-area is responsible for that part of 12 Corps area in rear of forward Div. areas.

7. Forward Inf. Bdes. will fight the battle in their present allotted areas. The garrisons of localities will hold out to the last, fighting the enemy on their own ground without thought of withdrawal or surrender, and inflicting the maximum toll on his forces; so that, even if his seaborne forces manage to fight their way inland, they will be disorganised, exhausted and seriously weakened before they meet our reserve formations.

Local reserves will be kept ready to take immediate and energetic offensive action against enemy penetrations from the coast, or against airborne landings in rear of beach defences.

8. **Right Forward Division**

(a) *Reserve Inf. Bde.* One Inf. Bde., with one Army Tank Bn. and one Coy. Reece. Bn. under command, will be located in the area LYMINGE 6059 – ARPINGE 6257 – POSTLING 5857 to deal with enemy airborne landings North of FOLKESTONE or the formation of an enemy beach-head on the DYMCHURCH – HYTHE – SANDGATE beach. (NOTE: reserve battalion of the centre forward Inf. Bde. is located to the North of the ROYAL MILITARY CANAL).

(b) *Recce. Bn.* (less one coy. with Res. Inf. Bde. as in sub-para. (a) above) will be positioned in area ROLVENDEN 2849 to deal with enemy airborne landings in that area or make initial contact with enemy seaborne penetration in the RYE area.

9. **Left Forward Division.**

(a) The left forward Inf. Bde. area of the left forward Div. (the area HERNE BAY – CANTERBURY – WHITSTABLE) is garrisoned by one Inf. Bde. Gp. of the reserve Division, under operational command of the left forward Division.

This Bde. will be kept assembled in the area and NOT dispersed on the coast to the North, which will be watched by Home Guard or military O.Ps as necessary.

The Bde. will be prepared to operate offensively in an Easterly direction to restore the situation in the ISLE OF THANET, or in a S.E. or Southerly direction against a threat to CANTERBURY. It will also be prepared to man the coast in the Sector HERNE BAY – WHITSTABLE should this be necessary.

One Bn. of the Bde. will be earmarked to reinforce the garrison of CANTERBURY should such action become necessary.

As long as communications exist, the Bde. will not be used by the left forward Div. without reference to Corps H.Q.

(b) Reserve Inf. Bde. with one Army Tank Bde. (less one Bn.) under command, will be located in the area TILMANSTONE 7369 – WALDERSHARE PARK 7266, so as to be able to manoeuvre to deal with the formation of an enemy beach-head on the beaches astride DEAL.

(c) Recce. Bn. will move out of 12 Corps and come under command NORTH KENT AND SURREY AREA.

10. **Reserves of Forward Divs.** Reserve Inf. Bdes. (including the Inf. Bde. mentioned in para. 9(a) which can also be regarded as in reserve

initially) and Army Tank and Recce. units will be kept so assembled that offensive action can be developed rapidly; on no account will they be dispersed over a wide area.

The reserve Inf. Bdes. whose role is the dealing with enemy beach-heads on the beaches astride HYTHE and DEAL respectively will be prepared to commence reducing these beach-heads within two hours of receiving the order to do so, or within one hour of first light should the landing take place at night. They must not be dispersed for the purpose merely of taking action against enemy airborne troops landed behind the bench defences in order to attack the latter from the rear.

11. **Reserve Division of 12 Corps.** One Inf. Bde. Gp. will be located North of CANTERBURY under operational command of left forward Div., vide para. 9(a). Remainder of Division (less Bns. providing immediate assistance for WEST MALLING and DETLING aerodromes, vide para. 14 below) will be concentrated in areas West and South of CANTERBURY.

One Inf. Bde. Gp. will be concentrated in area BARHAM 6468.

One Inf. Bde. Gp. will be concentrated in the area South of CANTERBURY and East of CHARTHAM 5573 with dets. holding the crossings over R. GREAT STOUR between excl. CANTERBURY and incl. GODMERSHAM 5068.

The Div. in conjunction with 31 Army Tank Bde. (less one Bn.) if allotted will be prepared to:

> (a) act offensively against enemy penetrations N.E. of CANTERBURY, westwards from the beaches astride DEAL, or northwards or N.W. from the beaches West of FOLKESTONE.
>
> (b) stabilise the situation South of CANTERBURY so as to create a favourable opportunity for the action of reserves placed at Corps disposal by Army H.Q. In this connection the importance of maintaining a secure bridgehead across R. GREAT STOUR between CANTERBURY and GODMERSHAM becomes obvious.
>
> (c) act offensively against enemy forces in and South of the ASHFORD area.

12. **Troop carrying transport for Reserve Div.** The Reserve Div. will have two Motor Coach Coys. under command.

13. **Employment of Army Tanks,**

> (a) Any Tanks under command 12 Corps will be employed for Co-operation with the reserve Inf. Bdes. of forward Divs. and the Inf. Bde. in the ISLE OF THANET in immediate action to reduce enemy "beach-heads" or deal     with large-scale airborne landings. As a Corps reserve to act either in co-operation with the reserve Div. or independently in counter-attacking enemy penetration.

(b) The two Army Tank Bdes. will be positioned as follows:
First Bde. Bde. (less one Bn.) in area HASTINGLEIGH 5363 under command of Corps. One Bn. Under reserve Inf. Bde., right forward Div.
Second Bde. Bde. under Comd. left Fwd. Div. having: Bde. (less one Bn.) under reserve Inf. Bde., left forward Div. One Bn. under Inf. Bde. in ISLE OF THANET.

14. **Artillery.** See below.

15. **Protection of Aerodromes**
(a) Each of the five aerodromes in 12 Corps area has a special garrison (provided by Coys. of independent battalions) under command of the R.A.F. Station Commander.
(b) Field force units, in addition, as follows, will be earmarked to provide immediate assistance to aerodromes by offensive action in the event of enemy airborne attack:

*Right Forward Div. area*
LYMPNE          Reserve Bn. of centre forward Inf. Bde.
HAWKINGE        One Bn. of left forward Inf. Bde.
*Left Forward Div. area*
MANSTON         Mob cols provided by Inf. Bde. on Isle of Thanet
MAIDSTONE Sub-Area
DETLING         One Bn. of Reserve Div.
EASTCHURCH      None at present.
NORTH KENT AND SURREY Area (outside 12 Corps)
WEST MALLING    One Bn. of Reserve Div.

(c) Units earmarked for immediate counter-attack of aerodromes will not be moved away from the aerodrome without reference to Corps H.Q.

16. **Moves to Assembly and Concentration Positions**. Where formations and units are not already in the assembly and concentration positions shown above, the necessary moves will be made on issue by Corps H.Q. of the code message "FORM CONCENTRATIONS".

17. **R.E.** Engineer personnel and resources will not be dissipated on the widespread manning of minor demolitions and similar tasks. The maximum number of R.E. units must be held suitably concentrated in reserve, so disposed that they will be available as required for the many R.E. tasks which are likely to develop as the battle progresses. The most important of these will be the maintenance of road communications. Responsibility for repair of these is laid down as follows. In order to conserve R.E. resources for such tasks not more than one Fd. Coy. in each forward Div. will be deployed as firing parties on demolitions,

petrol immobilisation and kindred tasks. Not more than one Section R.E. will be allocated as part of the garrison of any "Fortress".

18. **Demolition Policy**. See below.

19. **Air Co-operation.**

(a) Reconnaissance. One A.C. Sqn. is under comd. 12 Corps. Demands for Tac. R and Arty. R will be    submitted by Divs. to Corps H.Q.

(b) Army Air Support. Initially, the Army Comd. will himself retain control of such fighter and bomber sqns. as may be allotted to S.E. Army.

## HOME GUARD

20. The Home Guard in the Corps area will play a vital part in the plan for defeating enemy invasion by:

(a) Holding defensively their own towns and villages throughout KENT, so as to restrict enemy movement.

(b) Providing O.Ps and small scouting parties to observe, and report on, enemy air landings or other enemy movement.

(c) Providing the Regular Army with guides and information.

A pool of expert local guides will be maintained at every village post office in KENT.

## INTERCOMMUNICATION

21. H.Q. 12 Corps.

| | |
|---|---|
| TUNBRIDGE WELLS. | A mobile Adv. Corps H.Q. will move forward to HARRIETSHAM on or after "FORM CONCENTRATIONS" as Corps Comd. may direct at the time. |
| H.Q. Right forward Div. | SCHOOLS, SOUTH ASHFORD 441601 (moving there on "FORM CONCENTRATIONS"). |
| H.Q. Left forward Div. | CHAUCER BARRACKS, CANTERBURY 600765. |
| H.Q. Reserve Div. | Area MYSTOLE HO 5371. |
| H.Q. MAIDSTONE Sub-Area | AYLESFORD 1777 (moving shortly to MAIDSTONE). |

## PREPARATIONS FOR BATTLE

22. Commanders concerned will prepare their plans in accordance with the orders outlined above. These plans will not be called Defence Schemes, since this is liable to induce a defensive mentality. They will be called "Plans to Defeat Invasion".

## CONDUCT OF THE BATTLE

23. The longer the war goes on the clearer it becomes that success in battle can only be achieved by vigorous offensive action. If the enemy is allowed to obtain the initiative and to develop his plans, no defences, however strong, will prevent him from achieving his object. All ranks must, therefore, be thoroughly imbued with the offensive spirit. They must be trained to regard their defences:

Firstly, as a means of inflicting heavy losses upon the enemy in his first rush.

Secondly, as a means of denying to the enemy avenues of approach through which he must not pass.

Thirdly, as pivots round which reserves can manoeuvre to exploit enemy failures and temporary disorganisation.

Every opportunity to counter-attack the enemy effectively will be seized, and at once. For this purpose Comds. of all grades will keep their reserves concentrated, and will employ them unhesitatingly and unflinchingly when opportunity offers, without waiting for doubtful contingencies which may never arise. It is only by such methods that the initiative can be regained in the defensive battle, and without the initiative we cannot win.

*Lieutenant-General, Commander, 12 Corps.*
*(signed 11.00 hours) 26 Mar. '42*
*Home Forces.*

Appendix XXVI

# Moves of Reserve Formations South-Eastern Command, 19th January 1942

GENERAL

1. The area of England which is nearest to the enemy is EAST KENT and it is in this area that he is most likely to attempt the establishment of a bridgehead and lines of communication. Operations by reserve formations to destroy any enemy forces which have penetrated our defences in EAST KENT will depend to a large extent on the free use by the reserve formations of the roads between the Southern outskirts of LONDON and the SOUTH DOWNS. The destruction of any enemy forces which may have penetrated into SUSSEX is therefore complementary and vital to the defence of EAST KENT. Whilst it is not possible to make a detailed plan for every contingency this Instruction lays down the general principles upon which the moves of reserve formations will be based. Separate Instructions have been or will be issued regarding the probable roles of each reserve formation.

DEGREE OF READINESS

2. All reserve formations will be at 12 hours' notice prior to STAND TO and at 4 hours' notice after STAND TO. This implies that the heads of columns must be capable of passing Start Points in reasonable proximity at that notice.

CONCENTRATION AREAS

3. A list of selected divisional headquarters within these concentration areas is attached below.

4. Formations whether normally located in or outside the Command may be required to move to one of these areas either as a strategical move or immediately prior to deployment. The more likely concentration areas for each formation will be specified in the separate Instructions referred to in paragraph 1. Formations will carry out detailed reconnaissance of the areas so specified but will only be

required to carry out general reconnaissances of the remaining areas as opportunity affords.

ROADS

5. The main reinforcement routes to the EAST, SOUTH-EAST, SOUTH and SOUTH-WEST will be known by letters. No other lettering of roads in the Command which may cause confusion with these will be permitted.

ORDERING OF MOVES

6. When a reserve formation is required to carry out a move to a concentration area which involves passing through the Army Traffic Control area (see paragraph 10 below) or from one Corps district to another, Army Headquarters, when ordering the move, will lay down the routes to be used, start points, dispersal points if necessary, and block timings. Corps will be consulted as regards routes passing through Corps districts. Whenever such a move can be anticipated and has not been already covered by a specific Operation Instruction, the formation concerned will be given warning in advance of the probable concentration areas, routes, start points etc. so that the executive order for the move can be given by message consisting merely of the code name of the concentration area and the time for heads of columns to pass start points.

COMMAND

7. After ACTION STATIONS commanders of reserve formations will be prepared to report to Army Headquarters at short notice if required. On being placed under command of a Corps, reserve formation commanders will report to Corps Headquarters as soon as possible after issuing any necessary preliminary orders. Command will pass at a time to be laid down by Army Headquarters when ordering the move.

LIAISON

8. Liaison officers from reserve formations located in the Command will report to Army Headquarters on STAND TO. Liaison officers from reserve formations located outside the Command will report as soon as possible after the formation has been ordered to move into the Command. As soon as a reserve formation is placed under command of a Corps, the Liaison officer at Army Headquarters will be released and will return to his formation to give his Commander the latest available information about the situation.

SPEED AND DENSITY

9. An appendix below shows the speeds and densities which will be observed and the approximate road times required by armoured and infantry formations. It is NOT normally desirable for one formation to cross another while in movement but maintenance vehicles and other traffic will be allowed to pass through gaps in convoys at pre-arranged points.

TRAFFIC CONTROL

10. The Army Traffic Control area is shown on the map attached at Appendix 'A' and is defined in greater detail at Annexure 29 to Section XIII of SOUTH-EASTERN ARMY Standing Administrative Instructions. Within this area the Army Traffic Control organization will be established on a static basis, functioning primarily on the main reinforcement routes. Certain points will be permanently manned after ACTION STATIONS, while others will be manned as required. A list of these points is contained in Annexure 28 to the above Administrative Instructions.

11. Within the Army Traffic Control area, Army Headquarters will control all movement, selecting and establishing the necessary Regulating Headquarters, Sector Controls and Traffic Posts in consultation with the formation moving. The latter may be required to provide personnel to supplement the Army personnel either as pointsmen or for sector controls operating under command of Army Traffic Control. Any additional traffic control arrangements made by the formation from its own resources will be co-ordinated with and subject to Army Traffic Control. The formation moving will in all cases send representatives with suitable means of communication to Army Regulating Headquarters and if required also to Army Sector Controls.

12. For moves outside the Army Traffic Control area, traffic control will be the responsibility of the formation moving and Army Traffic Control personnel will not normally be available. In the case of moves which are partially outside the Army Traffic Control area the formation moving will if necessary set up its own Regulating Headquarters in conjunction with the Army Regulating Headquarters.

METHOD OF ARRANGING DETAILS OF TRAFFIC CONTROL

15. Representatives of Army Headquarters will visit the Headquarters of the moving formation as soon as possible after the issue of the warning order to move, taking with them information relating to operational restrictions or requirements and to other movement which may affect the move in question. They will be ready with a proposed traffic control layout, which will be modified to meet the wishes of the Commander of the moving formation so far as conditions allow. If time does not permit the issue of written orders, these representatives will be authorized to complete all arrangements on the spot.

14. Traffic Control before Start Points and after Dispersal Points within as well as outside the Army Traffic Control area will be the responsibility of the formation moving.

INTERRUPTION OF ROAD MOVEMENT BY ENEMY ACTION ETC.

15. Commanders of formations and units moving within the Army Traffic Control area will retain the right under active conditions to take temporary control of the move if in their opinion the local tactical situation so demands, always bearing in mind that any action taken by

them may affect other moves taking place at the same time. Any such action will be notified immediately to Army Traffic Control through the representatives of the moving formation at Army Regulating Headquarters, or Army Sector Controls.
OPERATION INSTRUCTION
16. SOUTH EASTERN COMMAND Operation Instruction No. 20 dated 22 Jul. '41 is cancelled and will be destroyed.
17. ACKNOWLEDGE.

*J.B. SINCLAIR, B.G.S.*
*Time of Signature 17.00 hrs.*
*S/J3*

*Annex 'B'*

## TO SOUTH -EASTERN ARMY STANDING OPERATION INSTRUCTION No.3
### Dated 19 January 1942

| Serial | Divisional Concentration Area Code name | Locations of selected divisional headquarters | Map Ref. | Telephone No. | Remarks |
|---|---|---|---|---|---|
| 1 | CEYLON | Colesdane, HARRIETSHAM | R.313722 | Maidstone 4758/9 | Present H.Q. of Res. Div. of 12 Corps |
| 2 | RANGOON | The Place, LINTON | R.199686 | Maidstone 4581 | Present Bn. H.Q |
| 3 | MILAN | Dene Park, MEREWORTH | R.039690 | | |
| 4 | CAPRI | Hanworth, Sole Street, COBHAM | R.100863 | Cobham 2121 | Formerly Sub-Area HQ |
| 5 | ADEN | Claremont, High Street, CRANBROOK | R.216545 | | |
| 6 | LISBON | BRIGHTLING area | R.1239 | | |
| 7 | JAFFA | Dewlands, Rotherfield, CROWBOROUGH | Q.9947 | | |
| 8 | KHARTOUM | Courtlands, Sharpthome, WEST HOATHLY | Q.820515 | Sharpthorne 3 | |

| 9 | TOKIO | Hobbs Barracks, LINGFIELD | Q.806603 399/408 | Lingfield | |
| 10 | PARIS | WISBOROUGH GREEN area | Q.4845 | | |
| 11 | MOSCOW | CRANLEIGH area | Q.4958 | | |
| 12 | BOMBAY | Tweenways, HINDHEAD | Q.324539 | Hindhead 633/4 | |
| 13 | TUNIS | CAMBERLEY area | Q.3080 | | |
| 14 | CAIRO | Moore Lodge, Pennyfathers Road, ALDERSHOT | Q.305728 | A.Mil 0420 | Present Div. H.Q. |

## *Annex 'E'*

## TO SOUTH -EASTERN ARMY STANDING OPERATION INSTRUCTION No.3
## Dated 19 January 1942

## DAY

## ARMOURED DIVISION

| | Cruisers | I Tanks | Wheels |
|---|---|---|---|
| Speed | 25 m.i.2h | 15 m.i.2h | 25 m.i.2h |
| Density v.t.m. | 20 | 20 | 15 |
| Times Past a Point in Hours: One Road | | | |
| F | 4.25 | 6.75 | 6.75 |
| A | 2.5 | 2.5 | 2.5 |
| B | 9 | 9 | 9 |
| *Total* | 15.75 | 18.25 | 18.25 |
| Times Past a Point in Hours: Two Roads | | | |
| F | 2.25 | 3.5 | 3.5 |
| A | 1.5 | 1.5 | 1.5 |
| B | 4.75 | 4.75 | 4.75 |
| *Total* | 8.5 | 9.75 | 9.75 |
| Times Past a Point in Hours: Three Roads | | | |
| F | 1.75 | 2.25 | 2.25 |
| A | 1.25 | 1.25 | 1.25 |
| B | 3 | 3 | 3 |
| *Total* | 6 | 6.5 | 6.5 |

## ARMOURED BRIGADE GROUP

|  | Cruisers | I Tanks | Wheels |
|---|---|---|---|
| Speed | 25 m.i.2h | 15 m.i.2h | 25 m.i.2h |
| Density v.t.m. | 20 | 20 | 15 |
| Times Past a Point in Hours: One Road | | | |
| F | 1.75 | 2.75 | 2.75 |
| A | .75 | .75 | .75 |
| B | 1.25 | 1.25 | 1.25 |
| *Total* | 3.75 | 4.75 | 4.75 |
| Times Past a Point in Hours: Two Roads | | | |
| F | 1 | 1.5 | 1.5 |
| A | .5 | .5 | .5 |
| B | .75 | .75 | .75 |
| *Total* | 2.25 | 2.75 | 2.75 |
| Times Past a Point in Hours: Three Roads | | | |
|  | .75 | 1 | 1 |
| A | .25 | .25 | .25 |
| B | .5 | .5 | .5 |
| *Total* | 1.5 | 1.75 | 1.75 |

## INFANTRY DIVISION

| | |
|---|---|
| Speed | 12.5 m.i.h |
| Density v.t.m. | 15 |
| Times Past a Point in Hours: One Road | |
| F | - |
| A | - |
| B | - |
| *Total* | 18 |
| Times Past a Point in Hours: Two Roads | |
| F | - |
| A | - |
| B | - |
| *Total* | 9 |
| Times Past a Point in Hours: Three Roads | |
| F | - |
| A | - |
| B | - |
| *Total* | 7.25 |

## INFANTRY BRIGADE GROUP

| | |
|---|---|
| Speed | 12.5 m.i.h |
| Density v.t.m. | 15 |
| Times Past a Point in Hours: One Road | |
| *Total* | 4.75 |

Times Past a Point in Hours: Two Roads
  *Total*                                     -
Times Past a Point in Hours: Three Roads
  *Total*                                     -

# NIGHT

## ARMOURED DIVISION

|                                            | I Tanks     | Wheels      |
| ------------------------------------------ | ----------- | ----------- |
| Speed                                      | 12 m.i.2h   | 12 m.i.2h   |
| Density v.t.m.                             | 30          | 30          |
| Times Past a Point in Hours: One Road      |             |             |
|   F                                        | 5.5         | 5.5         |
|   A                                        | 2.75        | 2.75        |
|   B                                        | 9.5         | 9.5         |
|   *Total*                                  | 17.75       | 17.75       |
| Times Past a Point in Hours: Two Roads     |             |             |
|   F                                        | 3           | 3           |
|   A                                        | 1.5         | 1.5         |
|   B                                        | 6           | 6           |
|   *Total*                                  | 10.5        | 10.5        |
| Times Past a Point in Hours: Three Roads   |             |             |
|   F                                        | 2           | 2           |
|   A                                        | 1.25        | 1.25        |
|   B                                        | 3           | 3           |
|   *Total*                                  | 6.25        | 6.25        |

## ARMOURED BRIGADE GROUP

|                                            | I Tanks     | Wheels      |
| ------------------------------------------ | ----------- | ----------- |
| Speed                                      | 12 m.i.2h   | 12 m.i.2h   |
| Density v.t.m.                             | 30          | 30          |
| Times Past a Point in Hours: One Road      |             |             |
|   F                                        | 2.25        | 2.25        |
|   A                                        | .75         | .75         |
|   B                                        | 1.25        | 1.25        |
|   *Total*                                  | 4.25        | 4.25        |
| Times Past a Point in Hours: Two Roads     |             |             |
|   F                                        | 1.25        | 1.25        |
|   A                                        | .5          | .5          |
|   B                                        | .75         | .75         |
|   *Total*                                  | 2.5         | 2.5         |
| Times Past a Point in Hours: Three Roads   |             |             |
|   F                                        | .75         | .75         |
|   A                                        | .25         | .25         |

| B | .5 | .5 |
|---|---|---|
| *Total* | 1.5 | 1.5 |

## INFANTRY DIVISION

| | |
|---|---|
| Speed | 7.5 m.i.h |
| Density v.t.m. | 15 |
| Times Past a Point in Hours: One Road | |
| *Total* | 28 |
| Times Past a Point in Hours: Two Roads | |
| *Total* | 14 |
| Times Past a Point in Hours: Three Roads | |
| *Total* | 11 |

## INFANTRY BRIGADE GROUP

| | |
|---|---|
| Speed | 7.5 m.i.h |
| Density v.t.m. | 15 |
| Times Past a Point in Hours: One Road | |
| *Total* | 6 |
| Times Past a Point in Hours: Two Roads | |
| *Total* | - |
| Times Past a Point in Hours: Three Roads | |
| *Total* | - |

NOTES:

(a) At night speeds may be slightly faster or slower according to the obscurity of the night and the lighting allowed.

(b) In an operational move of Armd. Div. only the Fighting Echelon will go forward. 'A' echelon or a proportion of it will come up at the end of the day to replenish the Fighting Echelon. 'B' echelon is unlikely to move from Rear Div. area.

(c) Calculations are based on Fighting Echelon at 15 m.i.2h and 'A' and 'B' echelons at 25 m.i.2h by day, and all at 12 m.i.2h by night.

(d) Armd. Bde. Gp. includes one Bty. R.H.A. – one Bty. A.Tk. – one Bty. Lt. A.A. – one Fd. Tp. R.E. – one Sec. Lt. Fd. Amb.

(e ) At night timing for cruisers and I tanks will be the same.

Appendix XXVII

# South-Eastern Command Appreciation for the Spring Of 1942

## DIRECTIVE

To:   Lieutenant-General F.P. Nosworthy, C.B., D.S.O., M.C., Commander, 4 Corps.
Lieutenant-General A.G.L. McNaughton, C.B., C.M.G., D.S.O., Commander, Canadian Corps.
Lieutenant-General B.L. Montgomery, C.B., D.S.O., Commander, 12 Corps.

1. Attached is an Appreciation of the defence problems facing the SOUTH-EASTERN Army. My intention is to fulfil the objects set forth in paragraph 2 of the Appreciation, namely:
    (a) to prevent the enemy establishing a bridgehead through which his main attack can be supplied and reinforced;
    (b) if the enemy succeeds nevertheless in establishing such a bridgehead, to stop and break up his main thrusts towards LONDON and to counter attack in order to recapture the enemy bridgehead.
2. In order to fulfil these objects the defence will be organized in accordance with the general principles defined in paragraph 25 of the Appreciation. I wish however to lay special emphasis on the following points.

## AREAS ESSENTIAL TO THE DEFENCE
3. The security of the beaches in SUSSEX and EAST KENT on which wheeled and tracked vehicles can land at all states of the tide and of the ports of SHOREHAM, NEWHAVEN, FOLKESTONE and DOVER is essential to the defence. Equally essential are the fighter aerodromes of the TANGMERE group, and REDHILL, BIGGIN HILL, GRAVESEND

and WEST MALLING. Accordingly, our forces will be disposed so that the maximum protection is given to these essential areas and risks will be accepted elsewhere if necessary. Special consideration is required in the case of the beaches at PEVENSEY BAY, which although not suitable for landing wheeled and tracked vehicles at all states of the tide, are of importance inasmuch as they might be used for an attack directed against the communications in rear of 12 Corps.

## NODAL POINTS

4. The object of the nodal point system is to delay the enemy's advance, if he should obtain a temporary success, until our reserve formations can be brought into action. The development of selected nodal points into fully tank-proof localities is next in importance only to the defences of the essential areas indicated in the preceding paragraph. In addition to the towns of CHICHESTER, HORSHAM, CANTERBURY, ASHFORD and CHATHAM where work on these lines is already in progress, I direct that GUILDFORD, DORKING, REDHILL-REIGATE, EAST GRINSTEAD, TONBRIDGE and MAIDSTONE shall be similarly developed. Furthermore, all other nodal points will be strengthened in so far as may be practicable, as additional weapons become available for their Home Guard garrisons.

## RESERVES

5. Reserves under the immediate control of Corps Commanders will be employed to counter-attack enemy forces which have overrun or are threatening any of the essential areas indicated in paragraph 3 (other than fighter aerodromes in the L of C area). Reserves under Army or GHQ control will be employed to counter-attack enemy forces which have penetrated further inland, possibly being placed under command of a Corps for that purpose. Reserve formations will in all cases be based on tank-proof localities or strong nodal points, so that they can manoeuvre from a secure pivot.

## CONDUCT OF THE DEFENCE

6. There will be no withdrawal in any circumstances and all ranks must be determined that every German who succeeds in setting foot in this country shall be killed.

*B. Paget,*
*Lieutenant-General, Commanding-in-Chief,*
*South-Eastern Command.*
*13 Oct. '41.*
*Time of Signature 11.30 hrs.*

*Annex*

APPRECIATION

*General*

1. In writing the following short Appreciation of the problems facing the SOUTH-EASTERN Army, no attempt has been made to argue in detail those factors which are already generally accepted, nor to tabulate established information.

2. In the event of invasion it is probable that the enemy will make his main attack against the SOUTH-EASTERN and EASTERN Armies, and that his immediate objective will be the occupation of LONDON. The primary objects of the SOUTH-EASTERN Army will therefore be:

(a) to prevent the enemy establishing a bridgehead through which his main attack can be supplied and reinforced;

(b) if the enemy succeeds nevertheless in establishing such a bridgehead, to stop and break up his main thrusts towards LONDON and to counter-attack in order to recapture the enemy bridgehead.

*Forces Available*

3. A comparison of the possible strength of the opposing land forces is necessarily of little value, as it is certain that, within wide limits, the enemy will be able to bring preponderating force to bear at the point where he decides to make his main attack. The possible scale of enemy attack against this country has however been calculated as follows:

(a) a "first Wave" of three armoured and four infantry divisions, carried in light craft and merchant vessels converted for running ashore and landing direct on to the beach

(b) this to be followed as quickly as possible by a further two armoured and three infantry divisions, in light craft

(c) a "main body" of four armoured and sixteen infantry divisions, carried in merchant vessels, to arrive as soon as arrangements have been made for their reception

(d) a further eleven infantry divisions to be used for diversions

(e) 55,000 airborne troops.

At least four of the armoured and eleven of the infantry divisions, and the whole of the airborne force, might, it is estimated, be employed against the SOUTH-EASTERN Army, whose forces will always be less than the ideal. The aim must therefore be to decide what areas are essential to the primary objects indicated in paragraph 2 and then to allocate to each of these areas the minimum proportion necessary of the available resources, keeping the maximum possible numbers in reserve.

4. The forces which, it is hoped, will be available for the SOUTH-EASTERN Army next Spring are as follows:

Two armoured divisions, one being in GHQ Reserve (instead of one as at present)

Three army tank brigades (instead of one as at present)

Seven infantry divisions, one being in GHQ Reserve (instead of nine as at present)

Two independent infantry brigades (each three battalions, instead of four as at present)

"X" force (infantry brigade group including 54 light tanks)

Two garrison battalions

Home Defence and Young Soldiers battalions as at present.

*Shipping*

5. At DOVER the distance between our forward defences and enemy-occupied territory is only 20 miles, but this distance increases rapidly as one proceeds WESTWARDS along the coast, until at BRIGHTON it is approximately 80 miles. In order that his shipping may avoid making either the outward or the return journey in daylight, or, alternatively, remaining during daylight hours off the English coast, the enemy is likely to select the shortest possible passage for his seaborne expedition.

6. From the enemy point of view the Dutch ports are much better equipped for handling a large expedition than are the French ports NORTH of CHERBOURG. If the Dutch ports are used the distance for transporting stores from GERMANY is to that extent shorter and use can be made of inland water transport facilities for this purpose. Shipping from Dutch ports can follow the normal deep-water channel close to the Belgian coast until opposite EAST KENT.

7. These factors indicate that, from the point of view of transportation, a large seaborne expedition can be more easily landed in EAST KENT than elsewhere on the sector of coast for which the SOUTH-EASTERN Army is responsible.

*Naval*

8. Within the narrow waters of the Straits of DOVER interception of enemy shipping may be even more costly to the Royal Navy than it was in the waters NORTH of CRETE. The short distance involved will make it possible in daylight for the enemy to provide continuous fighter protection for dive bombers directed against our naval vessels, while, if the enemy succeeds in establishing a bridgehead in EAST KENT, he will be able to cover the channel with artillery fire from both sides. At the same time he will be able to mine the approaches to the Channel and to watch the mine-fields with his submarines. As the length of the sea crossing increases the difficulties of interception from the point of view of the Royal Navy will proportionately diminish.

9. Owing to the lesser risk of interception by our Navy the enemy will, therefore, find it easier to maintain and reinforce a large-scale seaborne expedition in KENT than in SUSSEX.

*Air*

10. Local air superiority will be essential for both sides. This depends primarily on fighters whose bases must be secure. The British fighter aerodromes which it is essential to keep in use if the enemy is to be prevented from obtaining air superiority over the coastal area held by the SOUTH-EASTERN Army are shown. Certain fighter aerodromes near the coast which it may be impossible to keep in use during invasion, and which will, if necessary, be evacuated, are also shown. So long, however, as the essential fighter aerodromes are kept in use, and the enemy is thereby prevented from obtaining air superiority, it is unlikely that he, any more than we ourselves, will be able to use those aerodromes on the coast which we have been forced to evacuate, or any other aerodromes in the area held by the SOUTH-EASTERN Army; also arrangements have been made to destroy aerodromes near the coast, if they are liable to capture by the enemy.

11. There are areas suitable for large-scale landings of airborne troops both on the SOUTH DOWNS and in EAST KENT. An airborne landing, unless purely diversionary or having a limited objective, is likely to be associated with a seaborne landing. The enemy will, therefore, select the area for landing the bulk of his airborne troops not only on account of its physical suitability for that purpose but also on account of its tactical relationship to the section of coast where he intends to make his seaborne landing.

12. It is an obvious fact that enemy fighters operating over EAST KENT will be able to spend appreciably longer over their target than those operating over SUSSEX.

13. Nevertheless, although KENT once again presents greater advantages, it is clear that large-scale airborne landings combined with seaborne landings may take place both in SUSSEX and in KENT.

*Beaches*

14. To land, supply and reinforce his main attack, the enemy must select beaches on which he can land wheeled and tracked vehicles, unless he can obtain the use of suitable ports, a possibility on which he is unlikely to count. Between RYE and WHITSTABLE, out of a total coastline of 83 miles, no less than 32 miles are suitable at ALL states of the tide for landing wheeled and tracked vehicles, while only 14 miles are impracticable for this purpose at any tide. In this sector the ports of DOVER and FOLKESTONE would be of considerable utility to the enemy if he succeeded in capturing them.

15. Between CHICHESTER and RYE, out of a total coastline of 79 miles, a stretch of 12 miles between BOGNOR and WORTHING is suitable at ALL states of the tide for landing wheeled and tracked vehicles, while 22 miles are entirely impracticable for this purpose at any tide. In this sector are the smaller ports of NEWHAVEN and SHOREHAM.

16. Generally speaking, between BRIGHTON and RYE either the beaches are unsuitable for landing wheeled and tracked vehicles or the hinterland is unsuitable for the operation of A.F.Vs. A large seaborne landing in this sector is, therefore, unlikely, but it may be used for a subsidiary landing in connection with an attack on EAST KENT.

17. Thus, from the point of view of beaches and of the suitability of the country inland for A.F.Vs, the most likely areas for the enemy's large-scale seaborne landings are RYE – WHITSTABLE and BOGNOR – WORTHING.

*Road Communications*

18. Road communications in SUSSEX from the coast towards LONDON are excellent and would greatly assist an enemy attack towards the NORTH. In KENT they are more limited and the capture of ASHFORD and CANTERBURY would be essential to the enemy before he could develop his attack towards the NORTH-WEST. A subsidiary landing in the area PEVENSEY BAY with the aim of using the main roads leading NORTH from BEXHILL – HASTINGS in a thrust towards the rear of 12 Corps area might therefore present advantages for the enemy even though the beaches are possible only at certain states of the tide and the advance would pass through very close country.

19. The capture of crossings over the R. MEDWAY by the enemy, or action by hostile parachute troops to block the limited WEST – EAST communications from SURREY, would impede the movement of our reserves into KENT.

*Course of Action Open to the Enemy*

20. It has been shown that there are two areas where the enemy might launch a large-scale attack:

   (a) In EAST KENT (i.e. between RYE and WHITSTABLE) with a possible subsidiary landing between HASTINGS and BEXHILL.

   (b) In WEST SUSSEX (i.e. between BOGNOR and WORTHING).

Elsewhere, for reasons already indicated, conditions are suitable only for diversionary attacks.

21. In the case of EAST KENT the following advantages are apparent:

   (a) Short sea crossing (paragraph 5).

   (b) Number of suitable beaches (paragraph 14).

   (c) Existence of areas suitable for landing airborne troops in close relationship to beaches suitable for seaborne landings (paragraph 11).

   (d) Proximity to his fighter aerodromes in occupied France (paragraph 12).

The principal disadvantage is the fact, of which he is bound to be aware, that in this area our resistance will naturally be strongest.

22. In the case of WEST SUSSEX, the existence of the large expanse of the DOWNS, all of which is suitable for airborne landings, is a primary

advantage, but against that the sea crossing is four times as long, there are fewer suitable beaches, and the distance from his fighter aerodromes is appreciably greater. Whilst the distance from the coast to LONDON is shorter than in the case of EAST KENT and there are more good roads, these factors would scarcely outweigh the difficulties of maintaining and reinforcing a large force across 80 miles of sea in close proximity to PORTSMOUTH. In spite of these disadvantages, however, a landing in WEST SUSSEX is attractive from the enemy point of view, since the obvious threat to LONDON and PORTSMOUTH can be calculated to have the effect of pinning a large proportion of our reserves and thereby preventing or delaying their intervention in KENT.
23. Nevertheless, there are strong reasons for concluding that the main German attack will take place in EAST KENT, with landings at numerous points between RYE BAY and WHITSTABLE. A subsidiary attack from the area PEVENSEY BAY is also a likely move. There will also be large scale airborne landings on the SOUTH DOWNS probably combined with seaborne landings in WEST SUSSEX: these operations may well precede the main attack in EAST KENT in order to draw off our reserves.
24. Whatever course the enemy may adopt it is probable, however, that he will attempt to capture our vital fighter aerodromes with airborne forces either as a preliminary to or at the same time as the seaborne invasion.

*Defensive Policy of the South-Eastern Army*
25. The general policy is as follows:

(a) In order to retain the maximum forces in reserve, to use field troops for the defence primarily of those beaches and of the areas immediately in rear thereof, on which enemy sea landings are considered probable, and to rely on the Home Guard, where available, for the defence of the remaining beaches; where Home Guard are not available, the number of field troops employed for the defence of beaches on which enemy landings are considered unlikely to be kept to a minimum.

(b) As regards areas suitable for airborne landings, to use field troops for the defence only of those which are situated in the immediate vicinity of beaches where a seaborne landing is considered probable; the object in such cases being:

(i) to destroy enemy airborne troops before they can attack the beach defences from the rear,

(ii) in the case of the SOUTH DOWNS, to secure routes on to the DOWNS required by our reserve formations when counter-attacking an enemy seaborne force in the area of the beaches.

Special consideration however to be given to the protection of the R. MEDWAY crossings against attack by airborne troops.

(c) On the principle that modern war is without fronts, to strengthen the inland areas,

    (i) by improving the defences of all existing nodal points as more Home Guard weapons become available,

    (ii) by developing certain essential nodal points into fully tank-proof localities on the lines of CANTERBURY and ASHFORD.

(d) On the principle that infantry formations unsupported by tanks cannot be expected to attack armoured troops by day, to position our infantry reserve formations so that they can pivot on strong nodal points, in the defence of which their administrative echelons should be prepared to assist the Home Guard.

(e) The garrisons of nodal points, or the reserve formations pivoting on a group of nodal points, to have three roles:

    (i) To counter-attack any enemy whom it is within their power successfully to engage,

    (ii) To secure their position against attack by the enemy,

    (iii) To carry out raids by night against any enemy whom they are unable to counter-attack by day, with special attention to enemy A.F.Vs.

Nodal points, the garrison of which is limited to Home Guard or L of C troops, to concentrate on role (ii).

(f) Special protection to be given to essential fighter aerodromes, using field force troops for this purpose if available.

(g) In order to reinforce the garrisons of nodal points, to locate within them depots, small headquarters and L of C troops whenever possible.

(h) Depots, V.Ps, A.M.E.S. etc. which cannot be included within nodal points to be defended by static troops, thus forming with Home Guard defended villages a network of minor strong points throughout the Command.

*Conclusions*

26. The policy outlined in paragraph 25 will be adhered to, but, in view of the number of troops available, it will not be possible to strengthen the rear areas to the extent desired. For the purpose of illustrating this policy a suggested layout, down to brigades, has been shown on an accompanying map, although the detailed implementation of the policy is a matter for Corps Commanders to decide.

27. The localities which it is considered essential to hold comprise the following:

COASTAL AREAS

Bognor – Shoreham (beach)

The South Downs (East and West of Findon)

The South Downs (North of Brighton)

The South Downs (East and West of Lewes)
Winchelsea – Rye
Isle of Oxney (high ground)
Lydd – New Romney (nodal points)
Littlestone – Hythe (beach)
Ham Street – Lympne (high ground)
ST. Margaret's-at-Cliffe – Sandwich (beach)
Wingham – Ash (high ground)
Isle of Thanet (beaches)

## COASTAL TOWNS

Shoreham
Newhaven
Folkestone
Dover
Sheerness

## FIGHTER AERODROME LOCALITIES

Westhampnett
Tangmere
Merston
Ford
Redhill
Biggin Hill
Gravesend
West Malling

## KEY INLAND TOWNS

Chichester
Lewes
Horsham
East Grinstead
Dorking
Redhill – Reigate
Ashford
Canterbury
Tonbridge
Maidstone
Chatham
Guildford

28. Certain localities which it is desirable, but not essential, to hold are shown on a map in BLUE.

29. The dispositions shown on the map are intended to take effect on "STAND TO". During normal periods troops will occupy existing accommodation in coastal sectors, hutted camps etc.

*Oct. '41.*

Appendix XXVIII

# Air Defence Plan for the Spring of 1942

RE-DISTRIBUTION OF ANTI-AIRCRAFT RESOURCES IN THE
EVENT OF INVASION
Report by the Sub-Committee on the Allocation of Active Air
Defences

At their meetings on the 18th July, 1941, (C.O.S. (41) 252nd Meeting,
Item 4.) and on the 11th August, 1941 (C.O.S. (41) 283rd Meeting, Item
8.) the Chiefs of Staff gave approval to a plan for the re-distribution of
anti-aircraft defences in the event of invasion, as set out in C.O.S.(41)
439, and to the modifications to this plan as submitted in C.O.S.(41)
482.

2. From a study of the lessons learnt as a result of operations overseas
during the past year, the Air Officer Commanding-in-Chief, Fighter
Command came to the conclusion that the existing plan for the re-
distribution of anti-aircraft guns in Great Britain in the event of invasion
required drastic revision. Accordingly in consultation with the General
Officer Commanding-in-Chief, Anti-Aircraft Command, a revised plan
has been prepared in which the primary aim has been to concentrate
our anti-aircraft resources to provide an adequate defence against air
attack, in the first place for those aerodromes vital to our fighter force;
secondly for those aerodromes of Bomber and Coastal Commands and
for those objectives vital to the operation of our Naval and Army anti-
invasion forces.

3. The C.O.S.(A.A.) Sub-Committee have examined and endorsed the
scheme put forward by the Air Officer Commanding-in-Chief, Fighter
Command, which is attached at Annex 1.

4. From Appendix 'B' of the Annex it will be seen that a total of 2,048
heavy anti-aircraft guns and 1,278 light anti-aircraft guns are required
to implement the plan. It is emphasised that these figures represent the

371

absolute number of anti-aircraft guns required to provide that degree of security against air attack considered necessary for the successful operation of our anti-invasion forces and for the protection of vital targets. In the opinion of the Sub-Committee any deficiency in these numbers of heavy and light anti-aircraft guns would seriously imperil the safety of this country should invasion be attempted and the figures therefore represent the "dead line" up to which the weapon strength of A.D.G.B. should be built and below which it should in future not be allowed to fall.

5. The resources of heavy anti-aircraft guns now in A.D.G.B. are sufficient for this commitment; there is, however, a deficit of 230 light anti-aircraft guns.

6. The Joint Intelligence Sub-Committee have examined the likelihood of air attack on the United Kingdom during 1942 and concluded inter alia: "If the campaign against Russia were brought to a successful conclusion by the Germans during 1942, some three months would elapse before air operations against the British Isles could be developed to full intensity".

It is therefore concluded that 1st September may be regarded as the earliest date on which invasion can be attempted, and it is therefore desirable that A.D.G.B. should receive an allocation of 230 Light A.A. guns by the 1st August, 1942. This is essential in order that the training of the personnel who will man these guns may be completed before the anticipated date of invasion.

7. The scheme as attached in the Annex necessitates the movement of 360 static heavy anti-aircraft guns. Assuming that rail communications are not interrupted it will be some 2 months before these moves can be completed. Thus, to implement the plan very early warning of impending invasion must be given. In the event of this warning being insufficient or of there being some dislocation of communications it is emphasised that no rail moves can be initiated after the order "Action Stations" has been given, though of course those guns already in transit would proceed to their destinations.

8. The Chiefs of Staff are invited:

    (a) to approve the attached plan for the re-distribution of anti-aircraft resources in the event of invasion;

    (b) to endorse the proposal that 2,048 Heavy and 1,278 Light anti-aircraft guns represents the "dead line" up to which the weapon strength of A.D.G.B. should be built and below which it should not be allowed to fall;

    (c) to invite the War Office Sub-Committee of the London Munitions Assignment Board to consider the allocation of 230 light anti-aircraft guns to A.D.G.B. before the 1st August, 1942;

(d) to note that no rail moves of static heavy anti-aircraft guns will be initiated after the order "Action Stations" has been given.

*(Signed) J. Whitworth Jones,*
*Chairman, C.O.S.(A.A.) Sub-Committee.*
*Great George Street, S.W.1, 3rd April, 1942.*

*Annex*

## THE ANTI-AIRCRAFT DEFENCE OF GREAT BRITAIN AGAINST AIR ATTACK IN THE EVENT OF INVASION

It has become necessary to review the arrangements for the deployment of anti-aircraft guns for the protection of Great Britain in the event of invasion. I have come to the conclusion that the existing plans under the "Attic" scheme require drastic revision in the light of our experiences in overseas theatres during the past year, and also on account of the large withdrawals of A.A. equipments for despatch overseas.

2. It is now accepted by all three Services that the continuous operation of fighter aircraft is an essential element in any anti-invasion plan. We have already paid dearly in other campaigns for the failure to protect our fighter aerodromes with adequate A.A. defences, with the result that our fighters have been unable to operate effectively. The first essential therefore in any anti-invasion plan, is that our fighter aerodromes must be adequately protected with anti-aircraft guns, both Heavy and Light. So long as our fighters can continue to operate effectively, it would seem that no plan for the invasion of this country is likely to succeed. Consequently I am strongly of the opinion that all other interests must be subordinated to the security of our vital fighter aerodromes.

3. The scales of A.A. defence necessary to attain a reasonable degree of security have been the matter of discussion between the Commander-in-Chief, Anti-Aircraft Command and myself, bearing in mind the lessons learnt from the air attacks which have been made on our aerodromes in this and other countries. As a result we have come to the conclusion that the minimum scale of A.A. defence for our most important and vulnerable fighter aerodromes is 8 Heavy Anti-Aircraft guns and 16 Bofors guns. Certain other scales have been laid down, graduated according to the relative importance and vulnerability to attack of the aerodromes in question.

4. In passing, it should be noted that the scale mentioned above of 8 Heavy Anti-Aircraft guns and 16 Light Anti-Aircraft guns is less than

that which the enemy affords to his vital aerodromes under similar circumstances. The German Scale is –

       8 – 12 Heavy A.A. guns

      12 – 30 Light A.A. guns

5. Almost equally pressing are the claims for the A.A. defence of the chain of R.D.F. Stations round our coast, on which we rely for early warning of impending attacks. Almost equally important again are the vital operational control centres of Fighter Command and No. 11 Group. I am satisfied that the scales of defence for these R.D.F. and control centres need not be augmented when invasion occurs, but must not fall below the present number of guns allotted to them, which is a bare minimum.

6. In drawing up the new plan therefore for the deployment of A.A. guns in case of invasion, I have taken as the basic factor the allocation of a suitable scale of A.A. defence to the minimum number of fighter aerodromes which it is considered essential to protect in order to ensure freedom of action to the fighter squadrons on whose activities the whole fabric of our anti-invasion plan is based. The number of aerodromes which have been selected for defence amounts approximately to only 40% of the aerodromes of Fighter Command, but a plan must be made which bears some relation to the resources at present available, and which is in conformity with the present appreciation by the Chiefs of Staff of the most likely "venue" of the enemy's main attack. It will be necessary to take risks elsewhere, both as regards A.A. defence of the less important and more remote fighter aerodromes, as well as many vital points scattered throughout the country, in order to ensure that the essential fighter aerodromes of this country, will be able to continue operations over the most likely area of attack.

7. Having postulated as a first priority the needs of A.A. protection for fighter aerodromes and their necessary adjuncts, the next most important task is that of the defence of Bomber and Coastal Command aerodromes adjacent to the invasion area. The allotment made to these Commands (vide Appendix 'A') has of necessity been small, owing to the meagre resources available, and indeed only represents a fraction of the needs of these Commands. But, in the case of Bofors guns, even this allotment, plus the necessary allotments to fighter aerodromes, exceeds the existing number of Bofors guns now at our disposal.

8. The commitments to Home Forces under the "Bargain" scheme of four Heavy and four Light A.A. regiments must undoubtedly be met, although the deficiency of Bofors guns becomes still greater by so doing.

9. Next comes those other commitments already undertaken under the existing "Attic" scheme to Home Forces, The Royal Navy and those Heavy gun-defended areas at which a minimum of defences must, it is considered, remain "in situ".

To examine these in detail:

(i) *Home Forces Commitments.* These at present consist of a total of 254 Hy. A.A. guns and 16 Bofors. Under the present "Attic" scheme these guns are to be deployed mainly in the protection of roads and bottle-necks. To succeed in attacking such targets, it would be necessary for the enemy to deliver low flying attacks, which Heavy A.A. guns would be powerless to prevent. Further it is considered, that fighters can be relied on to provide a good protection by day and by night against any large scale attack delivered at these objectives.

It is therefore suggested that some of the A.A. commitments to Home Forces which exist in the present "Attic" scheme should now be cancelled, in view of the present shortage of equipments, and that Home Forces should provide any further protection which they may consider essential from the resources of their Bargain Regiments. Consequently a proportion only of the Hy. A.A. commitments to Home Forces have been retained and these are shown in Appendix 'A' to this letter. This list has been agreed to by Commander-in- Chief, Home Forces, but only as an irreducible minimum.

(ii) *Commitments to Royal Navy.* The picture to be seen here is very different. All the Naval V.Ps. due to receive protection are "fringe" targets, and therefore fighter protection to them cannot be guaranteed. I consider therefore that these commitments should be met if possible.

(iii) *Vital areas at which Heavy A.A. Defences only are to be kept up to a minimum scale under the present "Attic" Scheme.* Here a different factor has to be considered, that is the morale of the general public. Conditions remain unaltered with regard to this problem, and therefore I recommend that these commitments should remain as they stand.

10. So far as the Heavy A.A. guns are concerned, it will be seen that provided the administrative difficulties of transportation (which are dealt with in more detail below) can be overcome, then nearly all the commitments I have recommended can be fulfilled. But the Bofors situation is such that failing an allotment of additional guns of this type to A.A. Command the commitments for Light A.A. appear quite beyond our powers. The final deficiencies, if my proposals are accepted, are shown at Appendix B, and amount to a total of Nil Heavy A.A. guns and 230 Bofors guns.

11. A line has been drawn below Serial 9 in Appendix B. This represents the "Dead Line", and I consider the safety of this country will be seriously imperilled if invasion be attempted and the commitments down to this line are not fulfilled.

12. There has recently been a tendency to rely on ample warning being received of an attempt at the invasion of this country and to stress that, during this warning period, deficits in A.A. guns may be made up by diverting guns from production which are due for despatch overseas. It is felt that the dangers of this line of thought are threefold.

First it has not been the experience of this war so far that the enemy have given ample warning of their impending plans.

Secondly the rearrangement of A.A. weapons on a threat of invasion will automatically denude every factory in the country of its Light A.A. protection, thereby rendering them liable to attack and consequently to a falling off in their production.

Thirdly equipment issued in a hurry, at a late stage in the preparatory period, to A.A. personnel, who have until then been employed in manning Lewis guns or U.P. projectors is unlikely to be handled efficiently when the time comes to bring it into action.

13. It will therefore be seen that should the recommendation in this paper be accepted, a minimum of 230 Bofors guns must be released to A.A. Command before invasion appears imminent, in order to fulfil the minimum requirements shown down to the "dead-line".

**The Administrative Problem**

14. The problem of the transportation of these equipments to their invasion positions is a difficult one. Under the present "Attic" scheme a total of 240 static Hy. A.A. guns are due to be moved, and it has been calculated that these take at least one month to move, assuming that rail communications are working to full capacity. The scheme envisaged in this paper will entail the moves of a total of 360 static Hy. A.A. guns, and this will probably increase the time necessary for the completion of the moves to about 2 months, the limiting factor of the railway trucks available for this purpose remaining the same. Thus it will be seen that very early warning of impending invasion must be given if this scheme is to be fully implemented in time. This fortunately only applies to the static H.A.A. guns.

15. The mobile Hy. A.A. guns and the Bofors – the latter of which are in my opinion the more important requirement – can be brought into position within 14 days, assuming the present scales of transport to be available. In view of the number of vital industries which are now protected by these guns, and which will all be completely denuded of Bofors guns when this plan is brought into operation, it is considered that these guns should not be moved until the latest possible date compatible with safety, i.e. that the moves should not commence until it is considered that invasion might be attempted within three weeks. The static H.A.A. guns however should commence their moves as soon as any threat of invasion becomes apparent. These moves will seldom entail denuding but only a thinning out of the areas affected.

16. Full details of the proposed allocation of A.A. guns which are recommended are contained in Appendix A attached, while at Appendix B these details are summarised for the purpose of easy reference.

*(Signed) W.S. Douglas,*
*Air Marshal,*
*Air Officer Commanding-in-Chief, Fighter Command.*
*FC/S. 26542/Ops.2.*
*20.3.'42.*

*Appendix A*

1. A.A. equipments not available. Through inaccessibility and commitments to His Majesty the King and the Prime Minister.
**Hy. A.A.:**

| | | |
|---|---|---|
| N.I.D. | | 96 |
| *Orkney:* | Scapa | 80 |
| | Skeabrae | 4 |
| | Twatt | 4 |
| *Shetlands:* | Lerwick | 4 |
| | Scatsta | 4 |
| | Sumburgh | 4 |
| *Caithness:* | Wick | 4 |
| | Skitten | 4 |
| | Castletown | 4 |
| Oban | | 4 |
| Flatholme | | 8 |
| Windsor Castle | | 8 |
| *Total* | | *228* |

**Lt. A.A.:**

| | | |
|---|---|---|
| N.I.D. | | 48 |
| *Orkney:* | Scapa | 22 |
| | Skeabrae | 8 |
| | Twatt | 4 |
| | Grimsetter | 4 |
| | Hatston | 1 (+3 Mk.VIII) |
| | Stromness | 2 |
| *Shetlands:* | Lerwick | 2 |
| | Scatsta | 4 |
| | Sumburgh | 4 |
| | Skaw | 4 |
| | Noss Hill | 4 |

|  |  |  |
|---|---|---|
|  | Fair Isle | 2 |
| *Caithness*: | Wick | 8 |
|  | Skitten | 4 |
|  | Castleton | 8 |
| Flatholme |  | 2 |
| Scilly Isles |  | 2 |
| Windsor Castle |  | 4 |
| P.M. |  | 8 |
| *Total* |  | 145 |

2. R.A.F. Operational H.Q. and A.M.E. Stations (other than those in Orkneys), whose present scale of defences are a minimum which must be retained.

**Lt. A.A.:**

| Stanmore | 8 |
|---|---|
| Uxbridge | 8 |
| Leighton Buzzard | 4 |

**A.M.E. Stations:**

| Pevensey | 3 |
|---|---|
| Poling | 3 |
| Rye | 3 |
| Ventnor | 4 |
| Bawdsey | 3 |
| Darsham | 3 |
| Dover | 3 |
| Dunkirk | 3 |
| W. Prawle | 3 |
| Worth Matravers | 3 |
| Gibbett Hill | 4 |
| Stenigot | 4 |
| Stoke Holy Cross | 2 |
| W. Beckham | 3 |
| Staxton Wold | 2 |
| Drone Hill | 2 |
| Hillhead | 2 |
| Stonehaven | 3 |
| Danby Beacon | 2 |
| Douglas Wood | 2 |
| Daventry | 8 |
| *Total* | 85 |

3. R.A.F. Fighter aerodromes.

(a) 21 vital aerodromes which will be occupied by Fighter Squadrons and which require the full scale of defence of 8 Hy. And 16 Lt. A.A. guns.

| Aerodrome | Hy. A.A. | Lt. A.A. |
|---|---|---|
| 1. Duxford | 8 | 16 |

| | | |
|---|---|---|
| 2. Fowlmere | 8 | 16 |
| 3. Snailwell | 8 | 16 |
| 4. Debden | 8 | 16 |
| 5. Castle Camps | 8 | 16 |
| 6. Gt. Sampford | 8 | 16 |
| 7. N. Weald | 8 | 16 |
| 8. Hunsden | 8 | 16 |
| 9. Hornchurch | 8 | 16 |
| 10. Fairlop | 8 | 16 |
| 11. Biggin Hill | 8 | 16 |
| 12. Gravesend | 8 | 16 |
| 13. West Malling | 8 | 16 |
| 14. Kenley | 8 | 16 |
| 15. Croydon | 8 | 16 |
| 16. Redhill | 8 | 16 |
| 17. Northolt | 8 | 16 |
| 18. Heston | 8 | 16 |
| 19. Tangmere | 8 | 16 |
| 20. Merston | 8 | 16 |
| 21. Westhampnett | 8 | 16 |
| *Total* | *168* | *336* |

(b) 31 additional rearward and other important aerodromes in an invasion period. A small scale of 8 Hy. and 8 Lt. A.A. guns can be accepted owing to the longer approach.

| Aerodrome | Hy. A.A. | Lt. A.A. |
|---|---|---|
| 1. Stapleford | 8 | 8 |
| 2. Boscombe Down* | 8 | 8 |
| 3. Odiham | 8 | 8 |
| 4. White Waltham* | 8 | 8 |
| 5. Farnborough* | 8 | 8 |
| 6. Aldermaston* | 8 | 8 |
| 7. Benson* | 8 | 8 |
| 8. Hatfield* | 8 | 8 |
| 9. Cranfield | 8 | 8 |
| 10. Bassingbourne* | 8 | 8 |
| 11. Booker* | 8 | 8 |
| 12. Radlett* | 8 | 8 |
| 13. Twinwood Farm | 8 | 8 |
| 14. Steeple Morden* | 8 | 8 |
| 15. Henlow | 8 | 8 |
| 16. Wittering | 8 | 8 |
| 17. Collyweston | 8 | 8 |
| 18. Kingscliffe | 8 | 8 |
| 19. Middle Wallop | 8 | 8 |

| | | |
|---|---|---|
| 20. Chilbolton | 8 | 8 |
| 21. Ibsley | 8 | 8 |
| 22. Warmwell | 8 | 8 |
| 23. Hurn | 8 | 8 |
| 24. Exeter | 8 | 8 |
| 25. Harrowbeer | 8 | 8 |
| 26. Portreath | 8 | 8 |
| 27. Predannack | 8 | 8 |
| 28. Perranporth | 8 | 8 |
| 29. Coltishall | 8 | 8 |
| 30. Matlask | 8 | 8 |
| 31. Ludham | 8 | 8 |
| *Total* | *248* | *248* |

\* Subject to Air Ministry approval, but the numbers are not liable to alteration.

(c) Four Aerodromes, which will be evacuated by Squadrons, but will be used as long as possible as advance landing grounds. Full scale of 8 Hy. and 16 Lt. A.A. guns required.

| | *Hy. A.A.* | *Lt. A.A.* |
|---|---|---|
| 1. Manston | 8 | 16 |
| 2. Hawkinge | 8 | 16 |
| 3. Martlesham | 8 | 16 |
| 4. Southend | 8 | 16 |
| *Total* | *32* | *64* |

(d) Two aerodromes which it is intended to evacuate early and not to use thereafter. A scale of 4 Hy. and 4 Lt. A.A. guns is required.

| | *Hy. A.A.* | *Lt. A.A.* |
|---|---|---|
| 1. Bradwell | 4 | 4 |
| 2. Ford | 4 | 4 |
| *Total* | *8* | *8* |

Grand Total required for protection of Fighter Aerodromes:
456 Hy. A.A. guns
656 Lt. A.A. guns

4. A.A. defences needed for protection of 14 Bomber Command aerodromes. Minimum scale required of 8 Hy. A.A. and 8 Lt. A.A. guns.

| | *Hy. A.A.* | *Lt. A.A.* |
|---|---|---|
| 1. Bassingbourne | 8 | 8 |
| 2. Oakington | 8 | 8 |
| 3. Mildenhall | 8 | 8 |
| 4. Wyton | 8 | 8 |
| 5. Stradishall | 8 | 8 |
| 6. North Luffenham | 8 | 8 |

380

| | | |
|---|---|---|
| 7. Syerston | 8 | 8 |
| 8. Swinderby | 8 | 8 |
| 9. Waddington | 8 | 8 |
| 10. Scampton | 8 | 8 |
| 11. Marston Moor | 8 | 8 |
| 12. Linton | 8 | 8 |
| 13. Topcliffe | 8 | 8 |
| 14. Leeming | 8 | 8 |
| *Total* | *112* | *112* |

5. A.A. defences required for the defence of 8 Coastal Command aerodromes, four at a scale of 8 Hy. and 8 Lt. A.A. equipments, and four less vulnerable, on a scale of 8 Hy, A.A. and 4 Lt. A.A. equipments.

| | *Hy. A.A.* | *Lt. A.A.* |
|---|---|---|
| 1. St. Eval | 8 | 8 |
| 2. Thorney Island | 8 | 8 |
| 3. Bircham Newton | 8 | 8 |
| 4. North Coates | 8 | 8 |
| 5. Chivenor | 8 | 4 |
| 6. Leuchars | 8 | 4 |
| 7. Catfoss | 8 | 4 |
| 8. Docking | 8 | 4 |
| *Total* | *64* | *48* |

6. Bargain Regiments due to be transferred to Home Forces on Invasion. Total required:

| *Hy. A.A.* | *Lt. A.A.* |
|---|---|
| 96 | 144 |

7. Naval V.Ps. which are due to receive protection under the present Attic Scheme. Total required:

*Heavy A.A.:*

| | |
|---|---|
| Rosyth | 52 |
| Harwich | 24 |
| Humber | 50 |
| Lowestoft – Yarmouth | 24 |
| Thames and Medway | 80 |
| Portsmouth | 56 |
| Portland | 20 |
| Plymouth | 48 |
| Falmouth | 16 |
| Dartmouth | 8 |
| Dover (incl. R.D.F.) | 14 |
| Newhaven | 8 |
| Ramsgate | 8 |
| Milford Haven | 24 |

| | |
|---|---|
| Loch Ewe | 4 |
| Kyle of Lochalsh | 4 |
| *Total* | *440* |

**Light A.A.:**

| | |
|---|---|
| Harwich | 8 |
| Newhaven | 8 |
| Dartmouth | 4 |
| Plymouth | 4 |
| Falmouth | 8 |
| Milford Haven | 4 |
| Ramsgate | 8 |
| Immingham & Killingholme | 16 |
| Lowestoft – Yarmouth | 12 |
| Kyle of Lochalsh | 4 |
| Sheerness | 4 |
| Dover (incl. R.D.F.) | 8 |
| *Total* | *88* |

8. Vital areas at which Heavy A.A. defences only are to be kept up to a minimum scale under the present Attic Scheme. Total required:

**Heavy A.A.:**

| | |
|---|---|
| London I.A.Z. | 142 |
| Clyde | 40 |
| Tyne | 42 |
| Tees | 24 |
| Crewe | 8 |
| Birmingham & Wolver'on | 48 |
| Coventry | 24 |
| Scunthorpe | 4 |
| Sheffield | 24 |
| Leeds | 16 |
| Barrow | 8 |
| Liverpool | 40 |
| Manchester | 24 |
| Nottingham | 16 |
| Derby | 12 |
| Swansea | 12 |
| Cardiff, Newport | 16 |
| Cheltenham & Gloucester | 8 |
| Bristol | 20 |
| Southampton | 12 |
| *Total* | *540* |

9. V.Ps due to be protected in support of Home Forces. This represents some 50% of the V.Ps due to receive protection under the present Attic Scheme.

*Heavy A.A.:*

| | |
|---|---|
| Canterbury | 16 |
| Maidstone | 16 |
| Ashford | 8 |
| Oxford | 16 |
| Reading | 8 |
| Newbury | 8 |
| Carlisle | 8 |
| Bletchley | 8 |
| Cambridge | 8 |
| Didcot | 8 |
| Banbury | 8 |
| *Total* | *112* |

## Appendix 'B'

### SUMMARY OF PROPOSED ALLOCATION OF A.A. EQUIPMENTS FOR INVASION, IN ORDER OF PRIORITY

| | | Equipment now available | |
|---|---|---|---|
| *Serial No.* | *Commitment* | *Hy. A.A.* | *Lt. A.A.* |
| 1. | Not available | 228 | 145 |
| 2. | R.A.F.H.Q. and A.M.E. Stations | - | 85 |
| 3. | R.A.F. Fighter Aerodromes | 456 | 656 |
| 4. | Bomber Command Aerodromes | 112 | 112 |
| 5. | Coastal Command | 64 | 48 |
| 6. | Bargain Regiments | 96 | 144 |
| 7. | Naval V.Ps. | 440 | 88 |
| 8. | Vital Areas | 540 | - |
| 9. | Home Forces | 112 | - |
| | *Total available* | *2,048* | *1,048* |
| | *Balance* | *Nil* | *-230* |

Appendix XXIX

# Role, Organization and Dispositions of The Royal Air Force To Meet Invasion, 4th February 1942

ROLES OF THE ROYAL AIR FORCE

1. The principal roles of the Royal Air Force against invasion are:
(i) reconnaissance to obtain the earliest information of assembly and despatch of the invading forces;
(ii) attack of enemy aircraft wherever they are found, and the protection of our own aircraft and naval units from air attack;
(iii) defence of vital areas against air attack;
(iv) attack in co-operation with the other Services on:
(a) convoys and surface craft at their ports of departure;
(b) convoys and surface craft as they approach the British coast;
(c) enemy forces which succeed in reaching or establishing themselves in the British Isles.

ORGANISATION OF THE R.A.F. TO MEET THE THREAT

2. In general terms the anti-invasion organisation of the Royal Air Force provides for:
(i) Strategical Reconnaissance by Coastal Command units and P.R.U.
(ii) Tactical Reconnaissance by the Army Co-operation Squadrons under the control of army formations. In certain circumstances these squadrons may also be used to attack troops disembarking or ashore in this country.
(iii) Attack of enemy shipping and land forces by Bomber Command units and by Coastal Command units in collaboration with the Navy.
(iv) Attack of airborne forces, and defence against air attack, by Fighter Command units. Some of these units may be diverted to the attack with cannon, of armoured barges or A.F.V. in barges.

384

## STRENGTH AND DISPOSITION OF AIR FORCES

3. On 7th January the first line strengths of the R.A.F. Commands were:

(a) *Fighter Command*

| | |
|---|---|
| Day Fighter Squadrons | 66 |
| Night Fighter Squadrons | 25 |
| TOTAL I.E. | 1,484 |

(b) *Bomber Command_*

| | |
|---|---|
| Heavy Bomber Squadrons | 10 |
| Medium Bomber Squadrons | 33 |
| Light Bomber Squadrons | 4 |
| TOTAL I.E. | 832 |

In addition there are 1 Heavy, 2 Medium and 2 Light Bomber Squadrons which are non-operational, total I.E. = 80. The majority of them will be operational by 1st March and could therefore be called upon in the event of invasion.

(c) *Coastal Command*

| | |
|---|---|
| G.R. Squadrons | 20 |
| T.B. G.R. Squadrons | 3 |
| L.R.F. Squadrons | 5 |
| TOTAL I.E. | 448 |

These squadrons are at present employed mainly in trade protection duties but can be diverted at short notice to anti-invasion duties.

(d) *Army Co-operation Command*

| | |
|---|---|
| Bomber/Reece. Squadrons Blenheims | 2 |
| Fighter/Recce. Squadrons Tomahawks | 8 |
| Lysanders | 4 |
| Strat/Reece. Squadron | 1 |
| TOTAL I.E. | 120 |

The 15 Army Co-operation Squadrons are allotted to the various commands, corps and Armoured Divisions with the exception of the Strat, Recce. Squadron which is under the operation control of the C.-in-C., Home Forces. One Tomahawk squadron and one Lysander squadron are temporarily equipped with Hurricane II.Cs. In addition to the above there is one A.C. Squadron in N. Ireland re-equipping with Tomahawks.

## CONTROL

4. The calls on Bomber Command as between different types of targets are certain to be beyond its capacity. It will therefore be necessary for the Chiefs of Staff to lay down the broad allocation of the bomber effort.

The C.-in-C., Home Forces will indicate to the A.O.C.-in-C., Bomber Command the targets with which he is concerned in order of priority. The A.O.C.-in-C. will issue orders accordingly, and keep Home Forces informed of action taken. In the event of the breakdown of communications between Bomber and Fighter Commands and their respective groups, arrangements have been made to link Army Commands to appropriate R.A.F. Bomber and Fighter Group Headquarters. This list is given in Appendix 'A' to R.A.F. Organisation for Air Action Against Invasion of Great Britain. If R.A.F. stations are cut off, the Station Commander should obtain information regarding suitable targets either by reconnaissance or from the nearest Military Commander.

## PASSAGE OF INFORMATION

5. Up to the beginning of enemy operations, and during the "Approach" phase, the A.O.C.-in-C., Bomber Command is kept informed of the situation through the normal channels. When the enemy has reached the coast additional information regarding the military situation obtained through Army channels is passed to him under special arrangements at G.H.Q. Home Forces.

## IRELAND

6. R.A.F. Units in Northern Ireland at present consist of:
    Coastal Command:   3 Hudson Squadrons
                       1 Blenheim long range fighter squadron
                       1 Liberator (GR) squadron
                       1 Whitley (GR) squadron
                       1 Catalina (GR) squadron
    Fighter Command:   4 Spitfire squadrons (including 1 long range
                       squadron)
                       1 Defiant squadron
                       1 Beaufighter squadron
    Air Component:     1 fighter reconnaissance (Tomahawk) squadron
The Coastal Command and Fighter Command squadrons in Northern Ireland are operated under the orders of the C.-in-C. of Coastal and Fighter Commands through Nos. 15 and 82 Groups respectively. In the event of invasion of Ireland arrangements have been made to reinforce Northern Ireland with two light bomber squadrons and 3 fighter squadrons. These squadrons will be included in the Air Component. In addition, Nos. 82 and 226 light bomber squadrons which visit Northern Ireland for three weeks training every three months will proceed to Northern Ireland when Alert No. 1 is ordered.

## SCOTLAND

7. In view of the difficulties of control which may arise in the event of a successful enemy landing in Northern Scotland, it may be necessary to delegate operational control of the bomber forces in Scotland. In these circumstances control will be assumed by the A.O.C. No.18 Group who will employ his forces to meet requirements of the G.O.C.-in-C., Scottish Command. These forces will include the aircraft of those training establishments in Scotland which are affected by the Banquet "6 Group" and Banquet "EVANTON" schemes, together with any reinforcing bomber forces. If invasion of Scotland comes as a surprise, G.O.C.-in-C., Scottish Command will have at his disposal 12 aircraft and crews which have been specially made available for operations from the Training Units at Kinloss and Lossiemouth.

## CHEMICAL WARFARE

8. The following squadrons are trained and equipped for gas spray:

Bomber Command:   5 Wellington squadrons.
9 Blenheim squadrons.

In regard to the Blenheim squadrons, very few of these will be available at present, as one Squadron is maintaining two Blenheim squadrons at Malta, two squadrons are earmarked for temporary duty overseas, one squadron is standing by for No. 18 Squadron's commitment in Northern Ireland, Nos. 88 and 226 Sqns. are due to leave for Northern Ireland on Alert No. 1, and Nos. 107 and 105 are re-equipping with Bostons and Mosquitoes.

9. It takes approximately 4 hours to fit S.C.I.s on a Blenheim, and 8 hours to fit them on the Wellington. The following stocks of gas weapons are held at Home stations:

| WEAPONS | STOCK AT HOME STATIONS | STOCK AT MAINTENANCE UNITS |
|---|---|---|
| 250lb L.C. Bomb, filled Mustard | 7,553 | 5,482 |
| 30lb L.C. Bomb, filled Mustard | 7,068 | 22,679 |
| 30lb Mk.I 'M' Bomb, filled Mustard | 6,524 | 104 |
| 30lb Mk.II Bomb, filled Mustard | 22,760 | 24,676 |
| 65lb Bomb, filled Mustard | 22,729 | 19,271 |
| 100lb S.C.I. (Wellington) | 328 | 902 |
| 500lb S.C.I. (Blenheim) | 1,096 | 2,689 |
| 250lb S.C.I. (Blenheim) | 250 | 250 |

## SYSTEM OF ALERTS

10. In order to warn the operational and flying training commands of the R.A.F. of the imminence of an invasion attempt, so that they can

make the necessary preparations, a system of "ALERTS" is in force. The state of Alert in force is published daily in the Air Staff Operational Summary, any alteration being communicated by signal as necessary. A.O.s C.-in-C. are responsible for detailing the action to be taken within their own Commands when a change in the state of Alerts is notified.

11. The states of "ALERT" are:

| | |
|---|---|
| INVASION ALERT No.3 | When attack is regarded as improbable within the following three days, although an invasion threat is believed to exist. |
| INVASION ALERT No.2 | When attack is probable within the following three days. |
| INVASION ALERT No.1 | When attack is regarded as imminent, and likely to occur within the next 12 hours. |

*4.2.1942.*